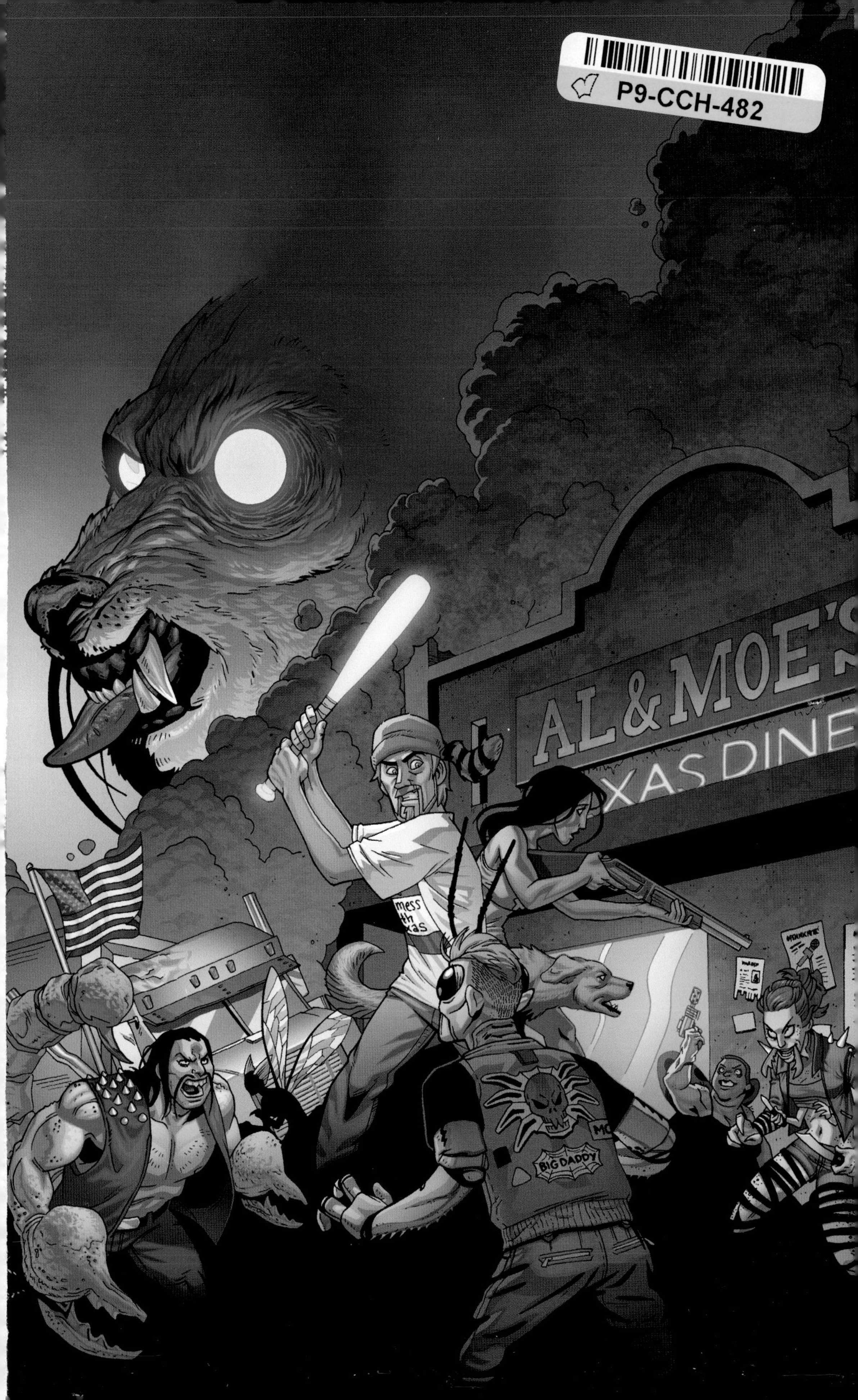
AL&MOE'
XAS DINE
BIG DADDY

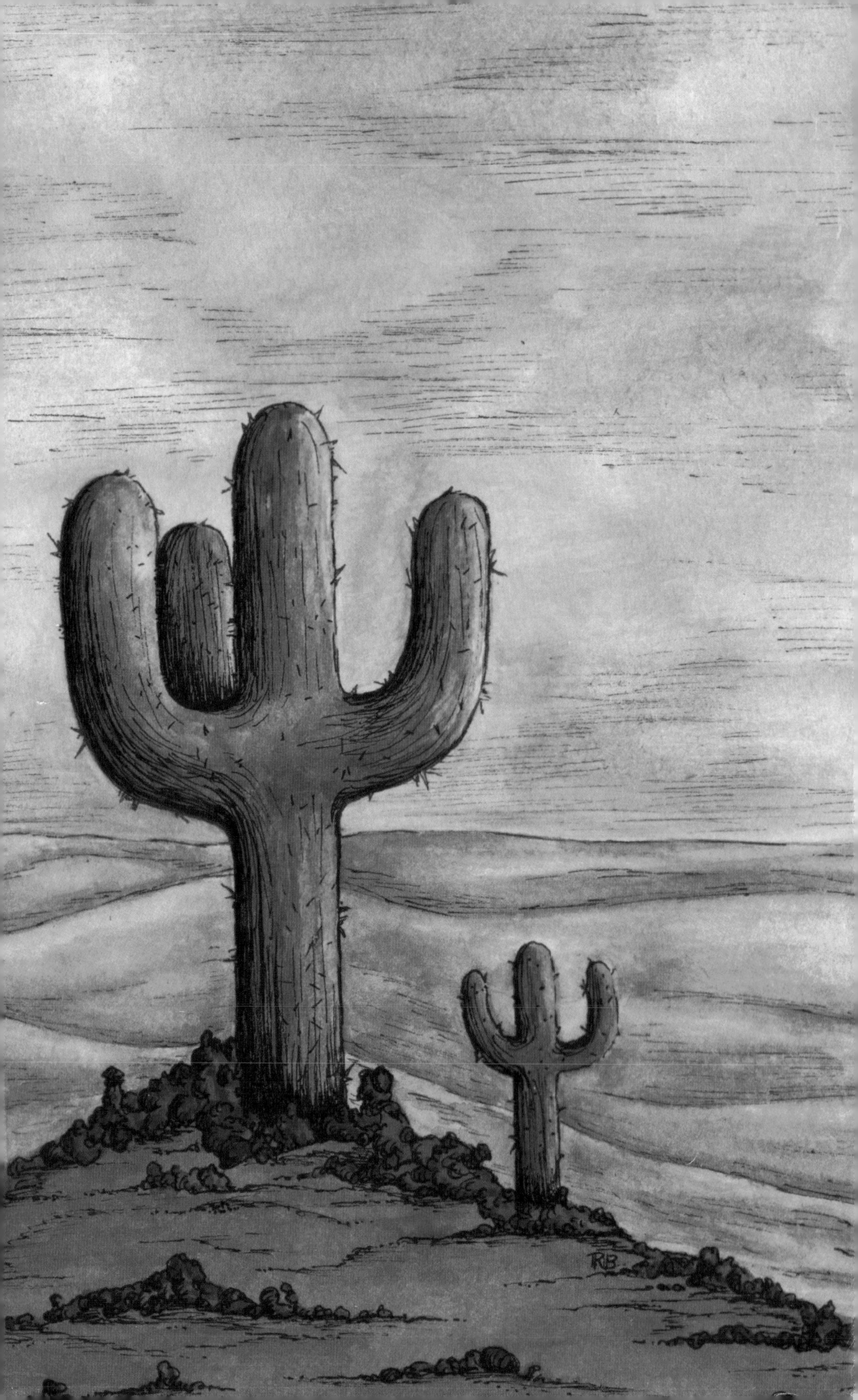

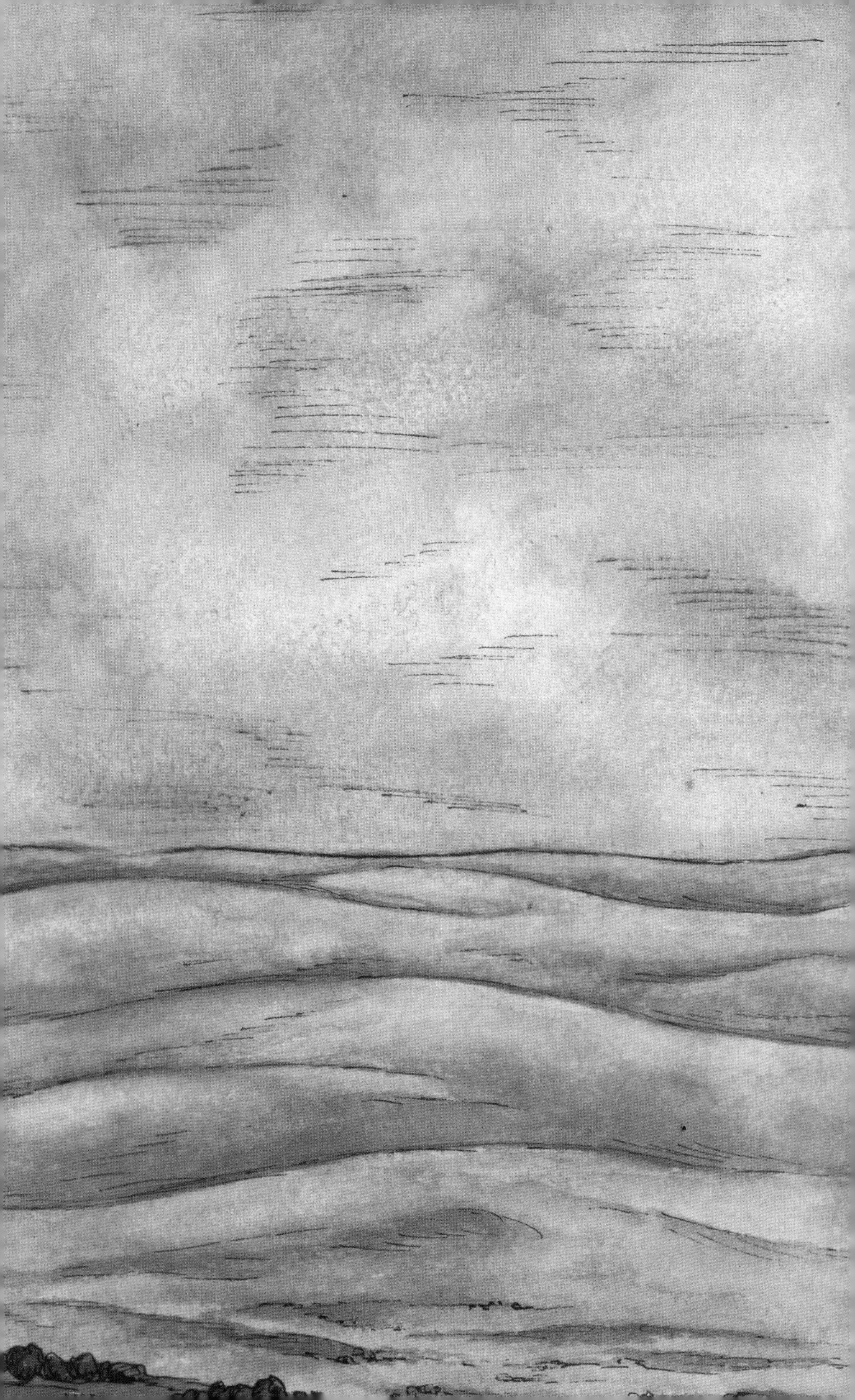

THANKS TO MOM, DAD, AND AMY, FOR THEIR NEVERENDING LOVE AND SUPPORT; DOUG MEYER FOR SHARING THE EXTENSIVE KNOWLEDGE IN HIS TRADE AS WELL AS HIS LIBRARY; KATE, REBEKAH, JOSH, AND SARAH FOR SUPPORTING MY WACKY ENDEAVORS AND FOR ALL THE LAUGHS; FOR TRANSLATION ASSISTANCE, BRIAN BENDER; FOR ALL OF THE HELP AND ENCOURAGEMENT... CHRISTINE MARTIN, MEGAN DEPUTY, ERAKLIS PETMEZAS, JASON LATOUR, RICO RENZI, ADAM AND SHAWN DAUGHEETEE, SETH AND HEATHER PEAGLER, JEREMY BROOKS, MIKE WIRTH, BROCKTON MCKINNEY, BO FADER, JONAS BRITT, STEVE SAFFEL, STEVE WHITE, CINDY KLINGBERG, AND MIKE MIGNOLA.

THANKS MOST OF ALL TO MY LOVE, JUSTIN CONNELL. LIFE IS AN ADVENTURE WITH YOU.

"THE MAN COMES AROUND" LYRICS USED WITH PERMISSION FROM THE HAL LEONARD CORPORATION.
"IF YOU WANNA GET TO HEAVEN" LYRICS USED WITH PERMISSION FROM NEW ERA PRODUCTIONS FOR THE OZARK MOUNTAIN DAREDEVILS.
COVER AND PAGE 1 BY BRIDGIT CONNELL. COLORED BY LUIS GUERRERO.
PAGES 133-136 AND 139-140 OF CHAPTER FIVE ARE CO-WRITTEN WITH PLAYWRIGHT AMY SCHEIDE CHEEK.
SPREADS IN THE FRONT AND BACK OF THE BOOK ARE MIXED MEDIA PAINTINGS BY REBEKAH BROWN.
BROTHER NASH LOGO DESIGNED BY RICO RENZI.

MANAGING & LAUNCH EDITOR
ANDREW JAMES

TITAN COMICS EDITORIAL
DAN BOULTWOOD
JAKE DEVINE

PRODUCTION ASSISTANT
RHIANNON ROY

PRODUCTION CONTROLLER
PETER JAMES

SENIOR PRODUCTION
CONTROLLER
JACKIE FLOOK

SENIOR DESIGNER
ANDREW LEUNG

ART DIRECTOR
OZ BROWNE

SENIOR SALES MANAGER
STEVE TOTHILL

CIRCULATION EXECUTIVE
FRANCES HALLAM

PRESS OFFICER
WILL O'MULLANE

BRAND MANAGER
CHRIS THOMPSON

DIRECT SALES &
MARKETING MANAGER
RICKY CLAYDON

ADVERTISING MANAGER
MICHELLE FAIRLAMB

ADS AND MARKETING ASSISTANT
BELLA HOY

HEAD OF RIGHTS
JENNY BOYCE

PUBLISHING MANAGER
DARRYL TOTHILL

PUBLISHING DIRECTOR
CHRIS TEATHER

OPERATIONS DIRECTOR
LEIGH BAULCH

EXECUTIVE DIRECTOR
VIVIAN CHEUNG

PUBLISHER
NICK LANDAU

COLLECTS BROTHER NASH #1-3.

ISBN: 9781785864568

FOR RIGHTS INFORMATION, CONTACT JENNY.BOYCE@TITANEMAIL.COM

BROTHER NASH, PUBLISHED BY TITAN COMICS, A DIVISION OF TITAN PUBLISHING GROUP, LTD. 144 SOUTHWARK STREET, LONDON SE1 0UP, UK.
TITAN COMICS IS A REGISTERED TRADEMARK OF TITAN PUBLISHING GROUP, LTD. ALL RIGHTS RESERVED.
BROTHER NASH AND ALL RELATED CHARACTERS ARE TRADEMARK ™ AND COPYRIGHT © 2018 BRIDGIT CONNELL. ALL RIGHTS RESERVED.

A CIP RECORD FOR THIS TITLE IS AVAILABLE FROM THE BRITISH LIBRARY.

FIRST EDITION: NOVEMBER 2018
10 9 8 7 8 6 5 4 3 2 1

PRINTED IN SPAIN.
TITAN COMICS.

BROTHER NASH

TITAN COMICS

WWW.TITAN-COMICS.COM

BECOME A FAN ON FACEBOOK.COM/COMICSTITAN

FOLLOW US ON TWITTER @COMICSTITAN

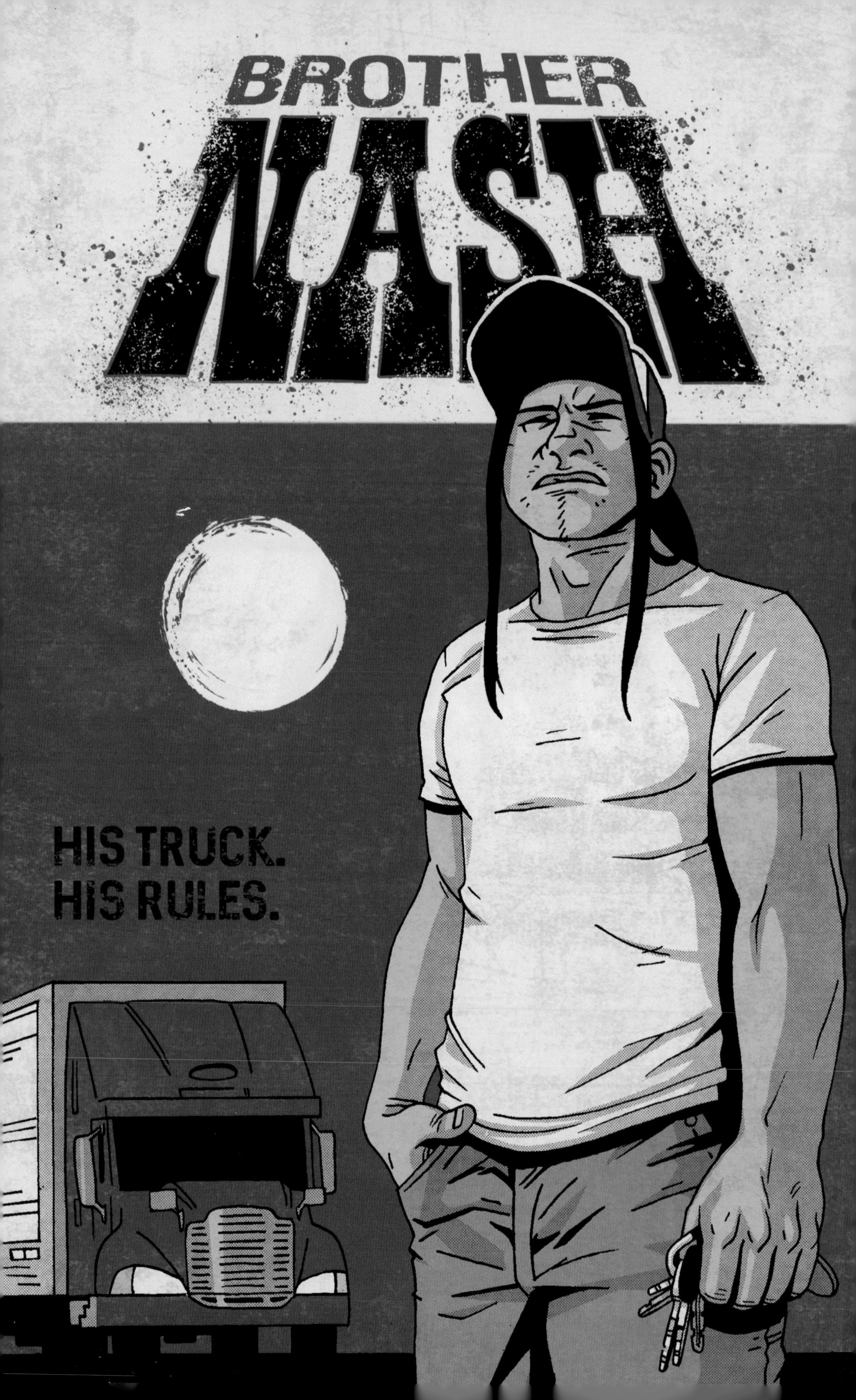
BROTHER
NASA
HIS TRUCK.
HIS RULES.

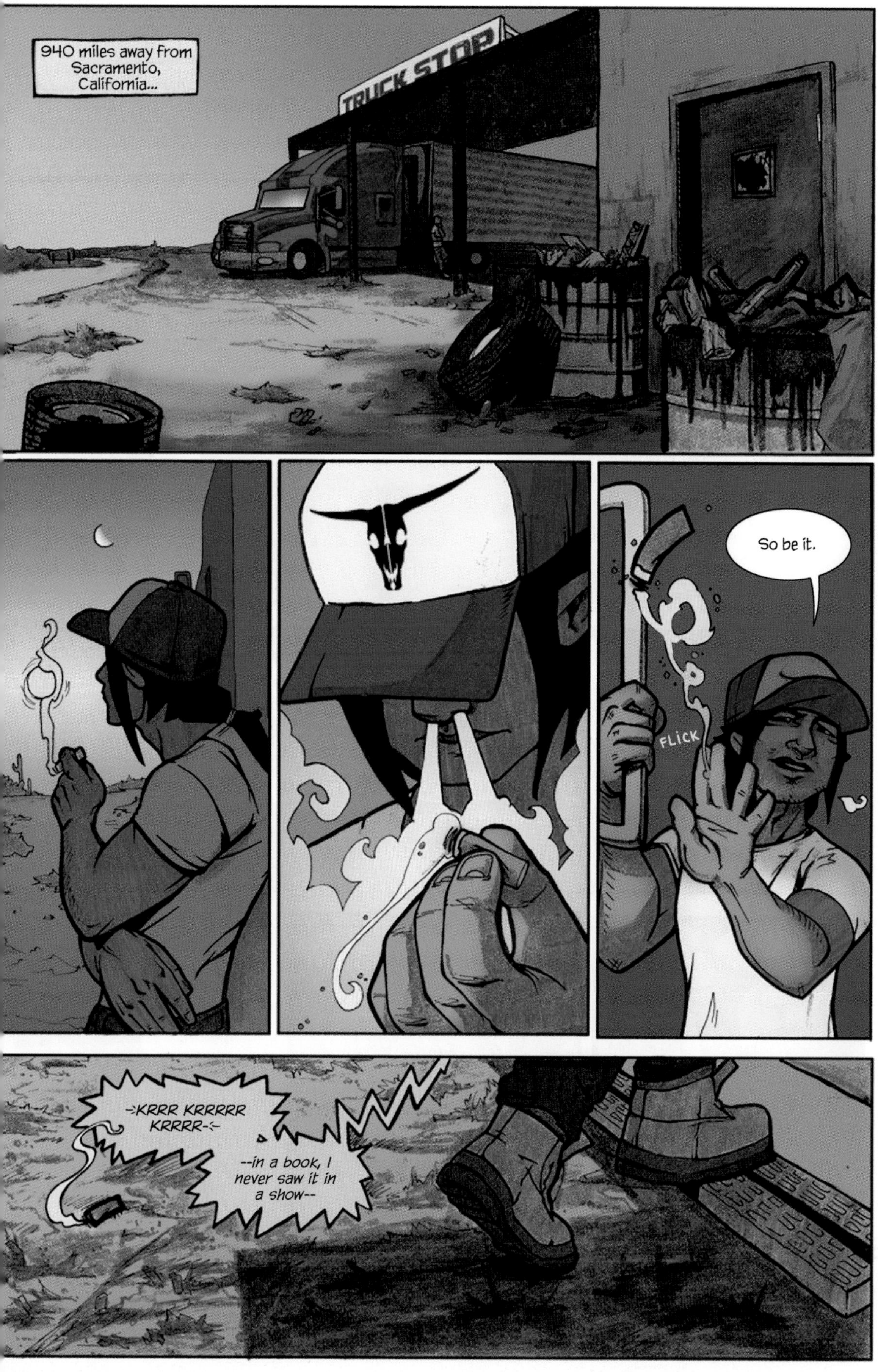

940 miles away from Sacramento, California...
TRUCK STOP
So be it.
FLICK
-KRRR KRRRRR KRRRR-
--in a book, I never saw it in a show--

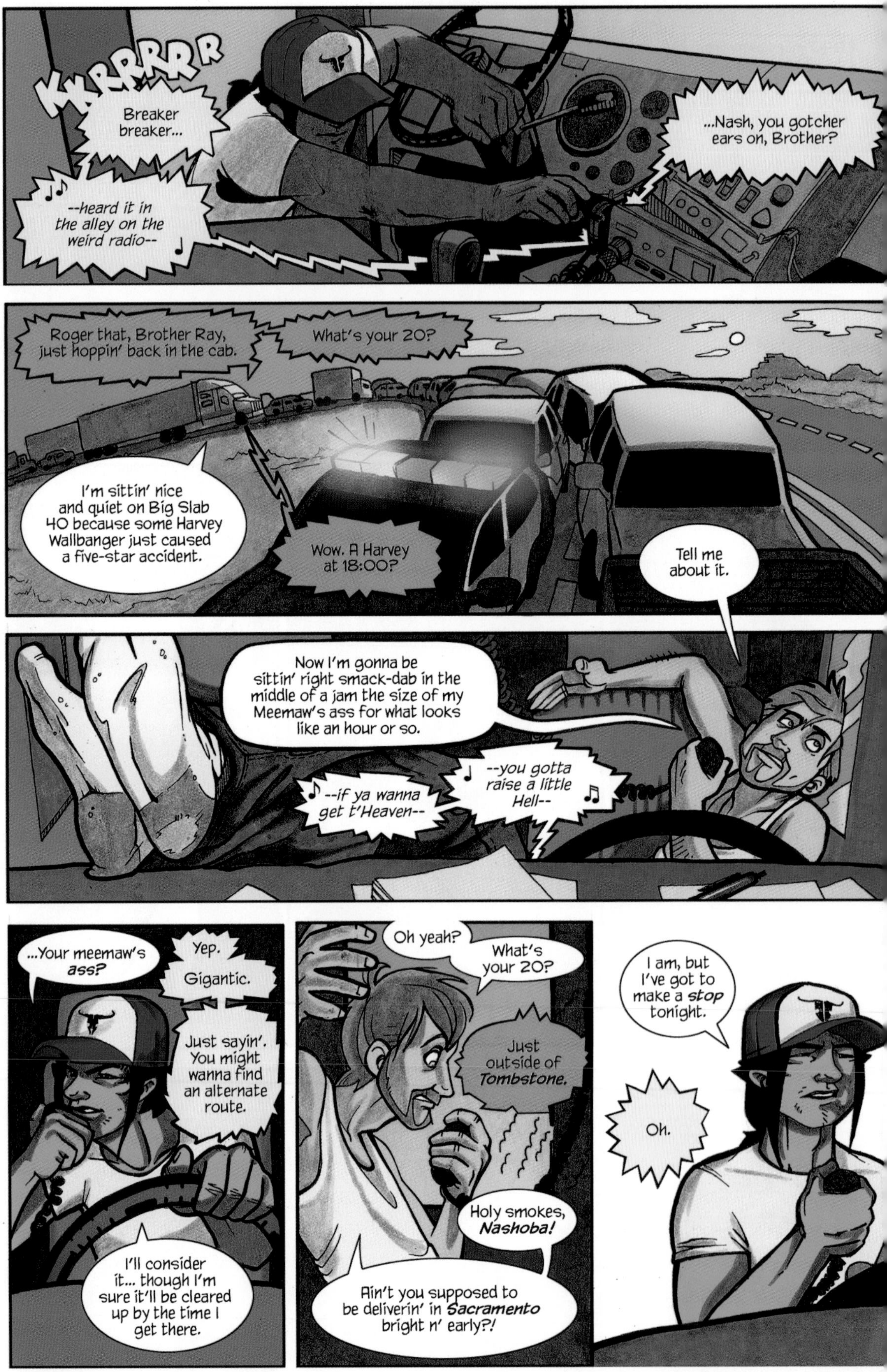
KKRRRRR
Breaker breaker...
...Nash, you gotcher ears on, Brother?
--heard it in the alley on the weird radio--
Roger that, Brother Ray, just hoppin' back in the cab.
What's your 20?
I'm sittin' nice and quiet on Big Slab 40 because some Harvey Wallbanger just caused a five-star accident.
Wow. A Harvey at 18:00?
Tell me about it.
Now I'm gonna be sittin' right smack-dab in the middle of a jam the size of my Meemaw's ass for what looks like an hour or so.
--if ya wanna get t'Heaven--
--you gotta raise a little Hell--
...Your meemaw's *ass?*
Yep.
Gigantic.
Just sayin'. You might wanna find an alternate route.
I'll consider it... though I'm sure it'll be cleared up by the time I get there.
Oh yeah?
What's your 20?
Just outside of *Tombstone.*
Holy smokes, ***Nashoba!***
Ain't you supposed to be deliverin' in *Sacramento* bright n' early?!
I am, but I've got to make a *stop* tonight.
Oh.

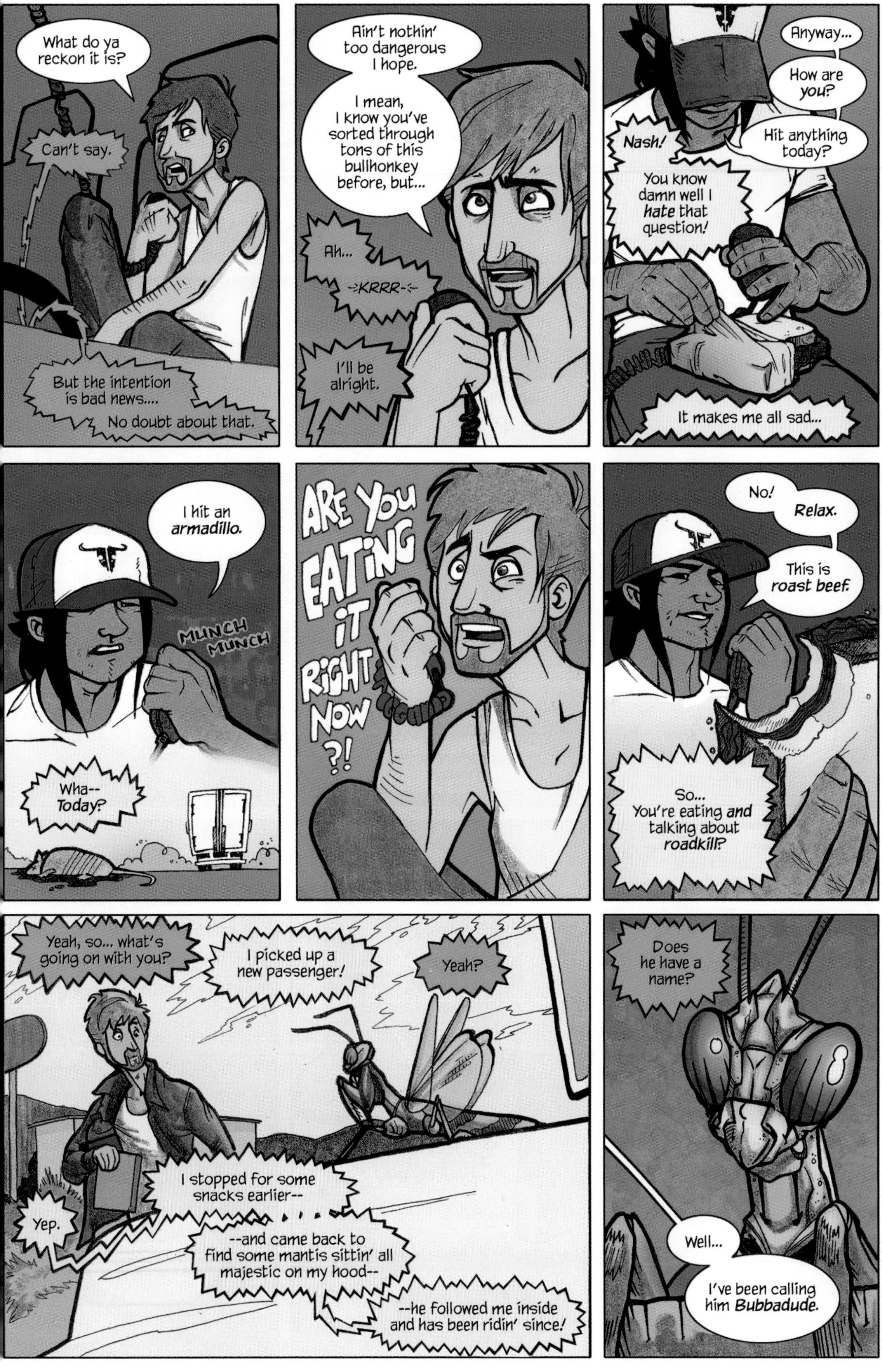
What do ya reckon it is?
Can't say.
But the intention is bad news....
No doubt about that.
Ain't nothin' too dangerous I hope.
I mean, I know you've sorted through tons of this bullhonkey before, but...
Ah...
-KRRR-
I'll be alright.
Anyway...
How are you?
Hit anything today?
Nash!
You know damn well I hate that question!
It makes me all sad...
I hit an armadillo.
MUNCH MUNCH
Wha-- Today?
ARE YOU EATING IT RIGHT NOW ?!
No! Relax.
This is roast beef.
So... You're eating and talking about roadkill?
Yeah, so... what's going on with you?
I picked up a new passenger!
Yeah?
I stopped for some snacks earlier--
Yep.
--and came back to find some mantis sittin' all majestic on my hood--
--he followed me inside and has been ridin' since!
Does he have a name?
Well...
I've been calling him Bubbadude.

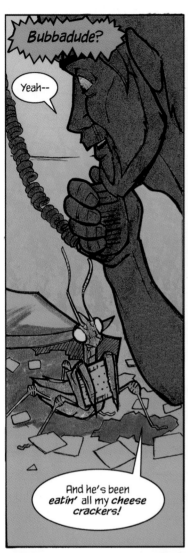

Bubbadude?

Yeah--

And he's been *eatin'* all my *cheese crackers!*

I'm not kidding, this guy loves them!

AHAA HA-HA HHA HHA HA!!

You're insane!

Say "Hi there", Bubbadude.

MUNCH MUNCH MUNCH

Did you hear that?

Wha--?

Negatory. I definitely did not hear that.

Bubbadude says, "Howdy".

Well. Since you seem to have done so yourself...

I'm gonna *bug out.*

HA HA HA

Roger that.

I'll letcha go.

But tonight you best be hammered down, supreme.

Roger that.

Supreme.

It won't take any time at all before I'm back on the big road again.

10-4.

And hey--

Be *safe*, man.

BWAMM BWAMM

You too, my southern brother. 10-4.

I'm gone.

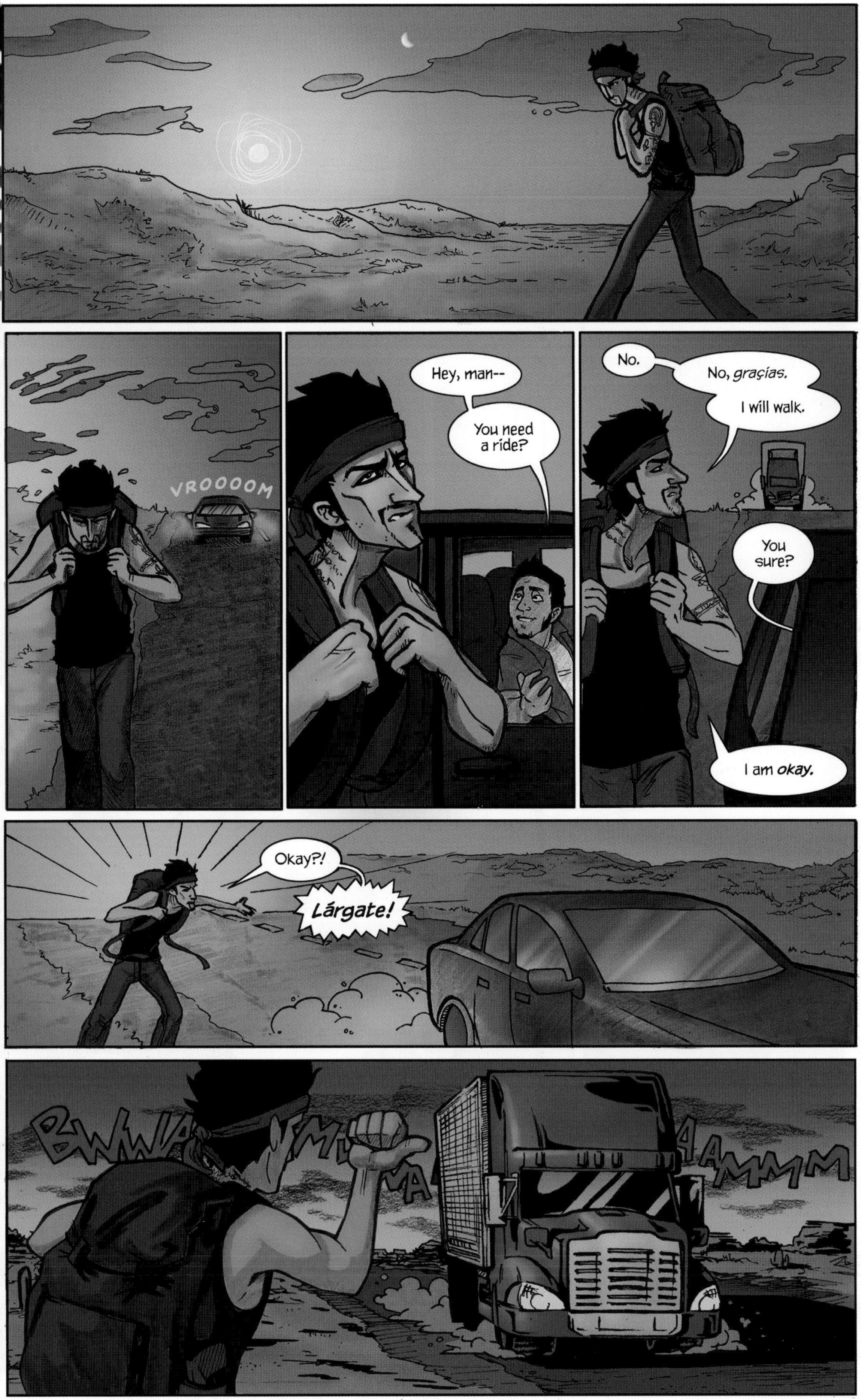
VROOOOM
Hey, man--
You need a ride?
No.
No, *gracías.*
I will walk.
You sure?
I am *okay.*
Okay?!
Lárgate!
BWWAAMMMMAAMMMM

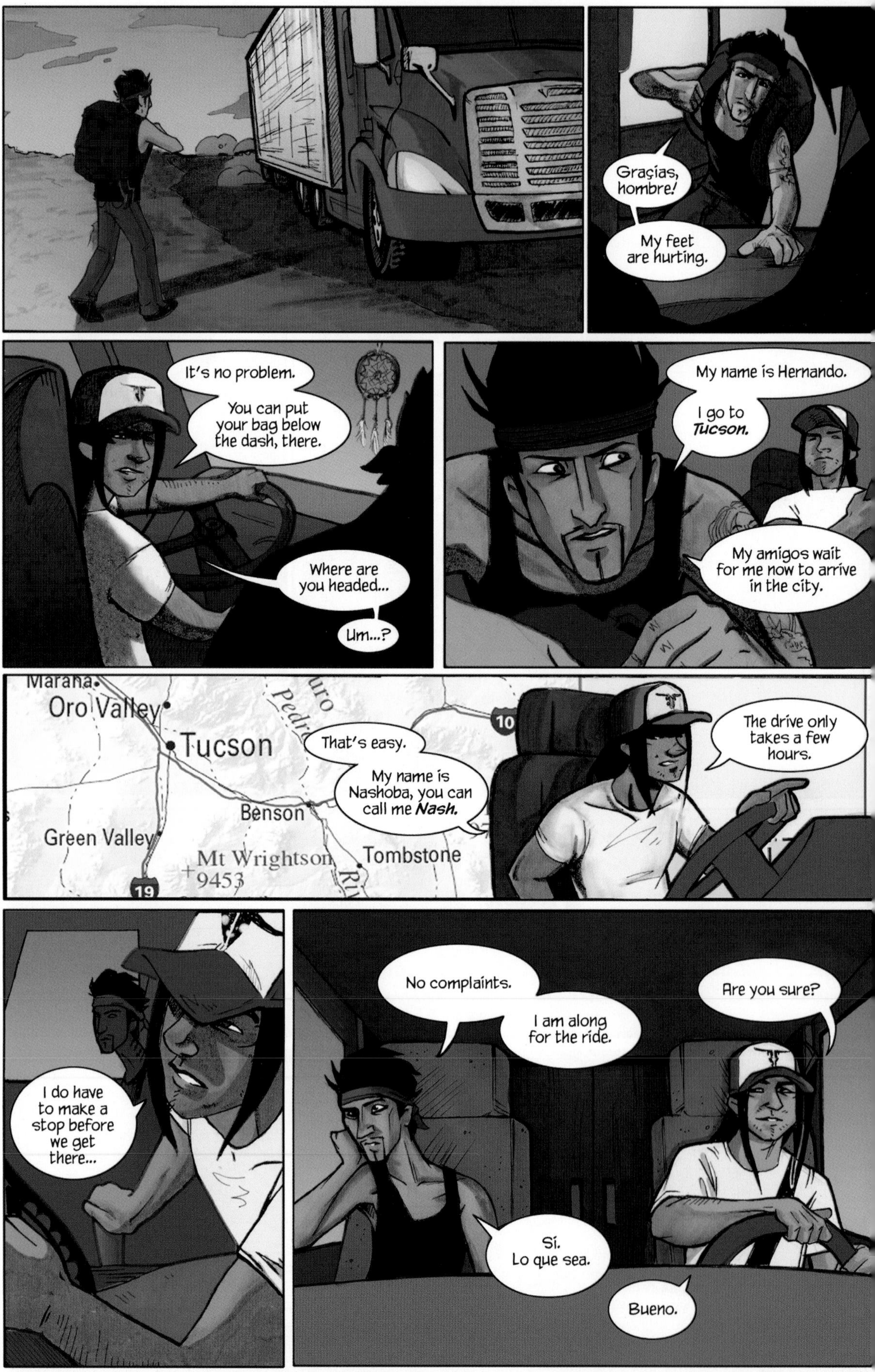
Graçias, hombre!
My feet are hurting.
It's no problem.
You can put your bag below the dash, there.
Where are you headed...
Um...?
My name is Hernando.
I go to *Tucson.*
My amigos wait for me now to arrive in the city.
Marana
Oro Valley
Tucson
Benson
Green Valley
Mt Wrightson 9453
Tombstone
10
19
That's easy.
My name is Nashoba, you can call me *Nash.*
The drive only takes a few hours.
I do have to make a stop before we get there...
No complaints.
I am along for the ride.
Are you sure?
Sí. Lo que sea.
Bueno.

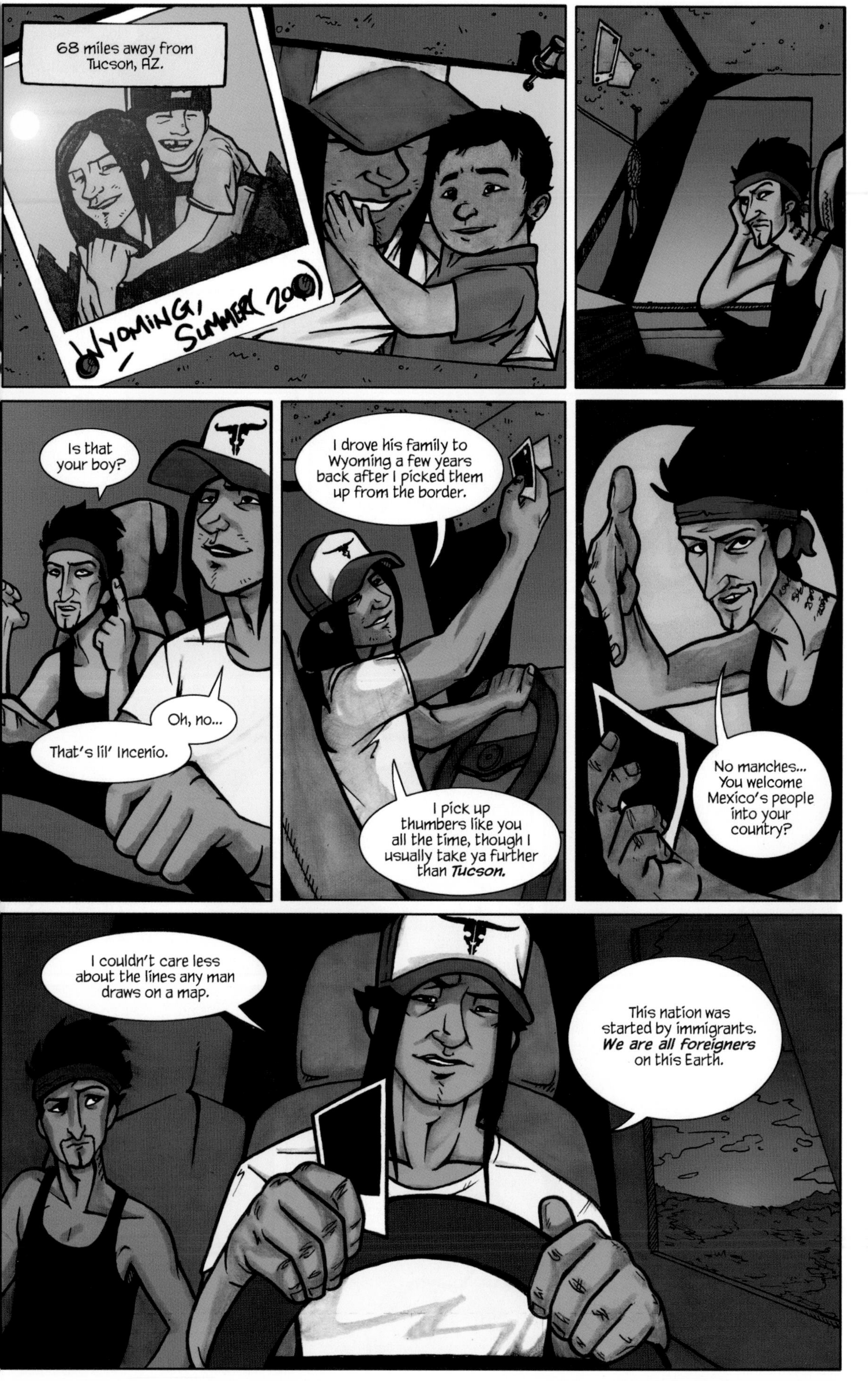
68 miles away from Tucson, AZ.
Wyoming, Summer 200_
Is that your boy?
Oh, no...
That's lil' Incenio.
I drove his family to Wyoming a few years back after I picked them up from the border.
I pick up thumbers like you all the time, though I usually take ya further than *Tucson.*
No manches... You welcome Mexico's people into your country?
I couldn't care less about the lines any man draws on a map.
This nation was started by immigrants. ***We are all foreigners*** on this Earth.

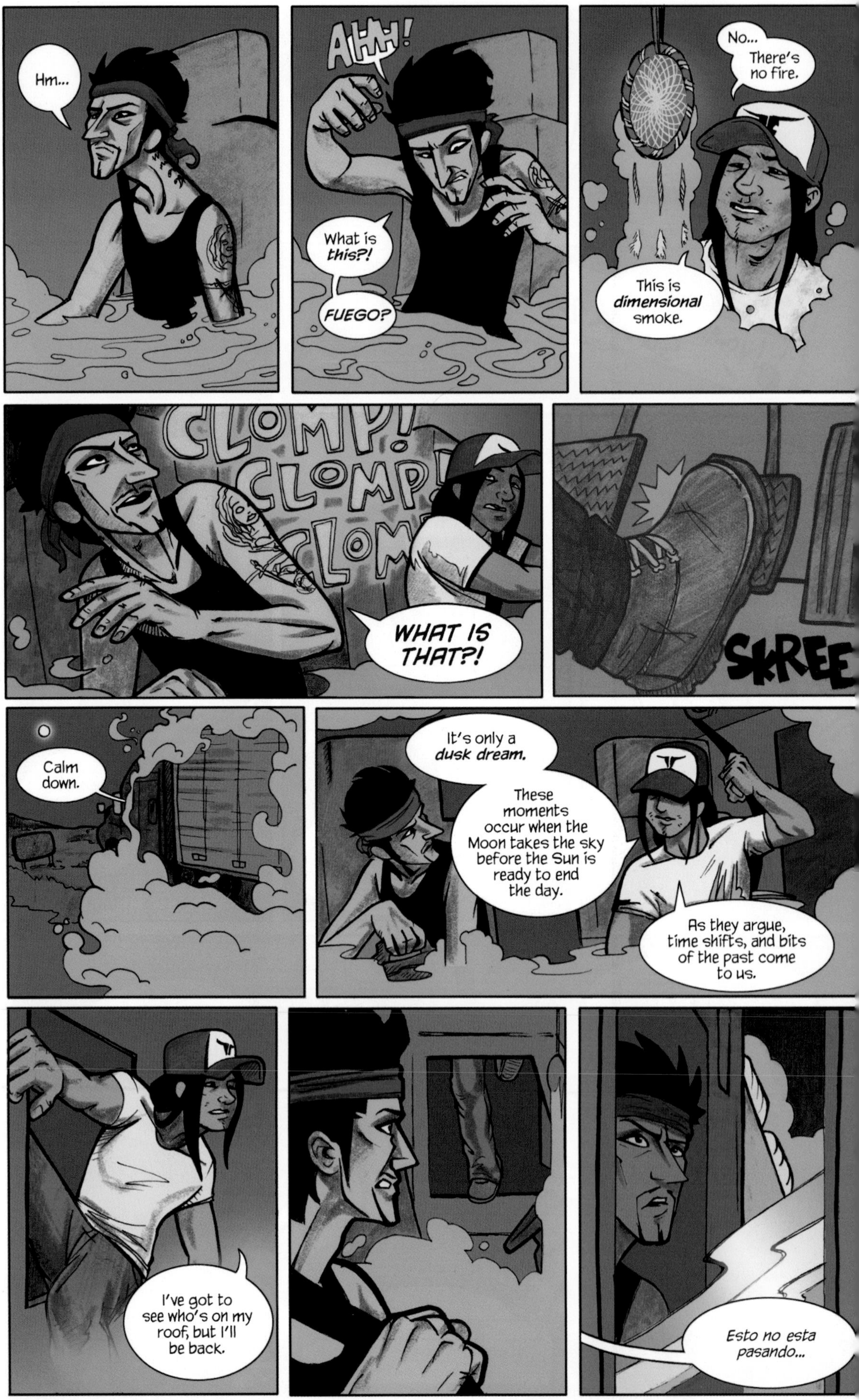
Hm...
AHH!
What is this?!
FUEGO?
No... There's no fire.
This is dimensional smoke.
CLOMP! CLOMP! CLOMP
WHAT IS THAT?!
SKREE
Calm down.
It's only a dusk dream.
These moments occur when the Moon takes the sky before the Sun is ready to end the day.
As they argue, time shifts, and bits of the past come to us.
I've got to see who's on my roof, but I'll be back.
Esto no esta pasando...

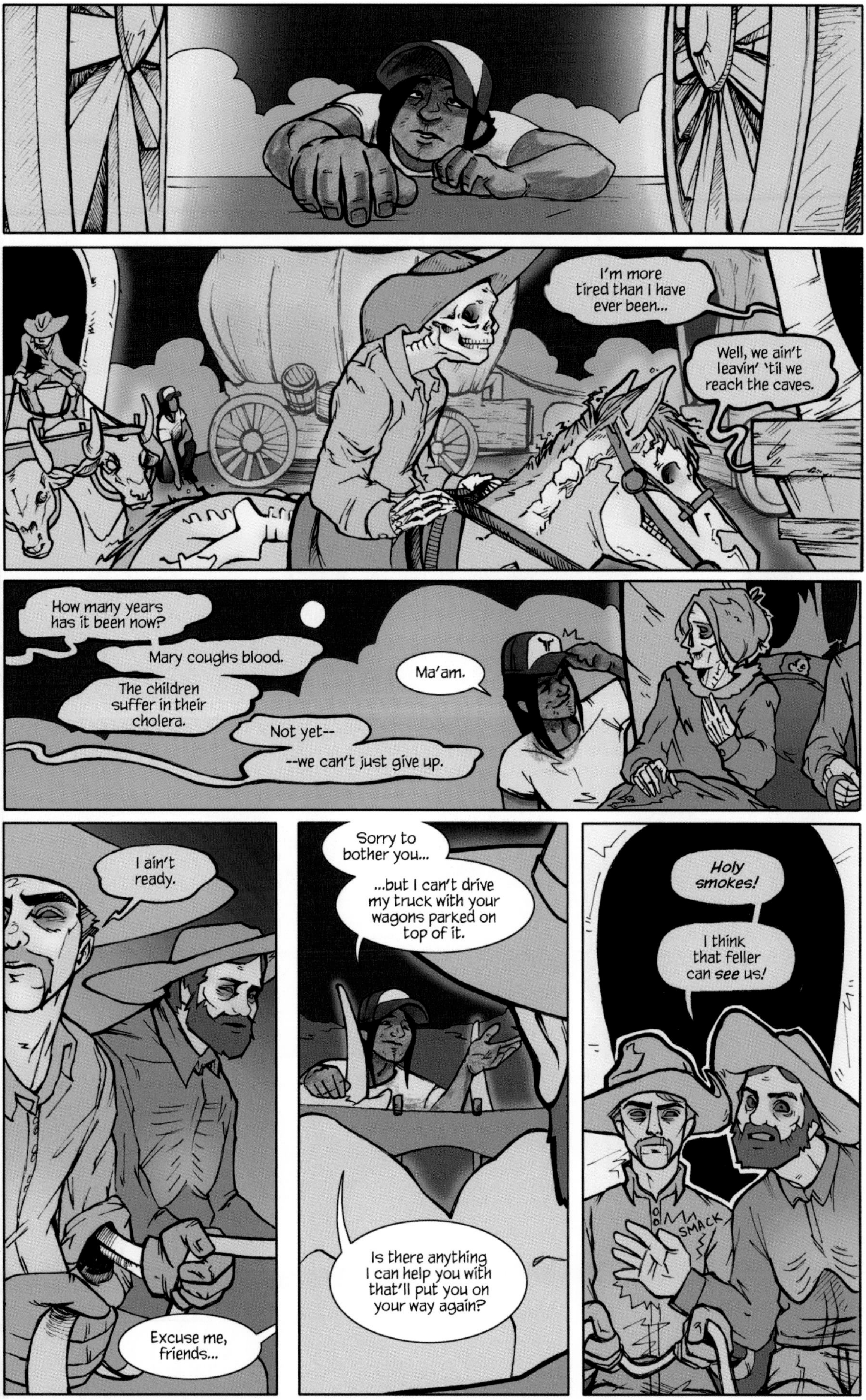
I'm more tired than I have ever been...
Well, we ain't leavin' 'til we reach the caves.
How many years has it been now?
Mary coughs blood.
The children suffer in their cholera.
Not yet--
--we can't just give up.
Ma'am.
I ain't ready.
Excuse me, friends...
Sorry to bother you...
...but I can't drive my truck with your wagons parked on top of it.
Is there anything I can help you with that'll put you on your way again?
Holy smokes!
I think that feller can see us!
SMACK

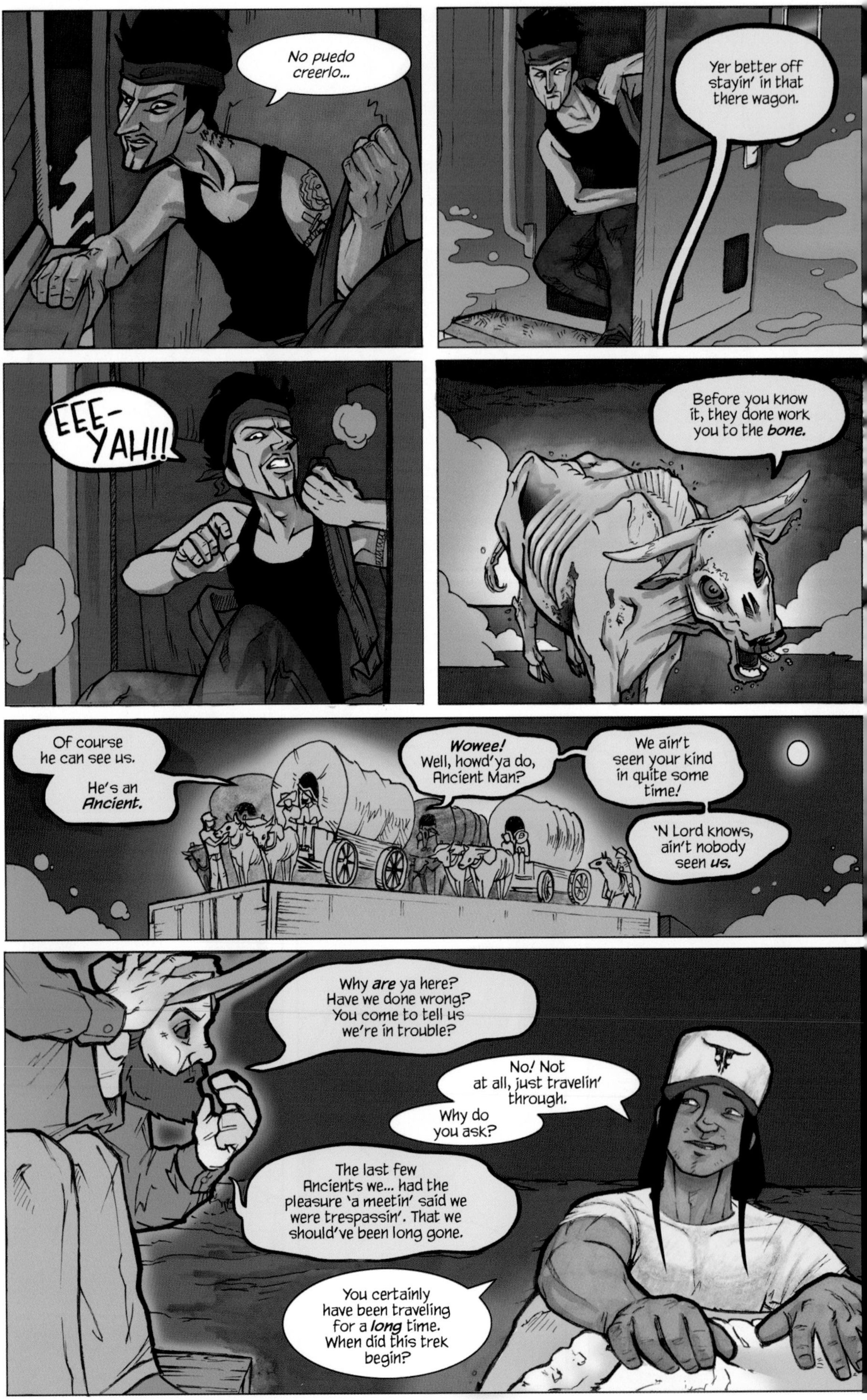
No puedo creerlo...
Yer better off stayin' in that there wagon.
EEE-YAH!!
Before you know it, they done work you to the bone.
Of course he can see us.
He's an Ancient.
Wowee! Well, howd'ya do, Ancient Man?
We ain't seen your kind in quite some time!
'N Lord knows, ain't nobody seen us.
Why are ya here? Have we done wrong? You come to tell us we're in trouble?
No! Not at all, just travelin' through.
Why do you ask?
The last few Ancients we... had the pleasure 'a meetin' said we were trespassin'. That we should've been long gone.
You certainly have been traveling for a long time. When did this trek begin?

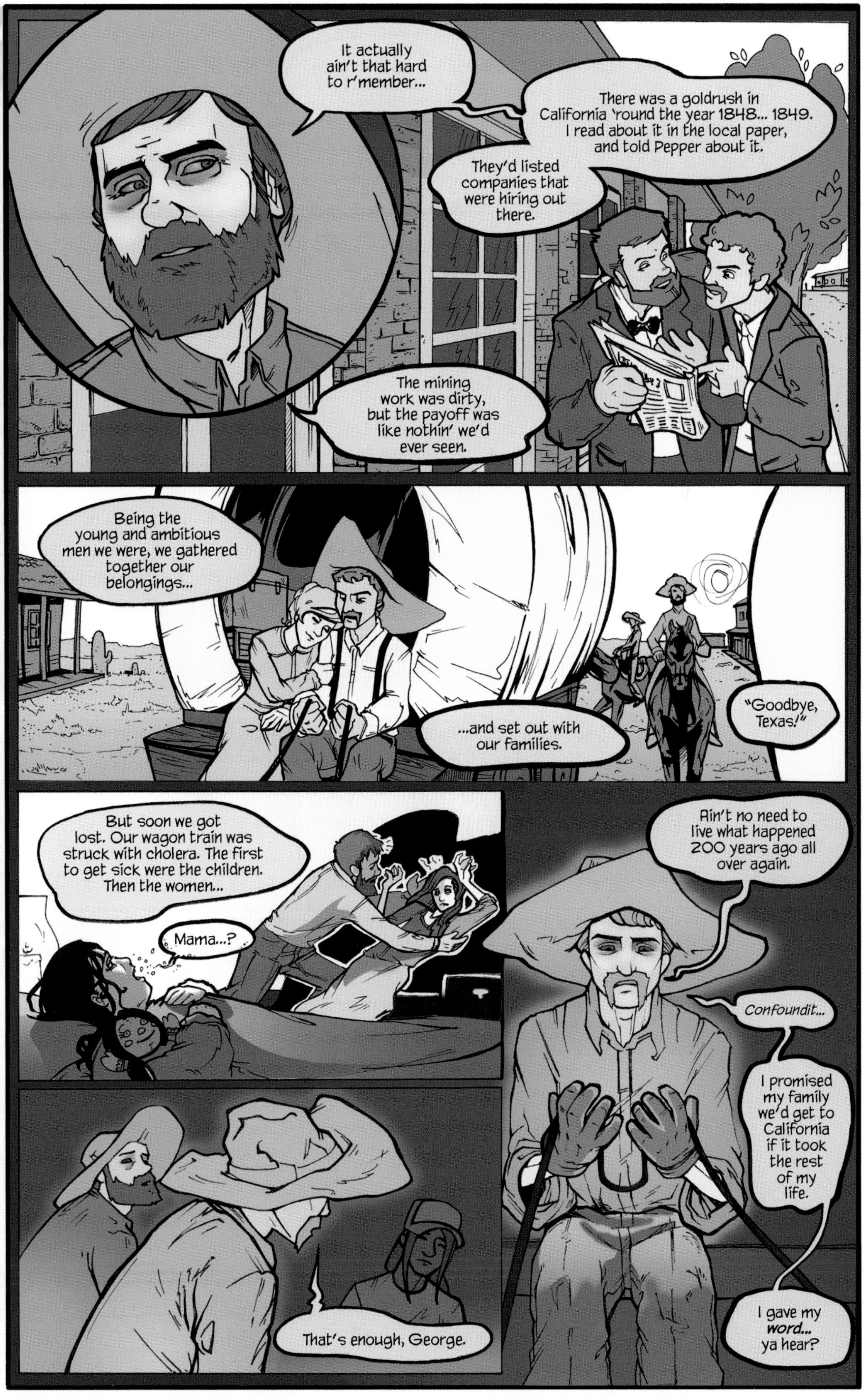
It actually ain't that hard to r'member...
There was a goldrush in California 'round the year 1848... 1849. I read about it in the local paper, and told Pepper about it.
They'd listed companies that were hiring out there.
The mining work was dirty, but the payoff was like nothin' we'd ever seen.
Being the young and ambitious men we were, we gathered together our belongings...
...and set out with our families.
"Goodbye, Texas!"
But soon we got lost. Our wagon train was struck with cholera. The first to get sick were the children. Then the women...
Mama...?
Ain't no need to live what happened 200 years ago all over again.
Confoundit...
I promised my family we'd get to California if it took the rest of my life.
I gave my *word...* ya hear?
That's enough, George.

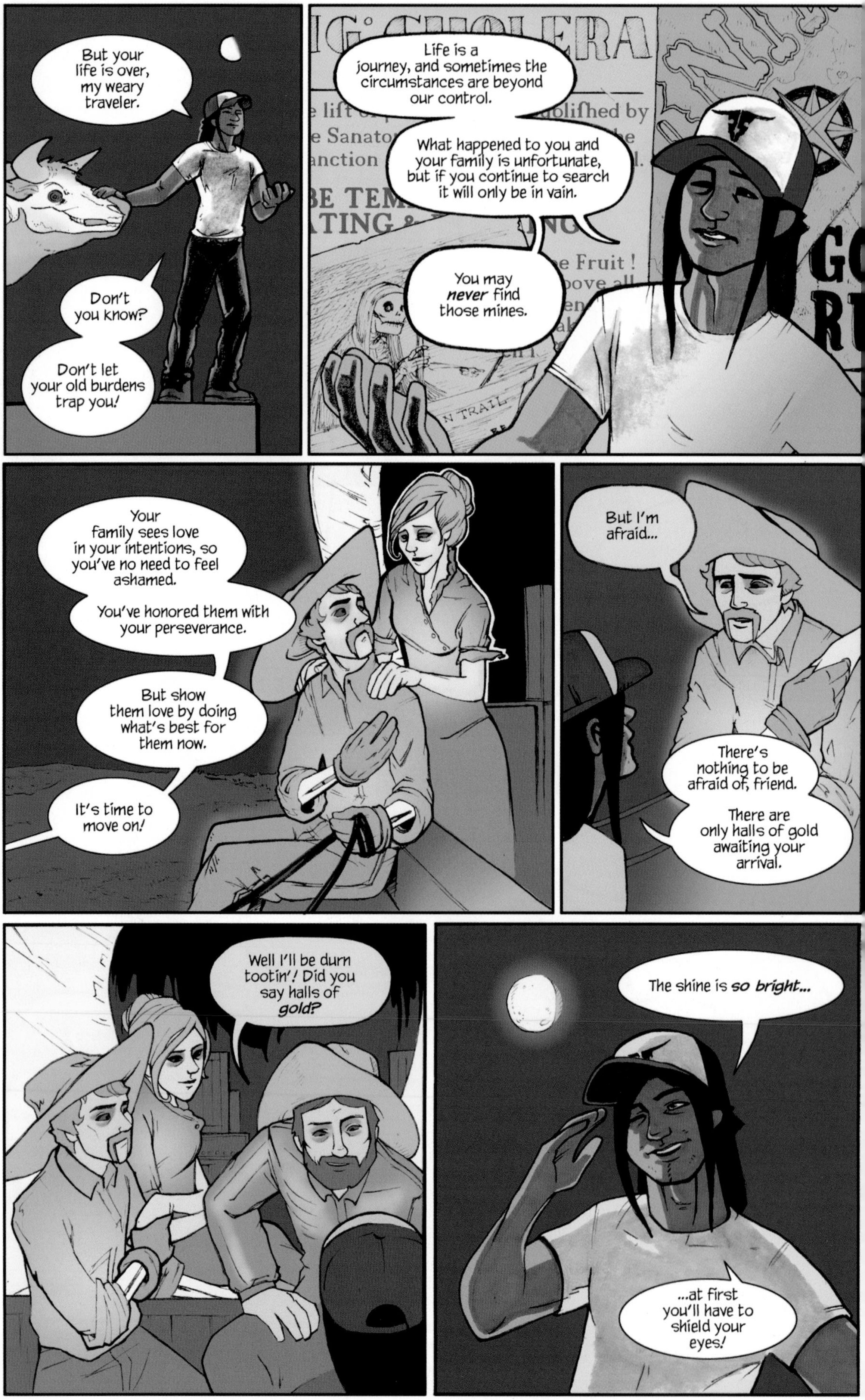
But your life is over, my weary traveler.
Don't you know?
Don't let your old burdens trap you!
Life is a journey, and sometimes the circumstances are beyond our control.
What happened to you and your family is unfortunate, but if you continue to search it will only be in vain.
You may *never* find those mines.
CHOLERA
BE TEM
ATING &
e Fruit !
N TRAIL
Your family sees love in your intentions, so you've no need to feel ashamed.
You've honored them with your perseverance.
But show them love by doing what's best for them now.
It's time to move on!
But I'm afraid...
There's nothing to be afraid of, friend.
There are only halls of gold awaiting your arrival.
Well I'll be durn tootin'! Did you say halls of *gold?*
The shine is *so bright...*
...at first you'll have to shield your eyes!

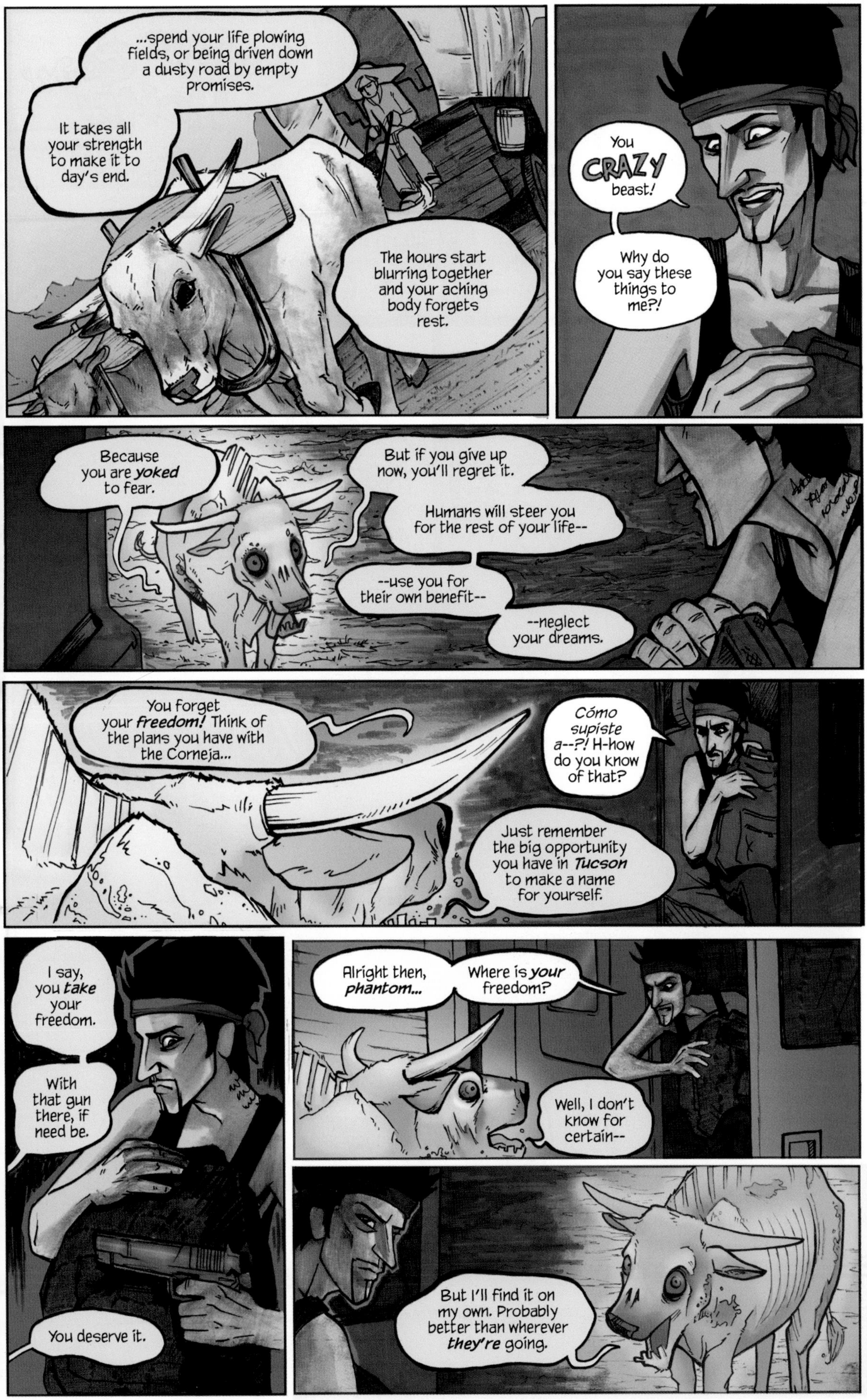
...spend your life plowing fields, or being driven down a dusty road by empty promises.
It takes all your strength to make it to day's end.
The hours start blurring together and your aching body forgets rest.
You CRAZY beast!
Why do you say these things to me?!
Because you are *yoked* to fear.
But if you give up now, you'll regret it.
Humans will steer you for the rest of your life--
--use you for their own benefit--
--neglect your dreams.
You forget your *freedom!* Think of the plans you have with the Corneja...
Cómo supiste a--?! H-how do you know of that?
Just remember the big opportunity you have in *Tucson* to make a name for yourself.
I say, you *take* your freedom.
With that gun there, if need be.
You deserve it.
Alright then, *phantom...*
Where is *your* freedom?
Well, I don't know for certain--
But I'll find it on my own. Probably better than wherever *they're* going.

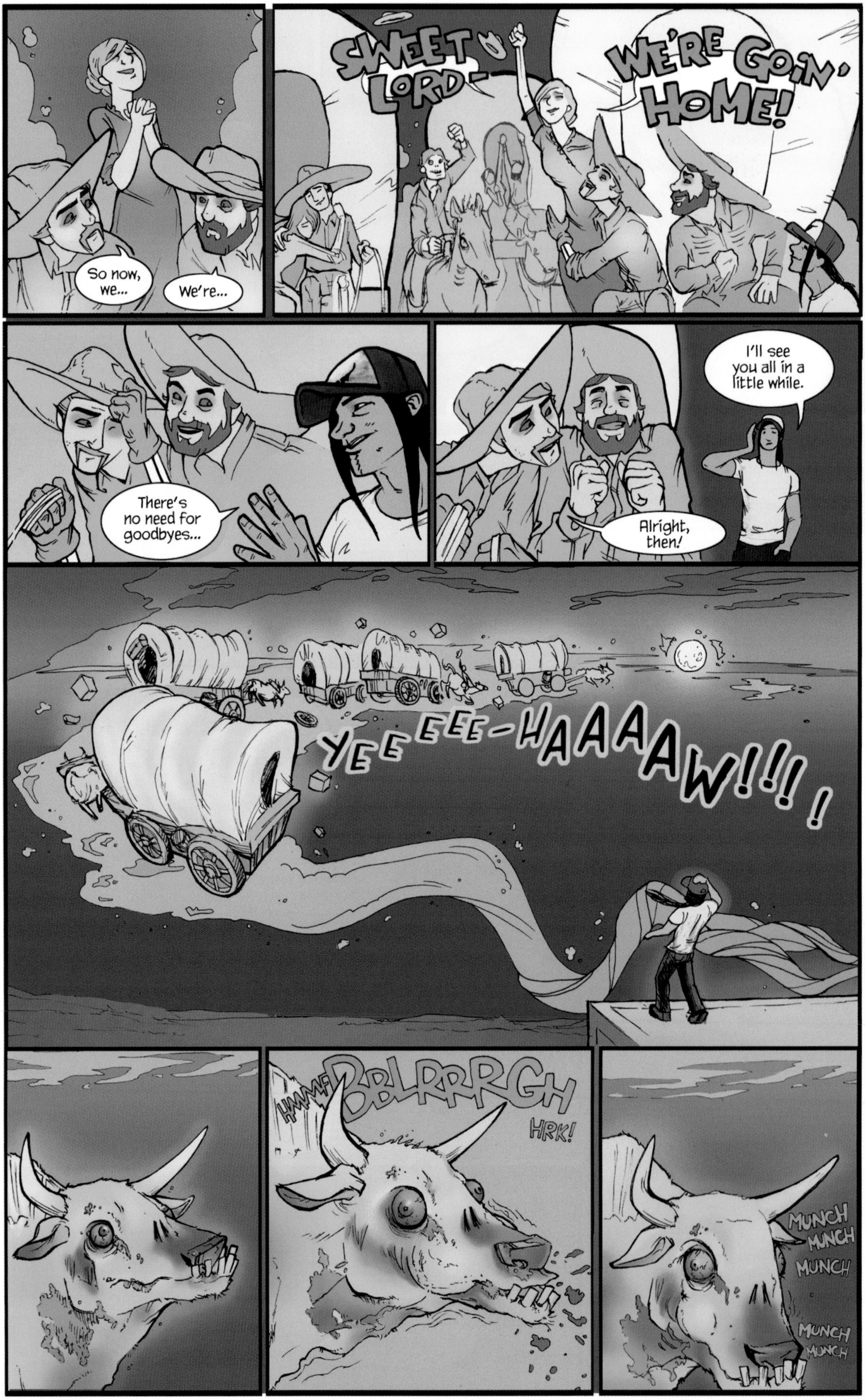
So now, we...
We're...
SWEET LORD-
WE'RE GOIN' HOME!
There's no need for goodbyes...
Alright, then!
I'll see you all in a little while.
YEEEEE-HAAAAAW!!!! !
HWWF BBLRRRGH
HRK!
MUNCH
MUNCH
MUNCH
MUNCH
MUNCH

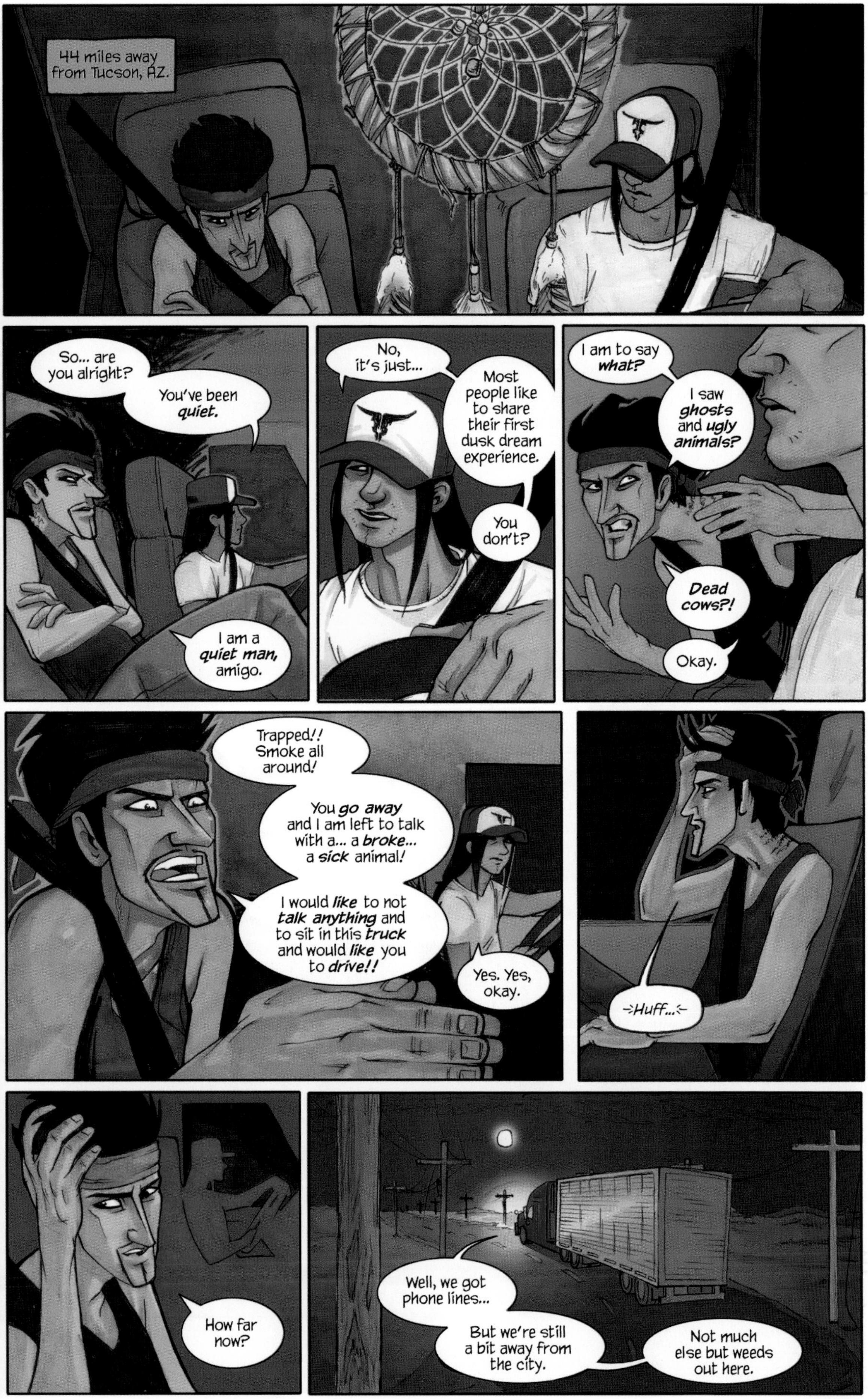

44 miles away from Tucson, AZ.
So... are you alright?
You've been *quiet.*
I am a *quiet man,* amigo.
No, it's just...
Most people like to share their first dusk dream experience.
You don't?
I am to say *what?*
I saw *ghosts* and *ugly animals?*
Dead cows?!
Okay.
Trapped!! Smoke all around!
You *go away* and I am left to talk with a... a *broke...* a *sick* animal!
I would *like* to not *talk anything* and to sit in this *truck* and would *like* you to *drive!!*
Yes. Yes, okay.
Huff...
How far now?
Well, we got phone lines...
But we're still a bit away from the city.
Not much else but weeds out here.

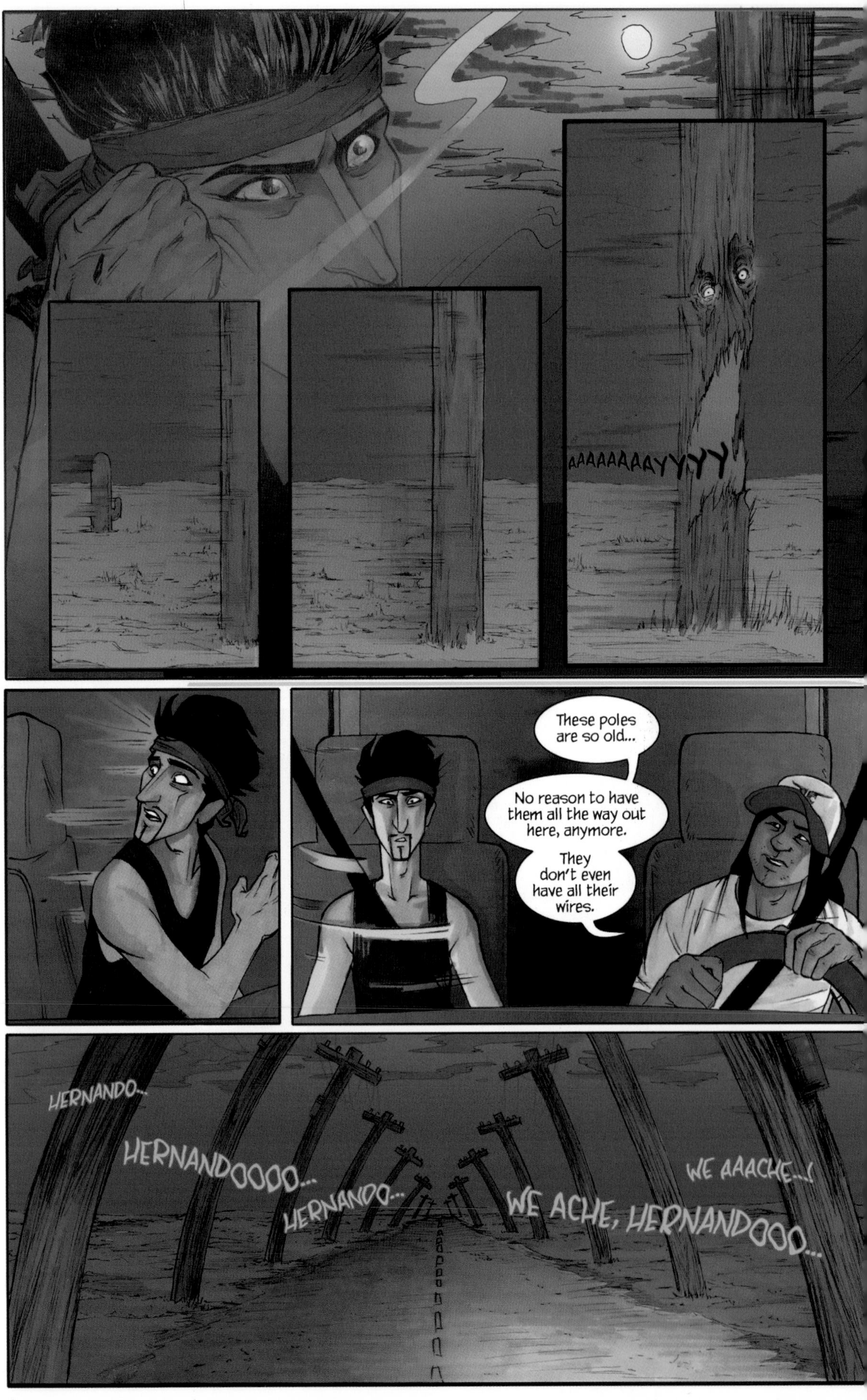
AAAAAAAAYYYYY
These poles are so old...
No reason to have them all the way out here, anymore.
They don't even have all their wires.
HERNANDO...
HERNANDOOOO...
HERNANDO...
WE ACHE, HERNANDOOO...
WE AAACHE...!

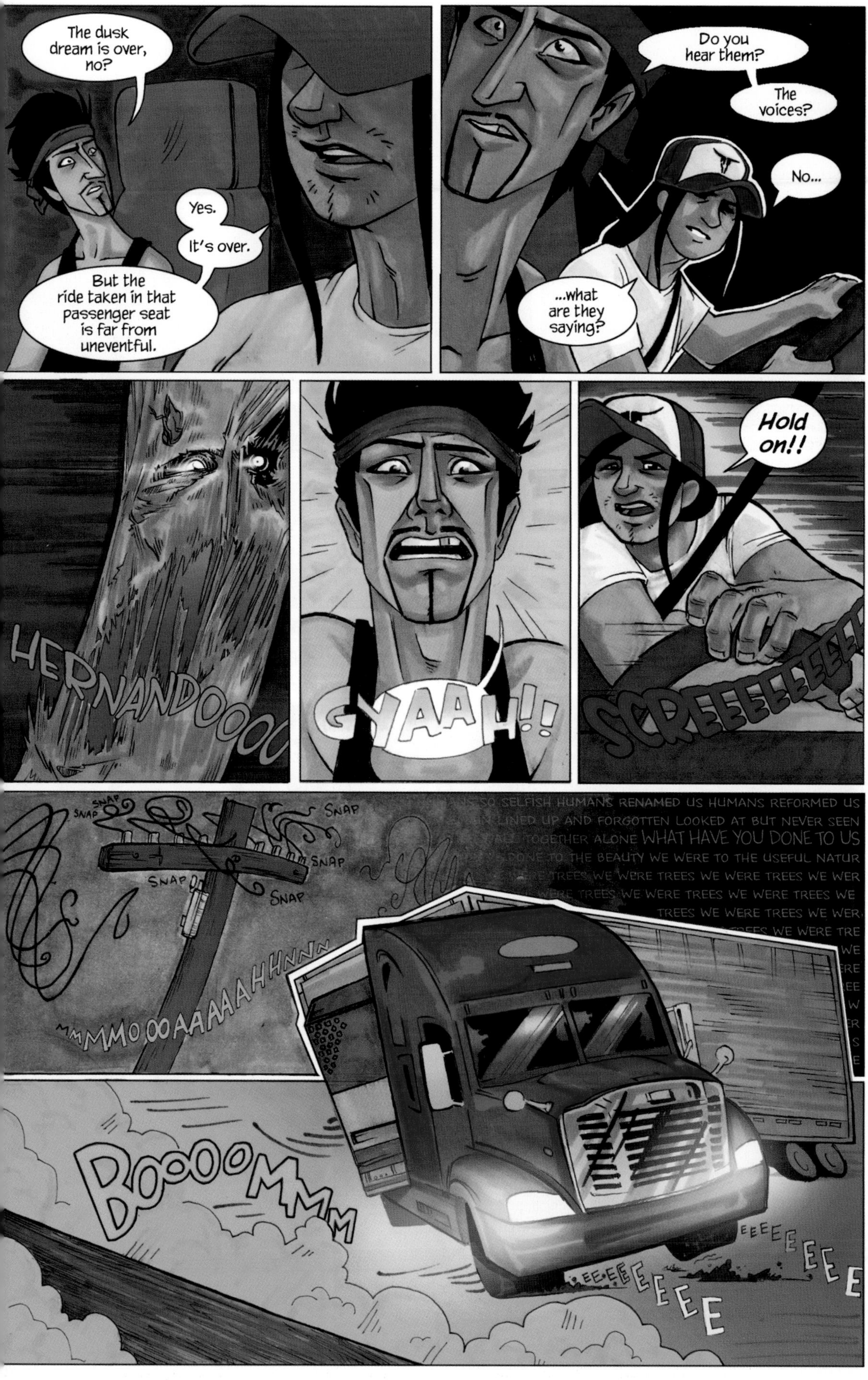
The dusk dream is over, no?
Yes.
It's over.
But the ride taken in that passenger seat is far from uneventful.
Do you hear them?
The voices?
No...
...what are they saying?
HERNANDOOOO
GYAAH!!
Hold on!!
SCREEEEEEEEE
SNAP
SNAP
SNAP
SNAP
SNAP
MMMOOOAAAAAHHNNN
SO SELFISH HUMANS RENAMED US HUMANS REFORMED US
LINED UP AND FORGOTTEN LOOKED AT BUT NEVER SEEN
TOGETHER ALONE WHAT HAVE YOU DONE TO US
TO THE BEAUTY WE WERE TO THE USEFUL NATUR
TREES WE WERE TREES WE WERE TREES WE WER
TREES WE WERE TREES WE WERE TREES WE
TREES WE WERE TREES WE WER
WE WERE TRE
BOOOOMMMM
EEEEEEEEEEEEEEE

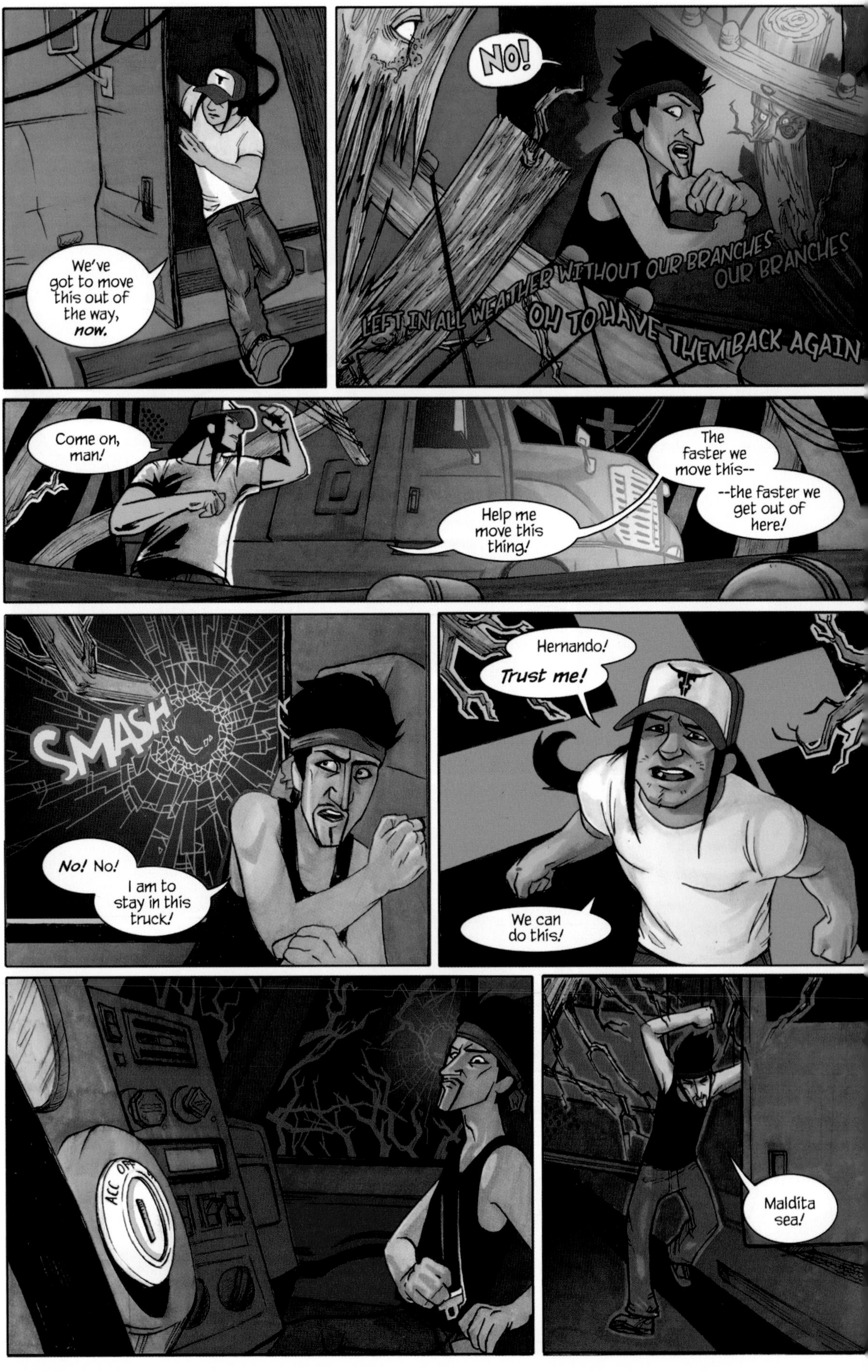
We've got to move this out of the way, *now.*
NO!
LEFT IN ALL WEATHER WITHOUT OUR BRANCHES
OUR BRANCHES
OH TO HAVE THEM BACK AGAIN
Come on, man!
Help me move this thing!
The faster we move this--
--the faster we get out of here!
SMASH
No! No!
I am to stay in this truck!
Hernando!
Trust me!
We can do this!
ACC OFF
Maldita sea!

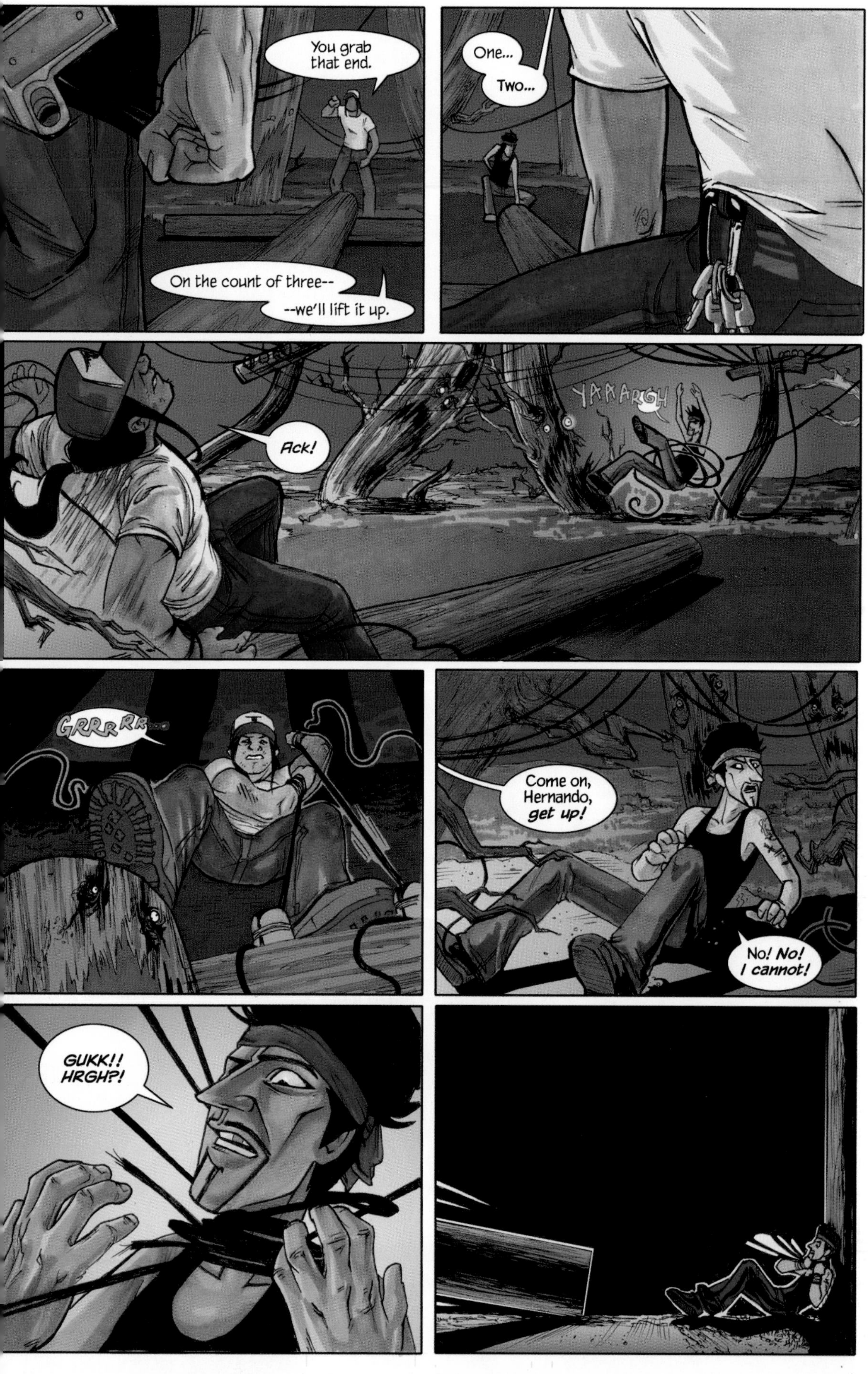
You grab that end.
On the count of three--
--we'll lift it up.
One...
Two...
Ack!
YARARGH
GRRRRR...
Come on, Hernando, *get up!*
No! *No!* I cannot!
GUKK!! HRGH?!

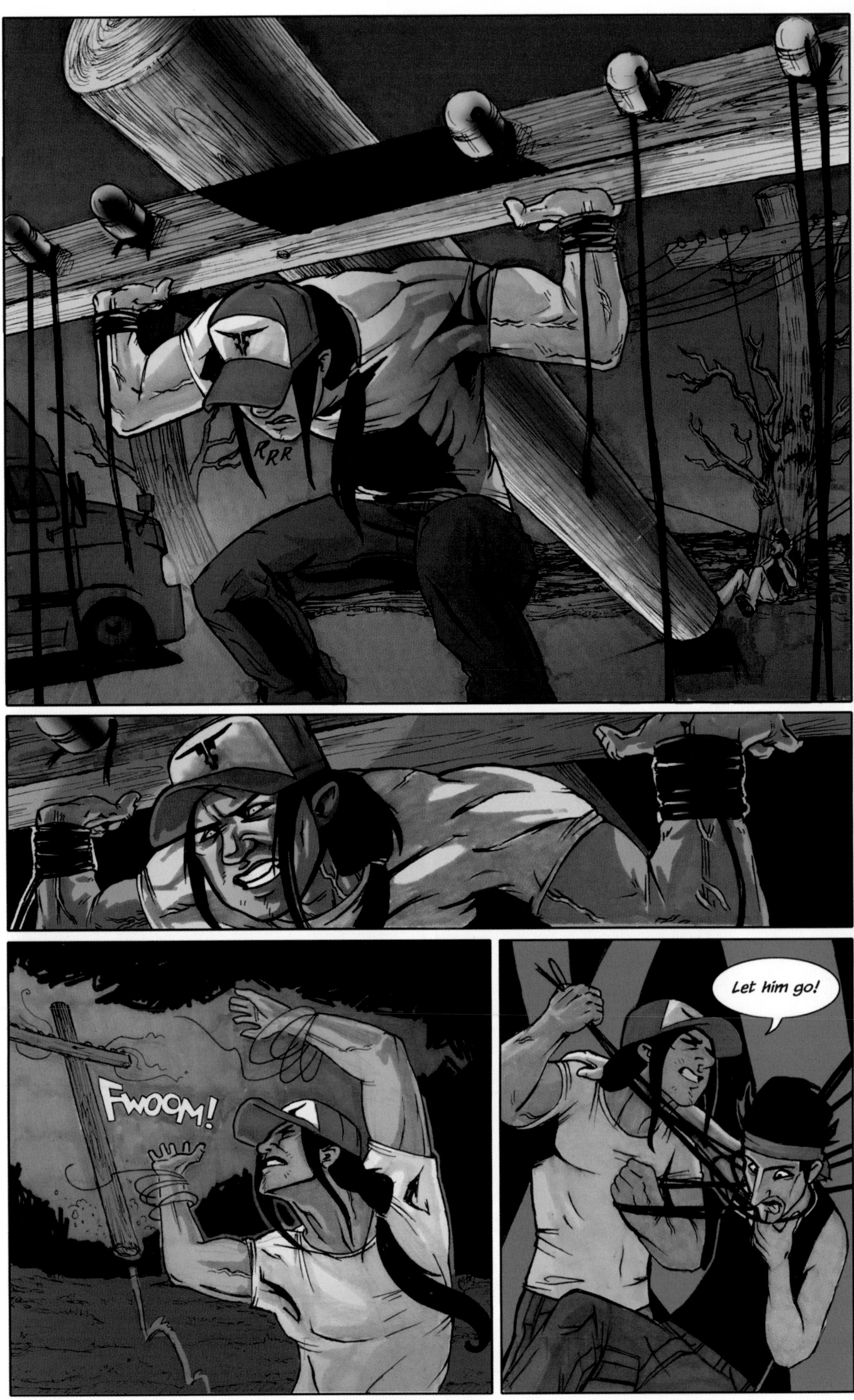
RRR
FWOOM!
Let him go!

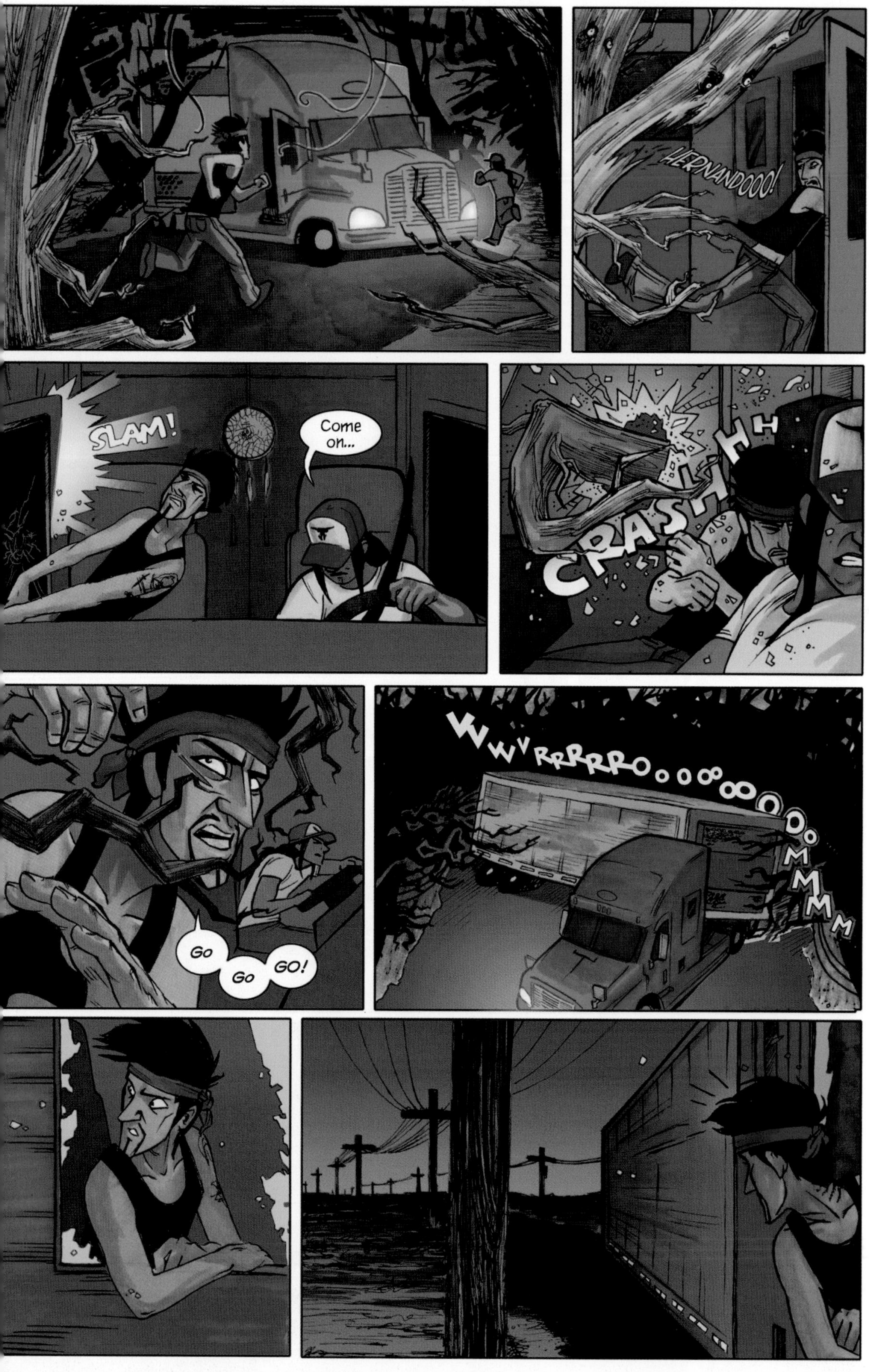
HERNANDOOO!
SLAM!
Come on...
CRASHHH
Go
Go
GO!
WWVRRRRROOOOOOOOMMMMM

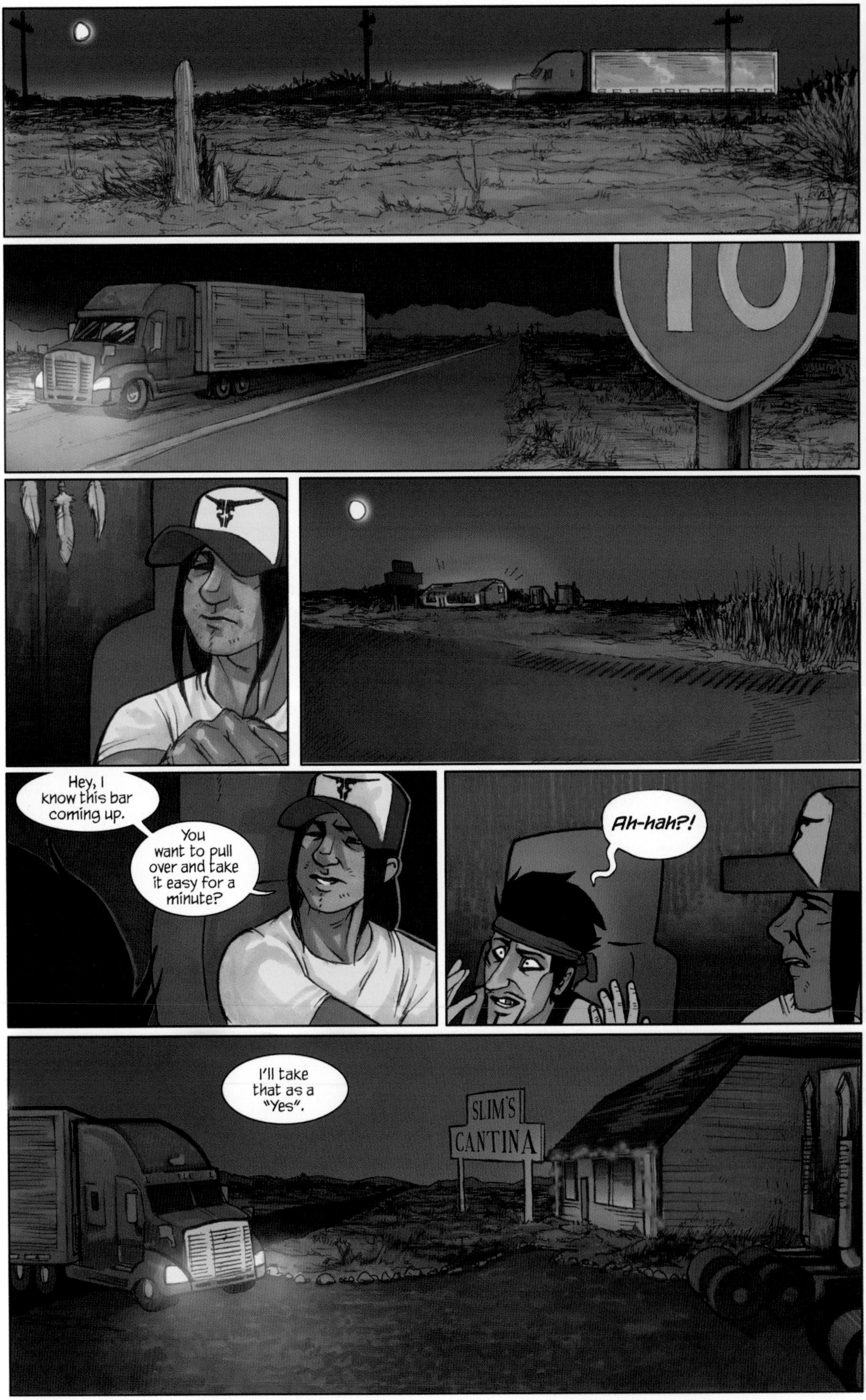
10
Hey, I know this bar coming up.
You want to pull over and take it easy for a minute?
Ah-hah?!
I'll take that as a "Yes".
SLIM'S CANTINA

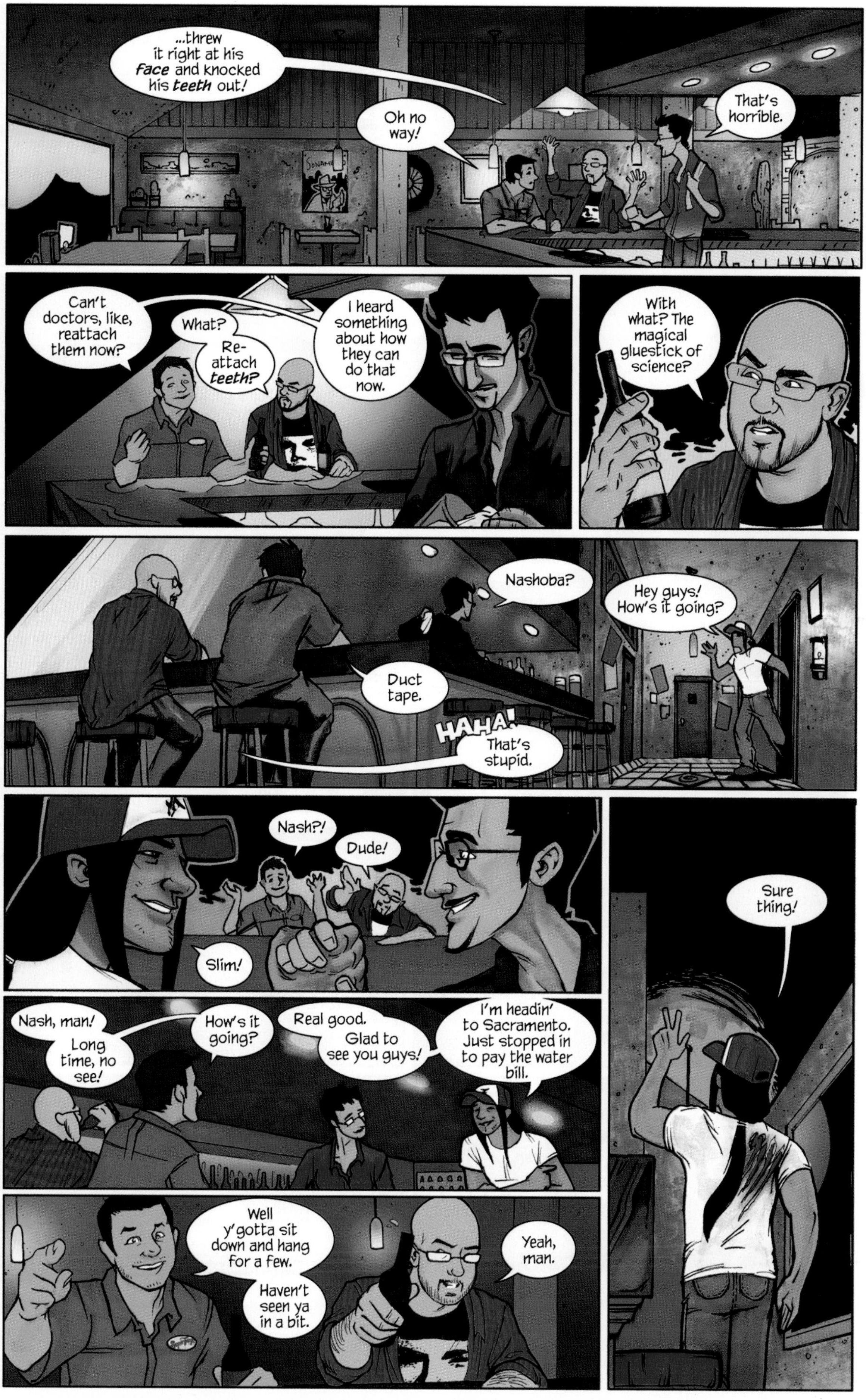
...threw it right at his *face* and knocked his *teeth* out!
Oh no way!
That's horrible.
Can't doctors, like, reattach them now?
What?
Re-attach *teeth*?
I heard something about how they can do that now.
With what? The magical gluestick of science?
Nashoba?
Hey guys! How's it going?
Duct tape.
HAHA!
That's stupid.
Nash?!
Dude!
Slim!
Sure thing!
Nash, man!
Long time, no see!
How's it going?
Real good.
Glad to see you guys!
I'm headin' to Sacramento. Just stopped in to pay the water bill.
Well y'gotta sit down and hang for a few.
Haven't seen ya in a bit.
Yeah, man.

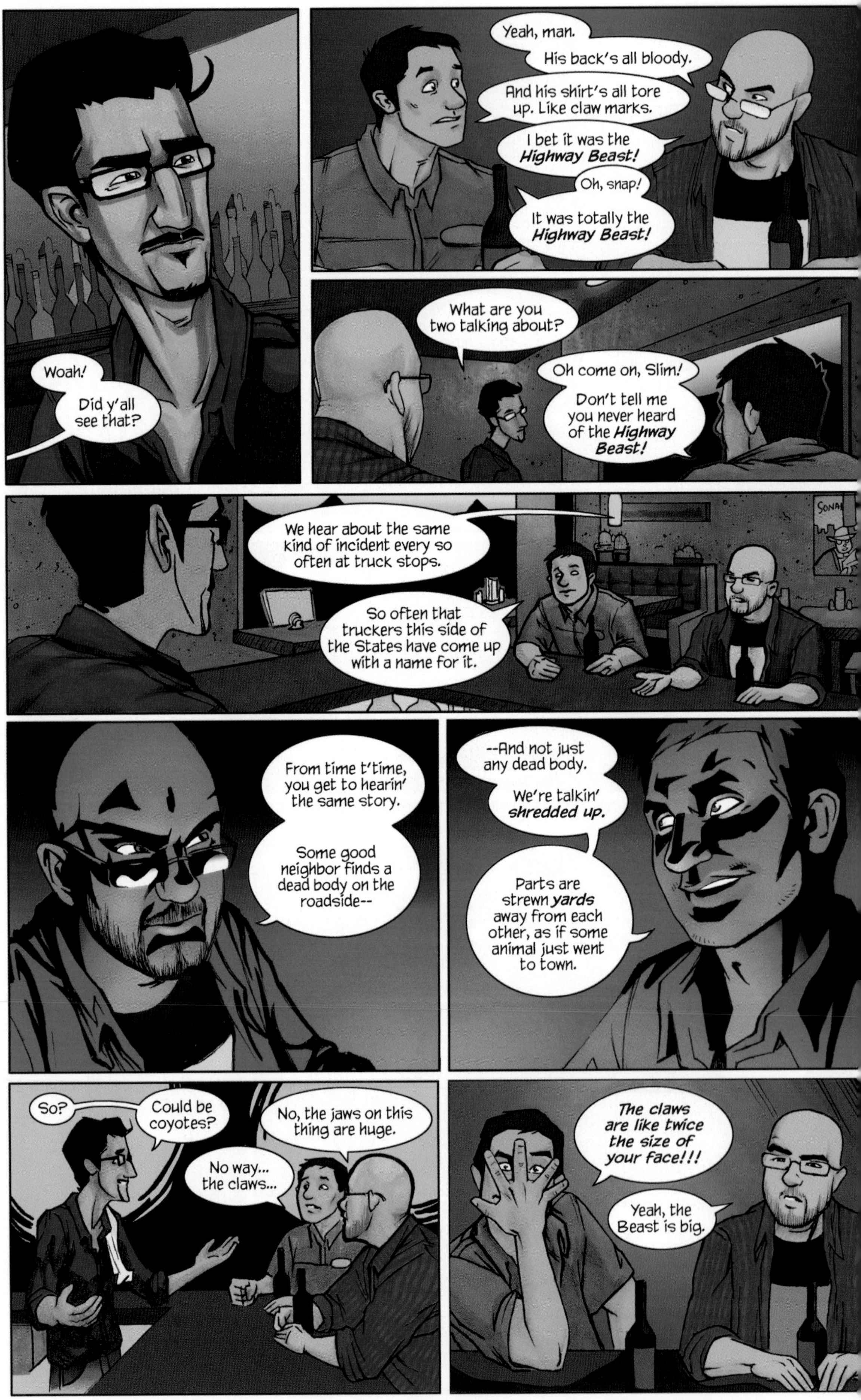
Woah!
Did y'all see that?
Yeah, man.
His back's all bloody.
And his shirt's all tore up. Like claw marks.
I bet it was the *Highway Beast!*
Oh, snap!
It was totally the *Highway Beast!*
What are you two talking about?
Oh come on, Slim!
Don't tell me you never heard of the *Highway Beast!*
We hear about the same kind of incident every so often at truck stops.
So often that truckers this side of the States have come up with a name for it.
From time t'time, you get to hearin' the same story.
Some good neighbor finds a dead body on the roadside--
--And not just any dead body.
We're talkin' *shredded up.*
Parts are strewn *yards* away from each other, as if some animal just went to town.
So?
Could be coyotes?
No, the jaws on this thing are huge.
No way... the claws...
The claws are like twice the size of your face!!!
Yeah, the Beast is big.

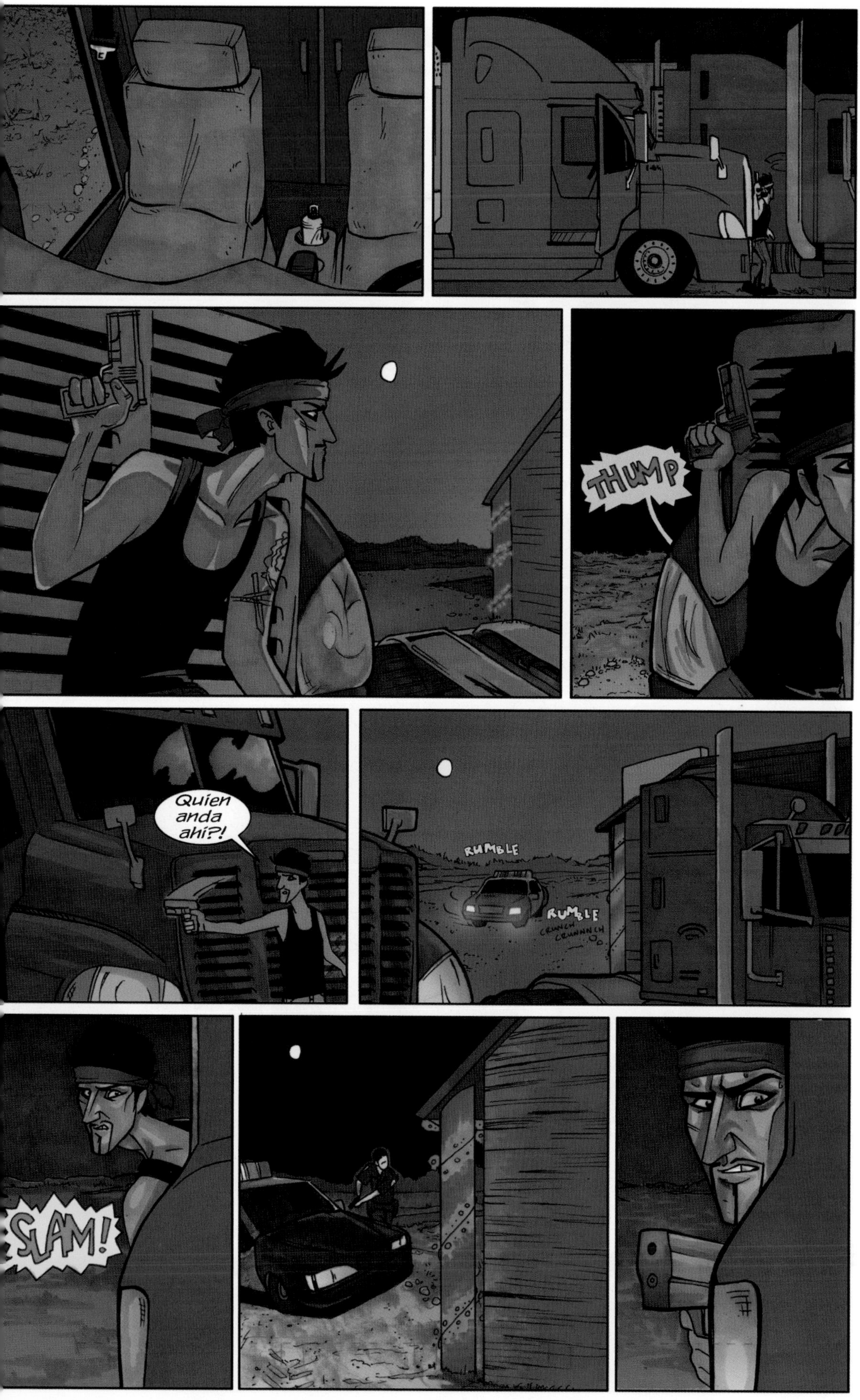
THUMP
Quien anda ahi?!
RUMBLE
RUMBLE
CRUNCH CRUNNNCH
SLAM!

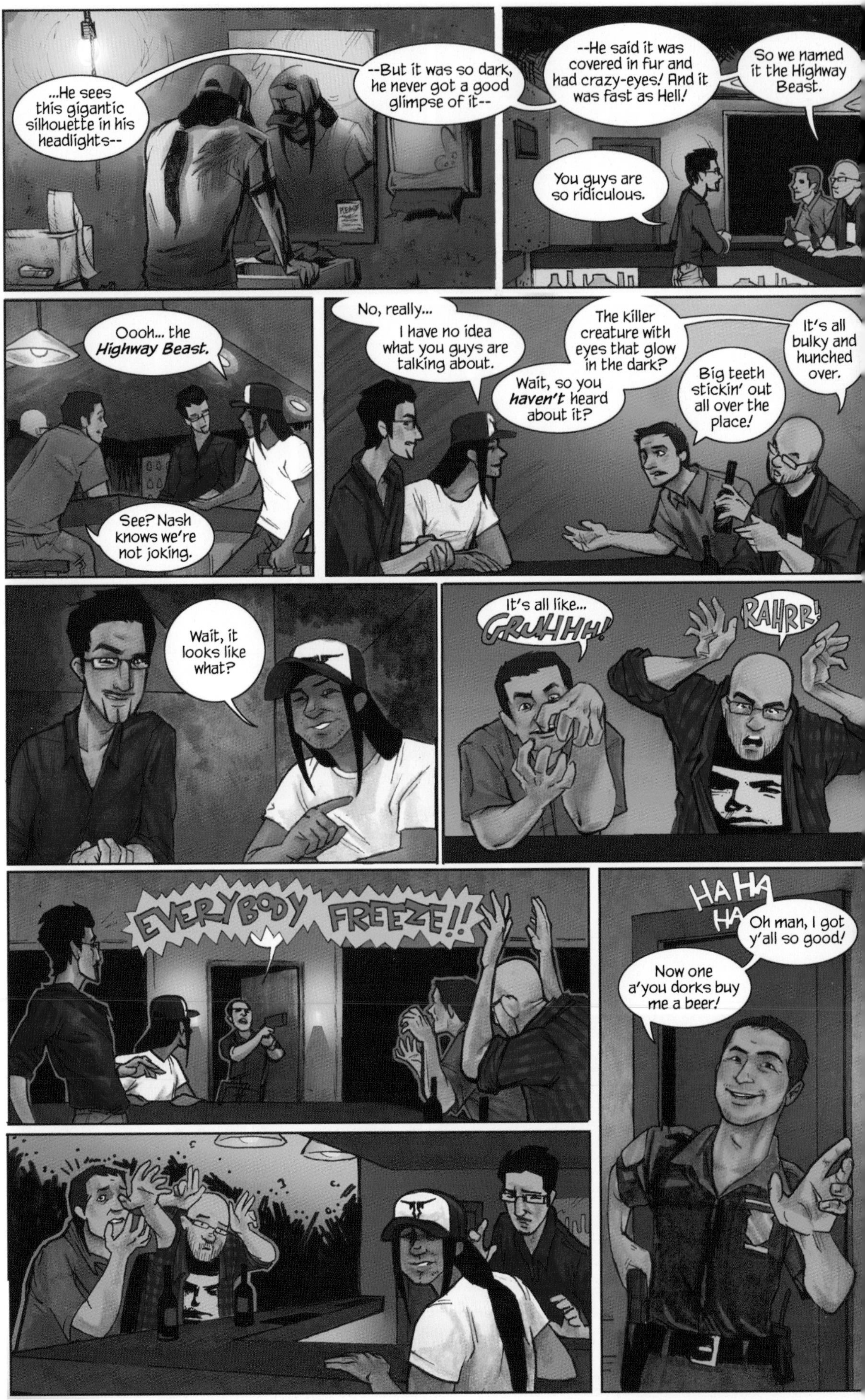
...He sees this gigantic silhouette in his headlights--
--But it was so dark, he never got a good glimpse of it--
--He said it was covered in fur and had crazy-eyes! And it was fast as Hell!
So we named it the Highway Beast.
You guys are so ridiculous.
Oooh... the *Highway Beast.*
See? Nash knows we're not joking.
No, really...
I have no idea what you guys are talking about.
Wait, so you *haven't* heard about it?
The killer creature with eyes that glow in the dark?
Big teeth stickin' out all over the place!
It's all bulky and hunched over.
Wait, it looks like what?
It's all like... GRUHHH!
RAHRR!
EVERYBODY FREEZE!!
HA HA HA
Oh man, I got y'all so good!
Now one a'you dorks buy me a beer!

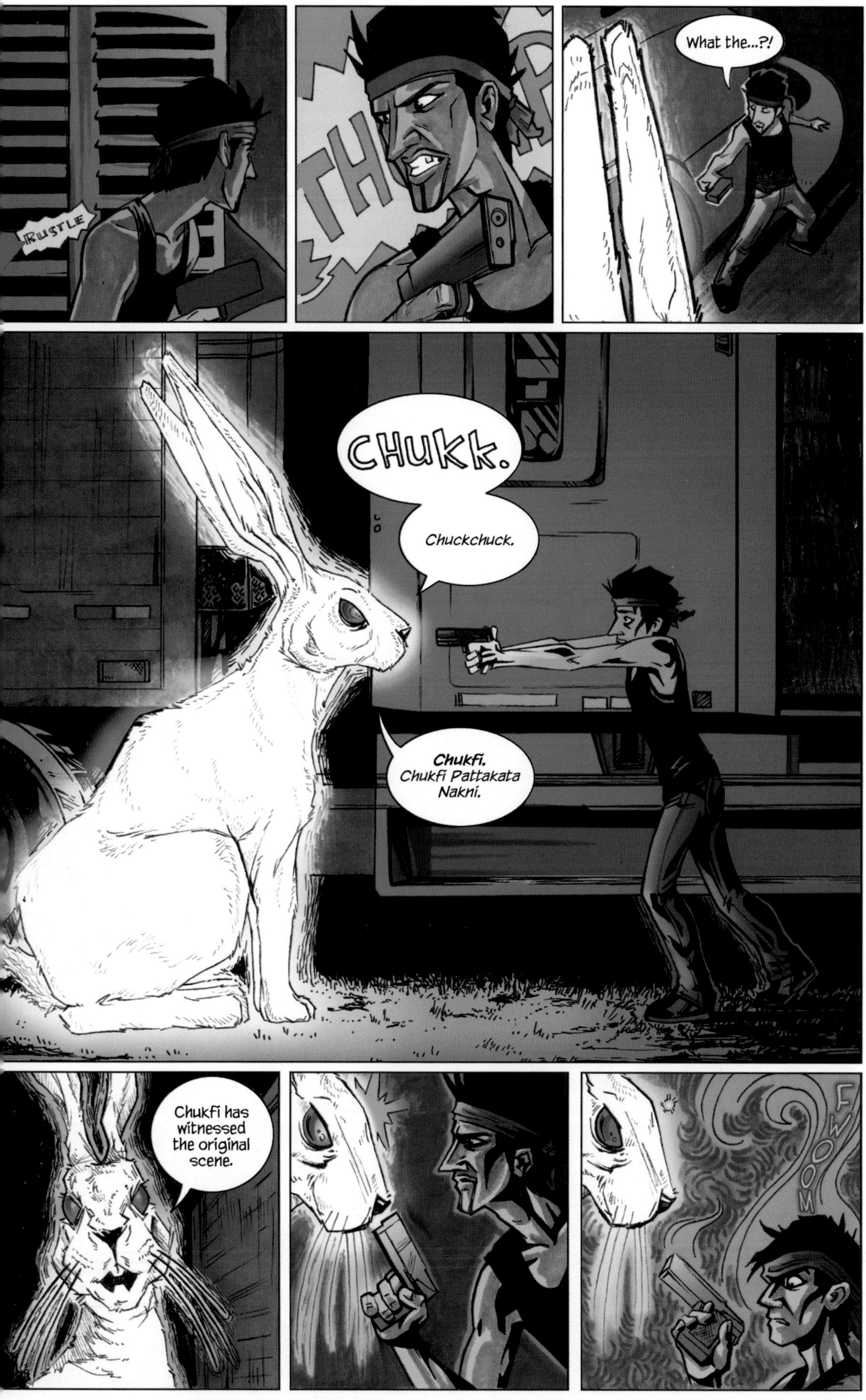
RUSTLE
What the...?!
CHUKK.
Chuckchuck.
Chukfi.
Chukfi Pattakata Nakni.
Chukfi has witnessed the original scene.
FWOOM

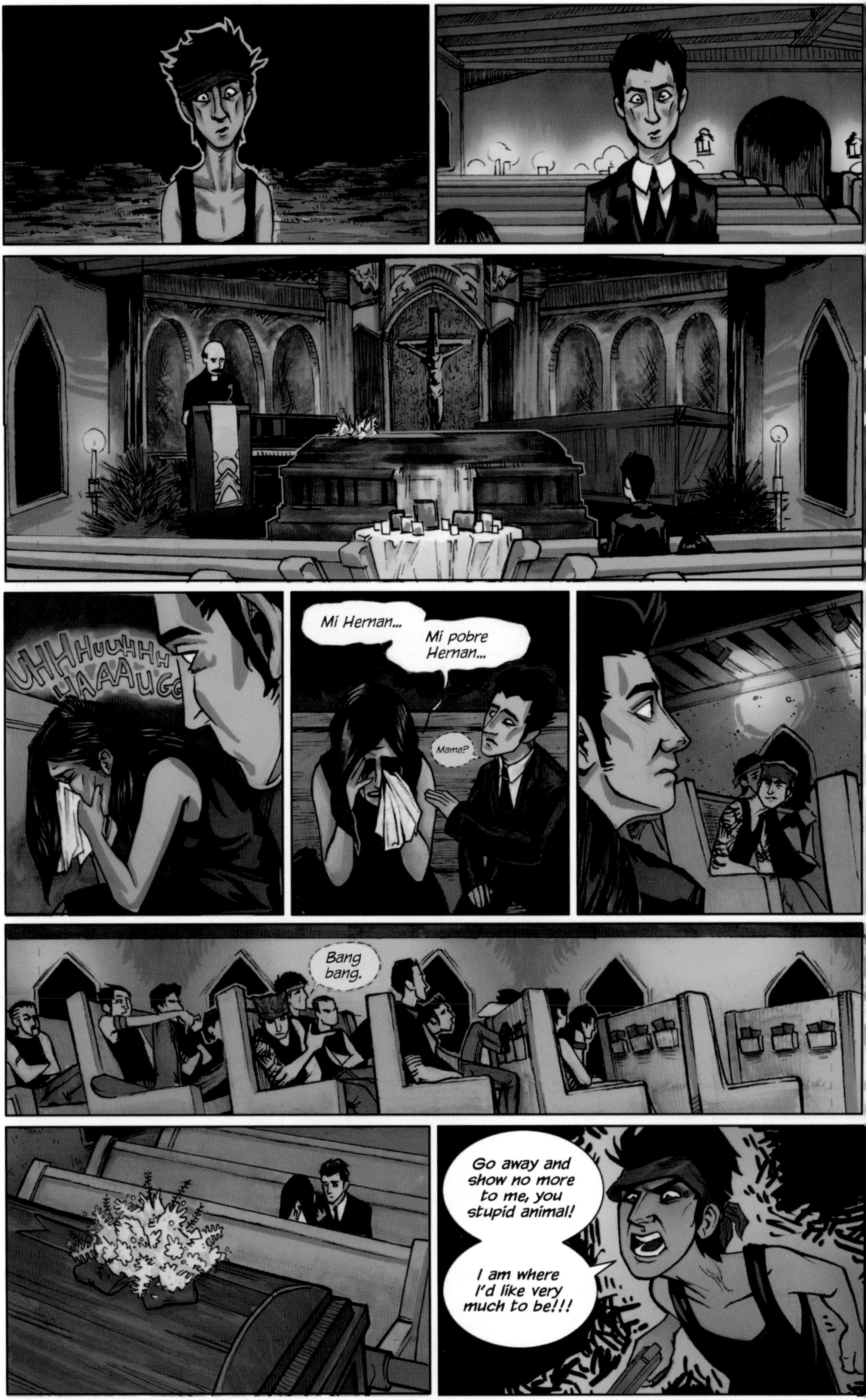
UHHHuuhhh HAAAUGG
Mí Hernan...
Mí pobre Hernan...
Mama?
Bang bang.
Go away and show no more to me, you stupid animal!
I am where I'd like very much to be!!!

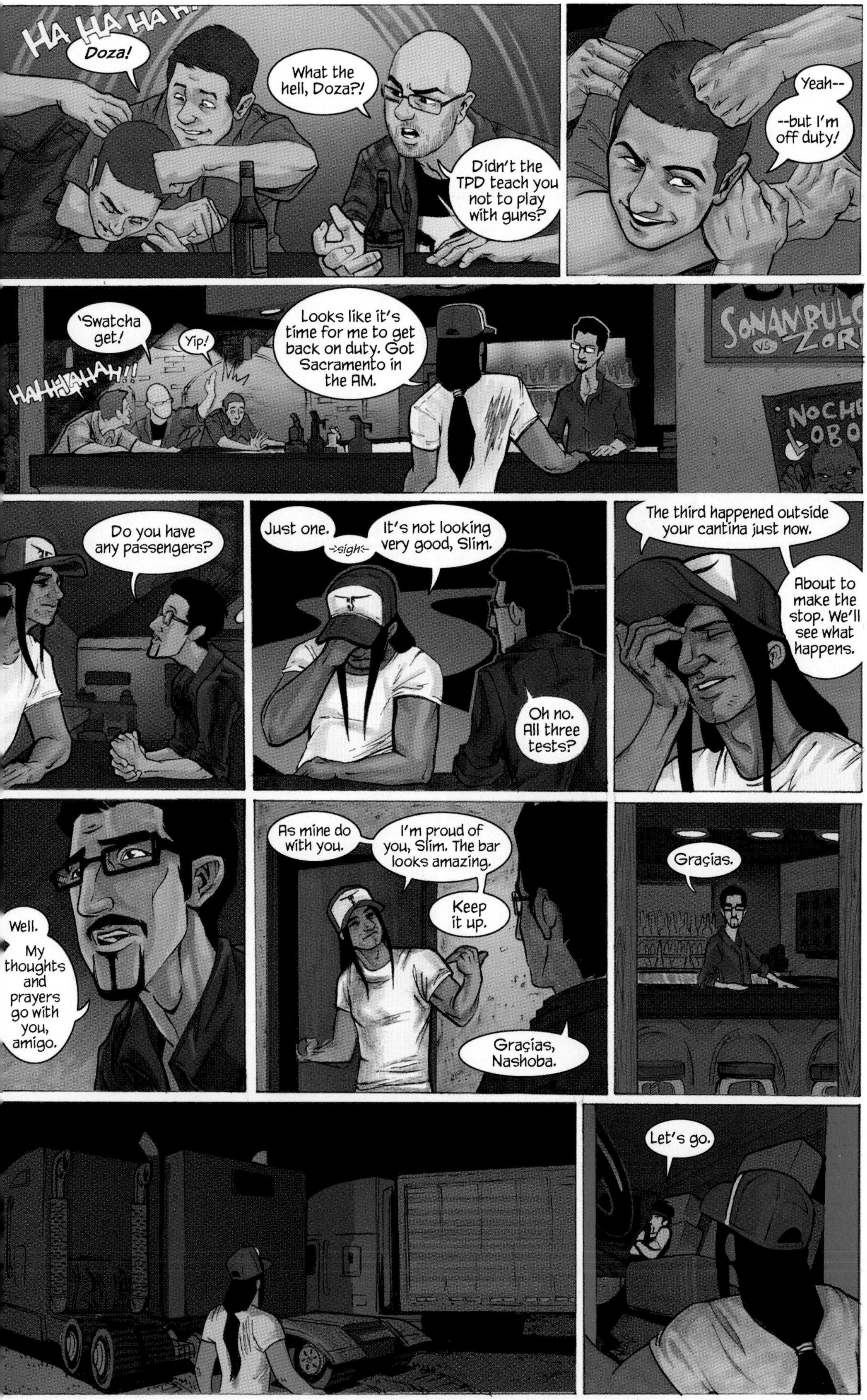
HA HA HA HA
Doza!
What the hell, Doza?!
Didn't the TPD teach you not to play with guns?
Yeah--
--but I'm off duty!
'Swatcha get!
Yip!
HAHHHAHAH!!
Looks like it's time for me to get back on duty. Got Sacramento in the AM.
SONAMBULO VS. ZOR
NOCHE LOBO
Do you have any passengers?
Just one.
~sigh~
It's not looking very good, Slim.
Oh no. All three tests?
The third happened outside your cantina just now.
About to make the stop. We'll see what happens.
Well.
My thoughts and prayers go with you, amigo.
As mine do with you.
I'm proud of you, Slim. The bar looks amazing.
Keep it up.
Graçias, Nashoba.
Graçias.
Let's go.

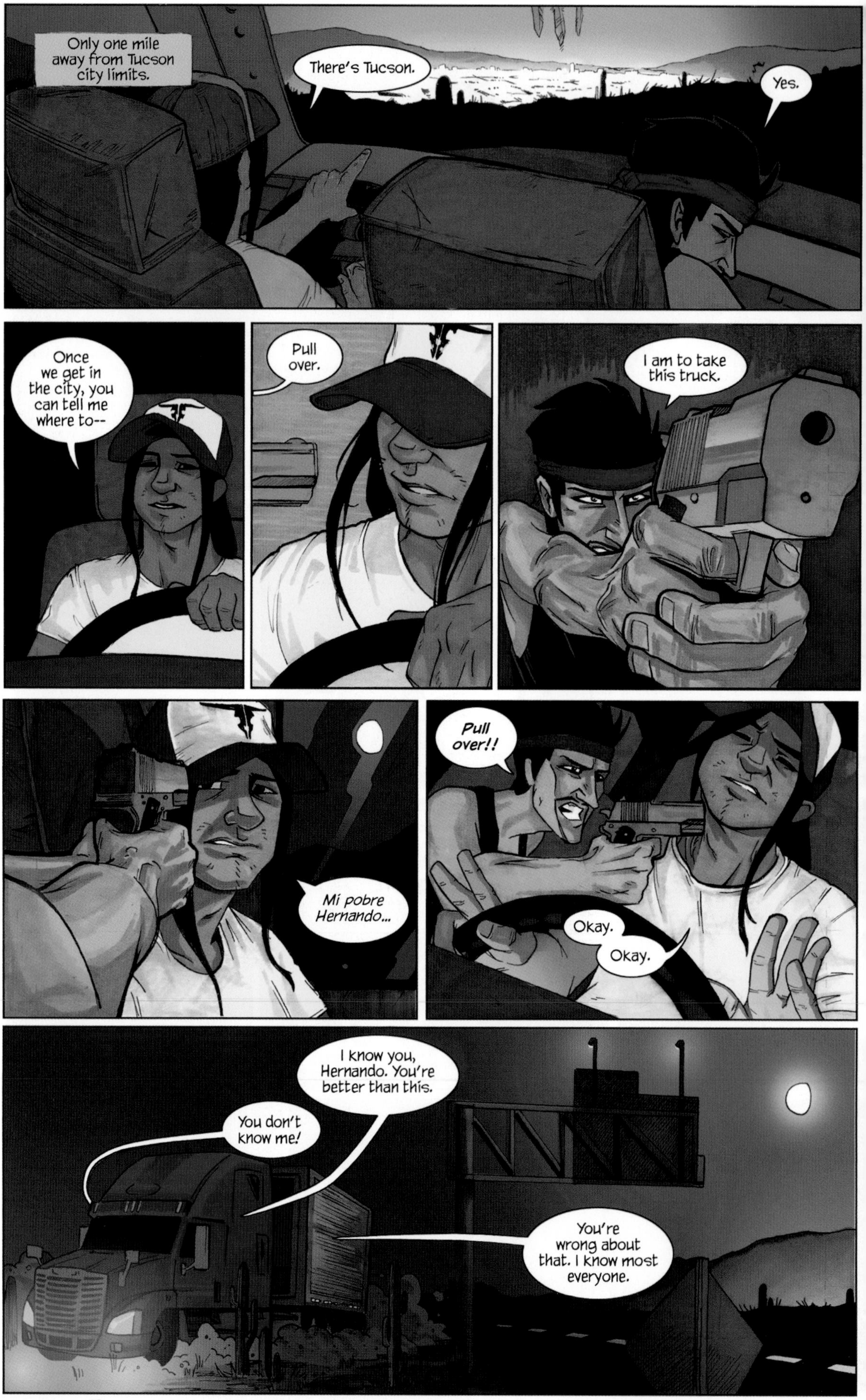
Only one mile away from Tucson city limits.
There's Tucson.
Yes.
Once we get in the city, you can tell me where to--
Pull over.
I am to take this truck.
Mi pobre Hernando...
Pull over!!
Okay. Okay.
I know you, Hernando. You're better than this.
You don't know me!
You're wrong about that. I know most everyone.

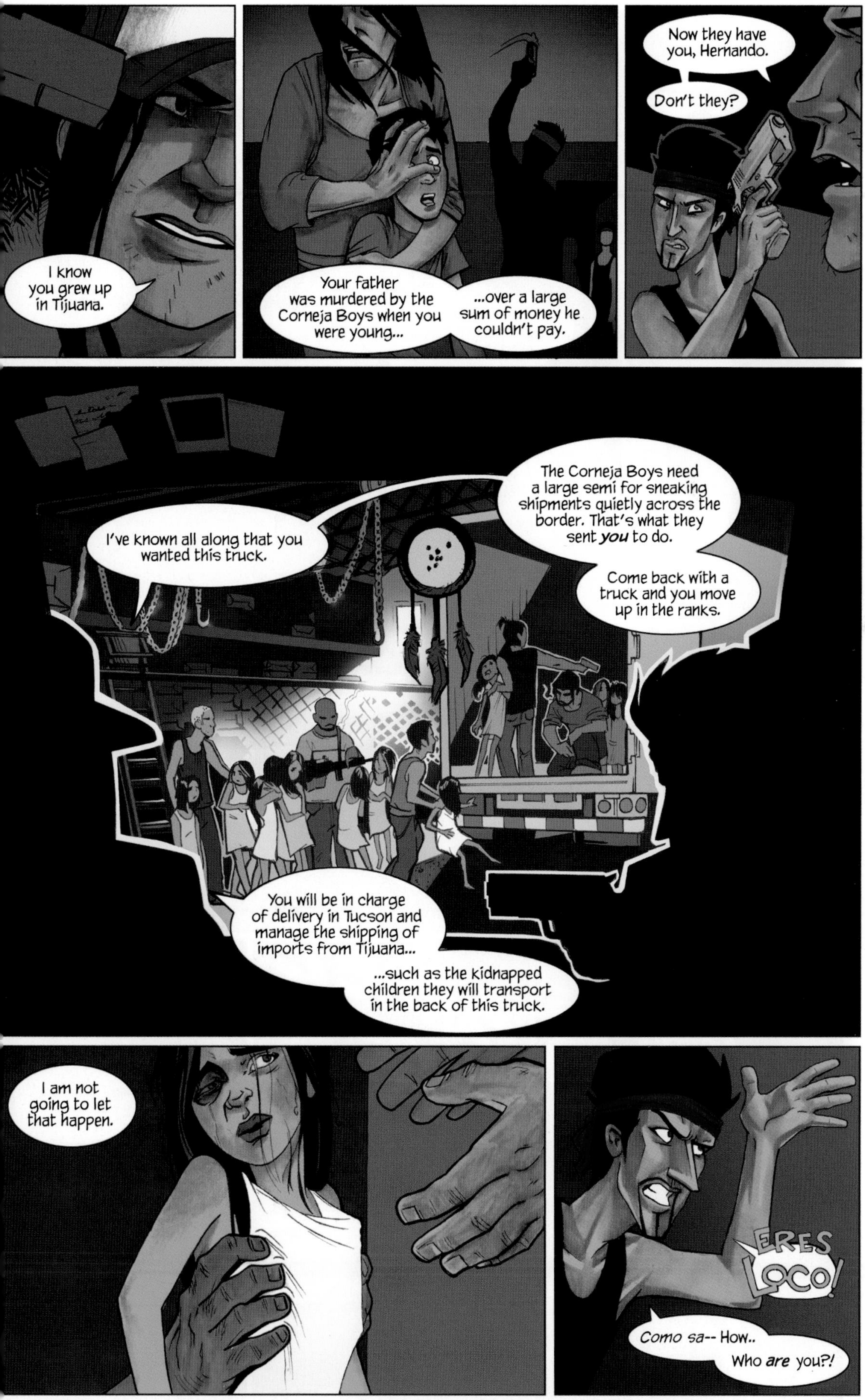
I know you grew up in Tijuana.
Your father was murdered by the Corneja Boys when you were young...
...over a large sum of money he couldn't pay.
Now they have you, Hernando.
Don't they?
I've known all along that you wanted this truck.
The Corneja Boys need a large semi for sneaking shipments quietly across the border. That's what they sent *you* to do.
Come back with a truck and you move up in the ranks.
You will be in charge of delivery in Tucson and manage the shipping of imports from Tijuana...
...such as the kidnapped children they will transport in the back of this truck.
I am not going to let that happen.
ERES LOCO!
Como sa-- How..
Who *are* you?!

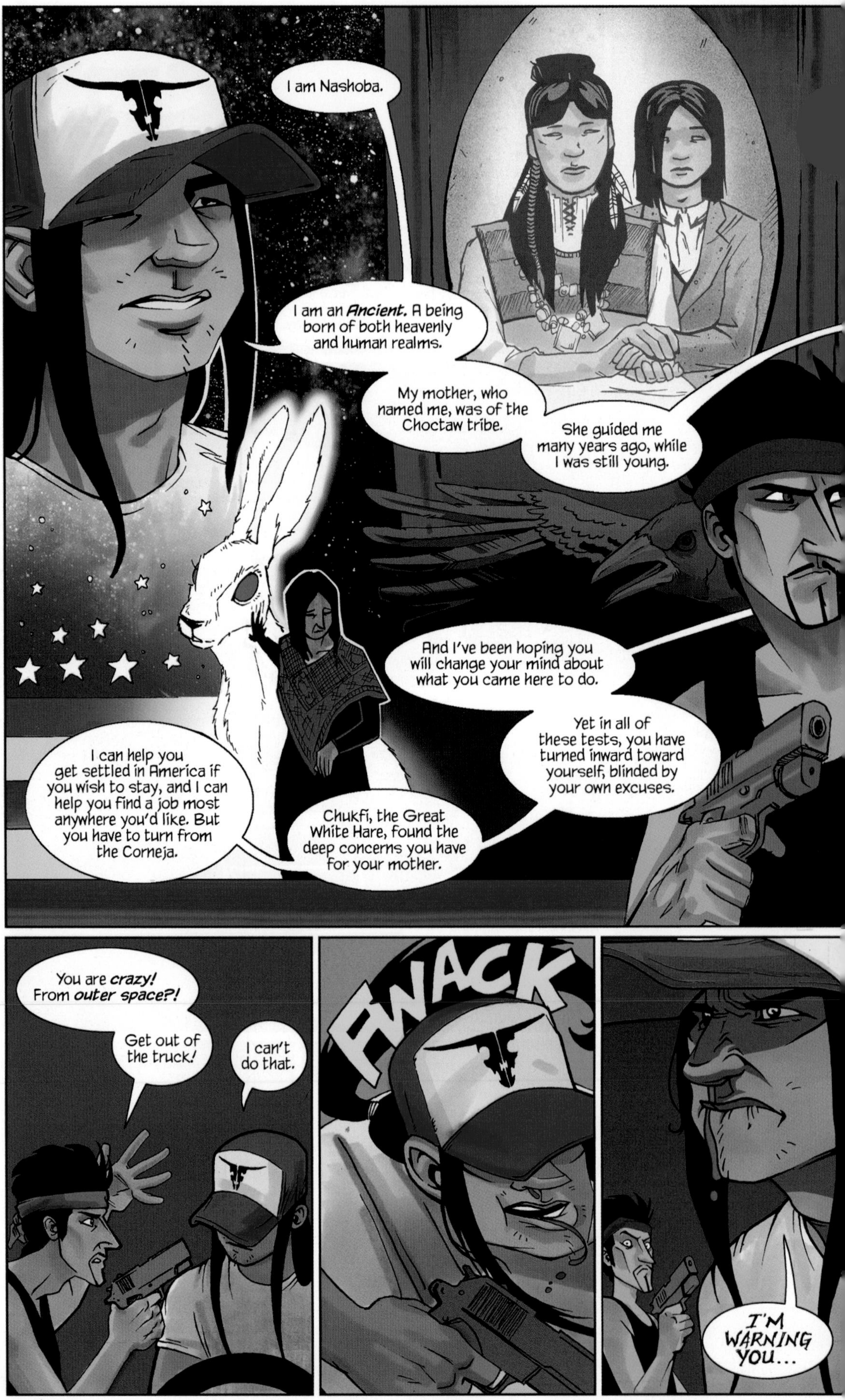
I am Nashoba.
I am an *Ancient.* A being born of both heavenly and human realms.
My mother, who named me, was of the Choctaw tribe.
She guided me many years ago, while I was still young.
And I've been hoping you will change your mind about what you came here to do.
Yet in all of these tests, you have turned inward toward yourself, blinded by your own excuses.
Chukfi, the Great White Hare, found the deep concerns you have for your mother.
I can help you get settled in America if you wish to stay, and I can help you find a job most anywhere you'd like. But you have to turn from the Corneja.
You are *crazy!* From *outer space?!*
Get out of the truck!
I can't do that.
FWACK
I'M WARNING YOU...

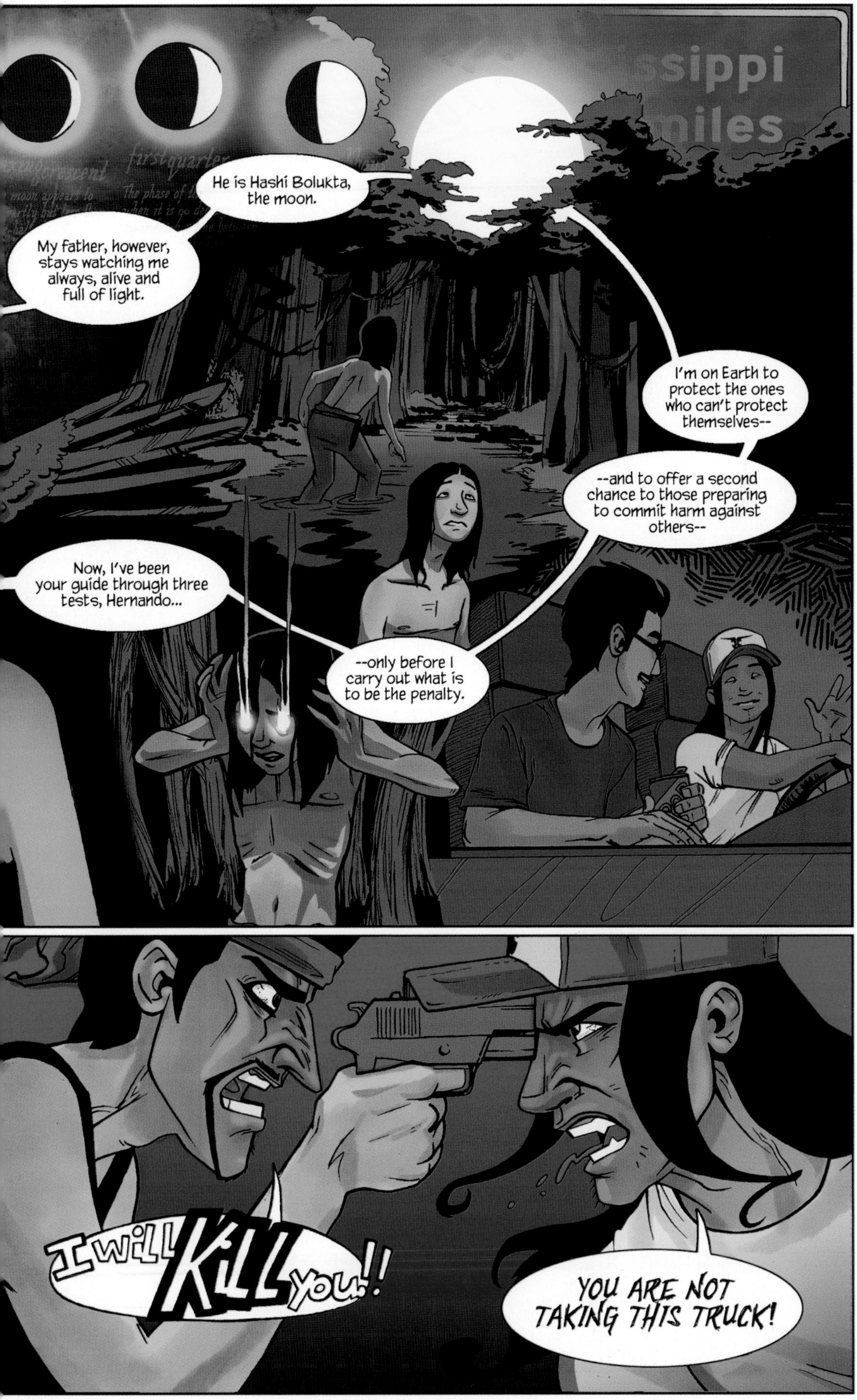

He is Hashi Bolukta, the moon.
My father, however, stays watching me always, alive and full of light.
I'm on Earth to protect the ones who can't protect themselves--
--and to offer a second chance to those preparing to commit harm against others--
Now, I've been your guide through three tests, Hernando...
--only before I carry out what is to be the penalty.
I will KILL you!!
YOU ARE NOT TAKING THIS TRUCK!

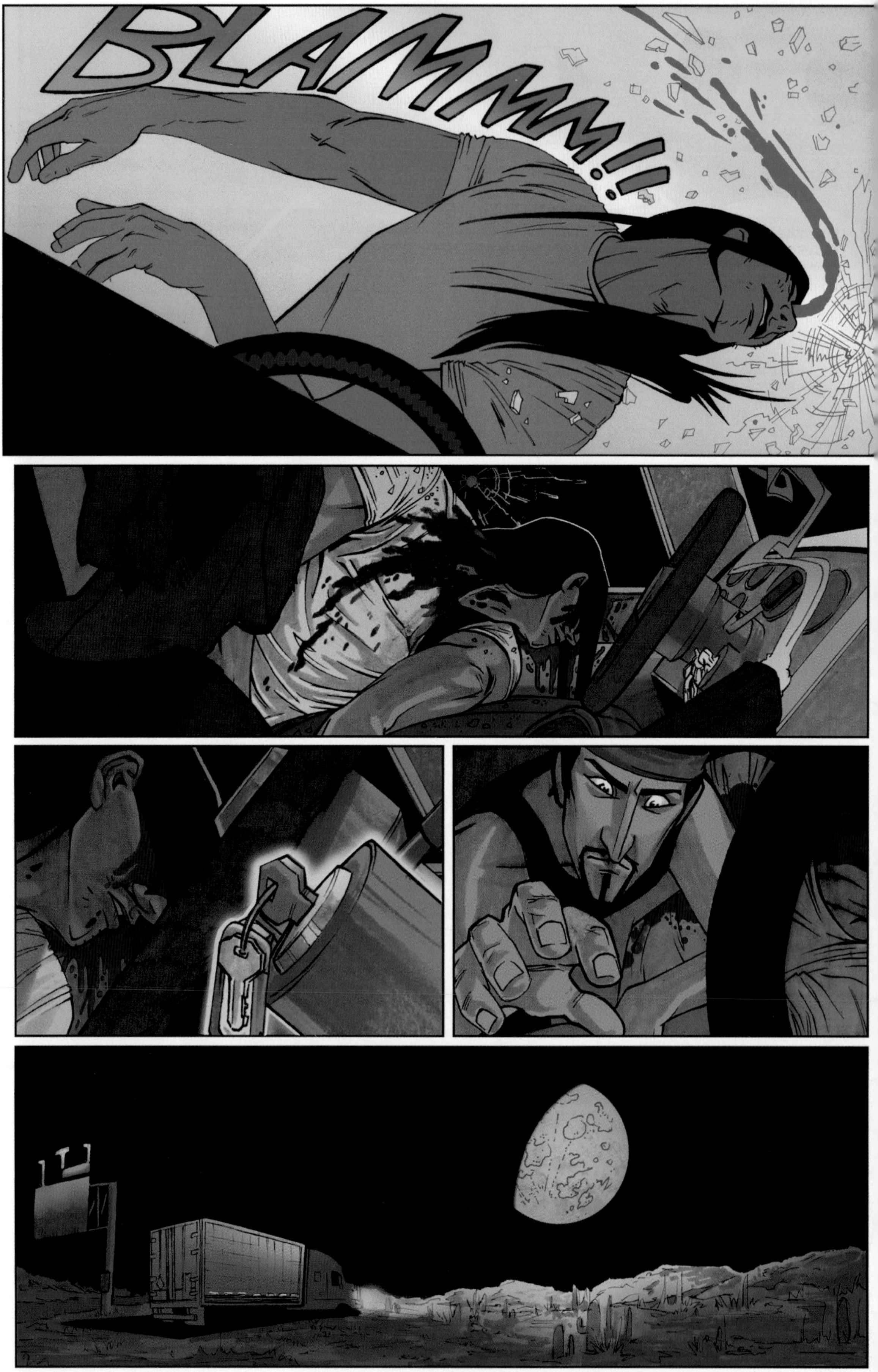
BLAMMM!!

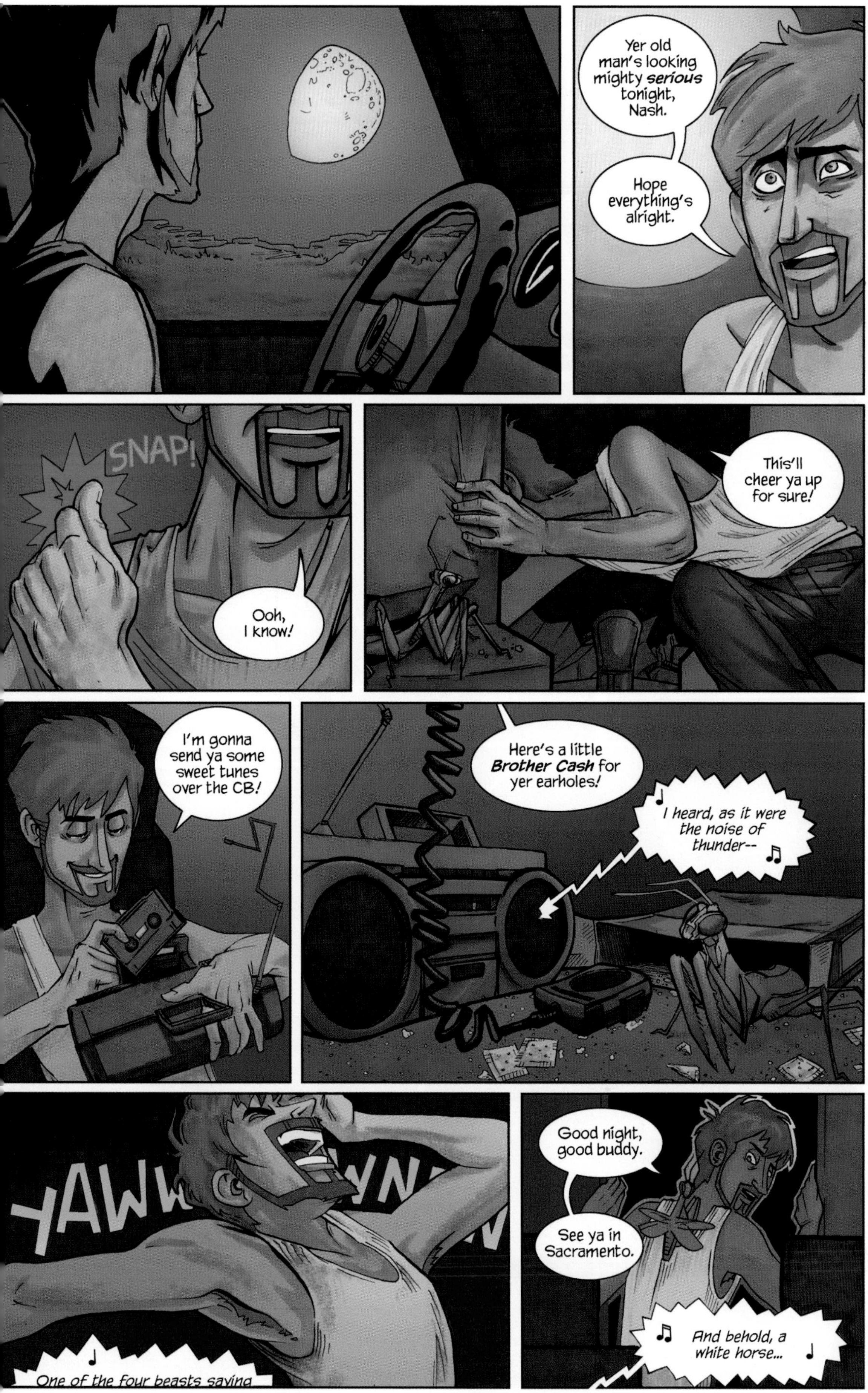
Yer old man's looking mighty **serious** tonight, Nash.
Hope everything's alright.
SNAP!
Ooh, I know!
This'll cheer ya up for sure!
I'm gonna send ya some sweet tunes over the CB!
Here's a little **Brother Cash** for yer earholes!
I heard, as it were the noise of thunder--
YAWWWWNNN
One of the four beasts saying
Good night, good buddy.
See ya in Sacramento.
And behold, a white horse...

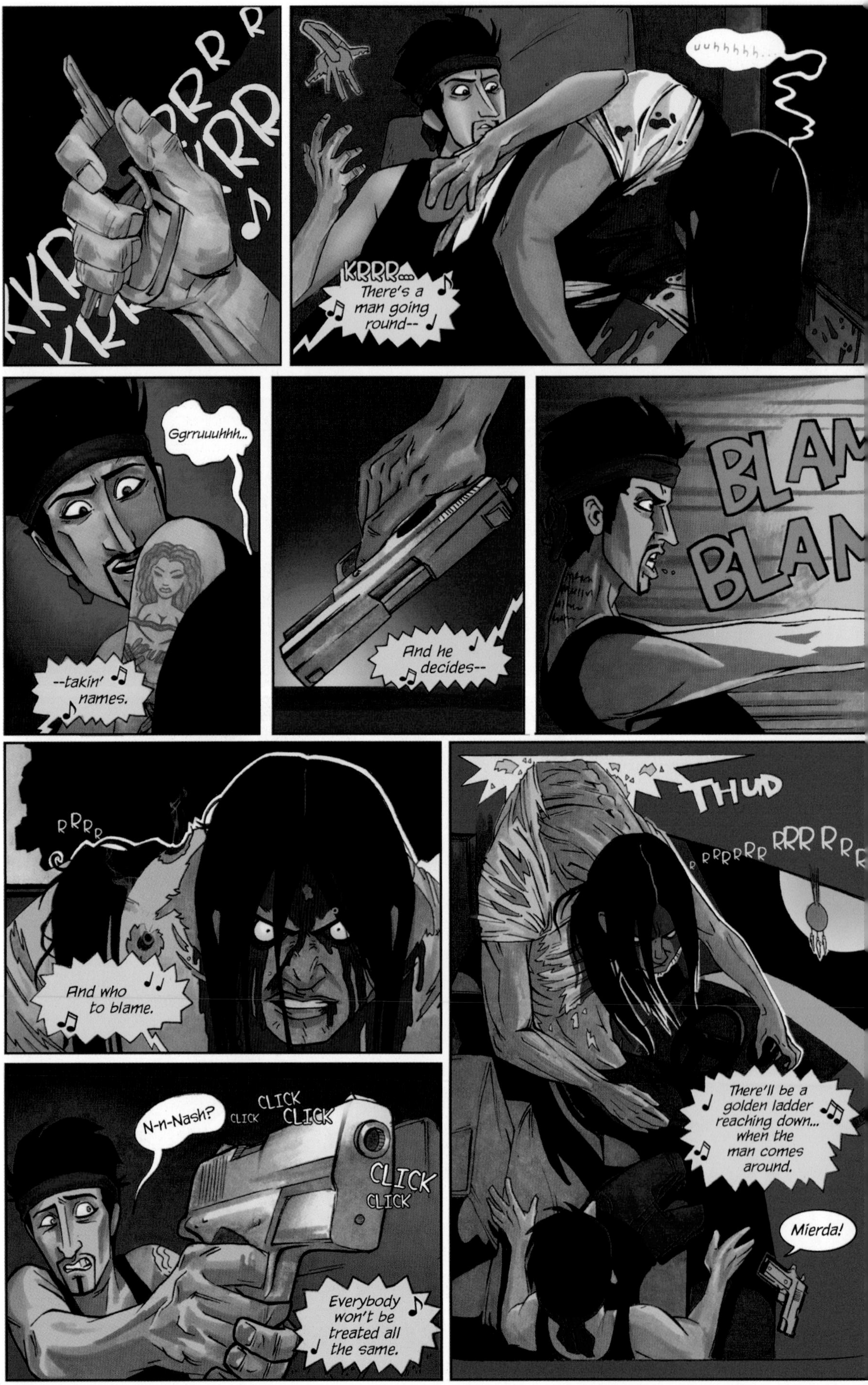
KRRRR R
KRRR
uuhhhhh...
KRRR...
There's a man going round--
Ggrruuuhhh...
--takin' names.
And he decides--
BLAM
BLAM
RRRR
And who to blame.
THUD
RRRRRR RRR RRR
There'll be a golden ladder reaching down... when the man comes around.
Mierda!
N-n-Nash?
CLICK
CLICK
CLICK
CLICK
CLICK
Everybody won't be treated all the same.

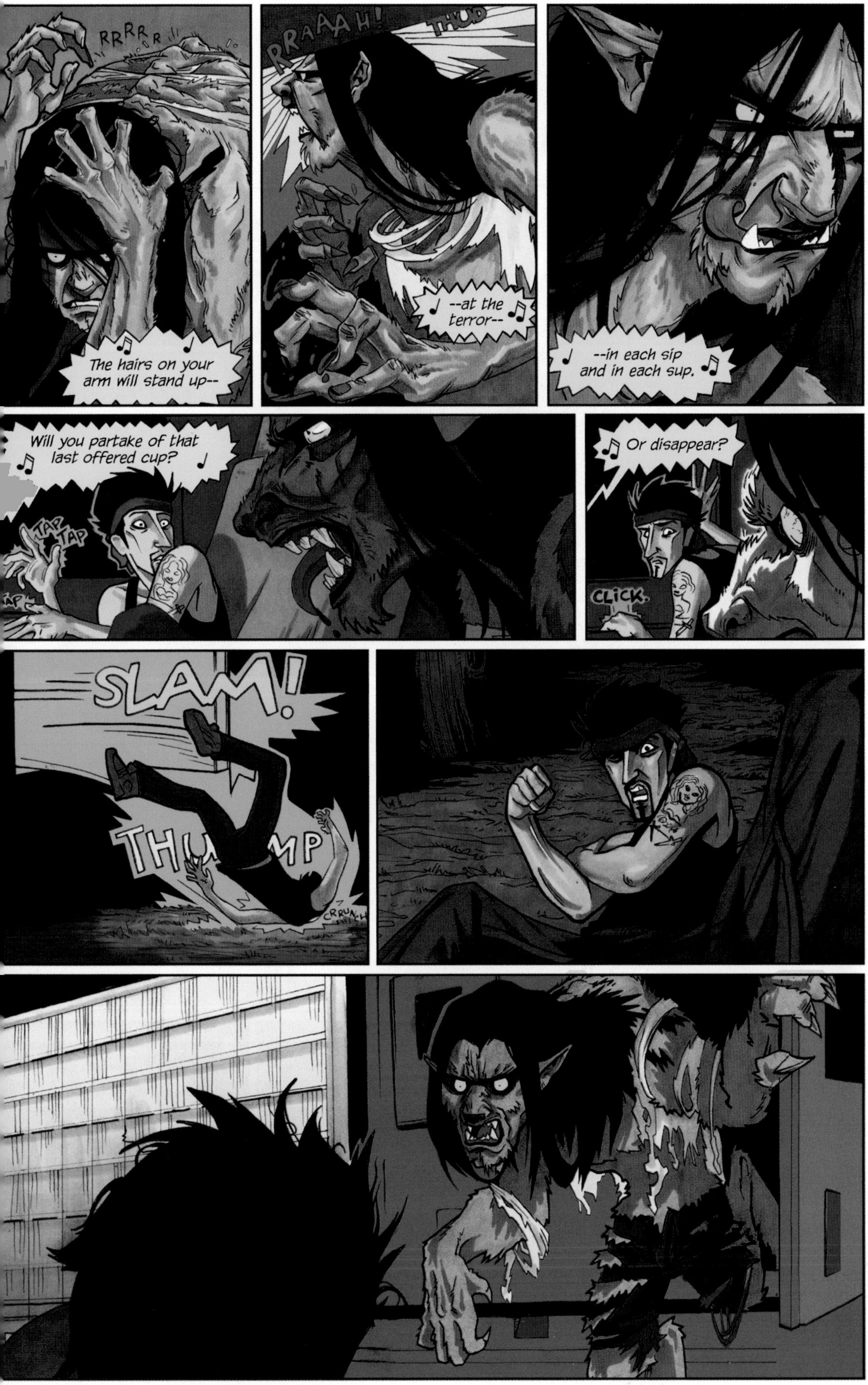
RRRRR
The hairs on your arm will stand up--
RRAAAAH!
THUD
--at the terror--
--in each sip and in each sup.
Will you partake of that last offered cup?
TAP TAP
Or disappear?
CLICK.
SLAM!
THUMP
CRRUNCH

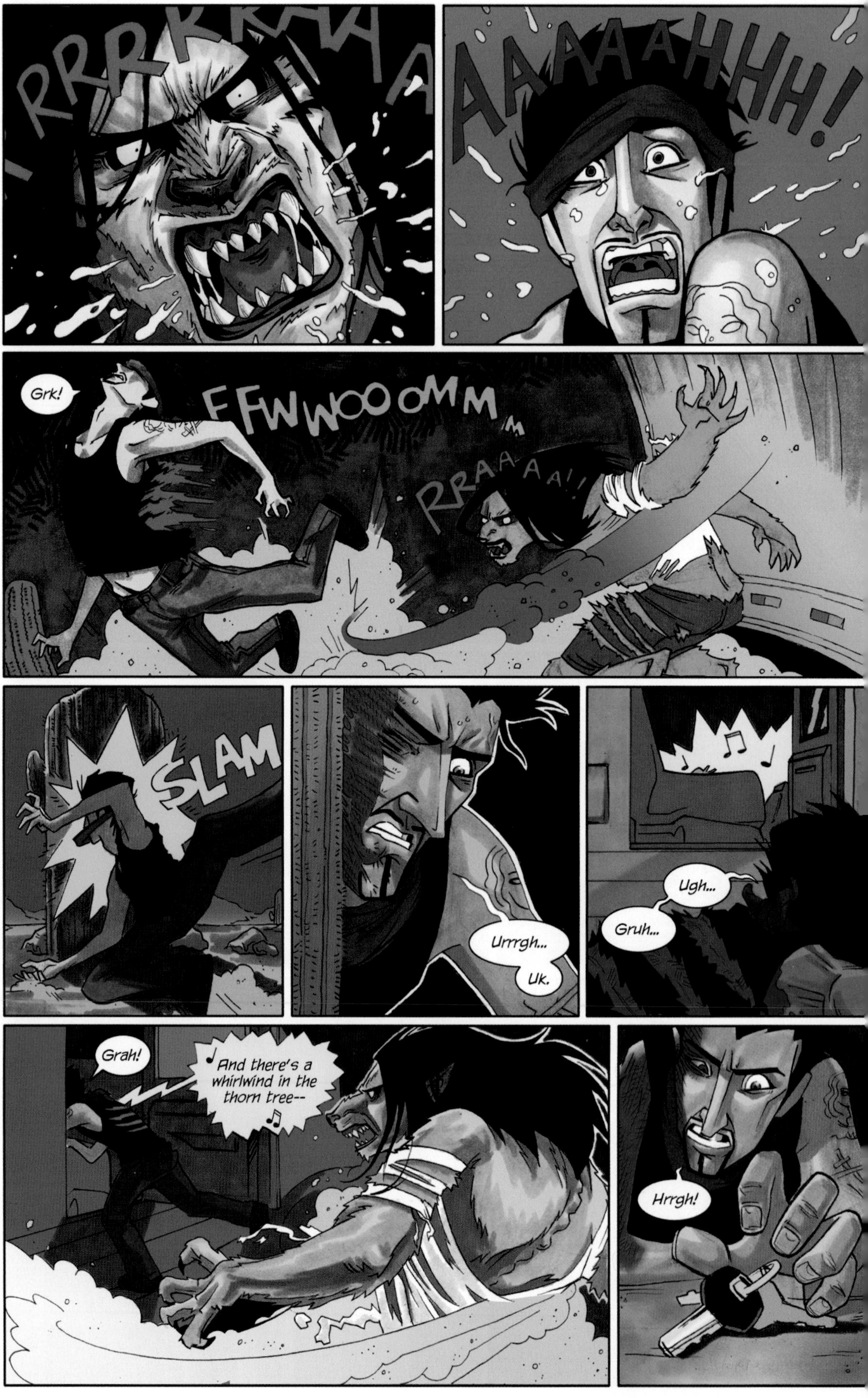
RRRRKRAAA
AAAAAHHH!
Grk!
FFWWOOOMM
M
RRAAAA!!
SLAM
Urrrgh...
Uk.
Ugh...
Gruh...
Grah!
And there's a whirlwind in the thorn tree--
Hrrgh!

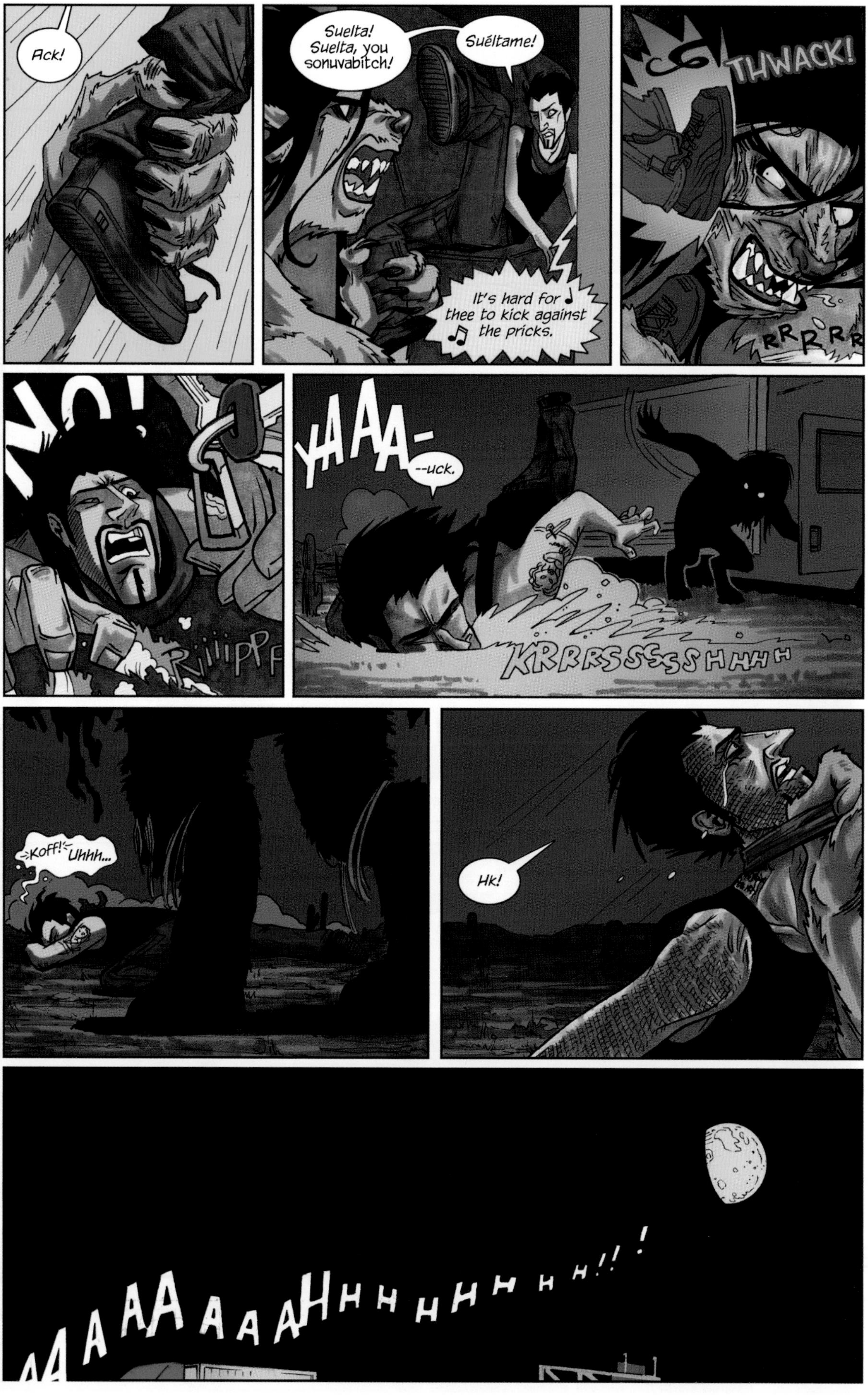
Ack!
Suelta! Suelta, you sonuvabitch!
Suéltame!
It's hard for thee to kick against the pricks.
THWACK!
RRRRR
NO!
RiiiPPF
YAAA-
--uck.
KRRRSSSSSSHHHH
KOFF! Uhhh...
Hk!
AAAAAAAAHHHHHHHH!!!

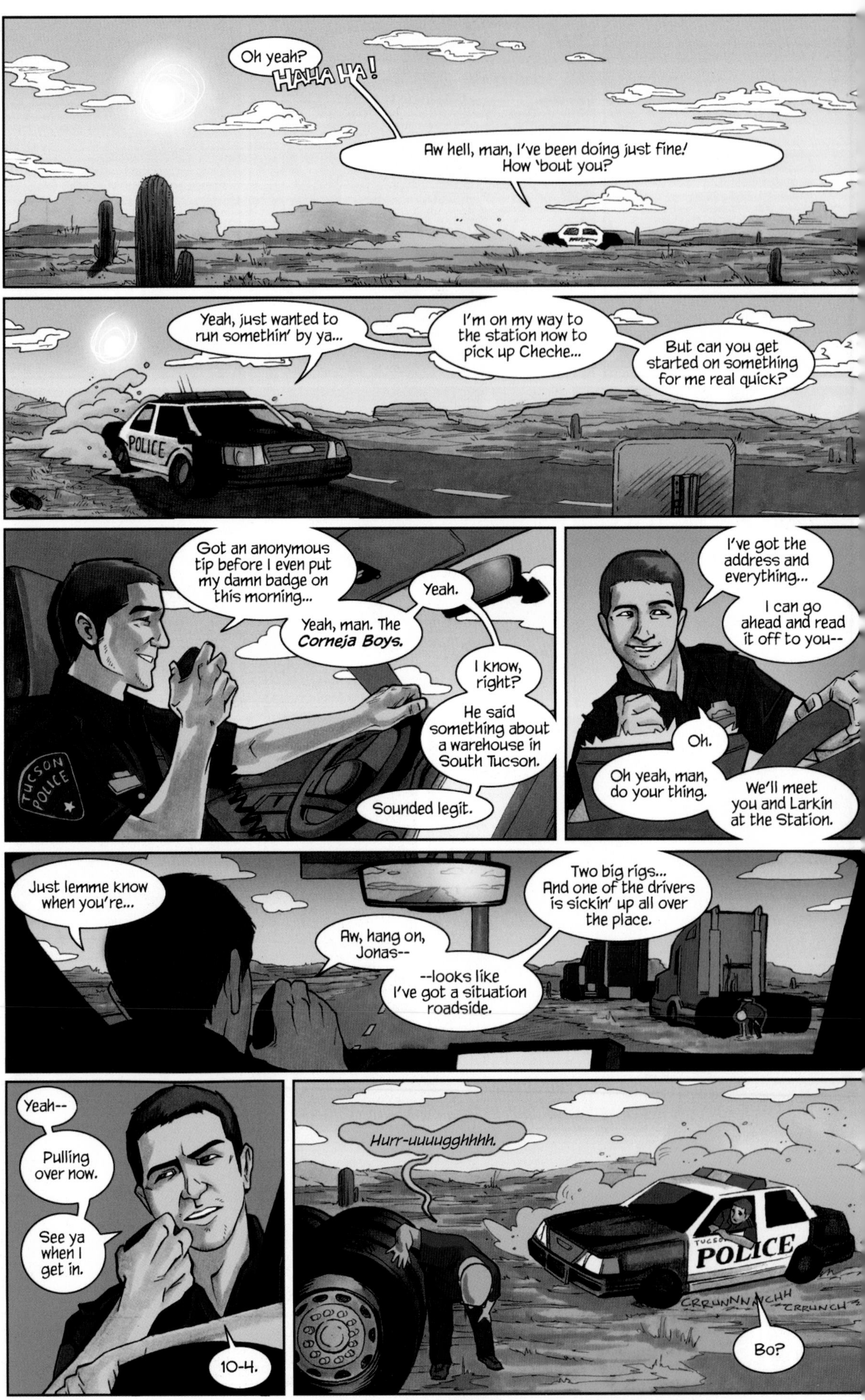
Oh yeah?
HAHA HA!
Aw hell, man, I've been doing just fine! How 'bout you?
Yeah, just wanted to run somethin' by ya...
I'm on my way to the station now to pick up Cheche...
But can you get started on something for me real quick?
Got an anonymous tip before I even put my damn badge on this morning...
Yeah.
Yeah, man. The *Corneja Boys.*
I know, right?
He said something about a warehouse in South Tucson.
Sounded legit.
I've got the address and everything...
I can go ahead and read it off to you--
Oh.
Oh yeah, man, do your thing.
We'll meet you and Larkin at the Station.
Just lemme know when you're...
Aw, hang on, Jonas--
--looks like I've got a situation roadside.
Two big rigs... And one of the drivers is sickin' up all over the place.
Yeah--
Pulling over now.
See ya when I get in.
10-4.
Hurr-uuuugghhhh.
CRRUNNNNCHH
CRRUNCH
Bo?
POLICE

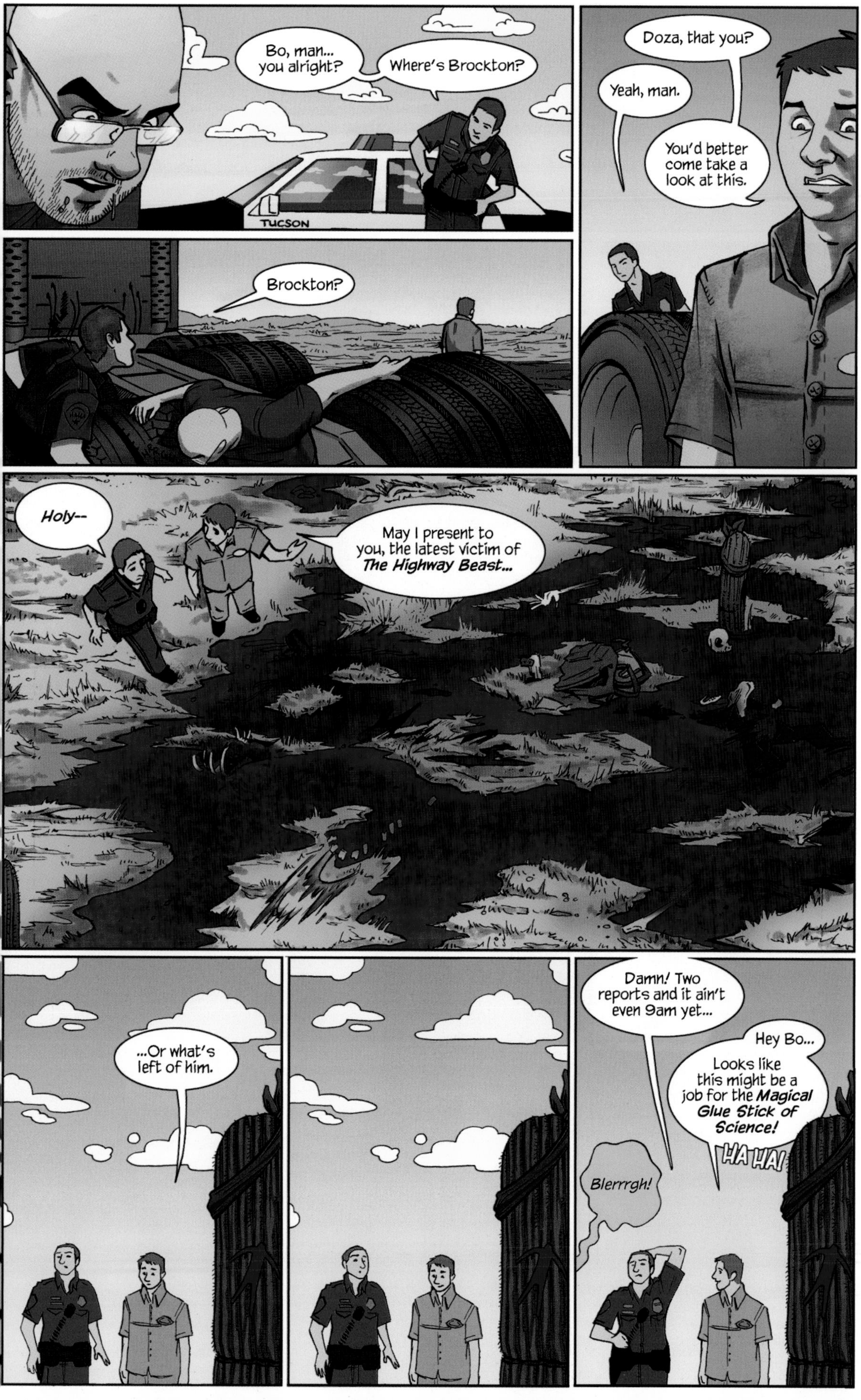

Bo, man...
you alright?
Where's Brockton?
TUCSON
Doza, that you?
Yeah, man.
You'd better come take a look at this.
Brockton?
Holy--
May I present to you, the latest victim of *The Highway Beast...*
...Or what's left of him.
Damn! Two reports and it ain't even 9am yet...
Hey Bo...
Looks like this might be a job for the *Magical Glue Stick of Science!*
HA HA!
Blerrrgh!

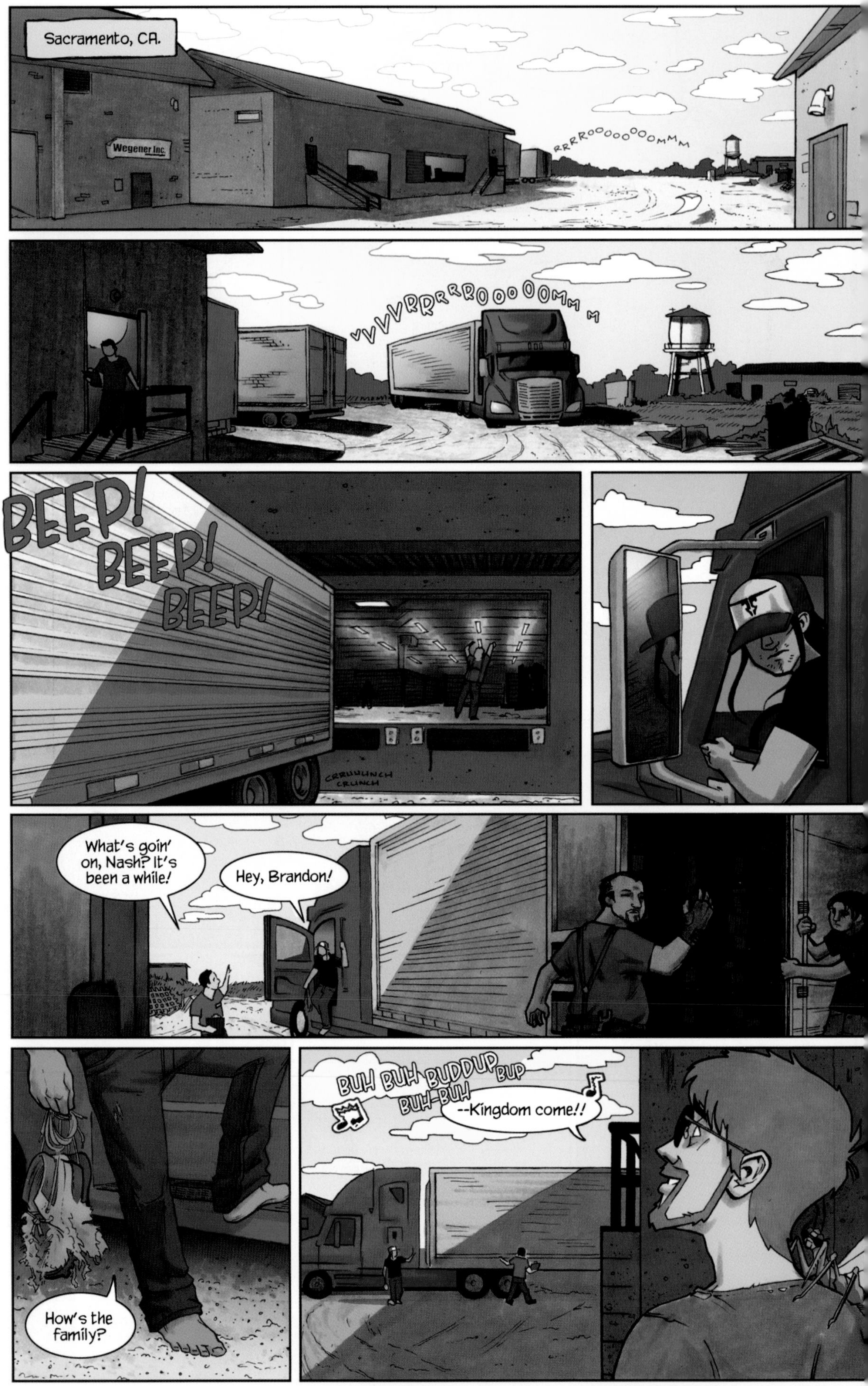

Sacramento, CA.
Wegener Inc.
RRRROOOOOOOOMMM
VVVRRRRRROOOOOOMM M
BEEP! BEEP! BEEP!
CRRUUUNCH CRUNCH
What's goin' on, Nash? It's been a while!
Hey, Brandon!
How's the family?
BUH BUH BUDDUP BUP BUH-BUH
--Kingdom come!!

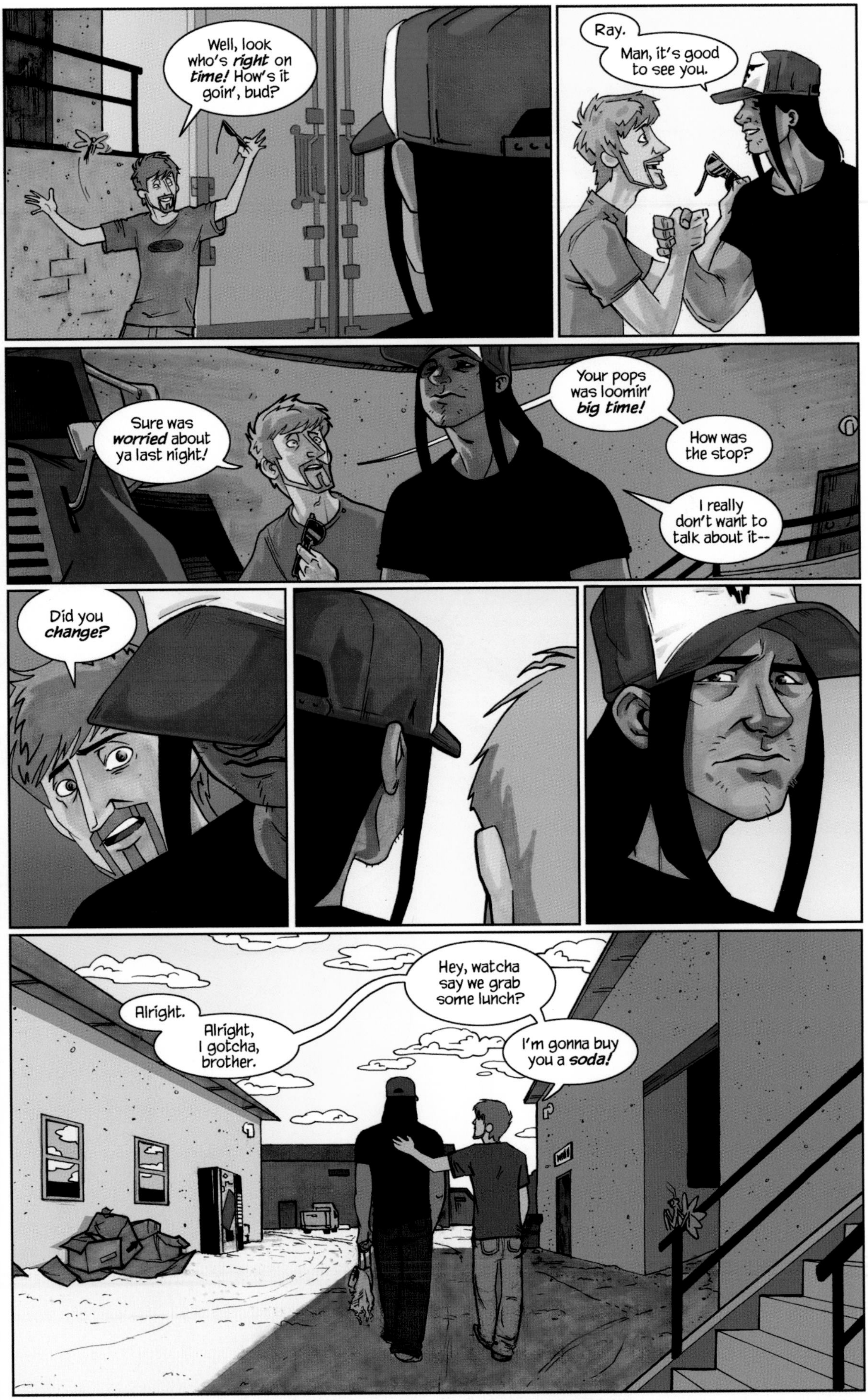
Well, look who's right on time! How's it goin', bud?
Ray.
Man, it's good to see you.
Your pops was loomin' big time!
Sure was worried about ya last night!
How was the stop?
I really don't want to talk about it--
Did you change?
Hey, watcha say we grab some lunch?
Alright.
Alright, I gotcha, brother.
I'm gonna buy you a soda!

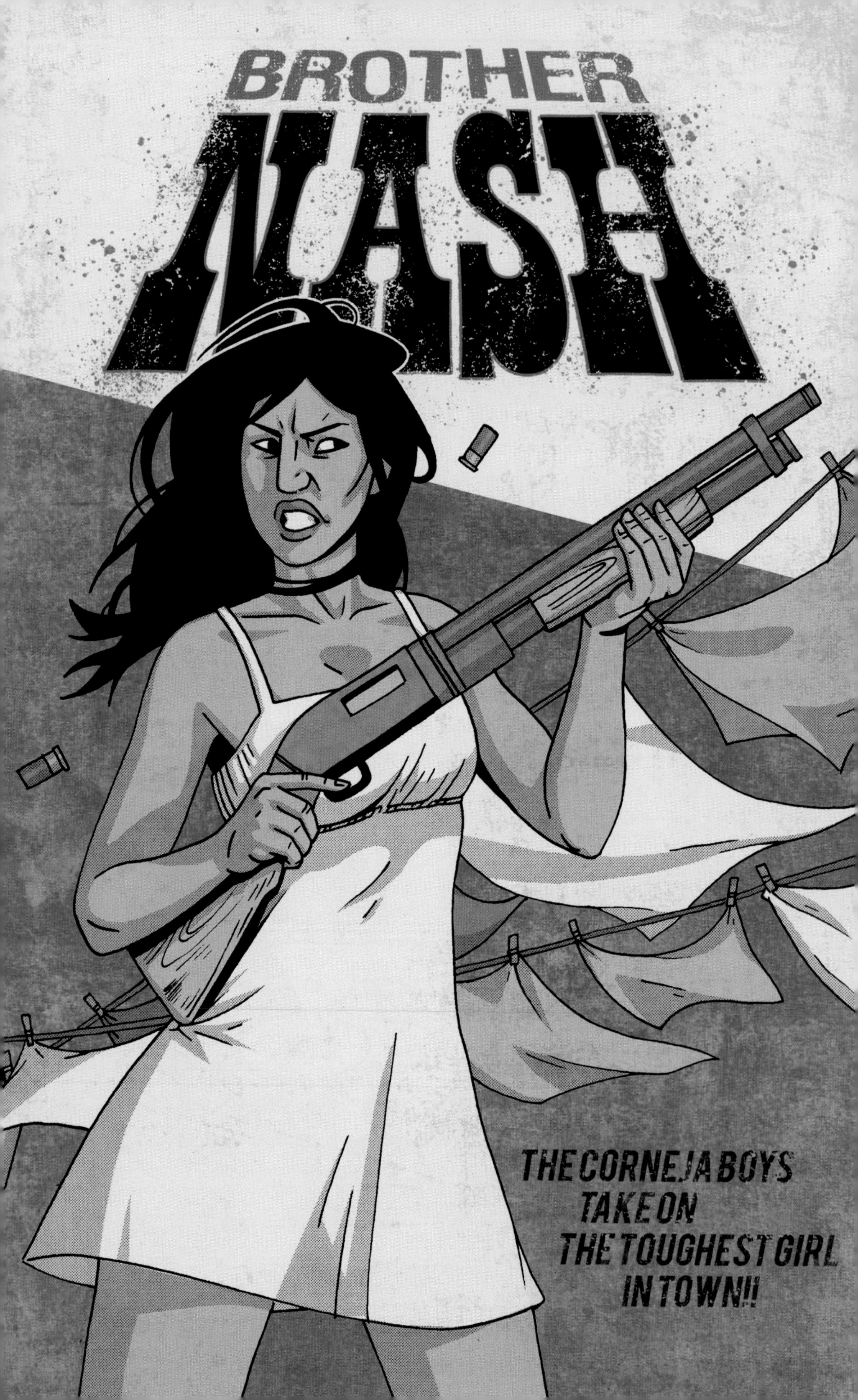
BROTHER
NASH
THE CORNEJA BOYS
TAKE ON
THE TOUGHEST GIRL
IN TOWN!!

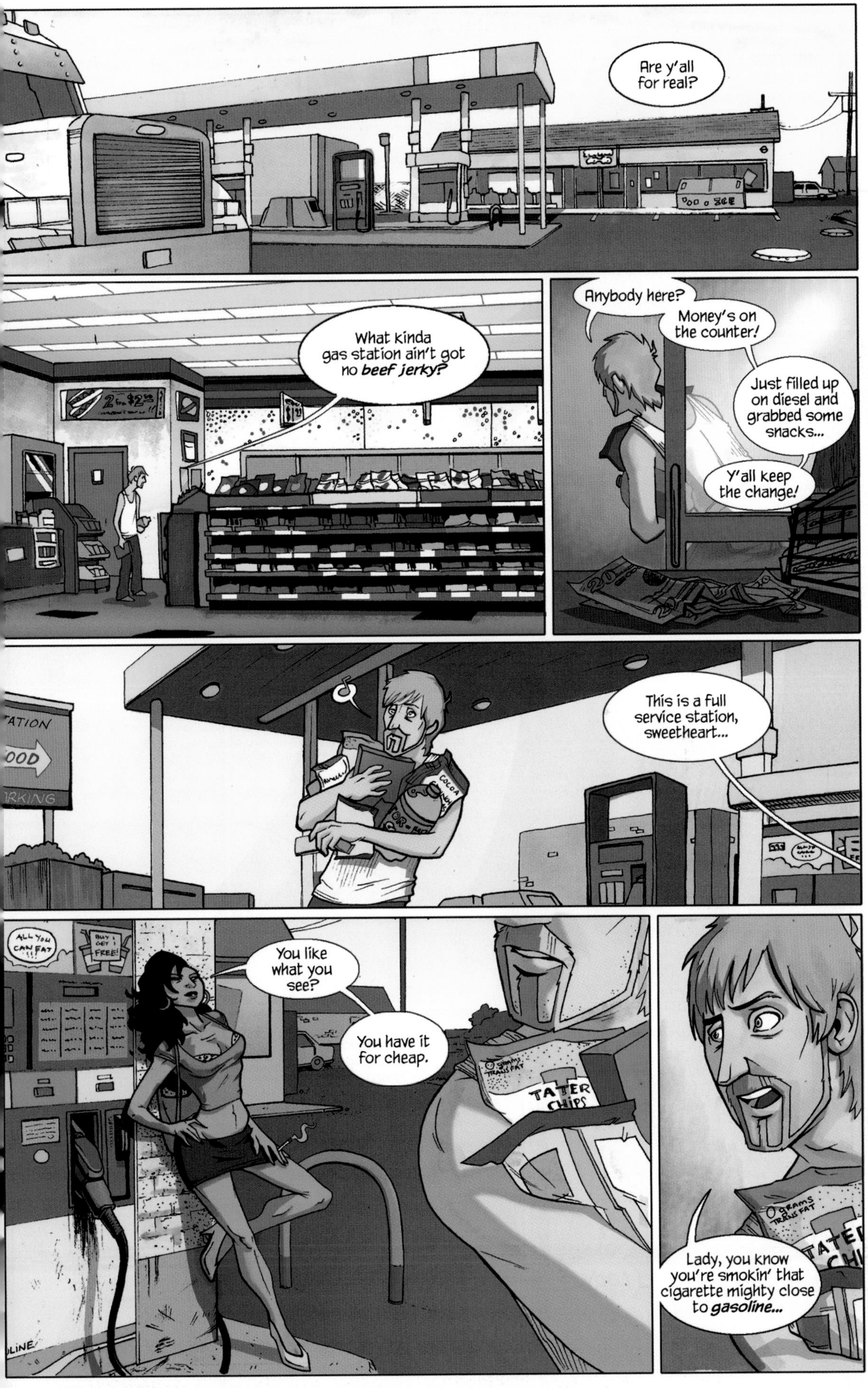
Are y'all for real?
What kinda gas station ain't got no *beef jerky?*
Anybody here?
Money's on the counter!
Just filled up on diesel and grabbed some snacks...
Y'all keep the change!
This is a full service station, sweetheart...
ALL YOU CAN EAT
BUY 1 GET 1 FREE!
You like what you see?
You have it for cheap.
TATER CHIPS
Lady, you know you're smokin' that cigarette mighty close to *gasoline...*

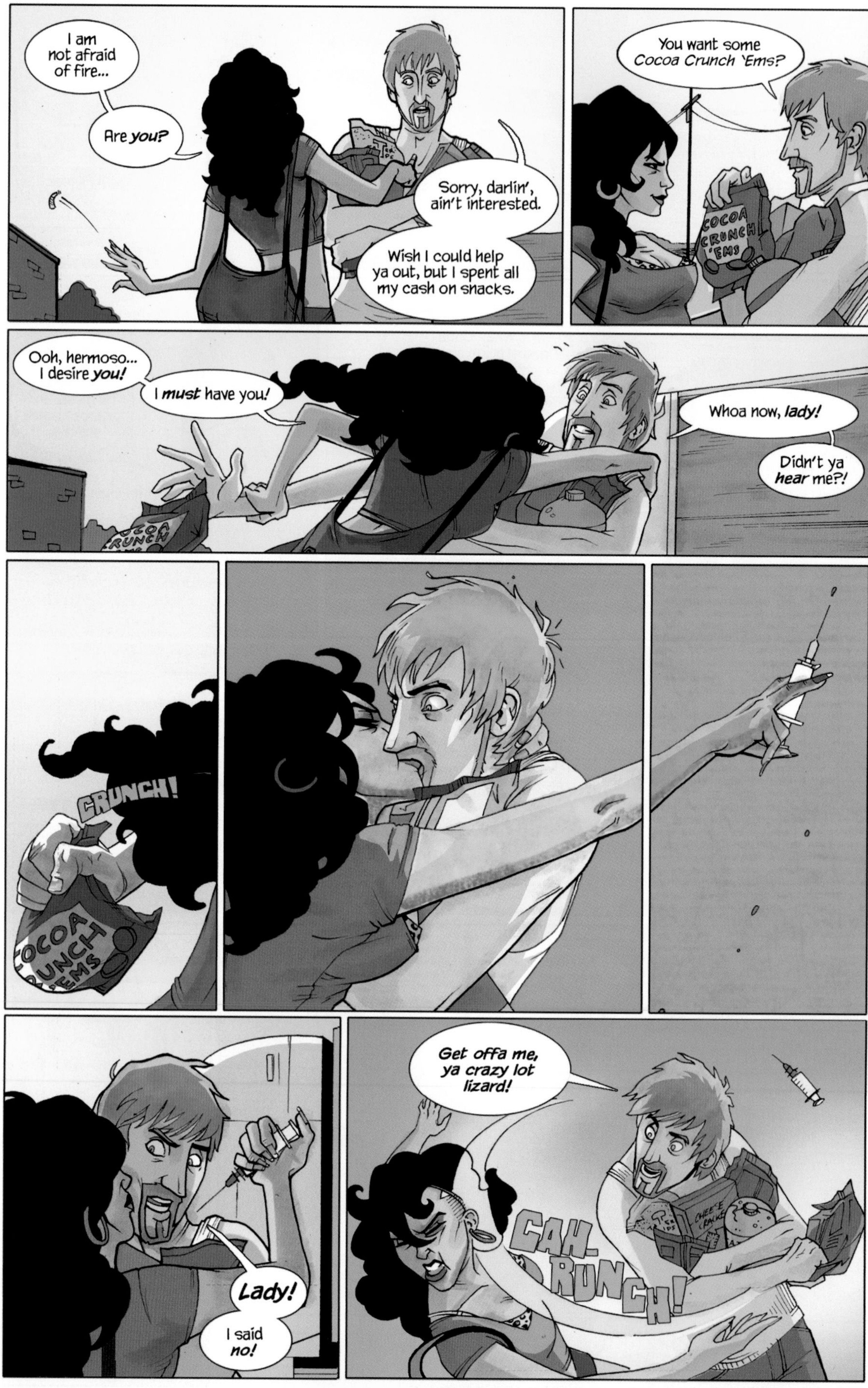
I am not afraid of fire...
Are you?
Sorry, darlin', ain't interested.
Wish I could help ya out, but I spent all my cash on snacks.
You want some Cocoa Crunch 'Ems?
COCOA CRUNCH 'EMS
Ooh, hermoso... I desire you!
I must have you!
Whoa now, lady!
Didn't ya hear me?!
CRUNCH!
Lady!
I said no!
Get offa me, ya crazy lot lizard!
CAH-RUNCH!

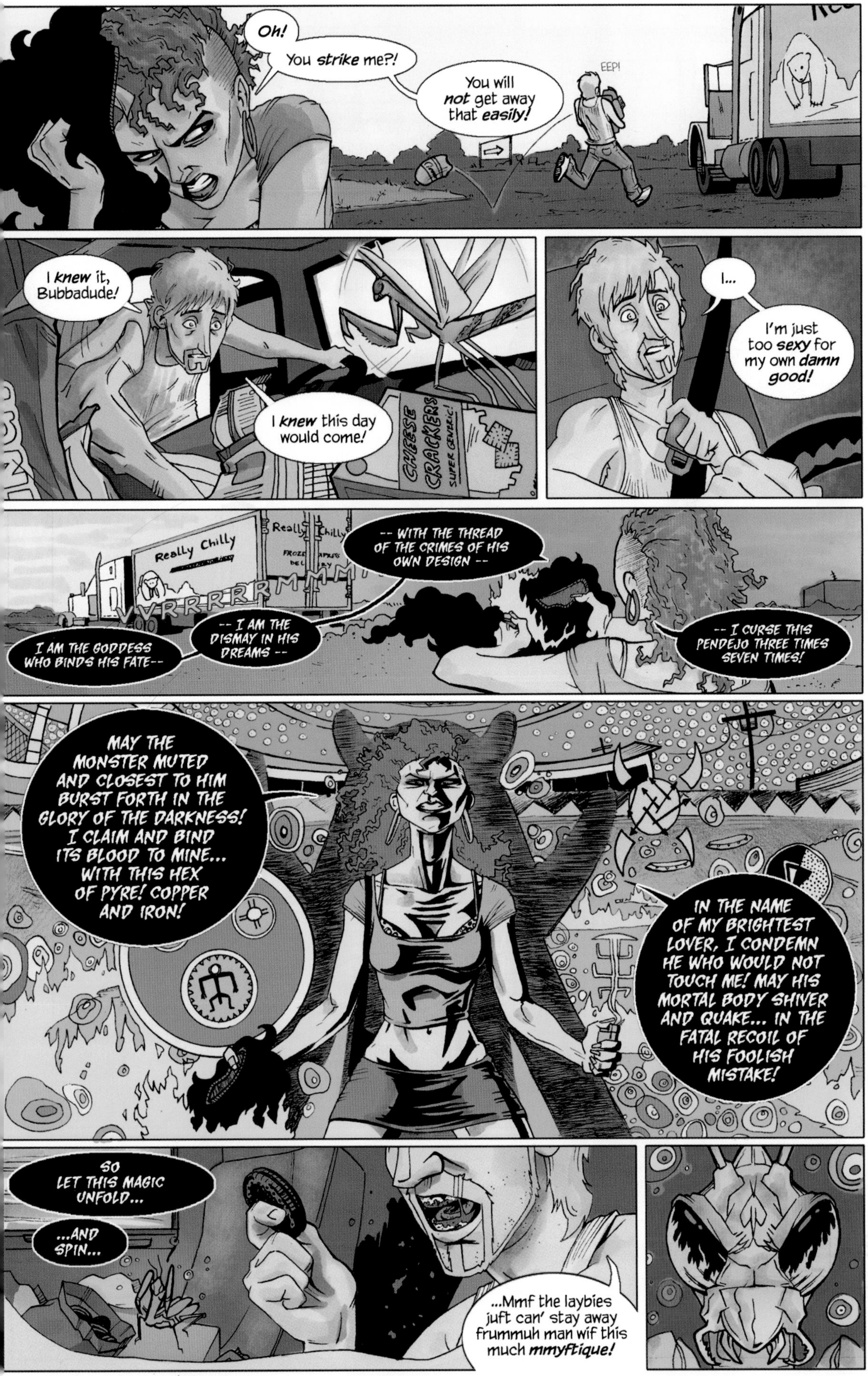
Oh!
You *strike* me?!
You will *not* get away that *easily!*
EEP!
I *knew* it, Bubbadude!
I *knew* this day would come!
CHEESE CRACKERS
SUPER GENERIC!
I...
I'm just too *sexy* for my own *damn good!*
Really Chilly
VVRRRRRRRMMMM
I AM THE GODDESS WHO BINDS HIS FATE--
-- I AM THE DISMAY IN HIS DREAMS --
-- WITH THE THREAD OF THE CRIMES OF HIS OWN DESIGN --
-- I CURSE THIS PENDEJO THREE TIMES SEVEN TIMES!
MAY THE MONSTER MUTED AND CLOSEST TO HIM BURST FORTH IN THE GLORY OF THE DARKNESS! I CLAIM AND BIND ITS BLOOD TO MINE... WITH THIS HEX OF PYRE! COPPER AND IRON!
IN THE NAME OF MY BRIGHTEST LOVER, I CONDEMN HE WHO WOULD NOT TOUCH ME! MAY HIS MORTAL BODY SHIVER AND QUAKE... IN THE FATAL RECOIL OF HIS FOOLISH MISTAKE!
SO LET THIS MAGIC UNFOLD...
...AND SPIN...
...Mmf the laybies juft can' stay away frummuh man wif this much *mmyftique!*

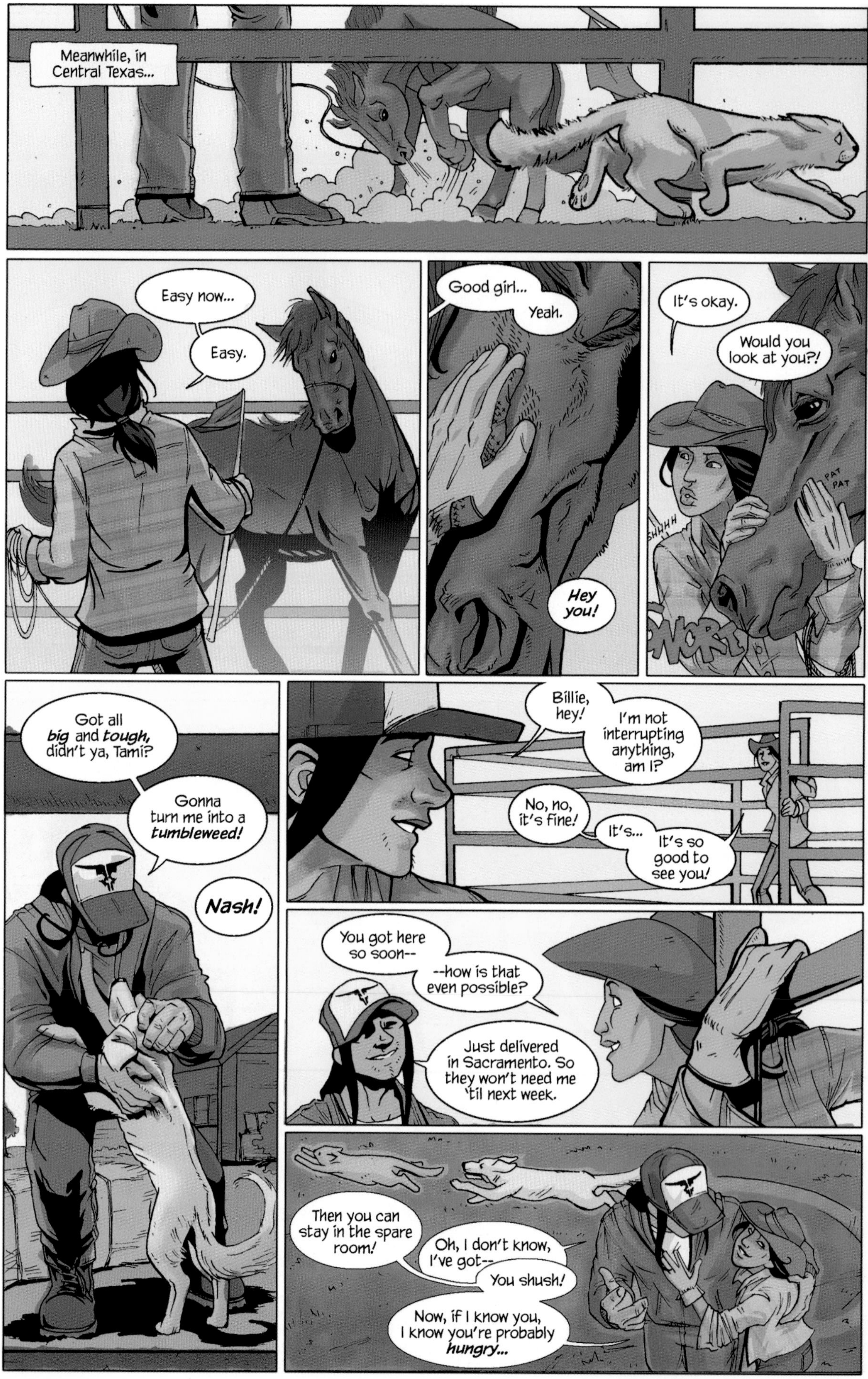

Meanwhile, in Central Texas...
Easy now...
Easy.
Good girl...
Yeah.
Hey you!
It's okay.
Would you look at you?!
PAT PAT
SHHHH
Got all *big* and *tough,* didn't ya, Tami?
Gonna turn me into a *tumbleweed!*
Nash!
Billie, hey!
I'm not interrupting anything, am I?
No, no, it's fine!
It's...
It's so good to see you!
You got here so soon--
--how is that even possible?
Just delivered in Sacramento. So they won't need me 'til next week.
Then you can stay in the spare room!
Oh, I don't know, I've got--
You shush!
Now, if I know you, I know you're probably *hungry...*

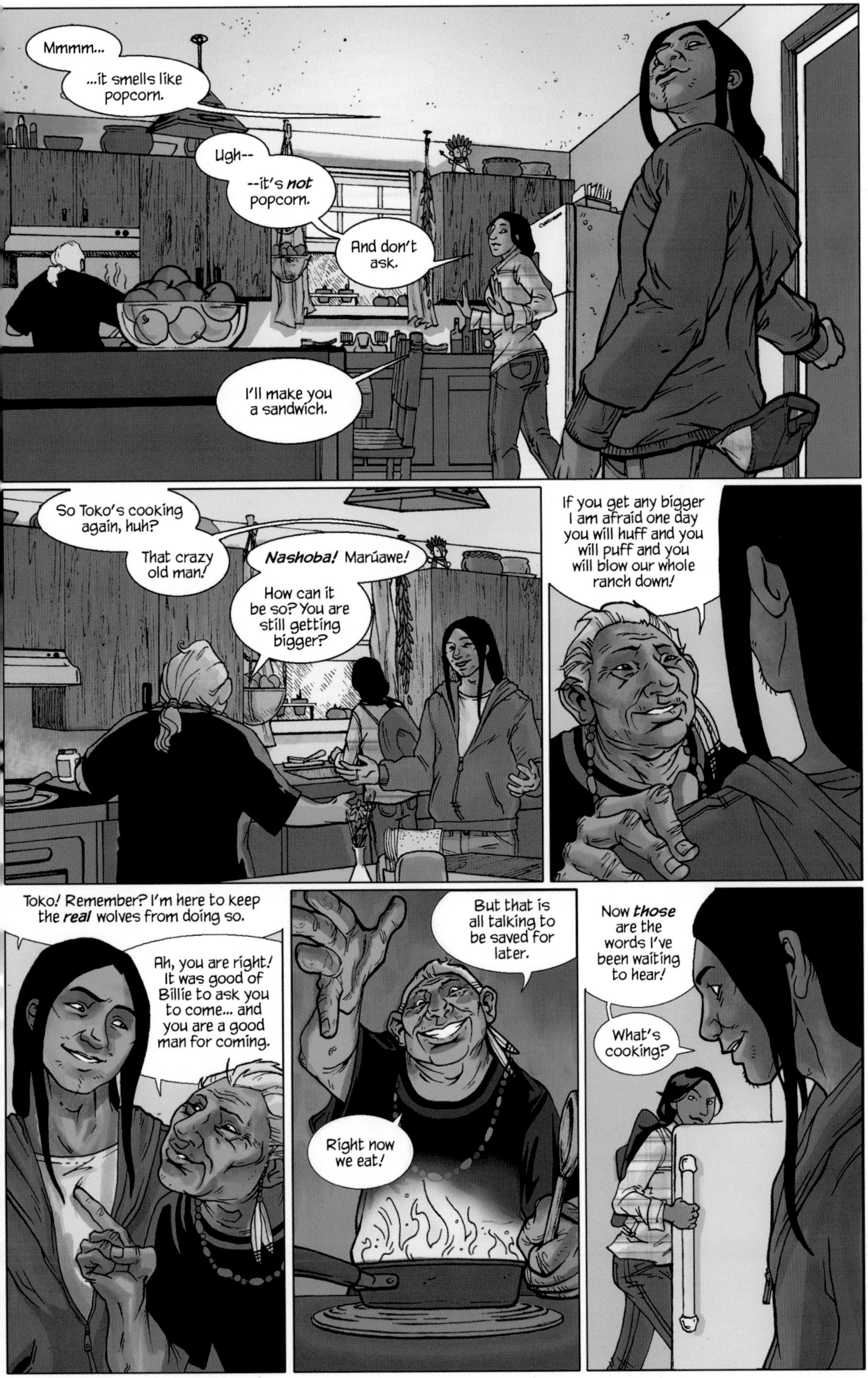

Mmmm...
...it smells like popcorn.
Ugh--
--it's **not** popcorn.
And don't ask.
I'll make you a sandwich.
So Toko's cooking again, huh?
That crazy old man!
Nashoba! Marúawe!
How can it be so? You are still getting bigger?
If you get any bigger I am afraid one day you will huff and you will puff and you will blow our whole ranch down!
Toko! Remember? I'm here to keep the **real** wolves from doing so.
Ah, you are right! It was good of Billie to ask you to come... and you are a good man for coming.
But that is all talking to be saved for later.
Right now we eat!
Now **those** are the words I've been waiting to hear!
What's cooking?

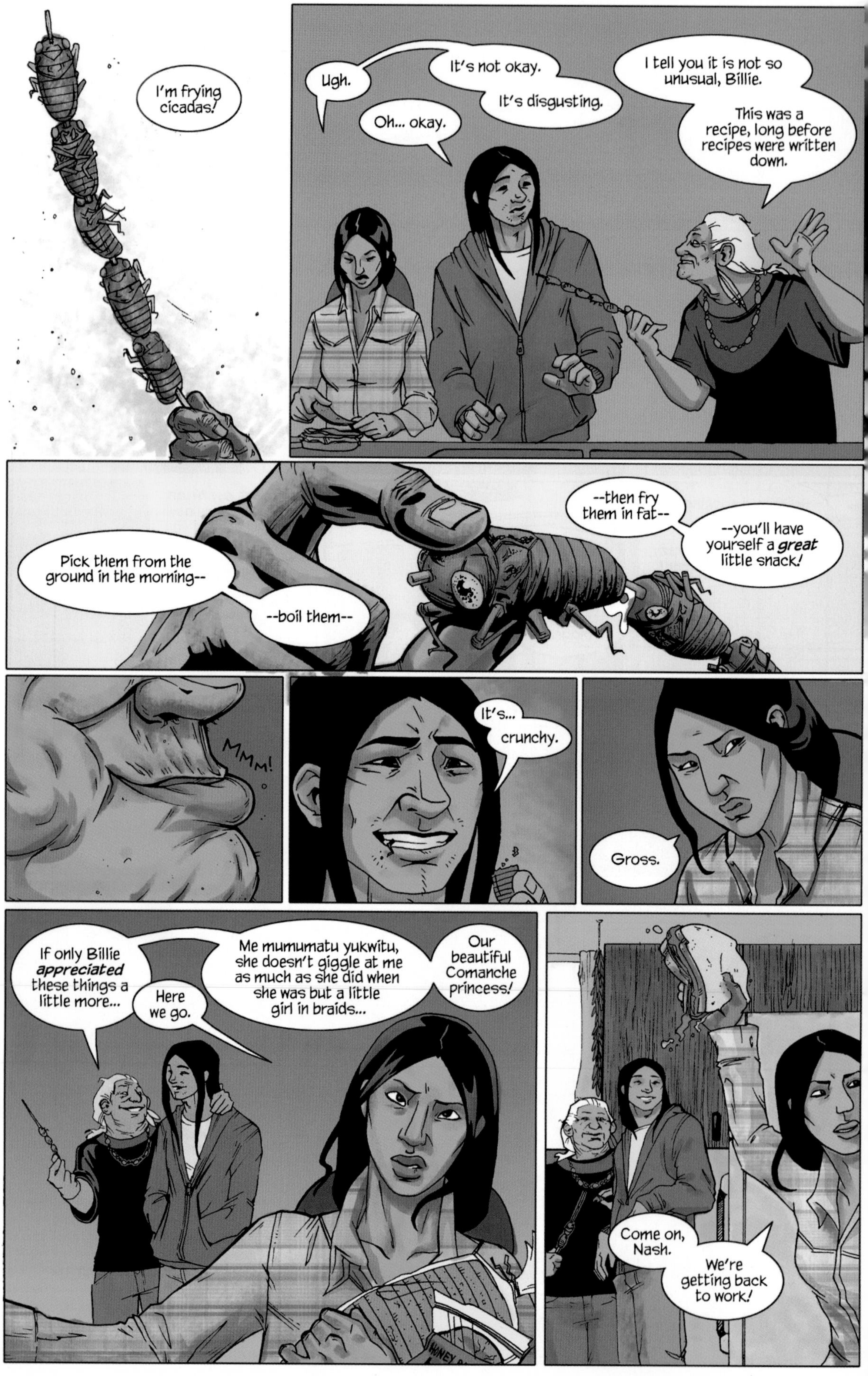
I'm frying cicadas!
Ugh.
It's not okay.
It's disgusting.
Oh... okay.
I tell you it is not so unusual, Billie.
This was a recipe, long before recipes were written down.
Pick them from the ground in the morning--
--boil them--
--then fry them in fat--
--you'll have yourself a great little snack!
MMM!
It's... crunchy.
Gross.
If only Billie appreciated these things a little more...
Here we go.
Me mumumatu yukwitu, she doesn't giggle at me as much as she did when she was but a little girl in braids...
Our beautiful Comanche princess!
Come on, Nash.
We're getting back to work!

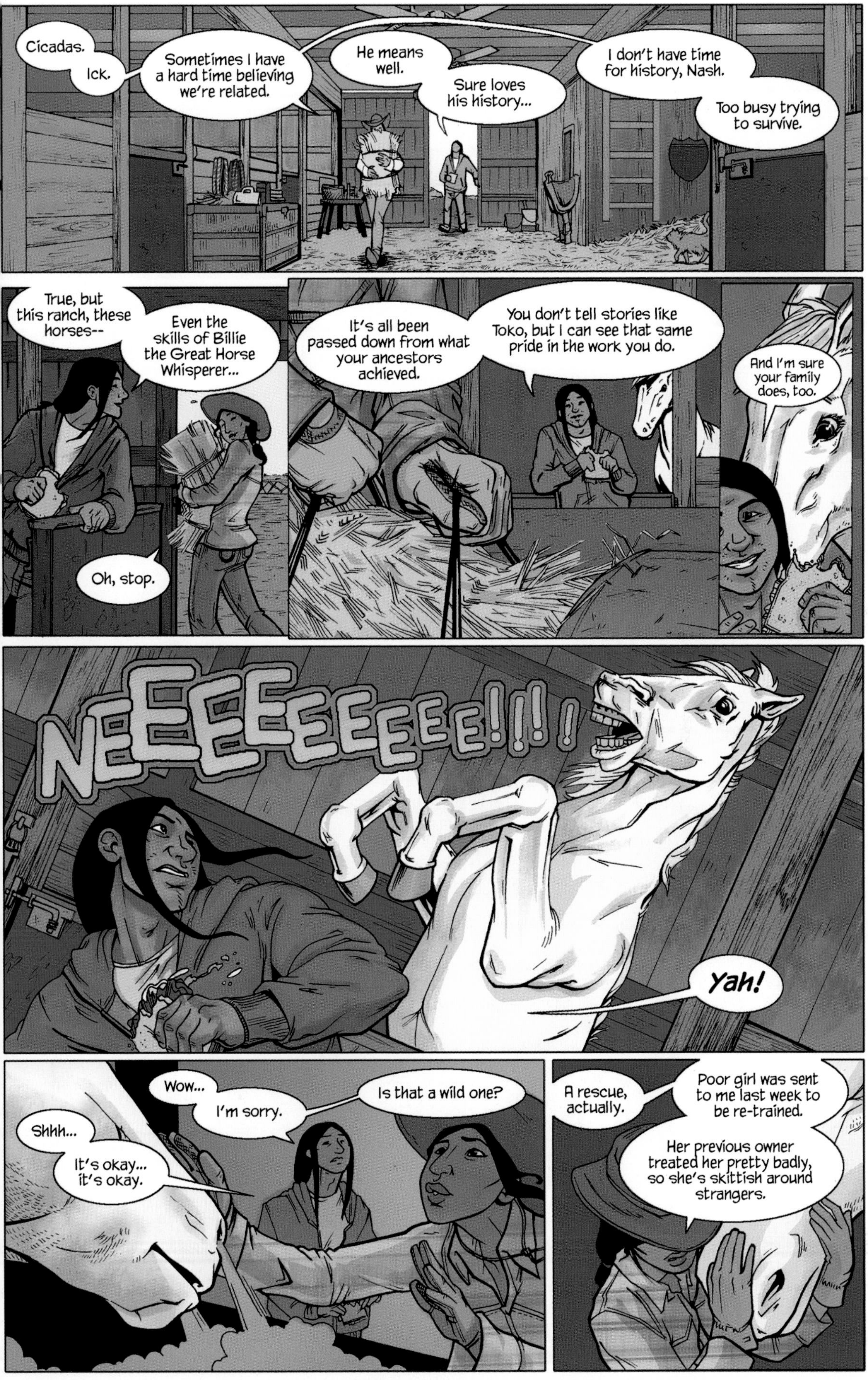
Cicadas.
Ick.
Sometimes I have a hard time believing we're related.
He means well.
Sure loves his history...
I don't have time for history, Nash.
Too busy trying to survive.
True, but this ranch, these horses--
Even the skills of Billie the Great Horse Whisperer...
Oh, stop.
It's all been passed down from what your ancestors achieved.
You don't tell stories like Toko, but I can see that same pride in the work you do.
And I'm sure your family does, too.
NEEEEEEEEE!!!!
Yah!
Wow...
I'm sorry.
Is that a wild one?
Shhh...
It's okay... it's okay.
A rescue, actually.
Poor girl was sent to me last week to be re-trained.
Her previous owner treated her pretty badly, so she's skittish around strangers.

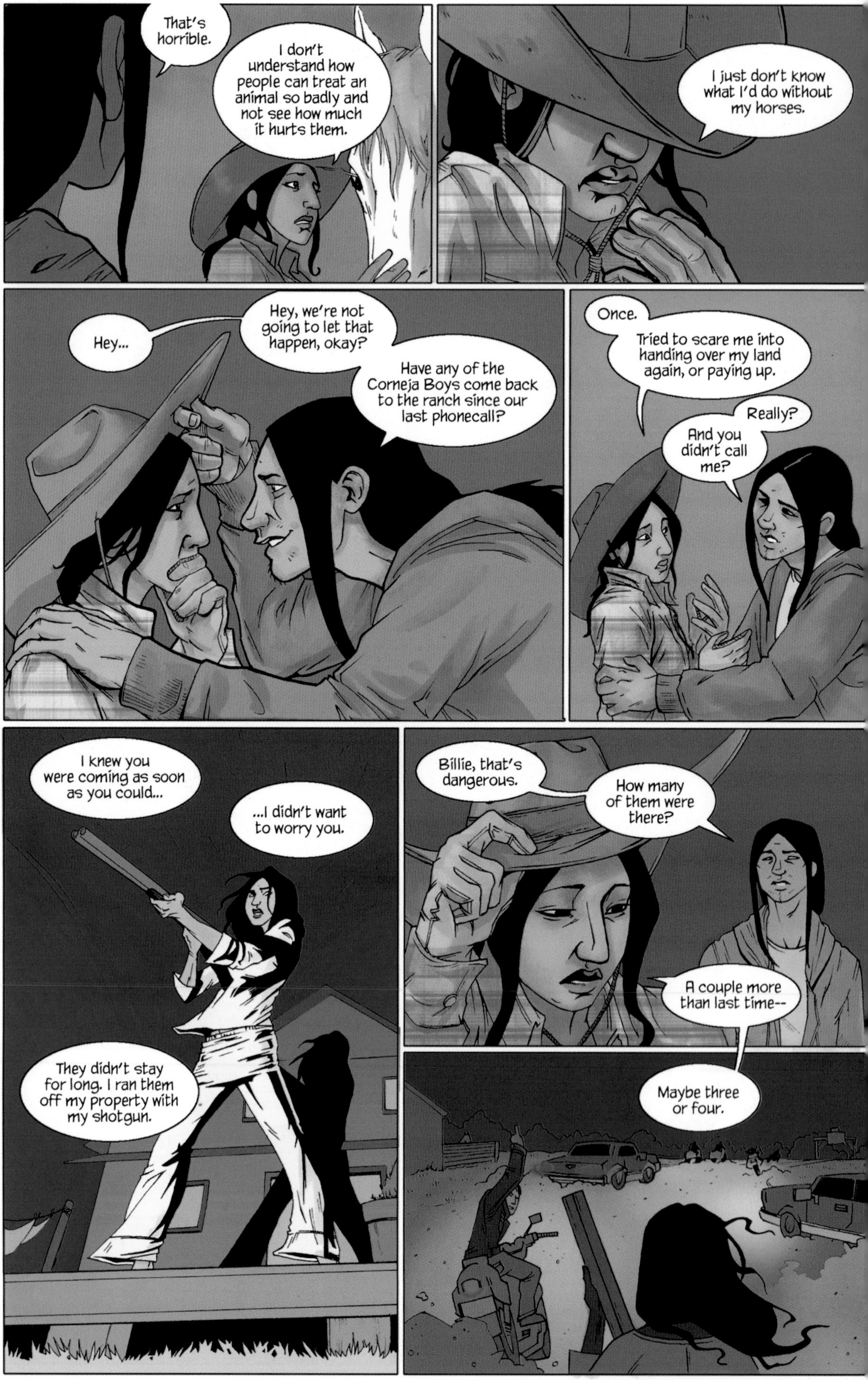
That's horrible.
I don't understand how people can treat an animal so badly and not see how much it hurts them.
I just don't know what I'd do without my horses.
Hey...
Hey, we're not going to let that happen, okay?
Have any of the Corneja Boys come back to the ranch since our last phonecall?
Once.
Tried to scare me into handing over my land again, or paying up.
Really?
And you didn't call me?
I knew you were coming as soon as you could...
...I didn't want to worry you.
They didn't stay for long. I ran them off my property with my shotgun.
Billie, that's dangerous.
How many of them were there?
A couple more than last time--
Maybe three or four.

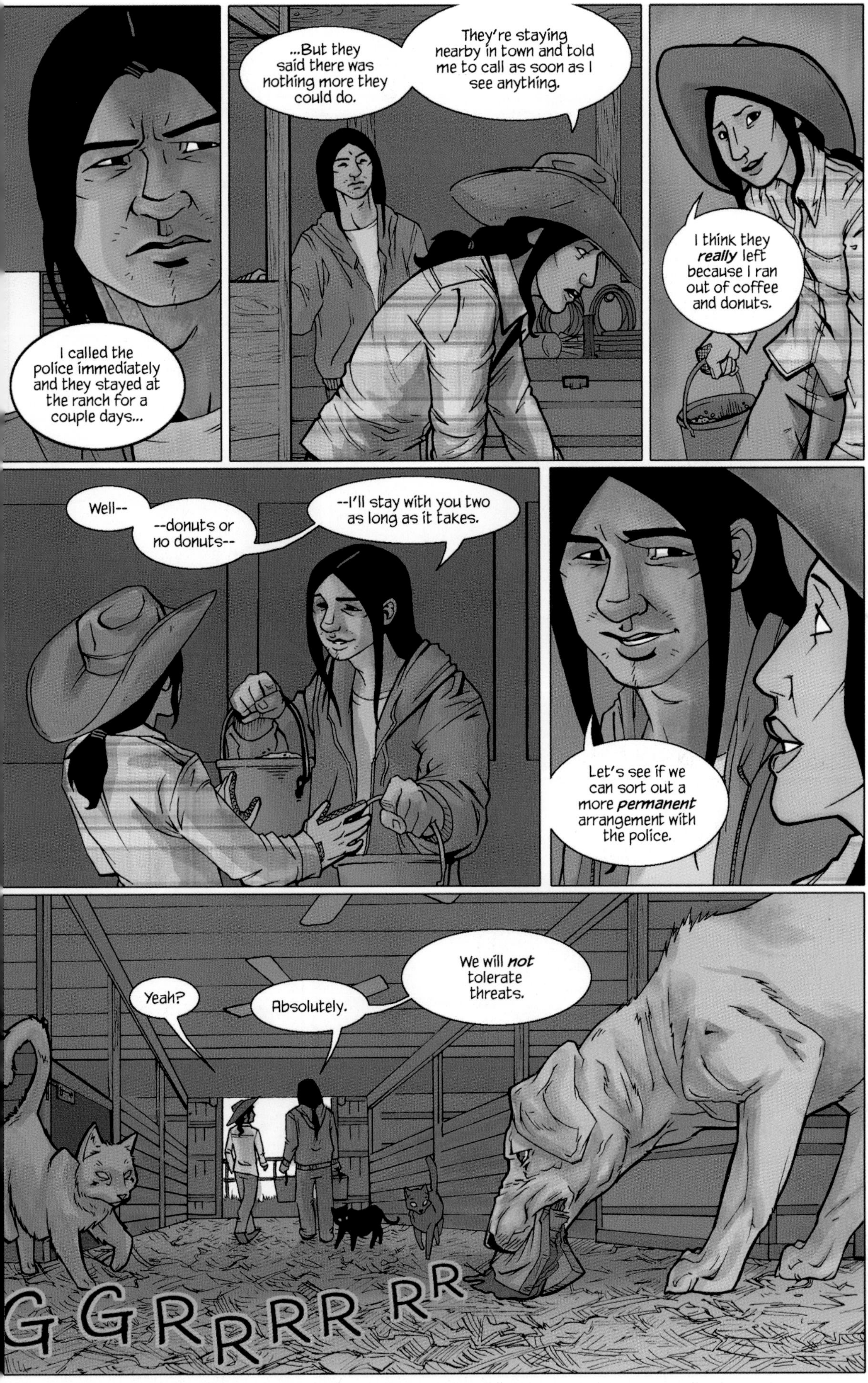

I called the police immediately and they stayed at the ranch for a couple days...
...But they said there was nothing more they could do.
They're staying nearby in town and told me to call as soon as I see anything.
I think they *really* left because I ran out of coffee and donuts.
Well--
--donuts or no donuts--
--I'll stay with you two as long as it takes.
Let's see if we can sort out a more *permanent* arrangement with the police.
Yeah?
Absolutely.
We will *not* tolerate threats.
GGRRRRR RR

Poot!

Toko?

You okay?

Mmf.

Those cicadas not sitting too well with you, old man?

Ugh, enough with the bugs already.

It's *something*.

Well, you take it easy, *Toko*. You want some water?

Yes, please.

Thank you, Nashoba.

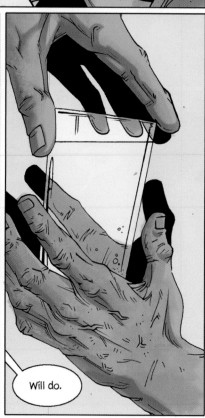

Nash...

I'm going to hop into the shower for a few minutes.

Go ahead and make yourself at home.

Will do.

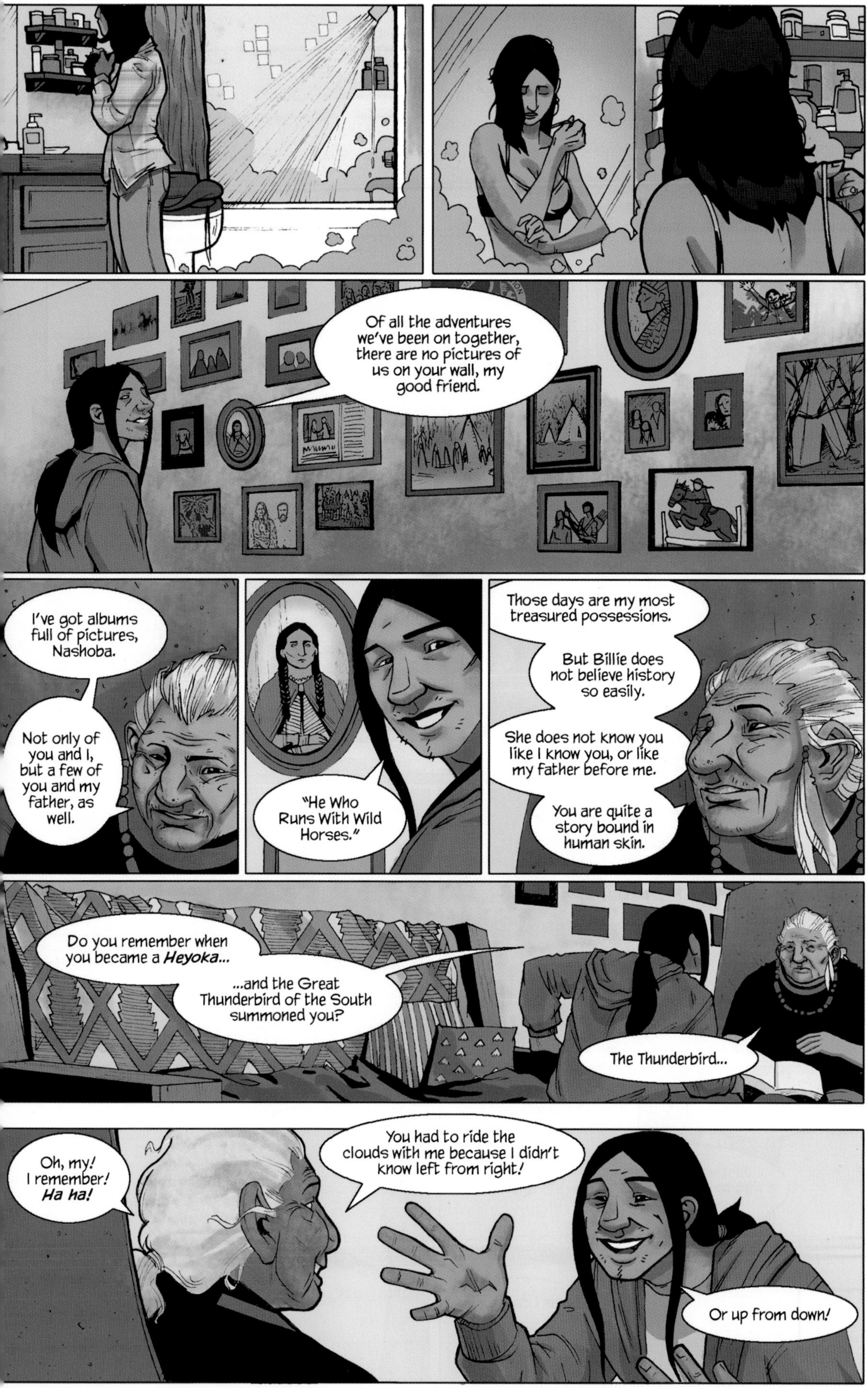
Of all the adventures we've been on together, there are no pictures of us on your wall, my good friend.
I've got albums full of pictures, Nashoba.
Not only of you and I, but a few of you and my father, as well.
"He Who Runs With Wild Horses."
Those days are my most treasured possessions.
But Billie does not believe history so easily.
She does not know you like I know you, or like my father before me.
You are quite a story bound in human skin.
Do you remember when you became a *Heyoka*...
...and the Great Thunderbird of the South summoned you?
The Thunderbird...
Oh, my! I remember! *Ha ha!*
You had to ride the clouds with me because I didn't know left from right!
Or up from down!

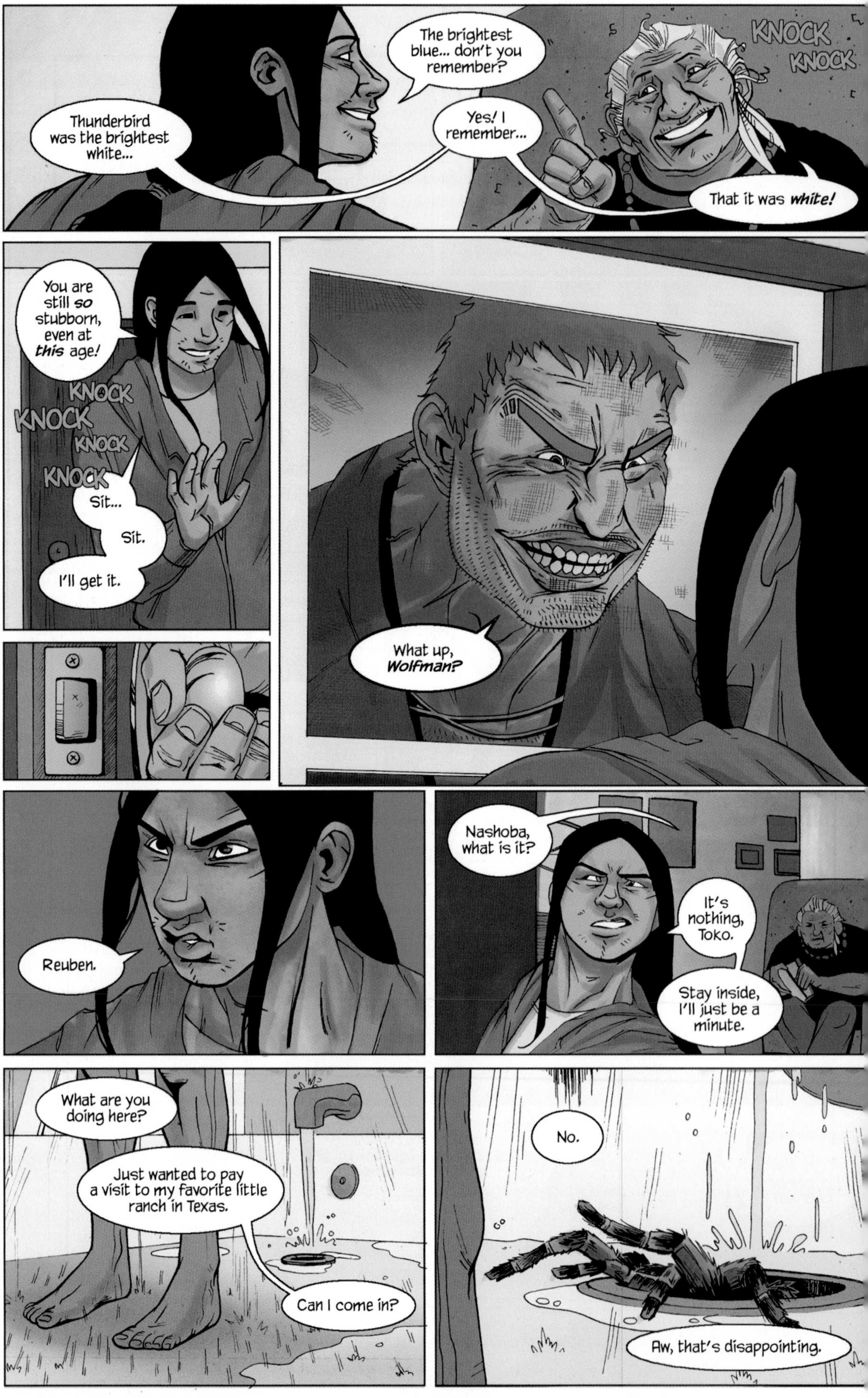
Thunderbird was the brightest white...
The brightest blue... don't you remember?
Yes! I remember...
That it was white!
KNOCK
KNOCK
You are still so stubborn, even at this age!
KNOCK
KNOCK
KNOCK
KNOCK
Sit...
Sit.
I'll get it.
What up, Wolfman?
Reuben.
Nashoba, what is it?
It's nothing, Toko.
Stay inside, I'll just be a minute.
What are you doing here?
Just wanted to pay a visit to my favorite little ranch in Texas.
Can I come in?
No.
Aw, that's disappointing.

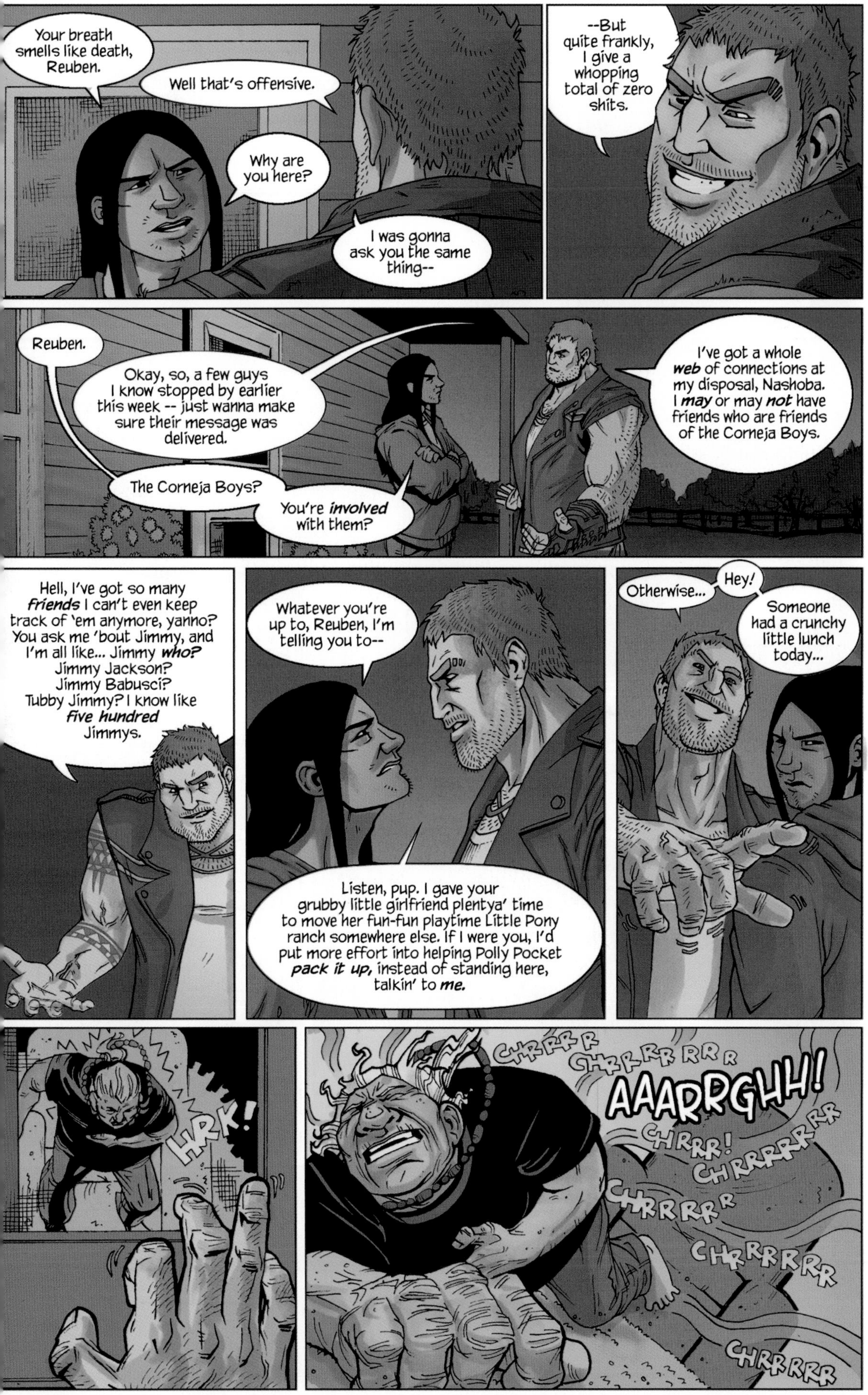

Your breath smells like death, Reuben.
Well that's offensive.
Why are you here?
I was gonna ask you the same thing--
--But quite frankly, I give a whopping total of zero shits.
Reuben.
Okay, so, a few guys I know stopped by earlier this week -- just wanna make sure their message was delivered.
The Corneja Boys?
You're *involved* with them?
I've got a whole *web* of connections at my disposal, Nashoba. I *may* or may *not* have friends who are friends of the Corneja Boys.
Hell, I've got so many *friends* I can't even keep track of 'em anymore, yanno? You ask me 'bout Jimmy, and I'm all like... Jimmy *who?* Jimmy Jackson? Jimmy Babusci? Tubby Jimmy? I know like *five hundred* Jimmys.
Whatever you're up to, Reuben, I'm telling you to--
Listen, pup. I gave your grubby little girlfriend plentya' time to move her fun-fun playtime Little Pony ranch somewhere else. If I were you, I'd put more effort into helping Polly Pocket *pack it up,* instead of standing here, talkin' to *me.*
Otherwise...
Hey!
Someone had a crunchy little lunch today...
HRK!
CHRRRR
CHRRRRRRR
AAARRGHH!
CHRRR!
CHRRRRRRR
CHRRRRR
CHRRRRRRR
CHRRRRRR

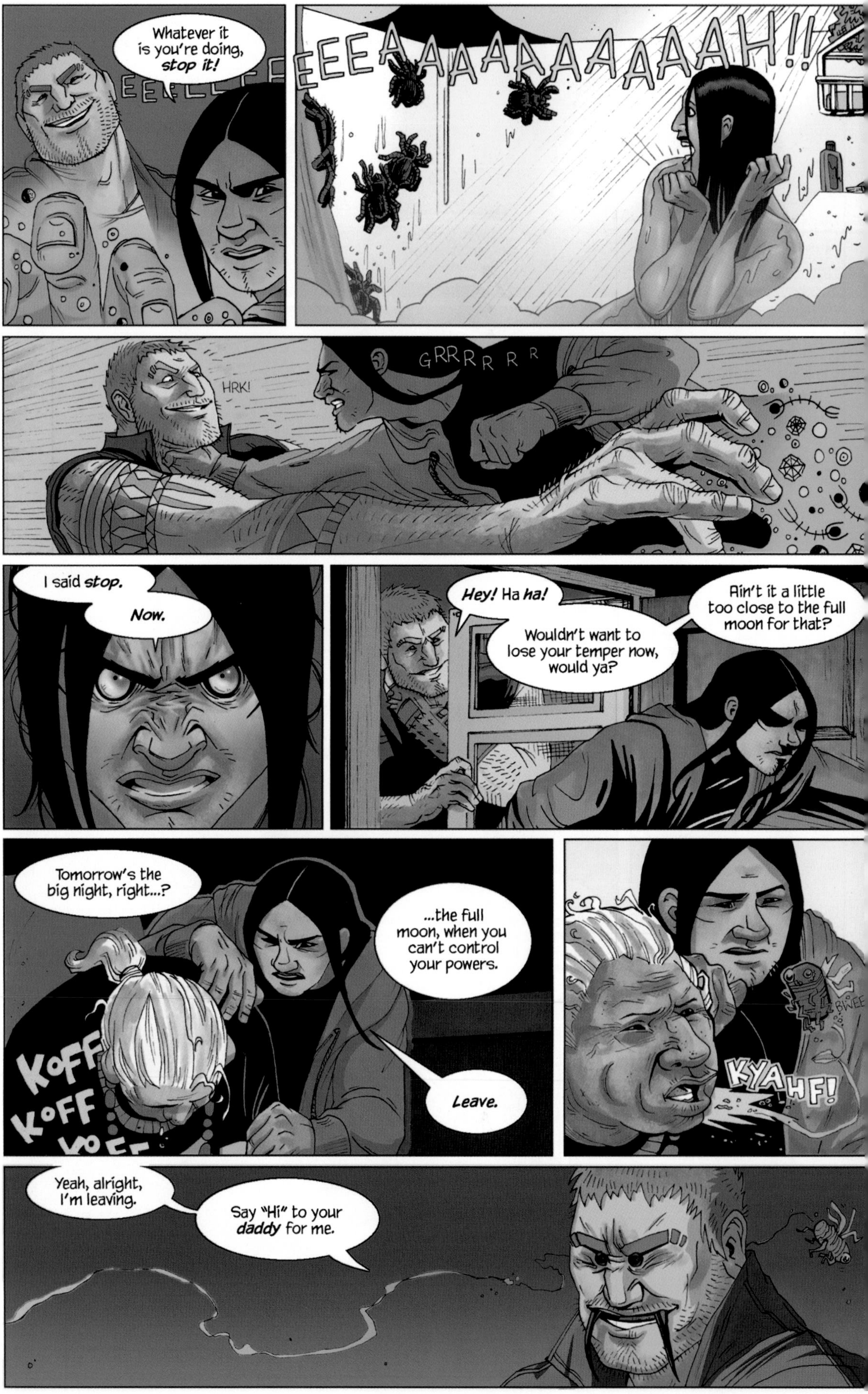
Whatever it is you're doing, *stop it!*
EEEEEEE
EEEEAAAAAAAAAAAH!!
GRRRRRRR
HRK!
I said *stop.*
Now.
Hey! Ha *ha!*
Wouldn't want to lose your temper now, would ya?
Ain't it a little too close to the full moon for that?
Tomorrow's the big night, right...?
...the full moon, when you can't control your powers.
Leave.
KOFF
KOFF
KYAHF!
BWEE
Yeah, alright, I'm leaving.
Say "Hi" to your *daddy* for me.

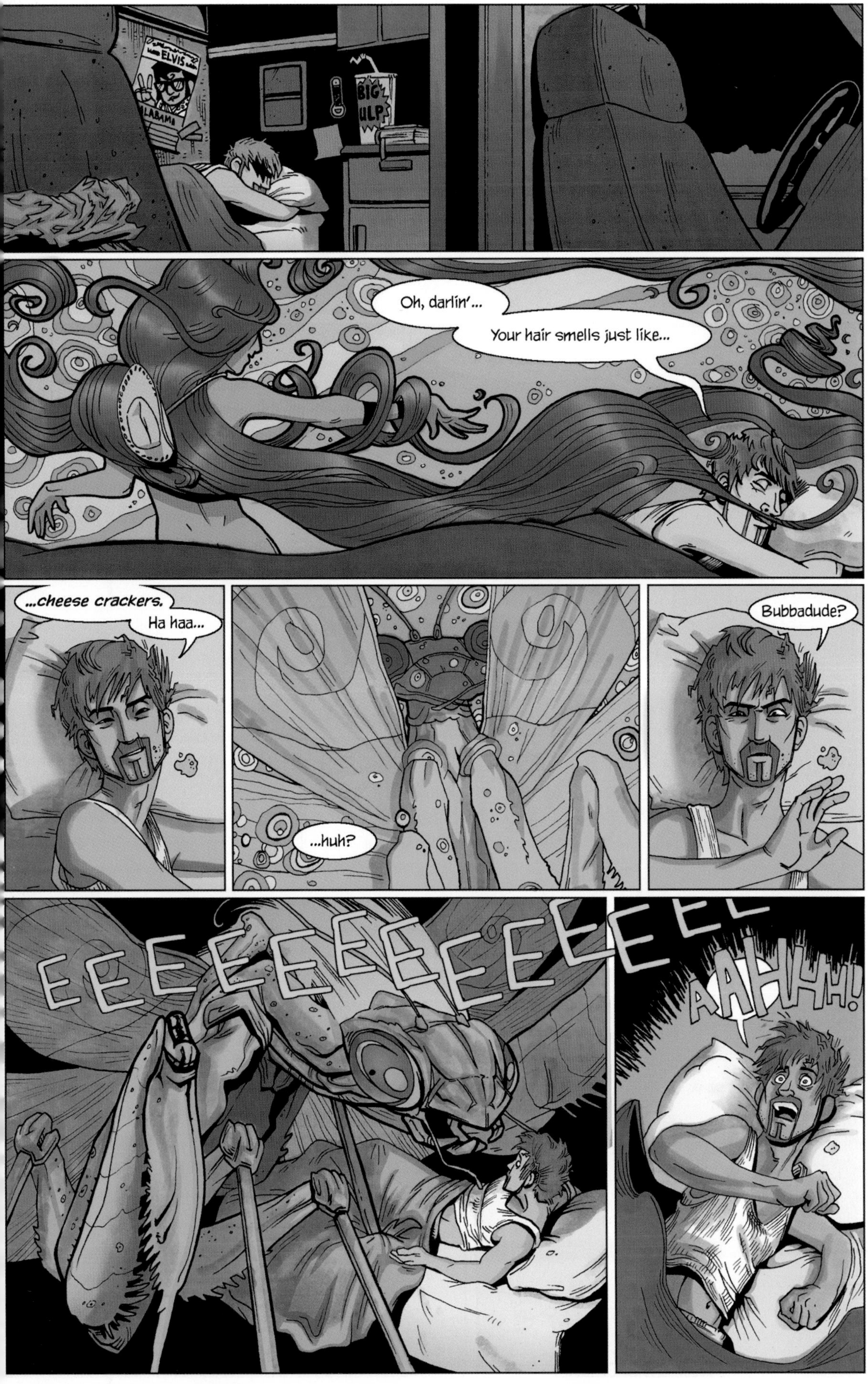

ELVIS
BIG ULP
Oh, darlin'...
Your hair smells just like...
...cheese crackers.
Ha haa...
...huh?
Bubbadude?
EEEEEEEEEEEEEEE
AAHHH!

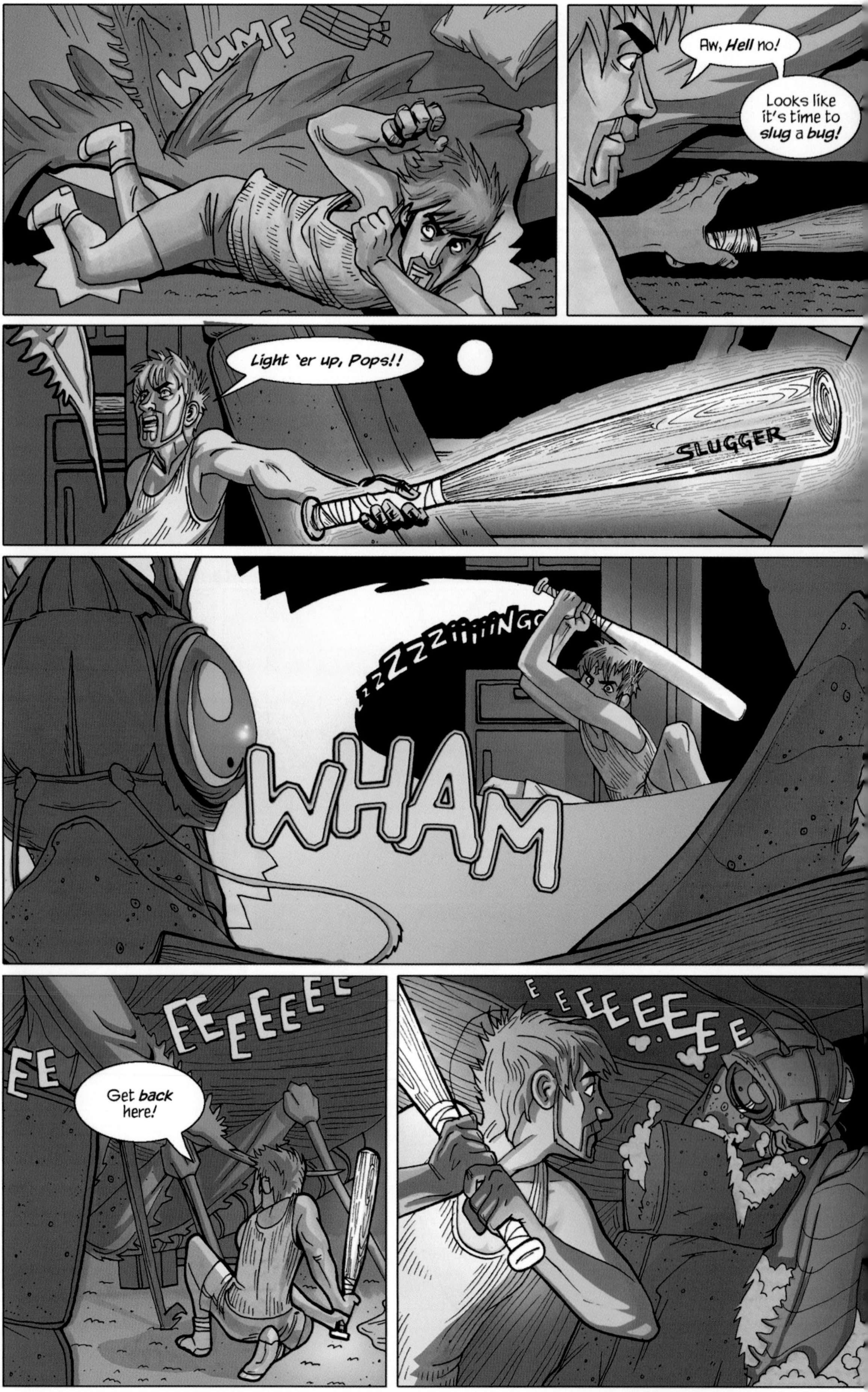
WUMF
Aw, Hell no!
Looks like it's time to slug a bug!
Light 'er up, Pops!!
SLUGGER
zzZZZiiiiiNG
WHAM
EEEEEEEE
Get back here!
EEEEEEEEEE

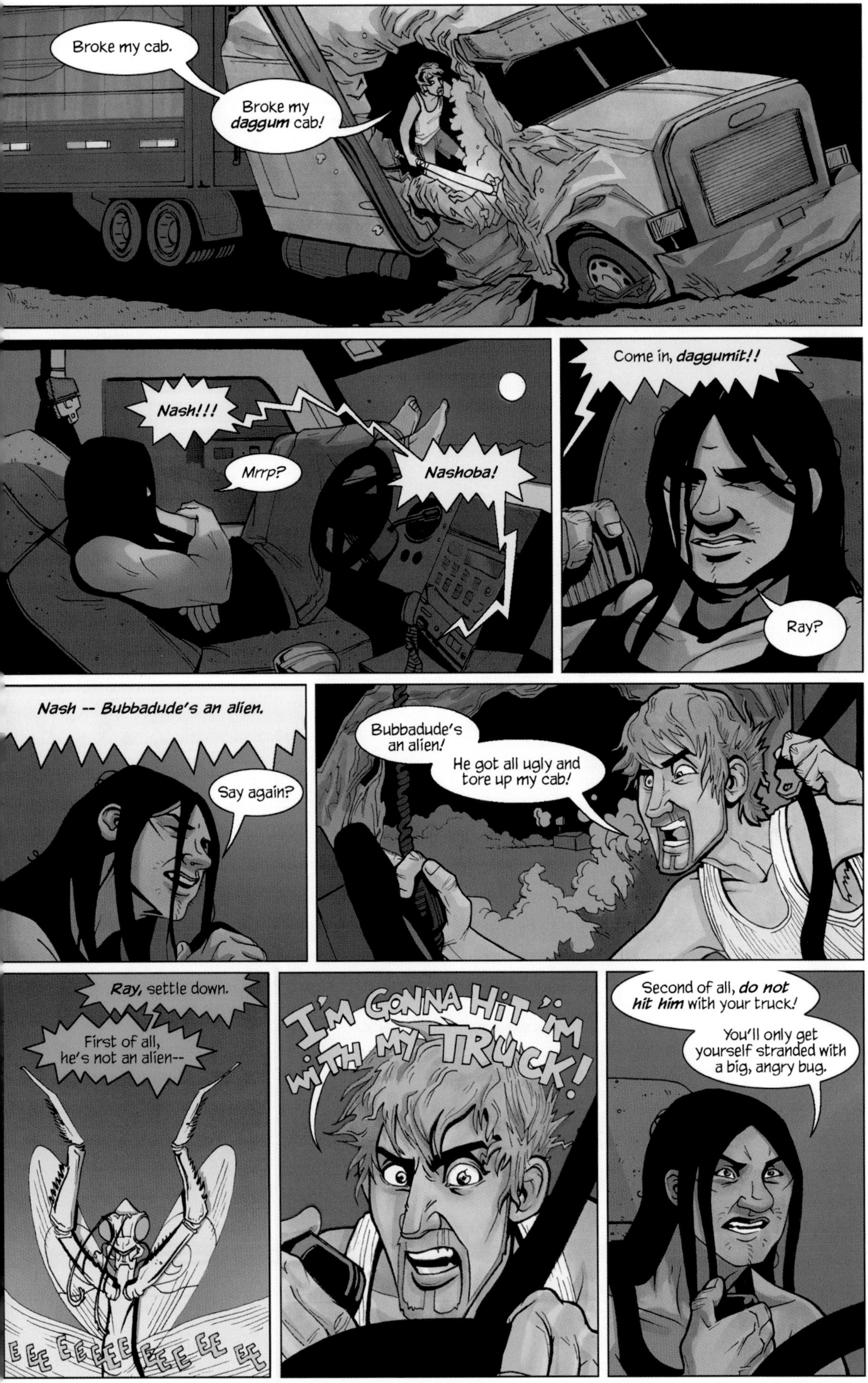
Broke my cab.
Broke my *daggum* cab!
Nash!!!
Mrrp?
Nashoba!
Come in, *daggumit!!*
Ray?
Nash -- Bubbadude's an alien.
Say again?
Bubbadude's an alien!
He got all ugly and tore up my cab!
Ray, settle down.
First of all, he's not an alien--
EEEEEEEEEEEEEEEEE
I'M GONNA HIT 'IM WITH MY TRUCK!
Second of all, ***do not hit him*** with your truck!
You'll only get yourself stranded with a big, angry bug.

Daggummit, I'm already stranded! **HE TRIED TO EAT ME IN MY SLEEP!** I'm not ev[...] in my [...]

POW!

[...] AT THE [...]

I'm [...] a make seriou[...] roadkill out of the [...] sonuva bit[...] Ain[...] Nash y[...]tta [...] come [...] and h[...] kill t[...] not [...] this [...]

No...

They must've come in a back way.

--before he *flies back* to the *mothership!*

Ray, listen...

If he tries to fly off, *let him!*

Where are you?

I'm on 10, just outside of Sonora.

'Bout two miles away from some diner called *Al and Moe's.*

Brother, stay safe. I gotta go.

I'll pick you up tomorrow.

10-4.

CLICK

CLICK

POW

Get off my property!!

I'm gonna call the police!

Pra-perr-ti!

Oh no, muchachos, my *pra-perr-ti!*

Ha ha *ha!* "The police"!

The police can't save you now, puta!

TOK

Aah!!

TOK

TOK

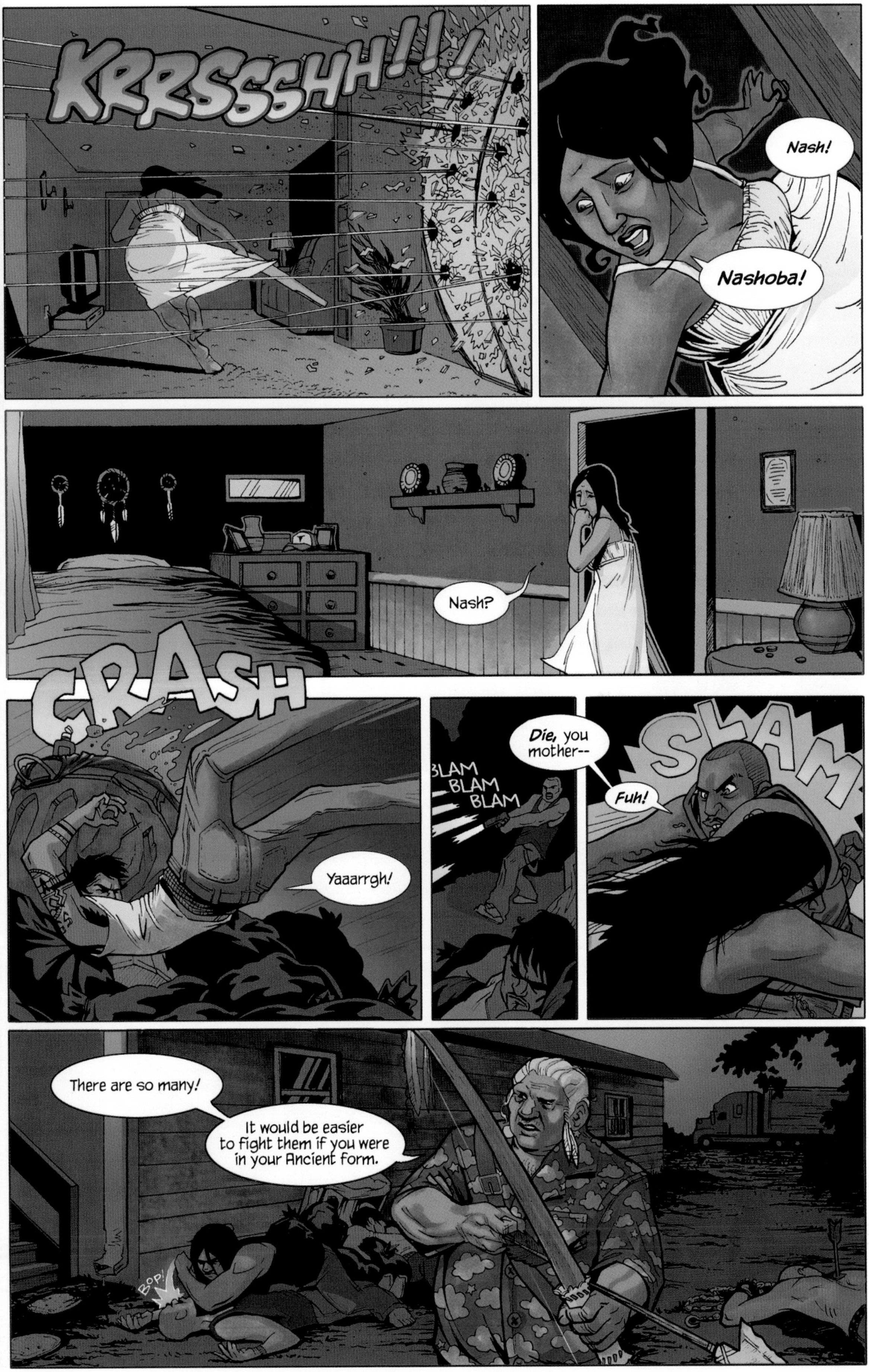
KRRSSSHH!!!!
Nash!
Nashoba!
Nash?
CRASH
Yaaarrgh!
BLAM
BLAM
BLAM
Die, you mother--
Fuh!
SLAM
There are so many!
It would be easier to fight them if you were in your Ancient form.
BOP!

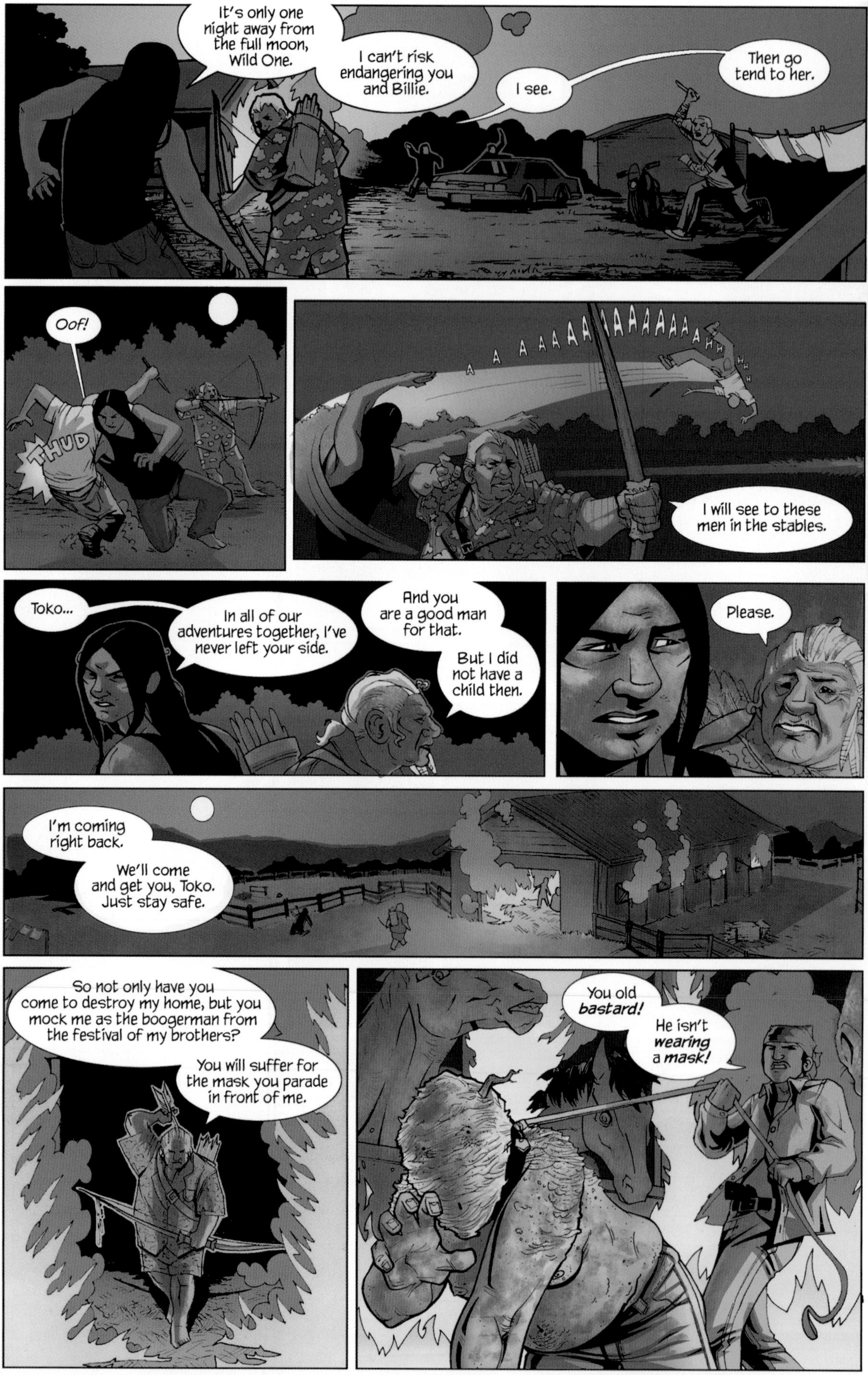
It's only one night away from the full moon, Wild One.
I can't risk endangering you and Billie.
I see.
Then go tend to her.
Oof!
THUD
AAAAAAAAAAAAAAAAAHHHHH
I will see to these men in the stables.
Toko...
In all of our adventures together, I've never left your side.
And you are a good man for that.
But I did not have a child then.
Please.
I'm coming right back.
We'll come and get you, Toko. Just stay safe.
So not only have you come to destroy my home, but you mock me as the boogerman from the festival of my brothers?
You will suffer for the mask you parade in front of me.
You old *bastard!*
He isn't *wearing* a *mask!*

THUD

Y-you bastards, coming here, showing off on your dumb bikes...

We don't scare you, eh?

You don't scare me!

You are a brave woman. Seems we must try a little harder...

FWAM

Billie, are you alright?

I-- I'm fine...

CRUMBLE CRUMBLE

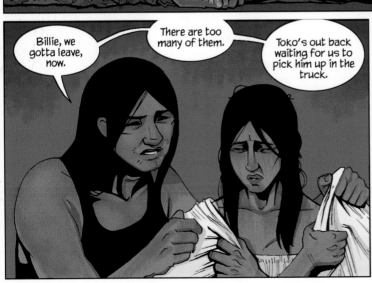

Billie, we gotta leave, now.

There are too many of them.

Toko's out back waiting for us to pick him up in the truck.

What about my horses?

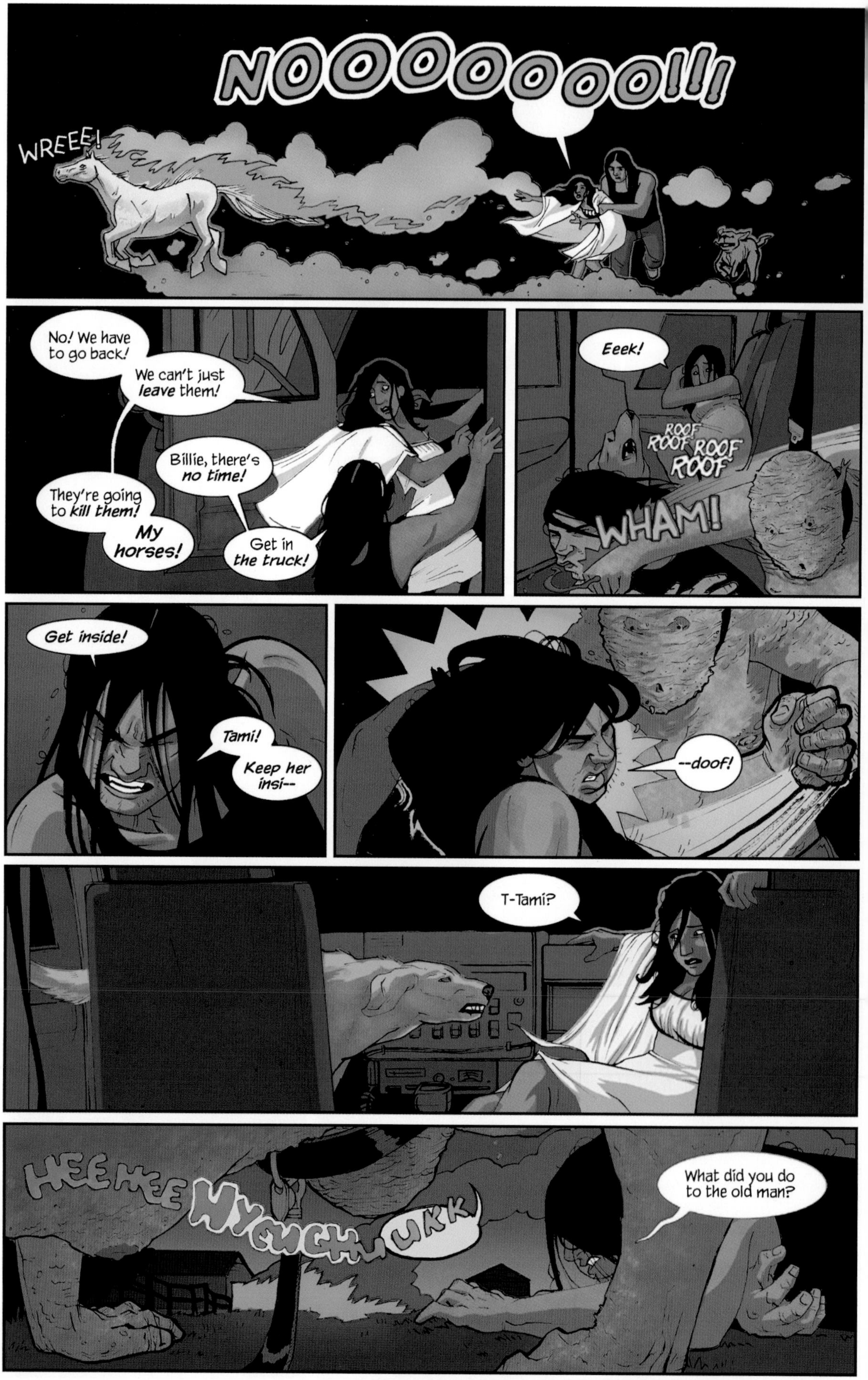
NOOOOOOO!!!
WREEE!
No! We have to go back!
We can't just *leave* them!
They're going to *kill them!*
My horses!
Billie, there's *no time!*
Get in *the truck!*
Eeek!
ROOF ROOF ROOF ROOF
WHAM!
Get inside!
Tami!
Keep her insi--
--doof!
T-Tami?
HEE HEE HYGUGH UKK
What did you do to the old man?

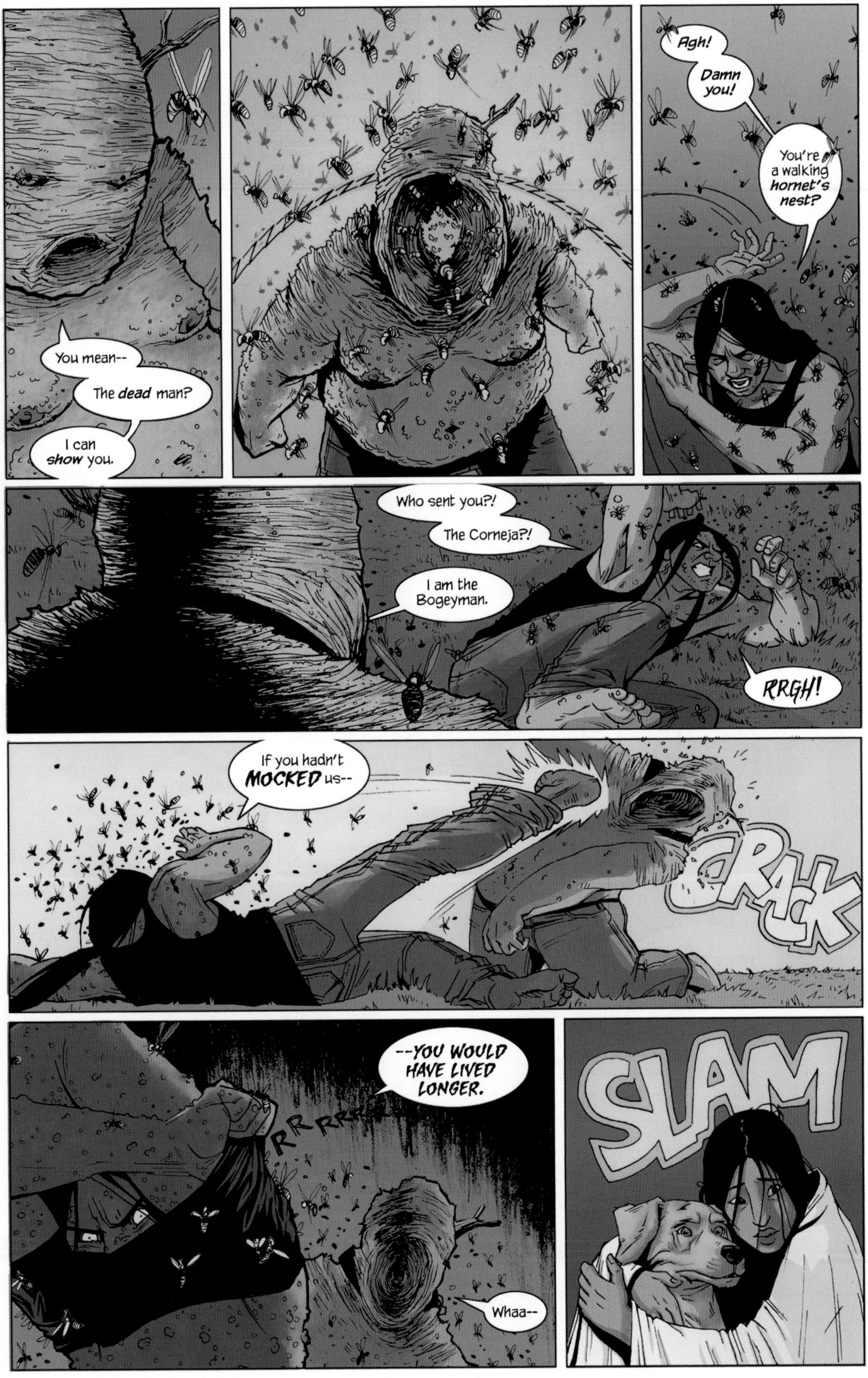
ZZ
You mean--
The *dead* man?
I can *show* you.
Agh!
Damn you!
You're a walking *hornet's nest*?
Who sent you?!
The Corneja?!
I am the Bogeyman.
RRGH!
If you hadn't *MOCKED* us--
CRACK
--YOU WOULD HAVE LIVED LONGER.
RR RRR
Whaa--
SLAM

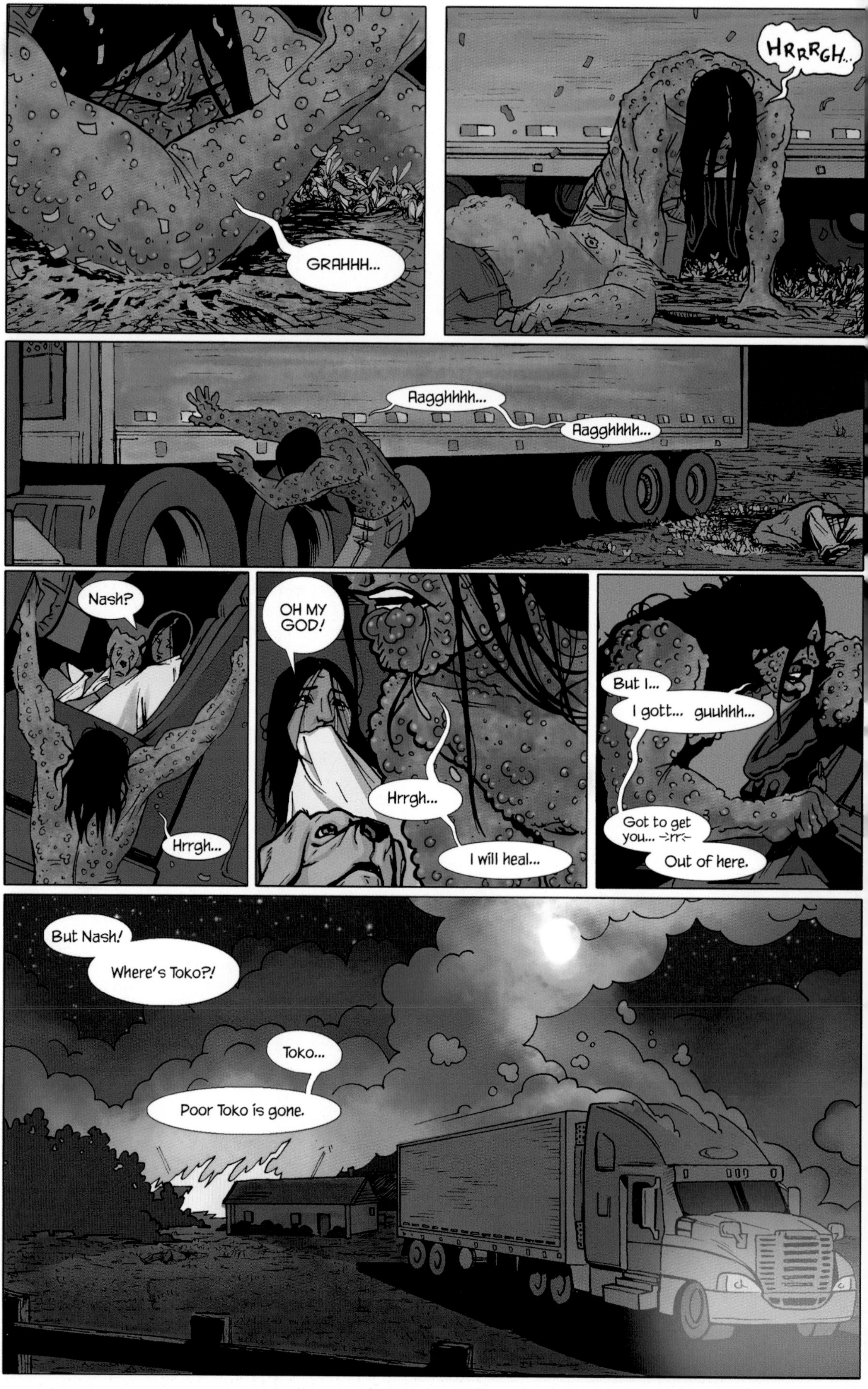
GRAHHH...
HRRRGH...
Aagghhhh...
Aagghhhh...
Nash?
Hrrgh...
OH MY GOD!
Hrrgh...
I will heal...
But I...
I gott... guuhhh...
Got to get you... rr
Out of here.
But Nash!
Where's Toko?!
Toko...
Poor Toko is gone.

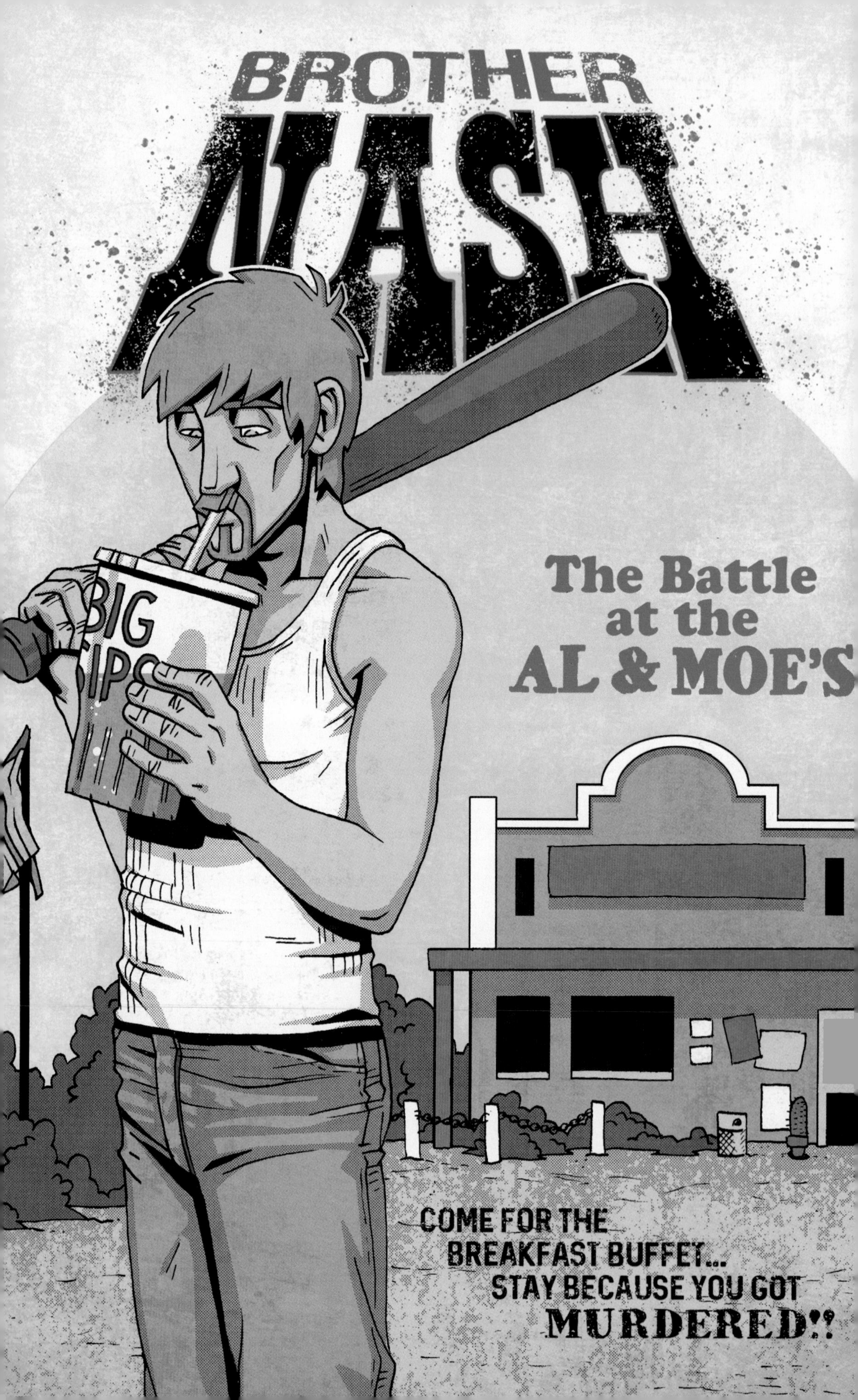
BROTHER NASH
The Battle at the AL & MOE'S
BIG SIPS
COME FOR THE BREAKFAST BUFFET... STAY BECAUSE YOU GOT MURDERED!?

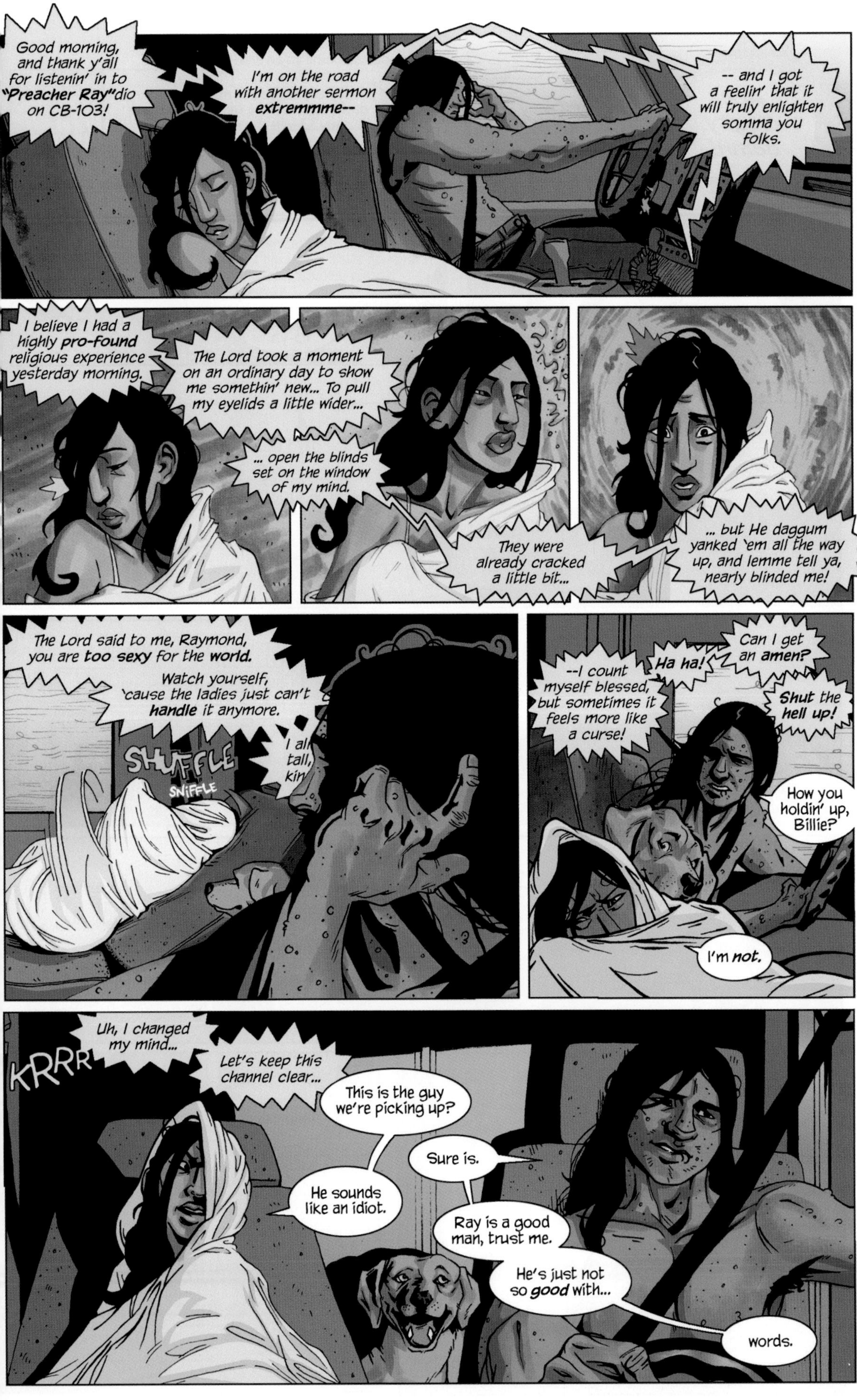

Good morning, and thank y'all for listenin' in to **"Preacher Ray"**dio on CB-103!
I'm on the road with another sermon **extremmme--**
-- and I got a feelin' that it will truly enlighten somma you folks.
I believe I had a highly **pro-found** religious experience yesterday morning.
The Lord took a moment on an ordinary day to show me somethin' new... To pull my eyelids a little wider...
... open the blinds set on the window of my mind.
They were already cracked a little bit...
... but He daggum yanked 'em all the way up, and lemme tell ya, nearly blinded me!
The Lord said to me, Raymond, you are **too sexy** for the **world.**
Watch yourself, 'cause the ladies just can't **handle** it anymore.
SHUFFLE
SNIFFLE
--I count myself blessed, but sometimes it feels more like a curse!
Ha ha!
Can I get an **amen?**
Shut the **hell up!**
How you holdin' up, Billie?
I'm ***not.***
KRRR
Uh, I changed my mind...
Let's keep this channel clear...
This is the guy we're picking up?
Sure is.
He sounds like an idiot.
Ray is a good man, trust me.
He's just not so ***good*** with...
words.

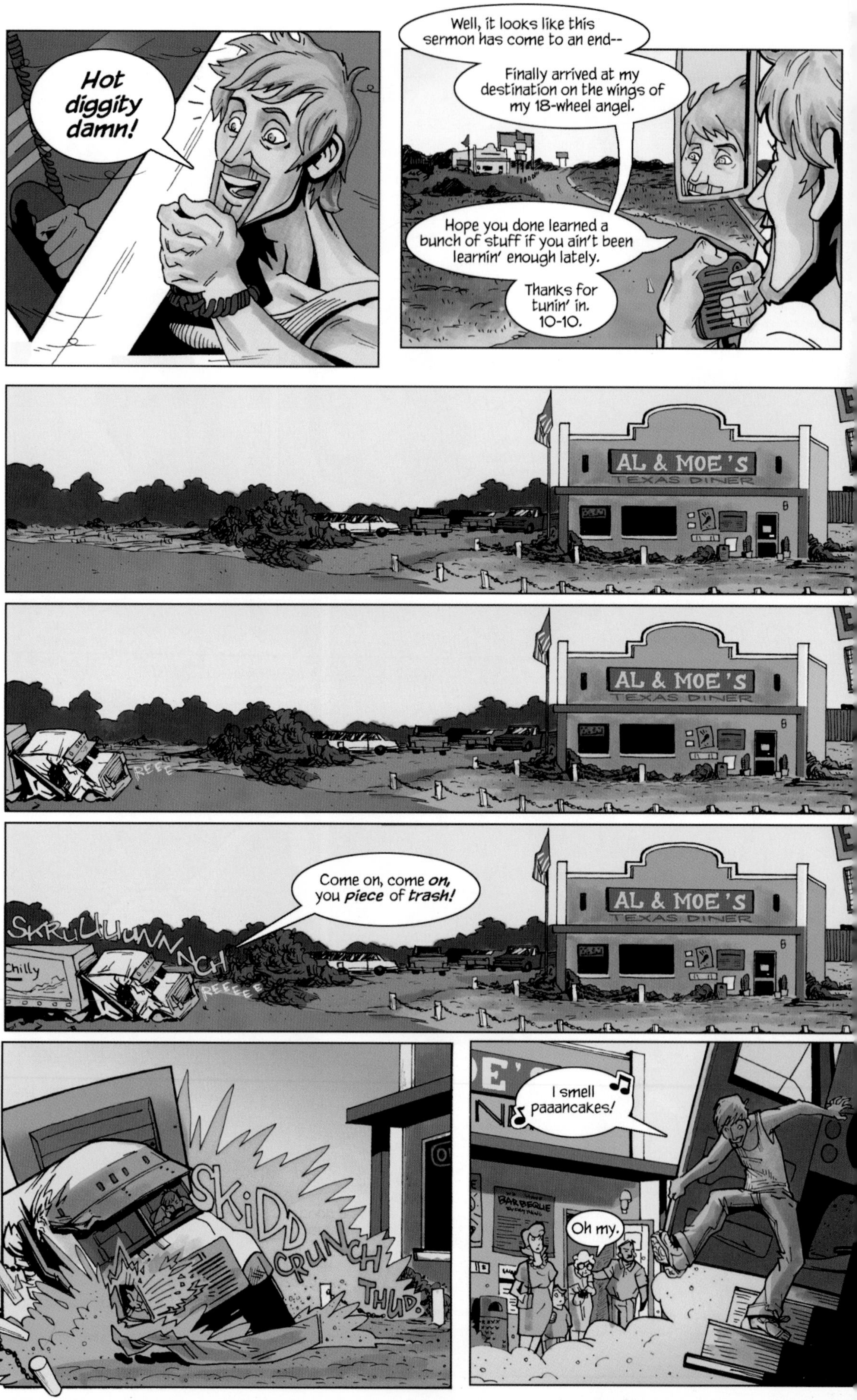
Hot diggity damn!
Well, it looks like this sermon has come to an end--
Finally arrived at my destination on the wings of my 18-wheel angel.
Hope you done learned a bunch of stuff if you ain't been learnin' enough lately.
Thanks for tunin' in. 10-10.
AL & MOE'S
TEXAS DINER
AL & MOE'S
TEXAS DINER
REEE
SKRUUUUUNNNCH
Chilly
REEEEEE
Come on, come *on*, you *piece* of *trash!*
AL & MOE'S
TEXAS DINER
SKIDD
CRUNCH
THUD.
I smell paaancakes!
BARBEQUE
Oh my.

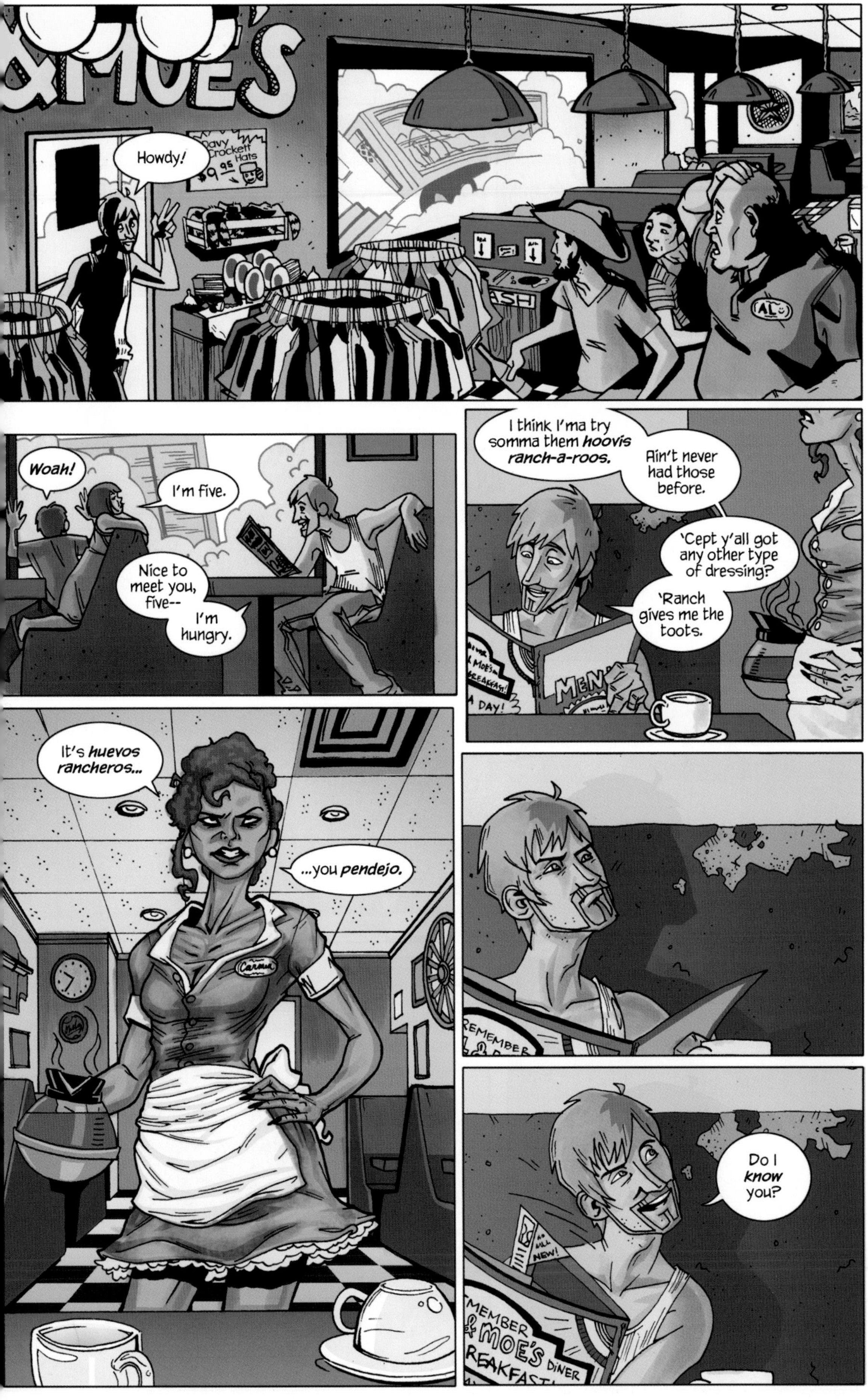
&MOE'S
Davy Crockett Hats $9.95
Howdy!
CASH
AL
Woah!
I'm five.
Nice to meet you, five--
I'm hungry.
I think I'ma try somma them *hoovis ranch-a-roos.*
Ain't never had those before.
'Cept y'all got any other type of dressing?
'Ranch gives me the toots.
MENU
It's *huevos rancheros...*
...you *pendejo.*
Carmen
REMEMBER
Do I *know* you?
ALL NEW!
REMEMBER &MOE'S DINER BREAKFAST

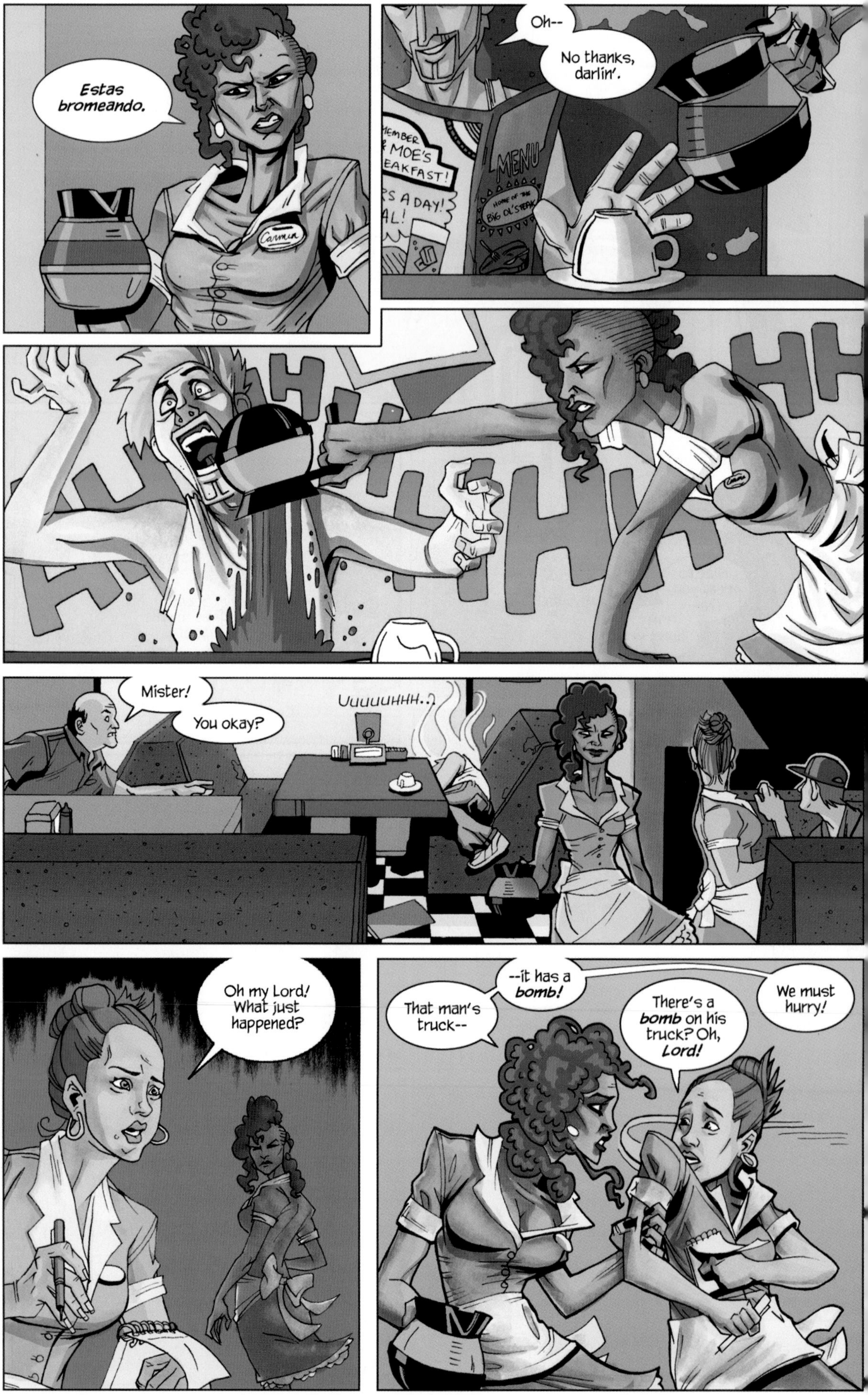

Estas bromeando.
Oh--
No thanks, darlin'.
MENU
HOME OF THE BIG OL'STEAK
Mister!
You okay?
Uuuuuhhh...
Oh my Lord! What just happened?
That man's truck--
--it has a bomb!
There's a bomb on his truck? Oh, Lord!
We must hurry!

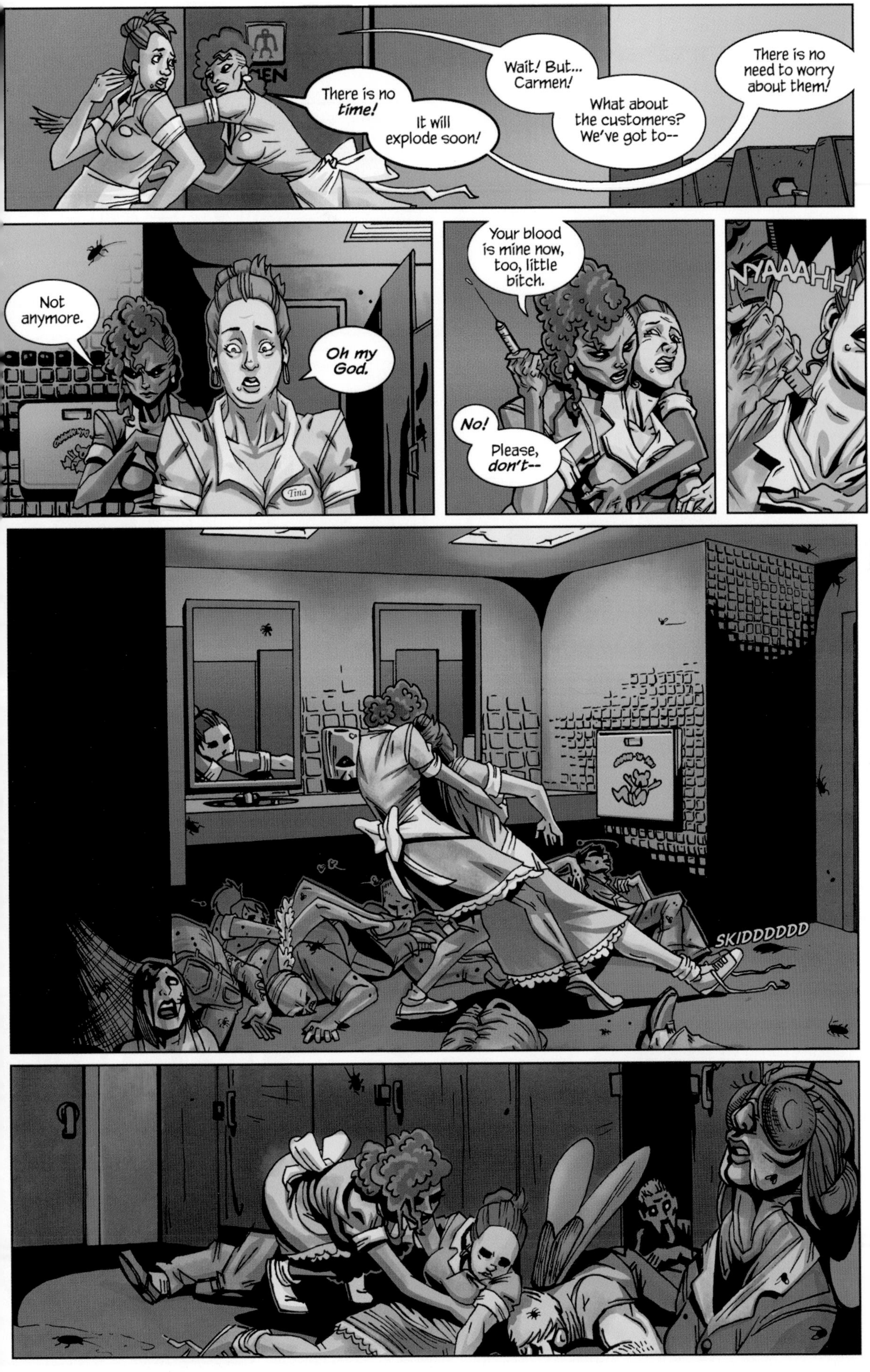
There is no *time!*
It will explode soon!
Wait! But... Carmen!
What about the customers? We've got to--
There is no need to worry about them!
Not anymore.
Oh my God.
Your blood is mine now, too, little bitch.
No!
Please, *don't--*
NYAAAHH!
SKIDDDDDD

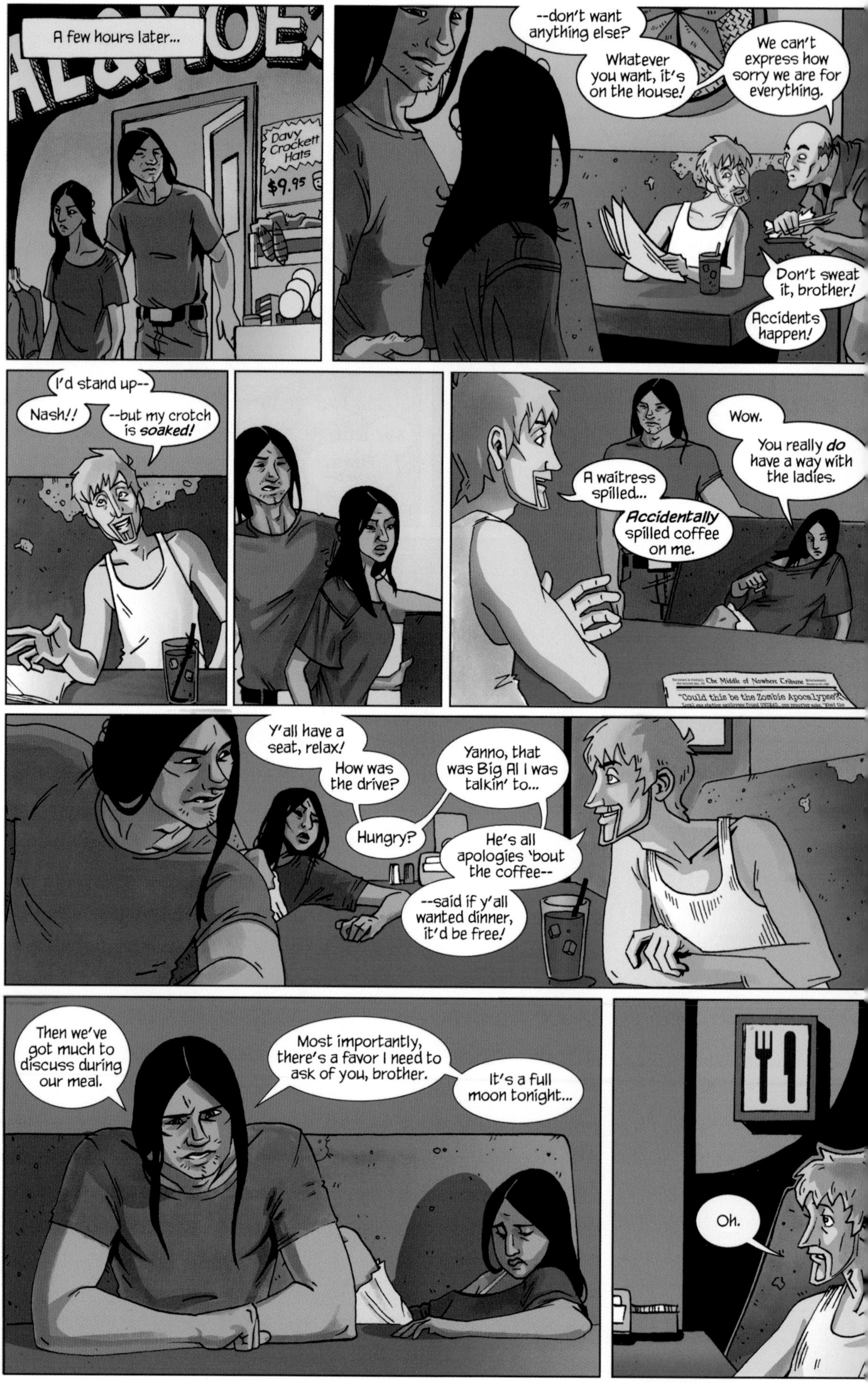
A few hours later...
Davy Crockett Hats
$9.95
--don't want anything else?
Whatever you want, it's on the house!
We can't express how sorry we are for everything.
Don't sweat it, brother!
Accidents happen!
I'd stand up--
Nash!!
--but my crotch is *soaked!*
A waitress spilled...
Accidentally spilled coffee on me.
Wow.
You really ***do*** have a way with the ladies.
The Middle of Nowhere Tribune
"Could this be the Zombie Apocalypse?"
Y'all have a seat, relax!
How was the drive?
Hungry?
Yanno, that was Big Al I was talkin' to...
He's all apologies 'bout the coffee--
--said if y'all wanted dinner, it'd be free!
Then we've got much to discuss during our meal.
Most importantly, there's a favor I need to ask of you, brother.
It's a full moon tonight...
Oh.

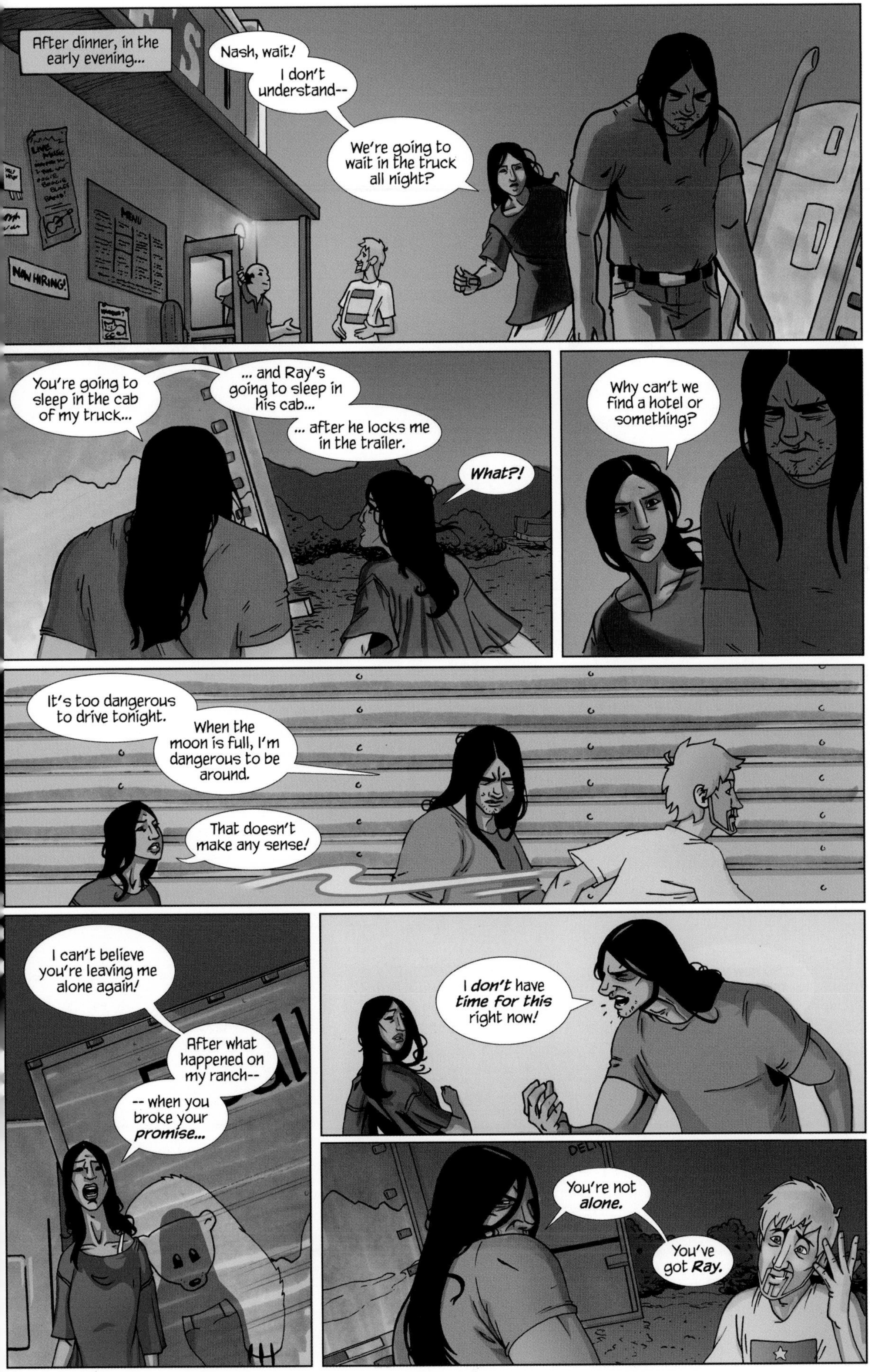
After dinner, in the early evening...
Nash, wait!
I don't understand--
We're going to wait in the truck all night?
NOW HIRING!
You're going to sleep in the cab of my truck...
... and Ray's going to sleep in his cab...
... after he locks me in the trailer.
What?!
Why can't we find a hotel or something?
It's too dangerous to drive tonight.
When the moon is full, I'm dangerous to be around.
That doesn't make any sense!
I can't believe you're leaving me alone again!
After what happened on my ranch--
-- when you broke your *promise...*
I ***don't*** have ***time for this*** right now!
You're not ***alone.***
You've got ***Ray.***

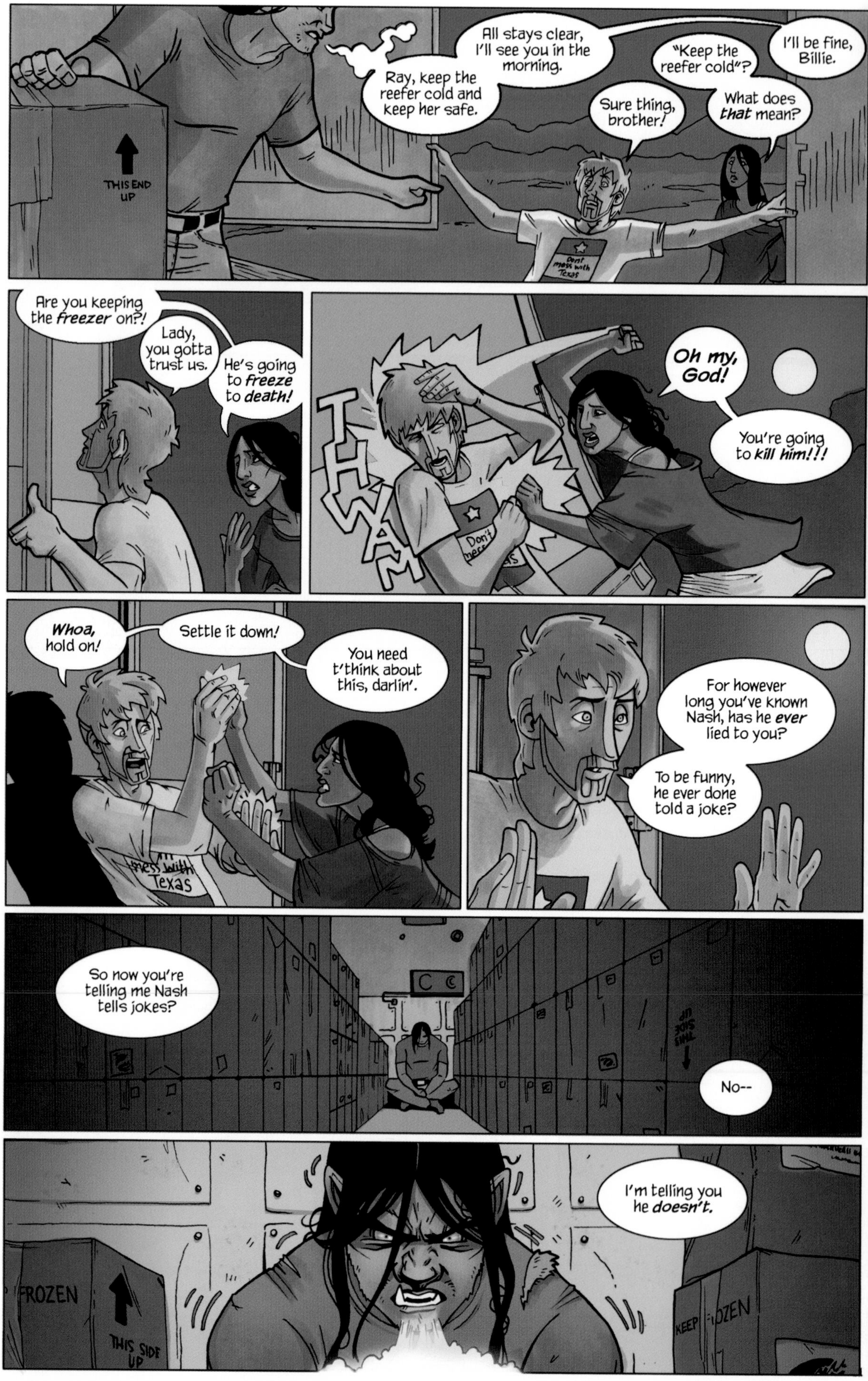

Ray, keep the reefer cold and keep her safe.
All stays clear, I'll see you in the morning.
Sure thing, brother!
"Keep the reefer cold"?
What does that mean?
I'll be fine, Billie.
THIS END UP
Don't mess with Texas
Are you keeping the freezer on?!
Lady, you gotta trust us.
He's going to freeze to death!
THWAM
Oh my, God!
You're going to kill him!!!
Whoa, hold on!
Settle it down!
You need t'think about this, darlin'.
For however long you've known Nash, has he ever lied to you?
To be funny, he ever done told a joke?
So now you're telling me Nash tells jokes?
No--
I'm telling you he doesn't.
FROZEN
THIS SIDE UP
KEEP FROZEN

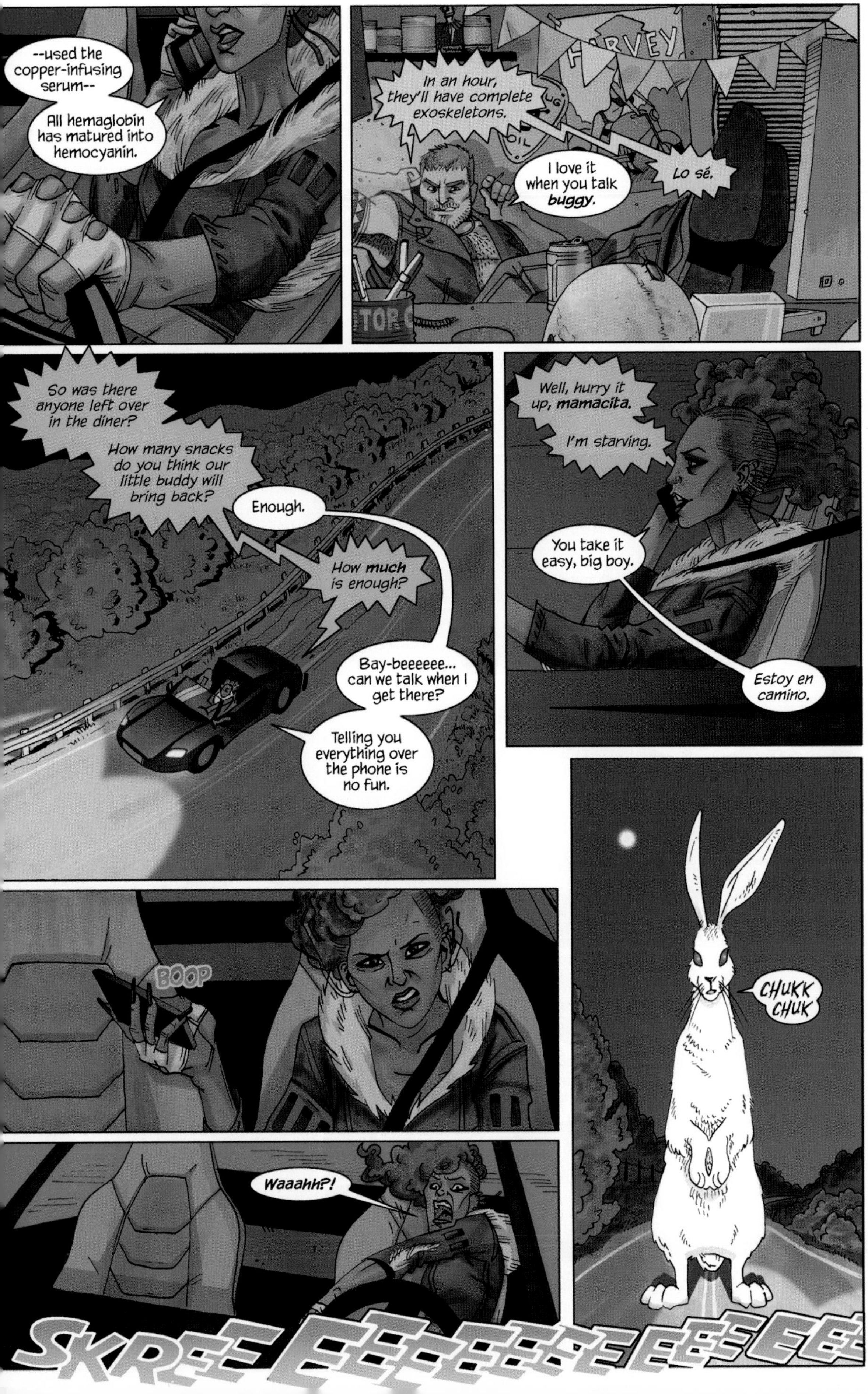
--used the copper-infusing serum--
All hemaglobin has matured into hemocyanin.
In an hour, they'll have complete exoskeletons.
I love it when you talk **buggy**.
Lo sé.
So was there anyone left over in the diner?
How many snacks do you think our little buddy will bring back?
Enough.
How **much** is enough?
Bay-beeeeee... can we talk when I get there?
Telling you everything over the phone is no fun.
Well, hurry it up, **mamacita**.
I'm starving.
You take it easy, big boy.
Estoy en camino.
BOOP
CHUKK CHUK
Waaahh?!
SKREEEEEEEEEEEEEEEEE

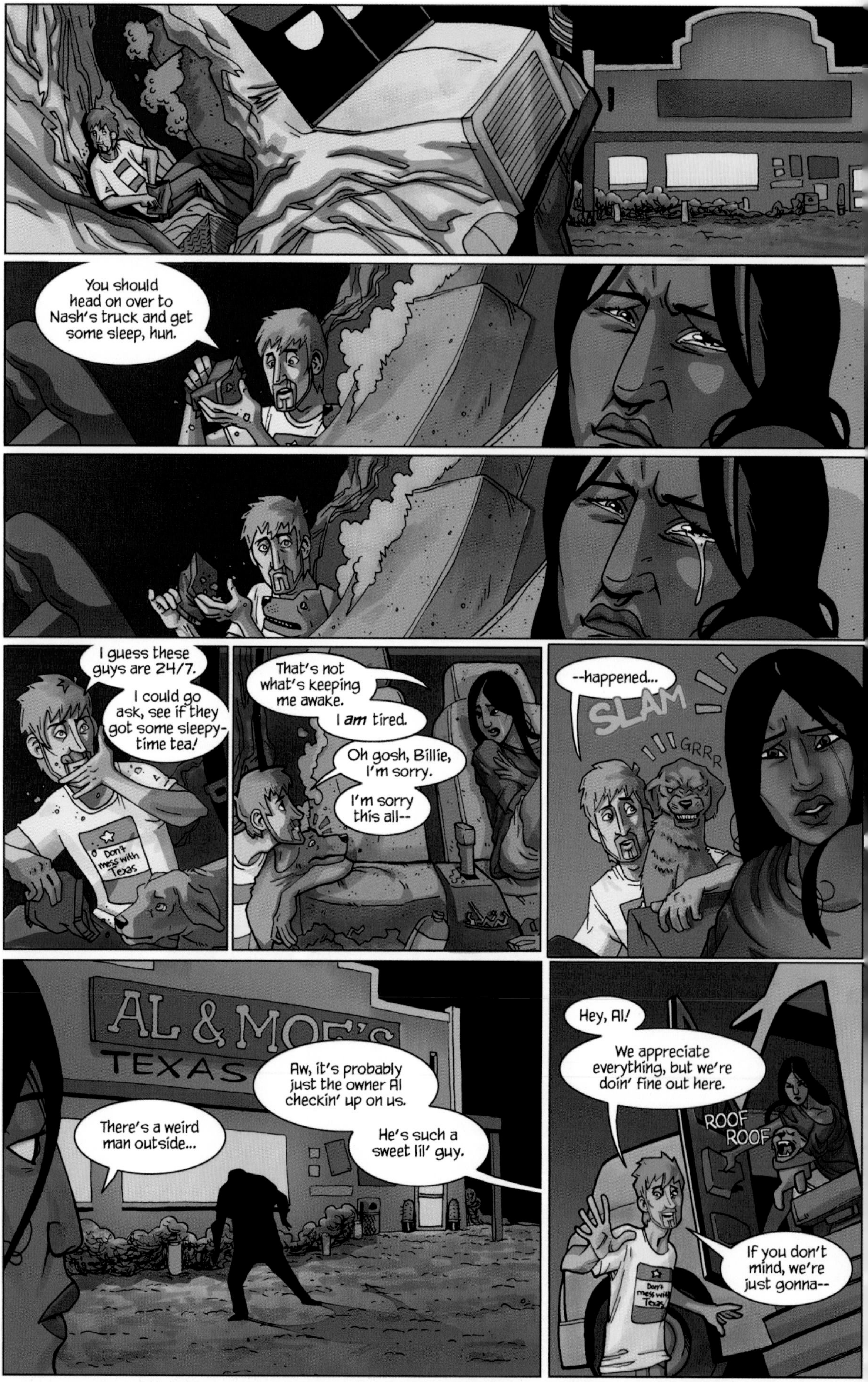
You should head on over to Nash's truck and get some sleep, hun.
I guess these guys are 24/7.
I could go ask, see if they got some sleepy-time tea!
Don't mess with Texas
That's not what's keeping me awake.
I *am* tired.
Oh gosh, Billie, I'm sorry.
I'm sorry this all--
--happened...
SLAM
GRRR
AL & MOE'S
TEXAS
There's a weird man outside...
Aw, it's probably just the owner Al checkin' up on us.
He's such a sweet lil' guy.
Hey, Al!
We appreciate everything, but we're doin' fine out here.
ROOF ROOF
If you don't mind, we're just gonna--
Don't mess with Texas

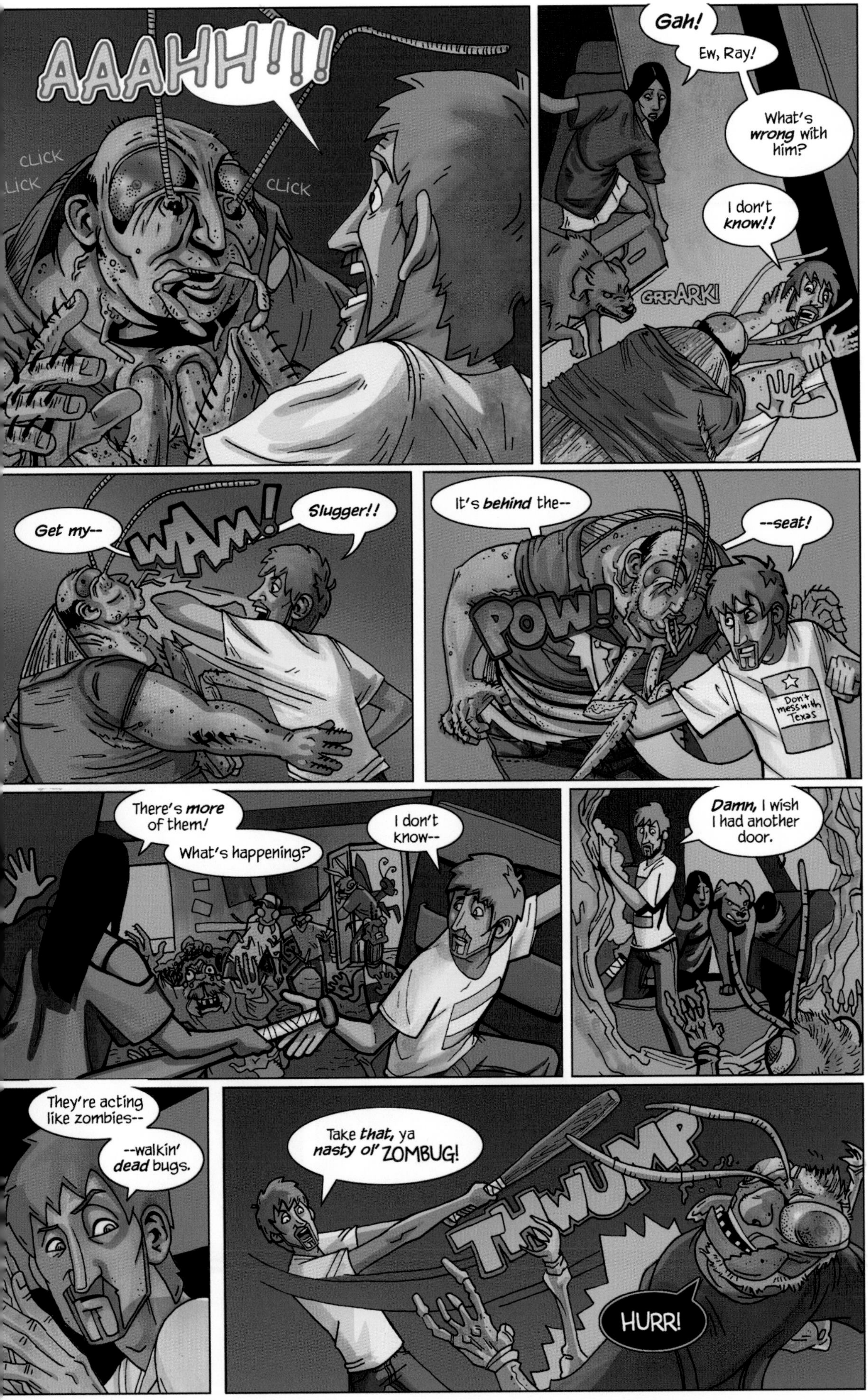

AAAHH!!!
CLICK
LICK
CLICK
Gah!
Ew, Ray!
What's wrong with him?
I don't know!!
GRRARK!
Get my--
WAM!
Slugger!!
It's behind the--
--seat!
POW!
Don't mess with Texas
There's more of them!
What's happening?
I don't know--
Damn, I wish I had another door.
They're acting like zombies--
--walkin' dead bugs.
Take that, ya nasty ol' ZOMBUG!
THWUMP
HURR!

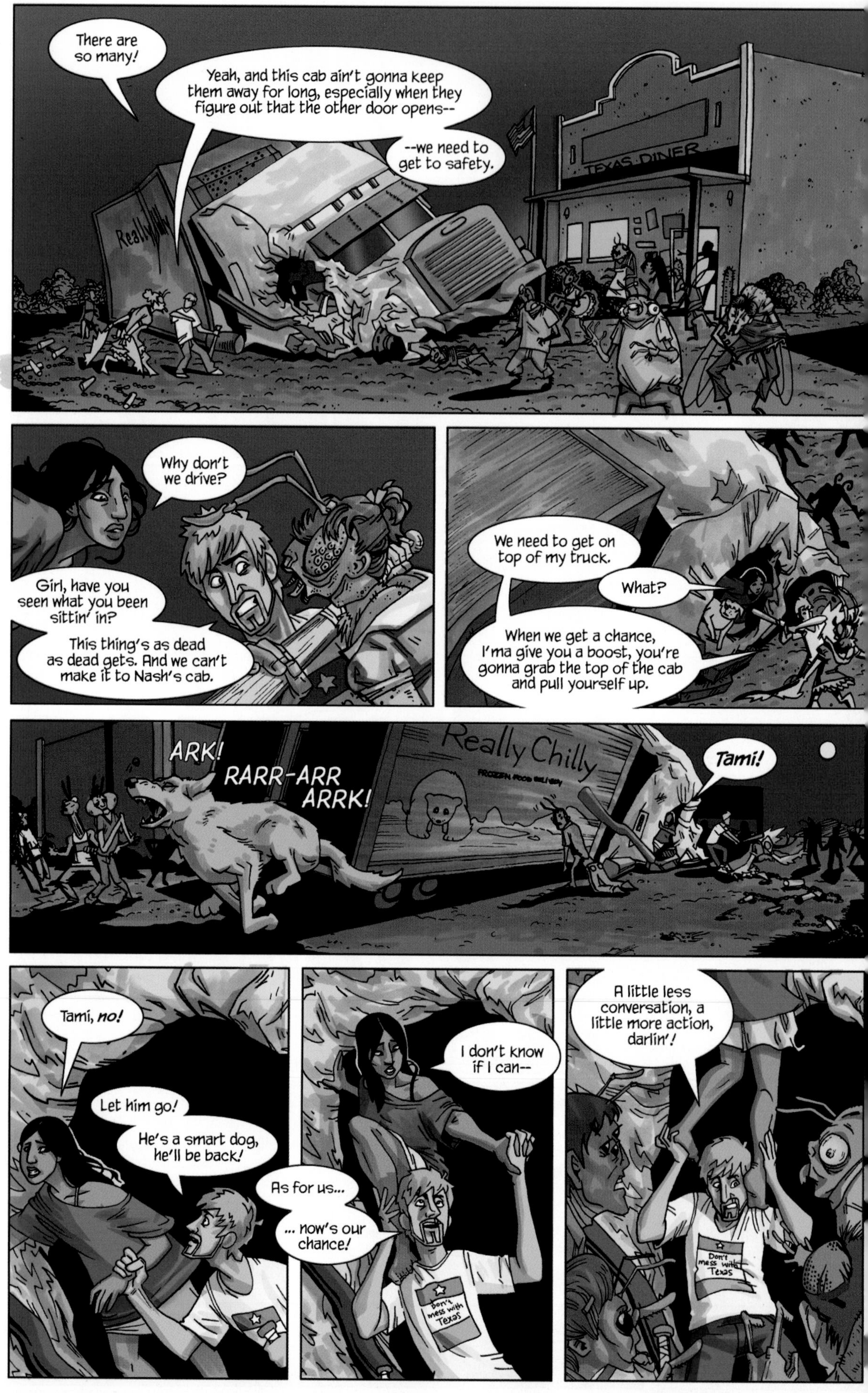

There are so many!
Yeah, and this cab ain't gonna keep them away for long, especially when they figure out that the other door opens--
--we need to get to safety.
TEXAS DINER
Really
Why don't we drive?
Girl, have you seen what you been sittin' in?
This thing's as dead as dead gets. And we can't make it to Nash's cab.
We need to get on top of my truck.
What?
When we get a chance, I'ma give you a boost, you're gonna grab the top of the cab and pull yourself up.
ARK!
RARR-ARR ARRK!
Really Chilly
FROZEN FOOD DELIVERY
Tami!
Tami, no!
Let him go!
He's a smart dog, he'll be back!
As for us...
... now's our chance!
I don't know if I can--
Don't mess with Texas
A little less conversation, a little more action, darlin'!
Don't mess with Texas

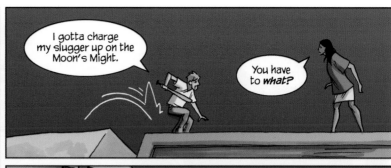

I gotta charge my slugger up on the Moon's Might.

You have to *what?*

Er... I call it Might...

Muh-tee-oo-lyne don't exactly roll off the tongue.

At least, if you ain't Algonquin.

M'teoulin? Isn't that the word for magic in some Penobscot stories?

You certainly got a lot to learn about the world if you're thinkin' that's just a story.

Nash bein' an Ancient and all, I thought you'd know about that.

An Ancient?

He's told you his mother was a woman and his father is the moon, right?

The... moon thing... it's just his way of dodging the subject of his father, because he doesn't want to talk about him.

Oh no, darlin'.

Nash can be mysterious for sure, but he always tells the truth.

He *was* talkin' about him.

Fine -- but how does that explain the *bat?*

You're not an Ancient, are you?

Nope, but if you're blessed by an Ancient, it allows you to access some powers of Might.

You're a SHAMAN?!

Don't mess with Texas

You can bet yer sweet britches I am!

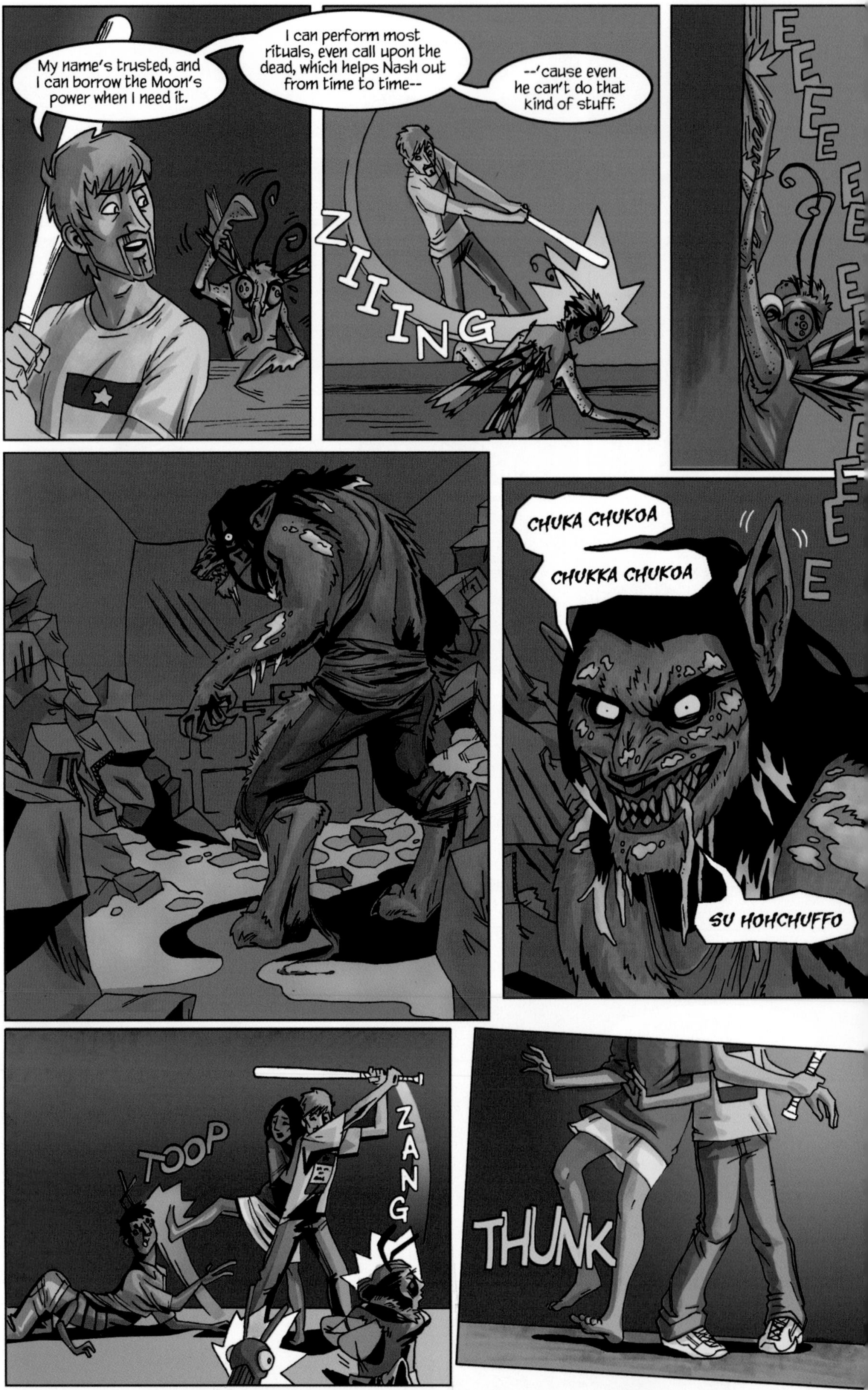
My name's trusted, and I can borrow the Moon's power when I need it.
I can perform most rituals, even call upon the dead, which helps Nash out from time to time--
--'cause even he can't do that kind of stuff.
ZIIING
EEEEEEEEEEEE
CHUKA CHUKOA
CHUKKA CHUKOA
SU HOHCHUFFO
TOOP
ZANG
THUNK

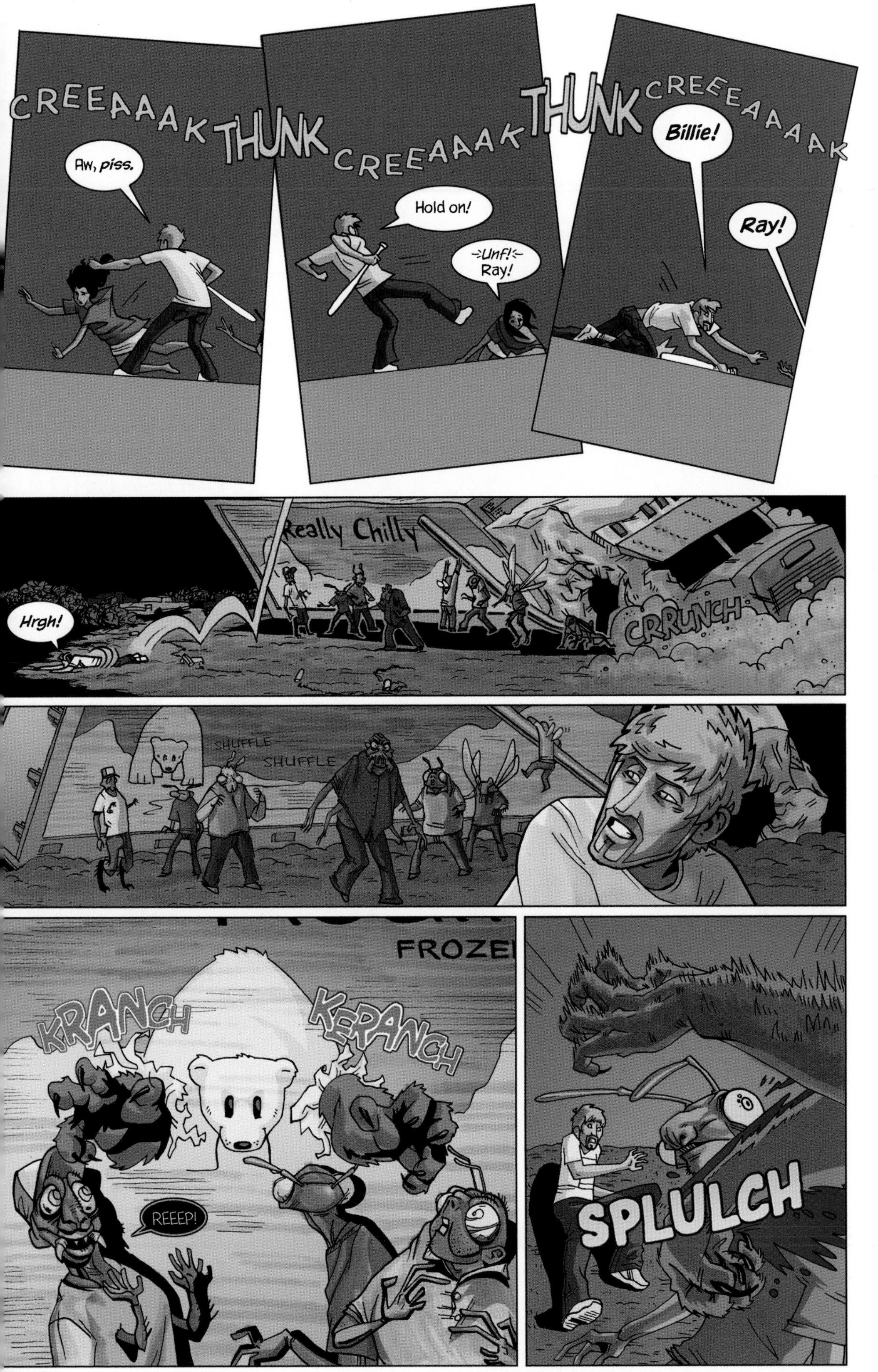
CREEAAAAK
THUNK
Aw, piss.
CREEAAAAK
Hold on!
Unf! Ray!
THUNK
CREEEAAAAK
Billie!
Ray!
Really Chilly
Hrgh!
CRRUNCH
SHUFFLE
SHUFFLE
FROZE
KRANCH
KERANCH
REEEP!
SPLULCH

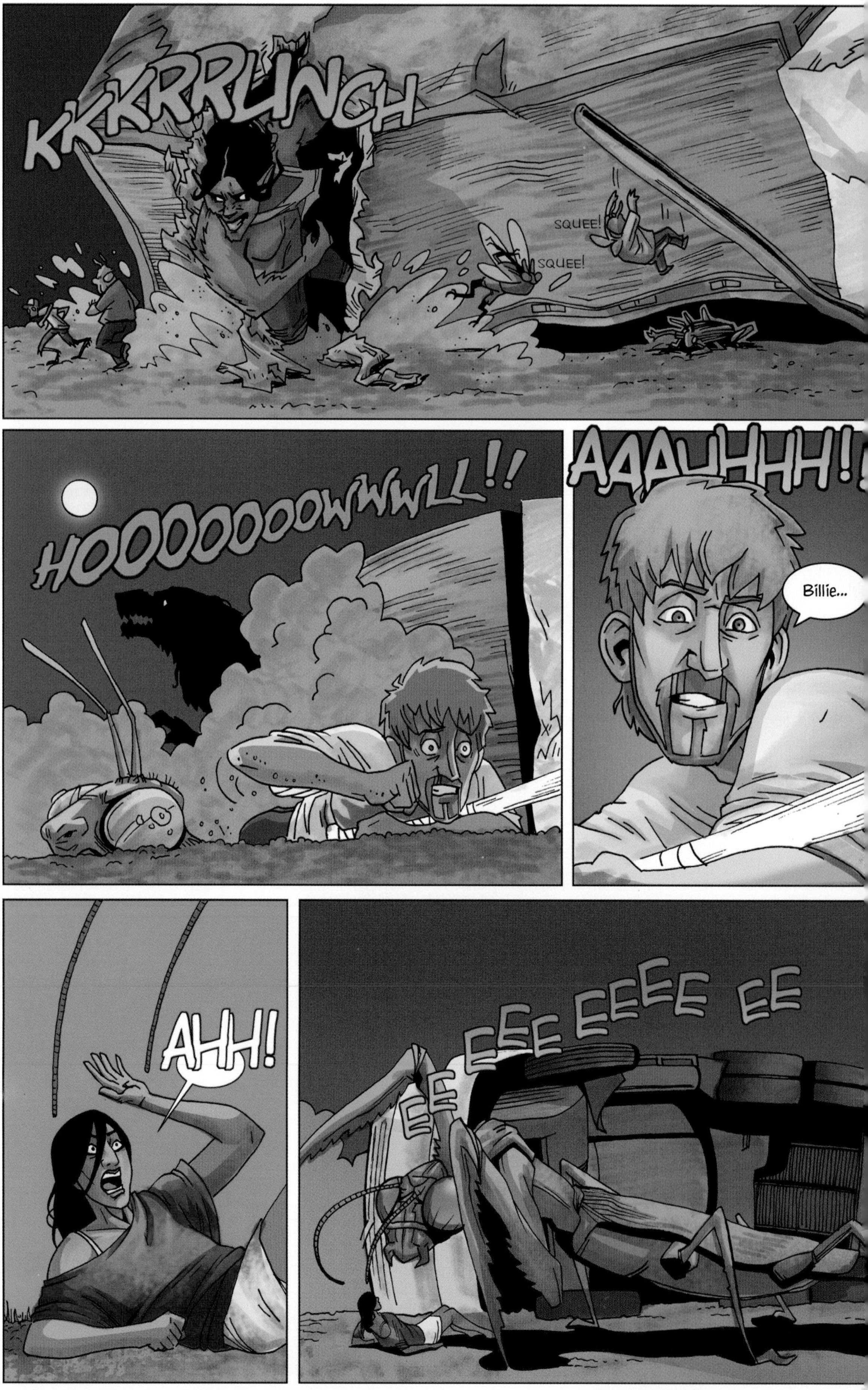
KKKRRUNCH
SQUEE!
SQUEE!
HOOOOOOOOWWLL!!
AAAUHHH!!
Billie...
AHH!
EE EEE EEEE EE

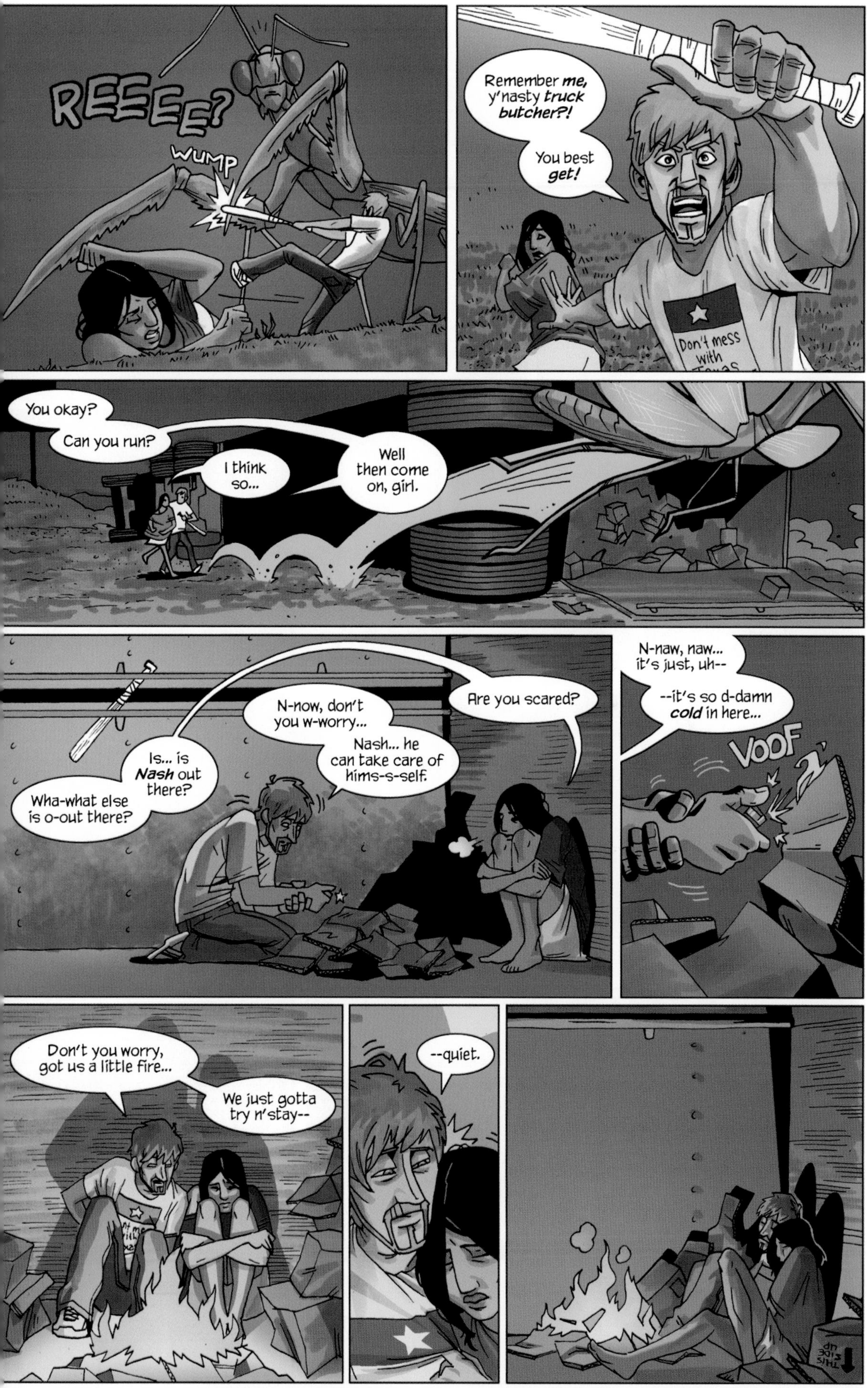
REEEEE?
WUMP
Remember me, y'nasty truck butcher?!
You best get!
Don't mess with
You okay?
Can you run?
I think so...
Well then come on, girl.
Are you scared?
N-now, don't you w-worry...
Nash... he can take care of hims-s-self.
Is... is Nash out there?
Wha-what else is o-out there?
N-naw, naw... it's just, uh--
--it's so d-damn cold in here...
VOOF
Don't you worry, got us a little fire...
We just gotta try n'stay--
--quiet.

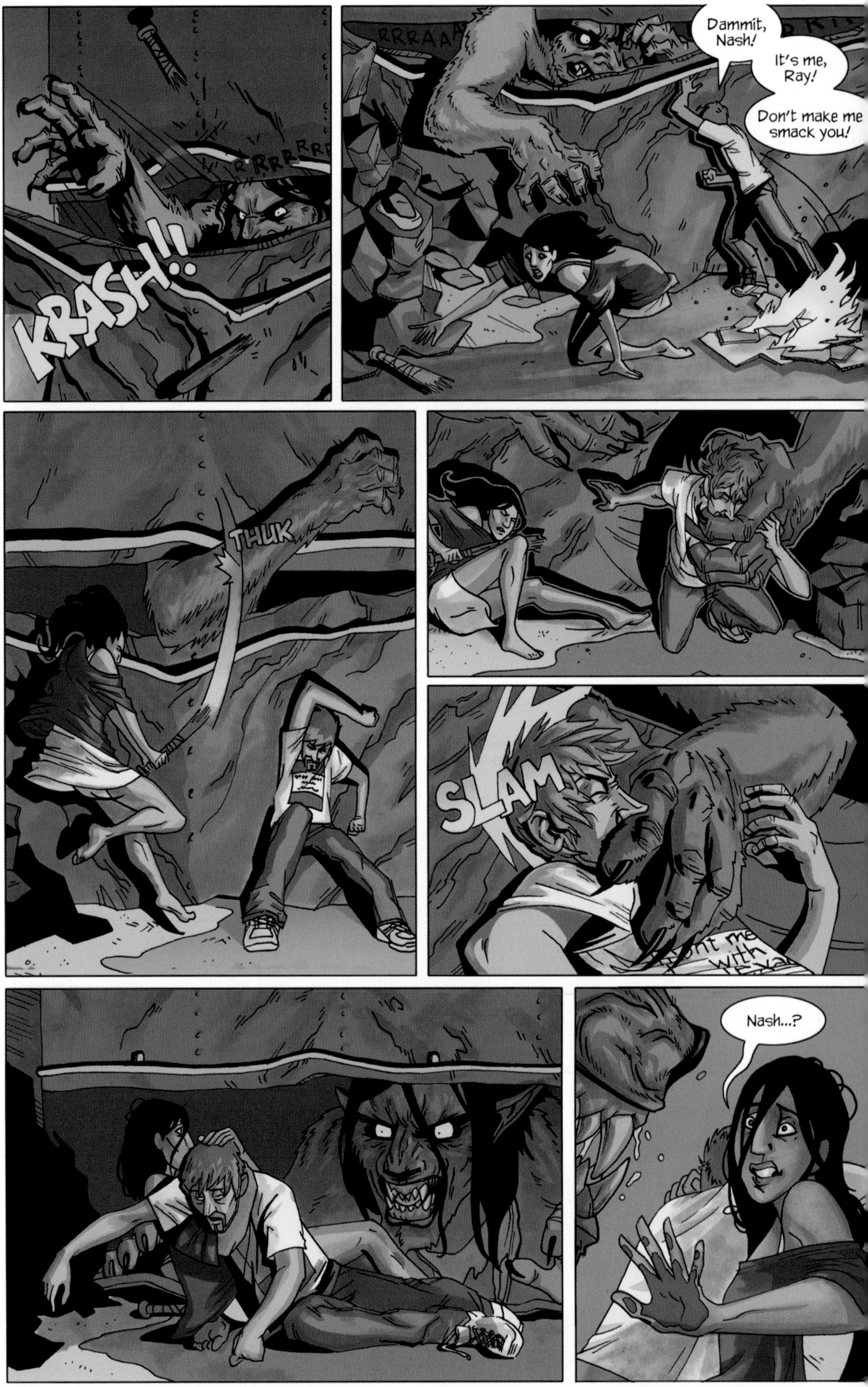
KRASH!!
Dammit, Nash!
It's me, Ray!
Don't make me smack you!
THUK
SLAM
Nash...?

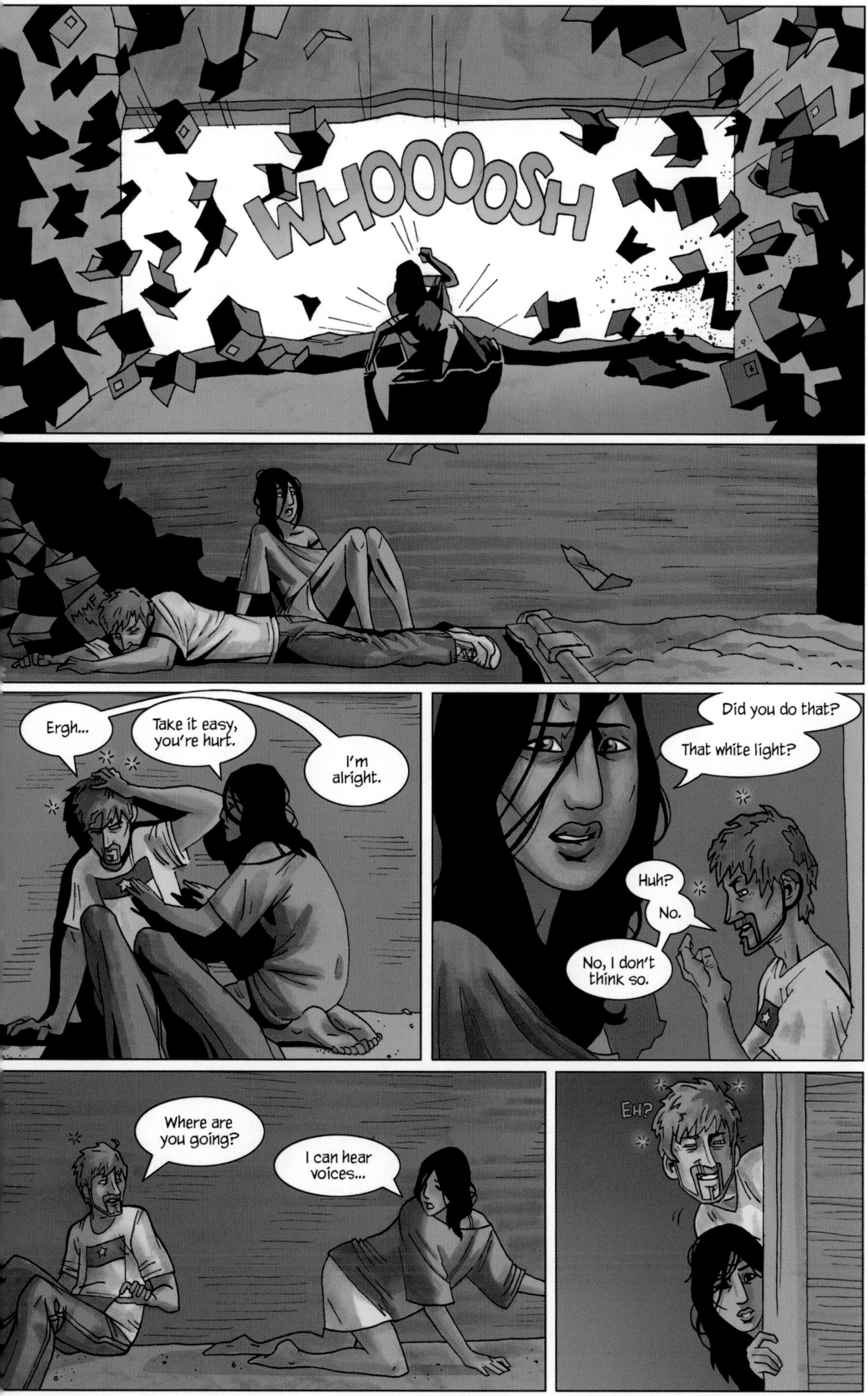
WHOOOOSH
MMF
Ergh...
Take it easy, you're hurt.
I'm alright.
Did you do that?
That white light?
Huh?
No.
No, I don't think so.
Where are you going?
I can hear voices...
EH?

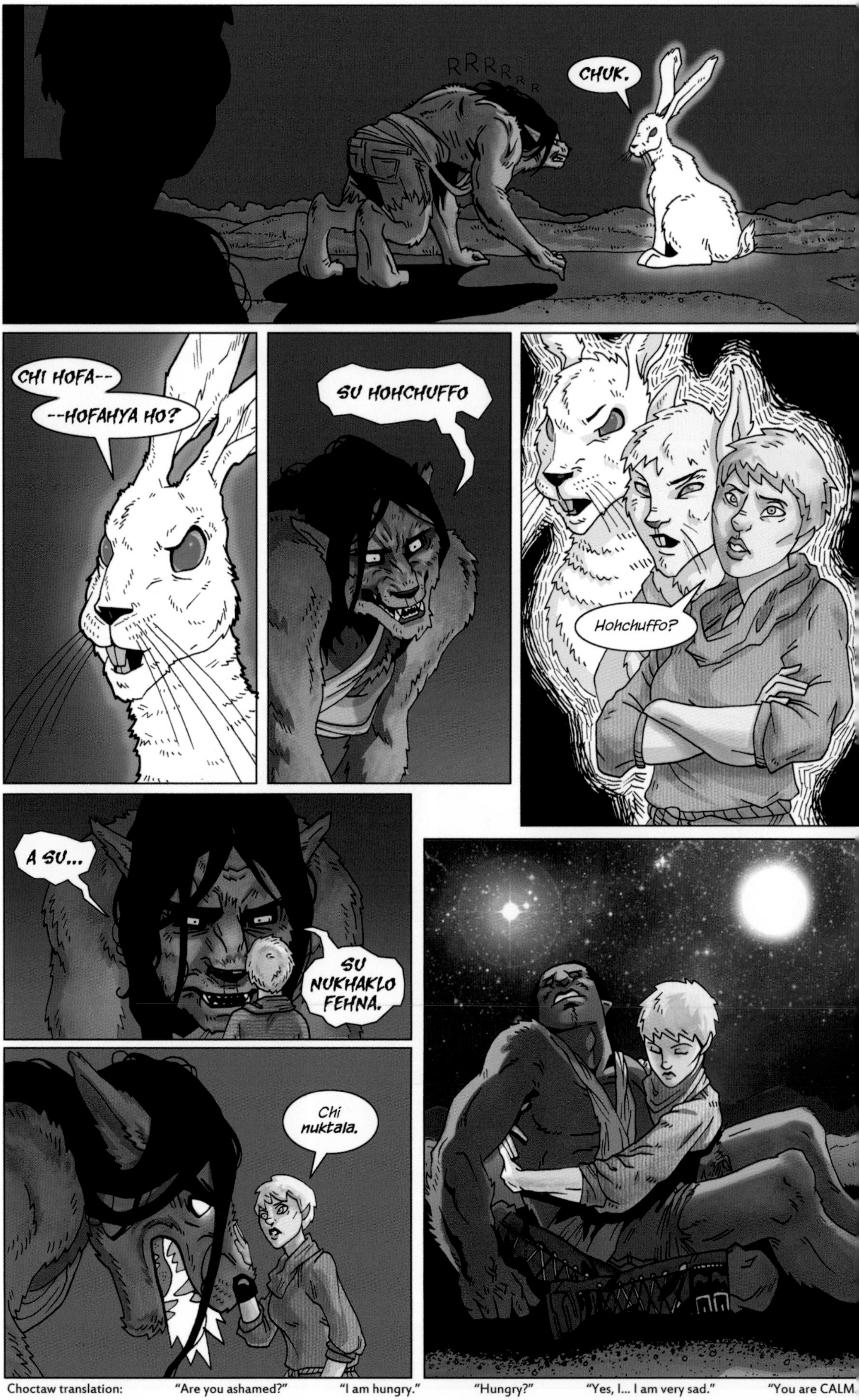
RRRRRRR
CHUK.
CHI HOFA--
--HOFAHYA HO?
SU HOHCHUFFO
Hohchuffo?
A SU...
SU NUKHAKLO FEHNA.
Chi nuktala.

Choctaw translation: "Are you ashamed?" "I am hungry." "Hungry?" "Yes, I... I am very sad." "You are CALM.

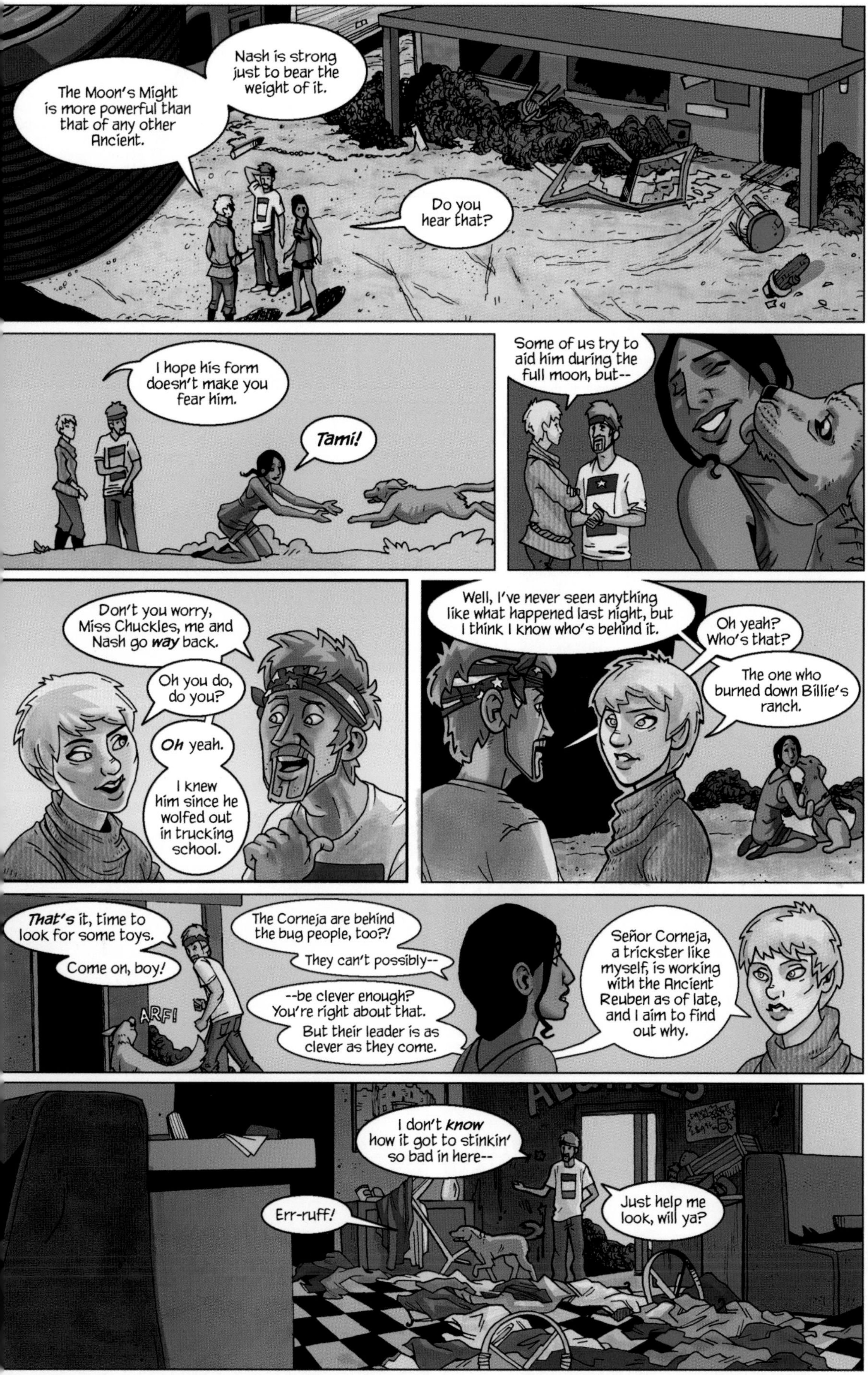
The Moon's Might is more powerful than that of any other Ancient.
Nash is strong just to bear the weight of it.
Do you hear that?
I hope his form doesn't make you fear him.
Tami!
Some of us try to aid him during the full moon, but--
Don't you worry, Miss Chuckles, me and Nash go way back.
Oh you do, do you?
Oh yeah.
I knew him since he wolfed out in trucking school.
Well, I've never seen anything like what happened last night, but I think I know who's behind it.
Oh yeah? Who's that?
The one who burned down Billie's ranch.
That's it, time to look for some toys.
Come on, boy!
ARF!
The Corneja are behind the bug people, too?!
They can't possibly--
--be clever enough? You're right about that.
But their leader is as clever as they come.
Señor Corneja, a trickster like myself, is working with the Ancient Reuben as of late, and I aim to find out why.
I don't know how it got to stinkin' so bad in here--
Err-ruff!
Just help me look, will ya?

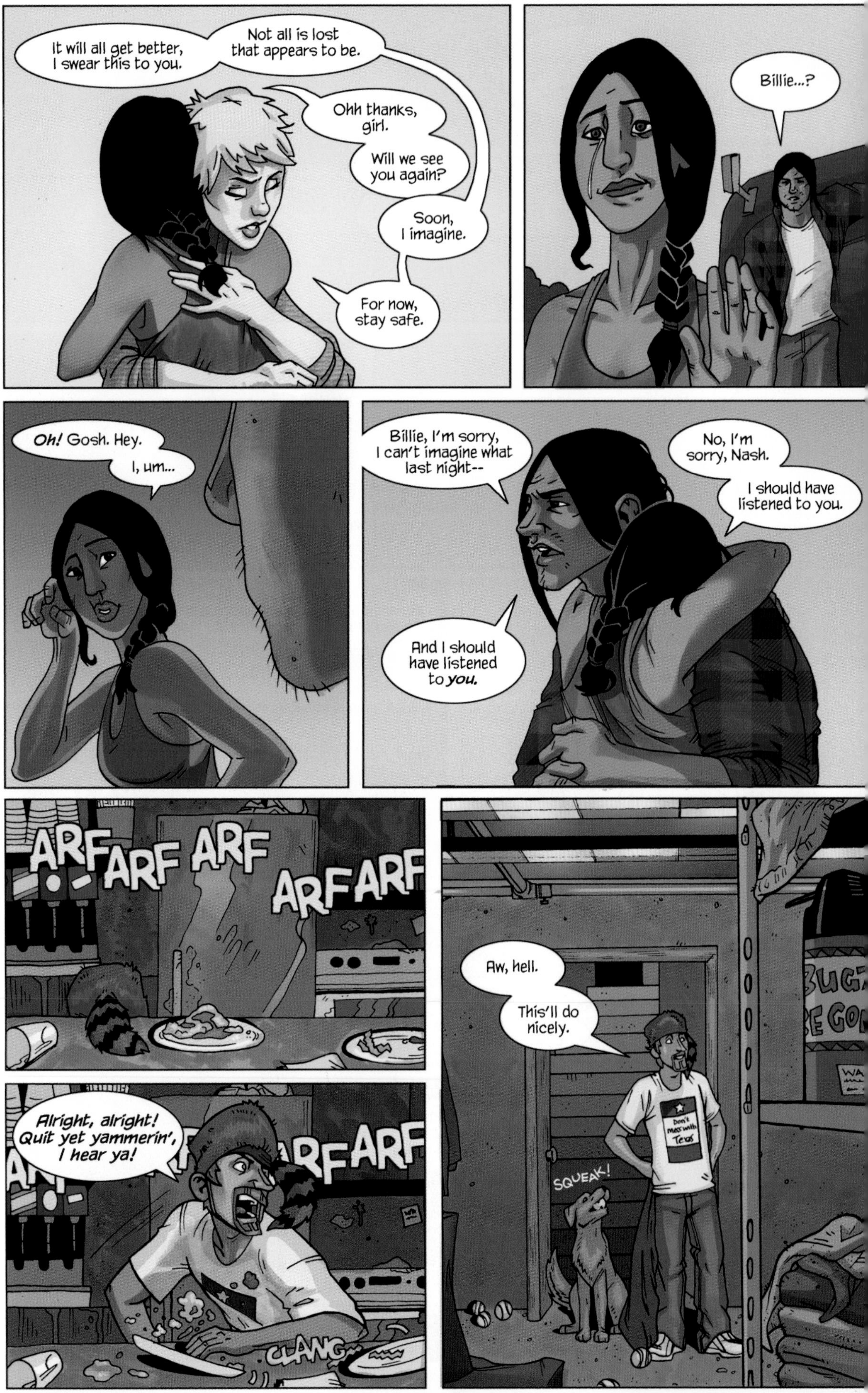
It will all get better, I swear this to you.
Not all is lost that appears to be.
Ohh thanks, girl.
Will we see you again?
Soon, I imagine.
For now, stay safe.
Billie...?
Oh! Gosh. Hey.
I, um...
Billie, I'm sorry, I can't imagine what last night--
No, I'm sorry, Nash.
I should have listened to you.
And I should have listened to *you.*
ARF ARF ARF
ARF ARF
Alright, alright! Quit yet yammerin', I hear ya!
ARF ARF
CLANG
Aw, hell.
This'll do nicely.
Don't mess with Texas
SQUEAK!

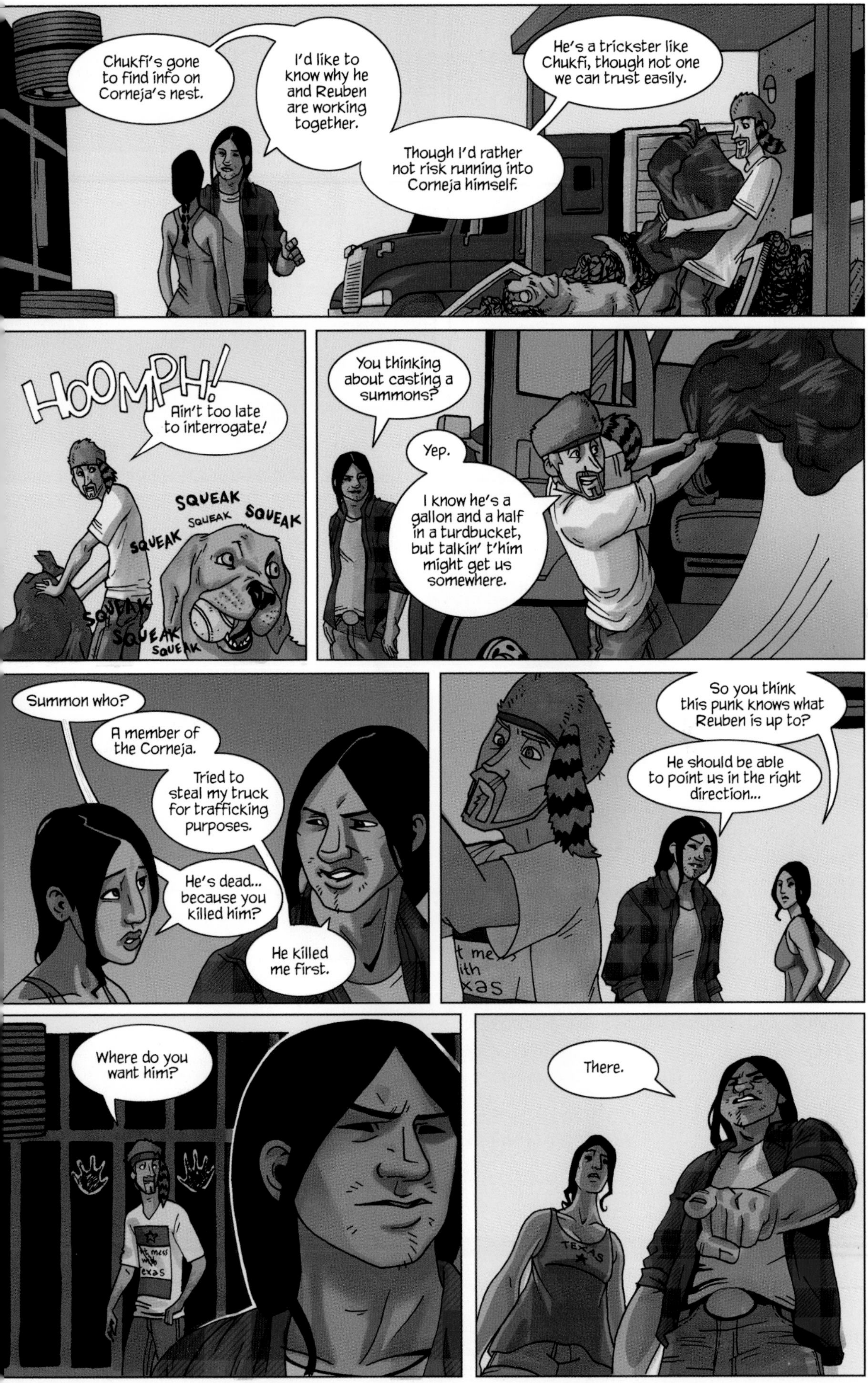
Chukfi's gone to find info on Corneja's nest.
I'd like to know why he and Reuben are working together.
Though I'd rather not risk running into Corneja himself.
He's a trickster like Chukfi, though not one we can trust easily.
HOOMPH!
Ain't too late to interrogate!
SQUEAK SQUEAK SQUEAK SQUEAK SQUEAK SQUEAK SQUEAK
You thinking about casting a summons?
Yep.
I know he's a gallon and a half in a turdbucket, but talkin' t'him might get us somewhere.
Summon who?
A member of the Corneja.
Tried to steal my truck for trafficking purposes.
He's dead... because you killed him?
He killed me first.
So you think this punk knows what Reuben is up to?
He should be able to point us in the right direction...
Where do you want him?
There.

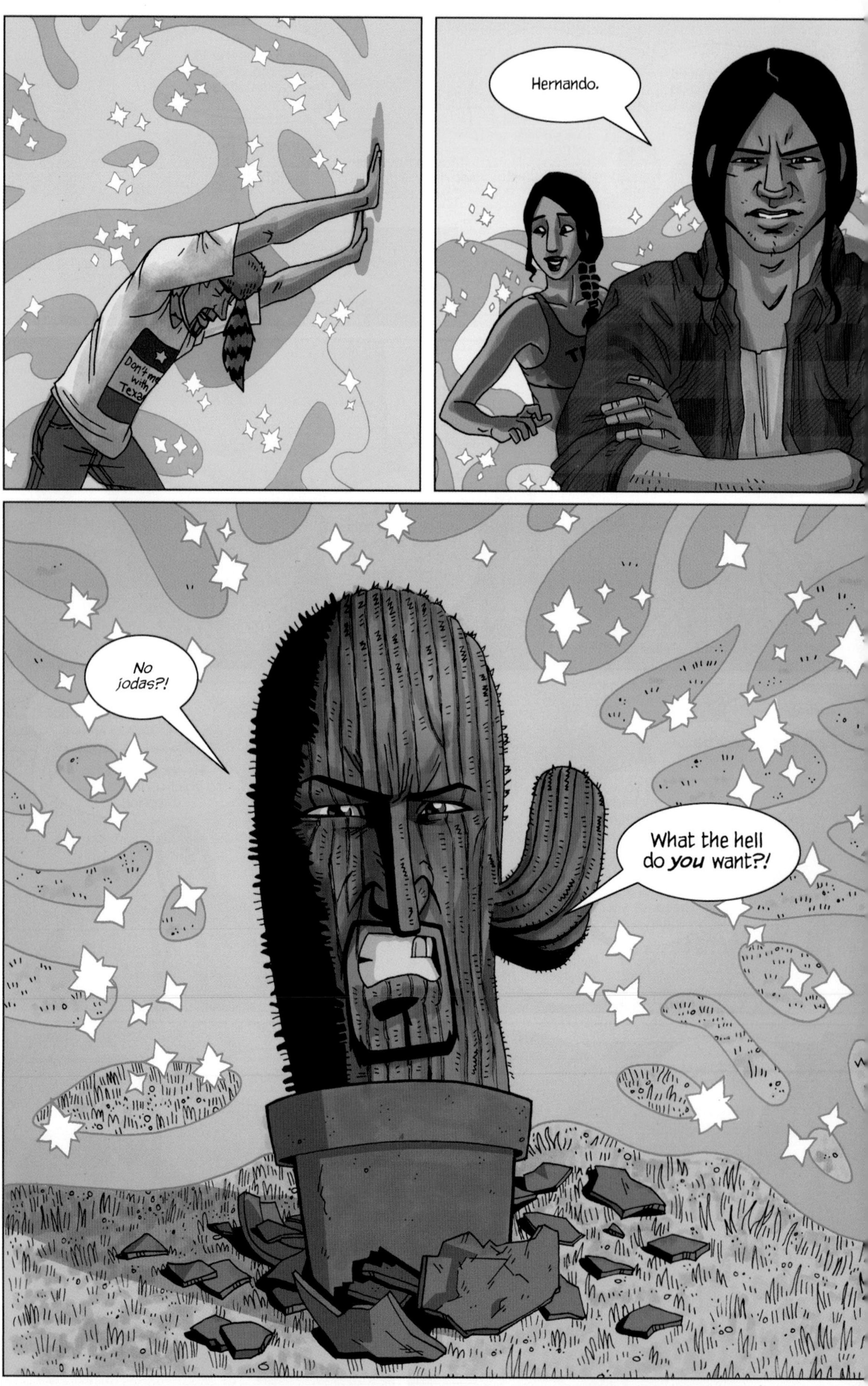
Hernando.
No jodas?!
What the hell do *you* want?!

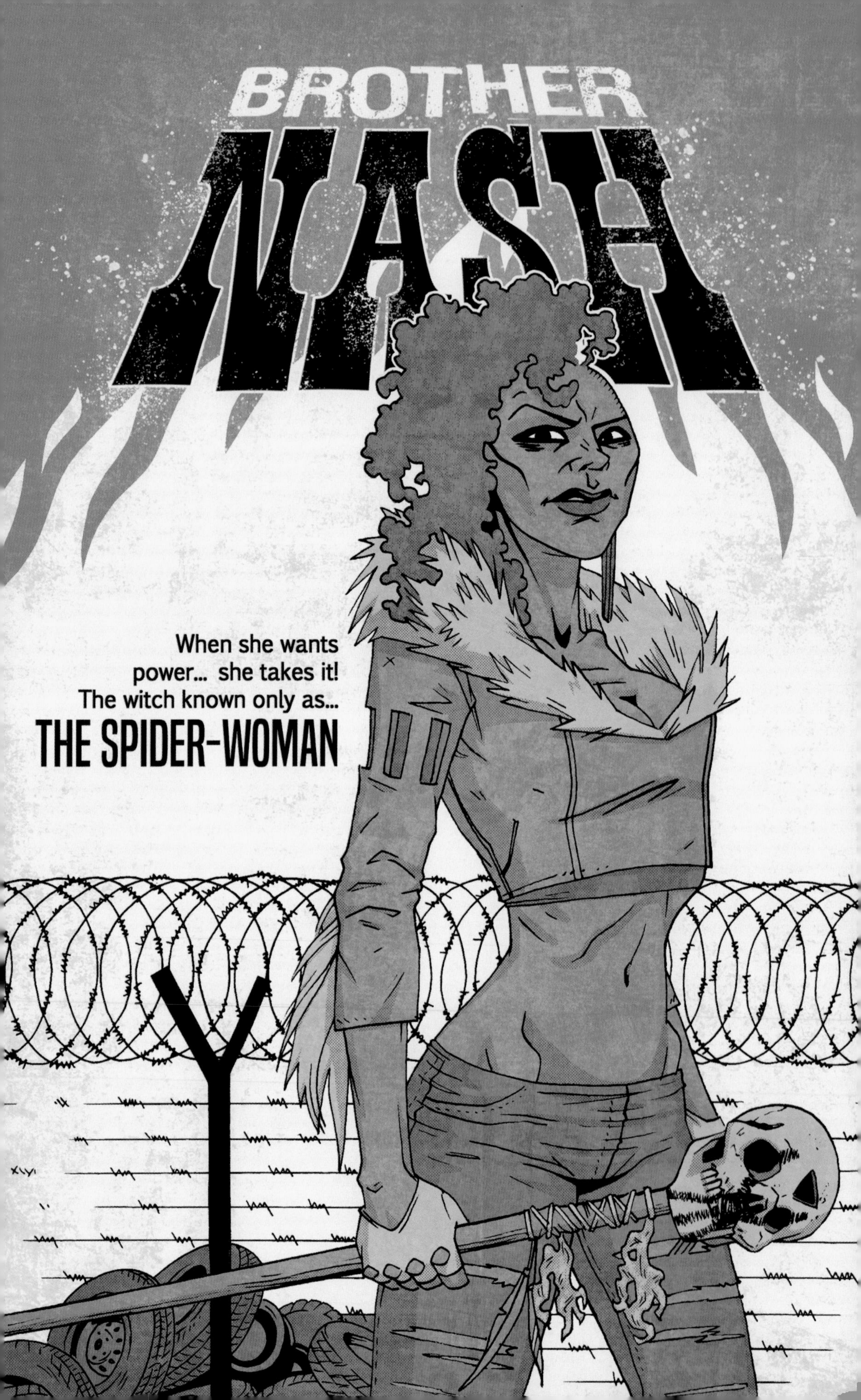
BROTHER
NASH
When she wants
power... she takes it!
The witch known only as...
THE SPIDER-WOMAN

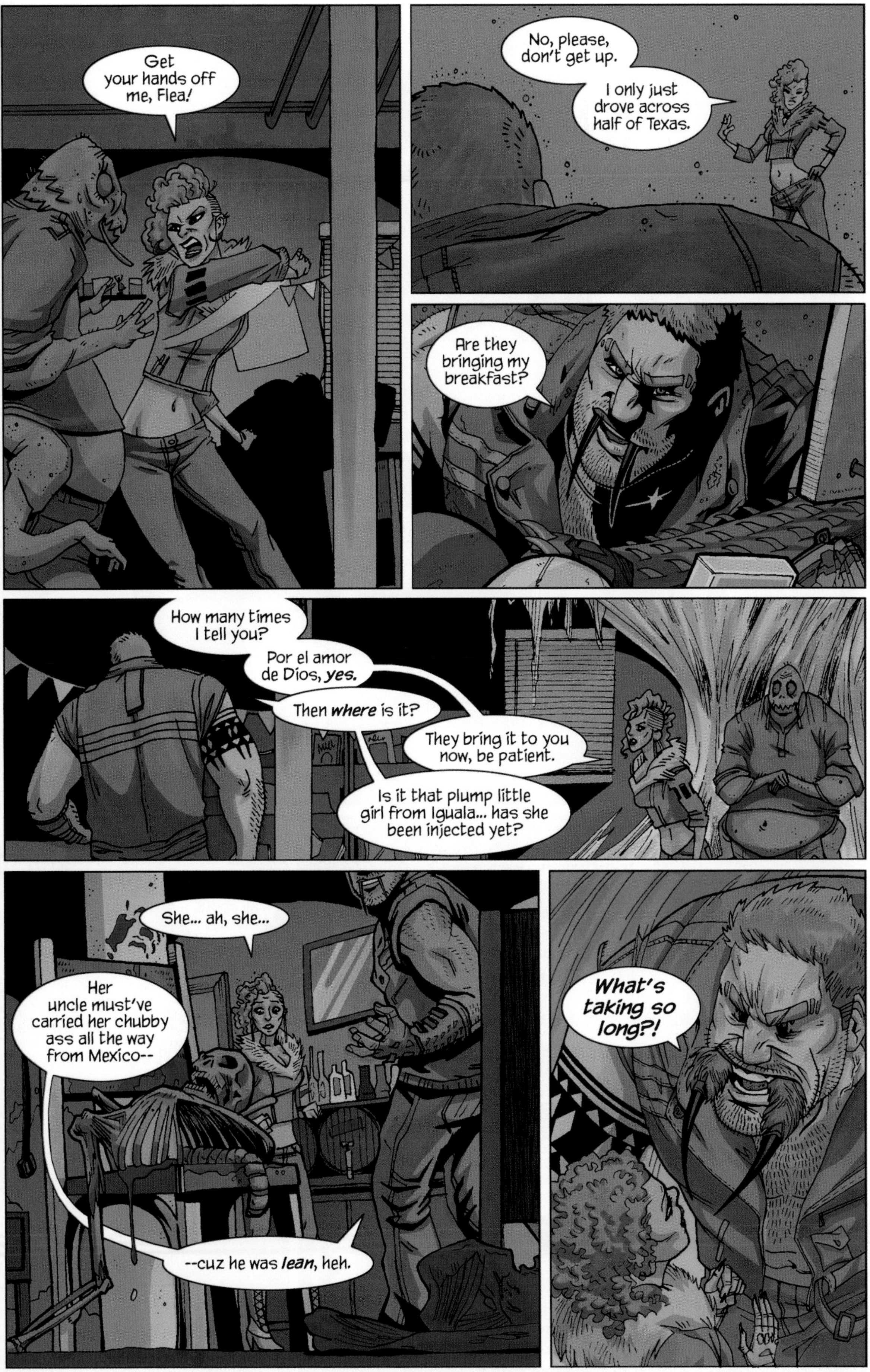
Get your hands off me, Flea!
No, please, don't get up.
I only just drove across half of Texas.
Are they bringing my breakfast?
How many times I tell you?
Por el amor de Dios, *yes.*
Then *where* is it?
They bring it to you now, be patient.
Is it that plump little girl from Iguala... has she been injected yet?
She... ah, she...
Her uncle must've carried her chubby ass all the way from Mexico--
--cuz he was *lean*, heh.
What's taking so long?!

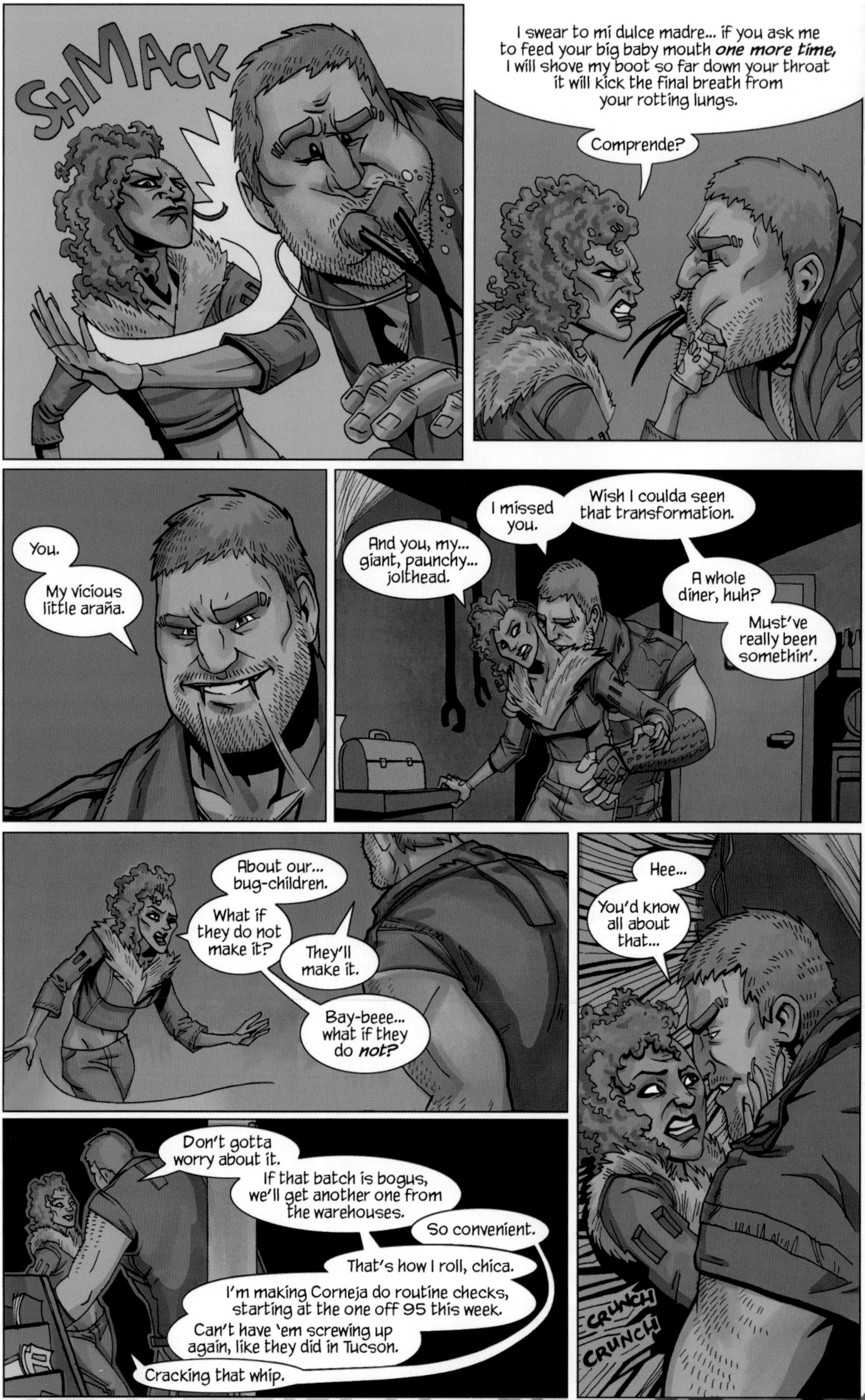
SHMACK
I swear to mi dulce madre... if you ask me to feed your big baby mouth *one more time,* I will shove my boot so far down your throat it will kick the final breath from your rotting lungs.
Comprende?
You.
My vicious little araña.
I missed you.
Wish I coulda seen that transformation.
And you, my... giant, paunchy... jolthead.
A whole diner, huh?
Must've really been somethin'.
About our... bug-children.
What if they do not make it?
They'll make it.
Bay-beee... what if they do *not?*
Hee...
You'd know all about that...
Don't gotta worry about it.
If that batch is bogus, we'll get another one from the warehouses.
So convenient.
That's how I roll, chica.
I'm making Corneja do routine checks, starting at the one off 95 this week.
Can't have 'em screwing up again, like they did in Tucson.
Cracking that whip.
CRUNCH
CRUNCH

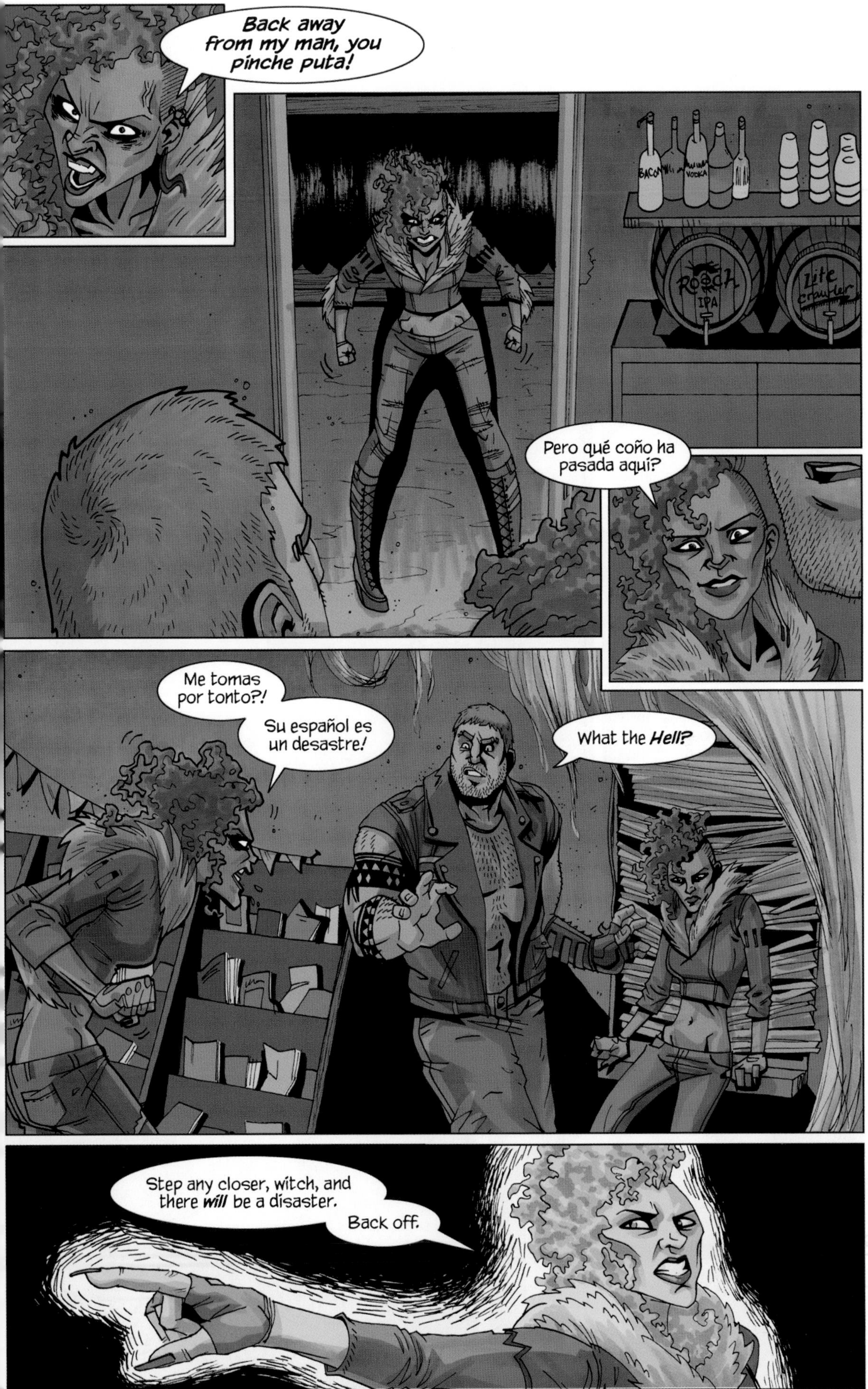
Back away from my man, you pinche puta!
Pero qué coño ha pasada aquí?
Me tomas por tonto?!
Su español es un desastre!
What the Hell?
Step any closer, witch, and there will be a disaster.
Back off.

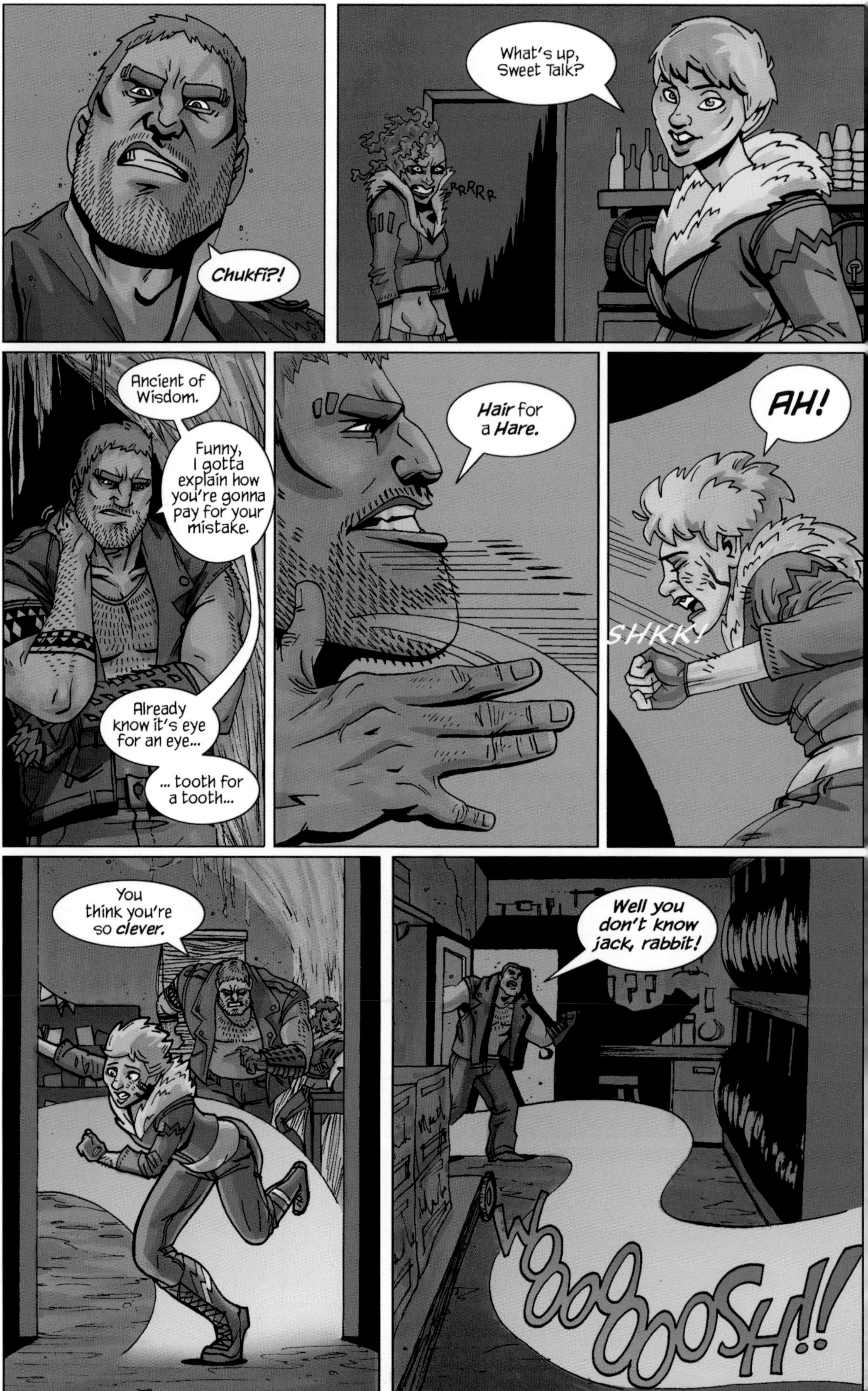
Chukfi?!
What's up, Sweet Talk?
RRRRR
Ancient of Wisdom.
Funny, I gotta explain how you're gonna pay for your mistake.
Already know it's eye for an eye...
... tooth for a tooth...
Hair for a Hare.
AH!
SHKK!
You think you're so clever.
Well you don't know jack, rabbit!
WOOOOOOOOSH!!

Hernando.

We need you to tell us why your boss murdered everyone in this entire diner.

PITTEW

Me cago en la madre que te parió!

So you wanna get prickly?

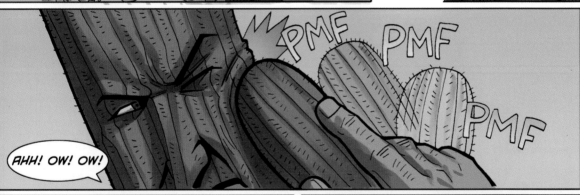

PMF PMF PMF

AHH! OW! OW!

Alright, alright, come on, mang!

You already turned me into a friggin' plant, give me a break!

The warehouse shipments--

--the *people*--

--where did they go?

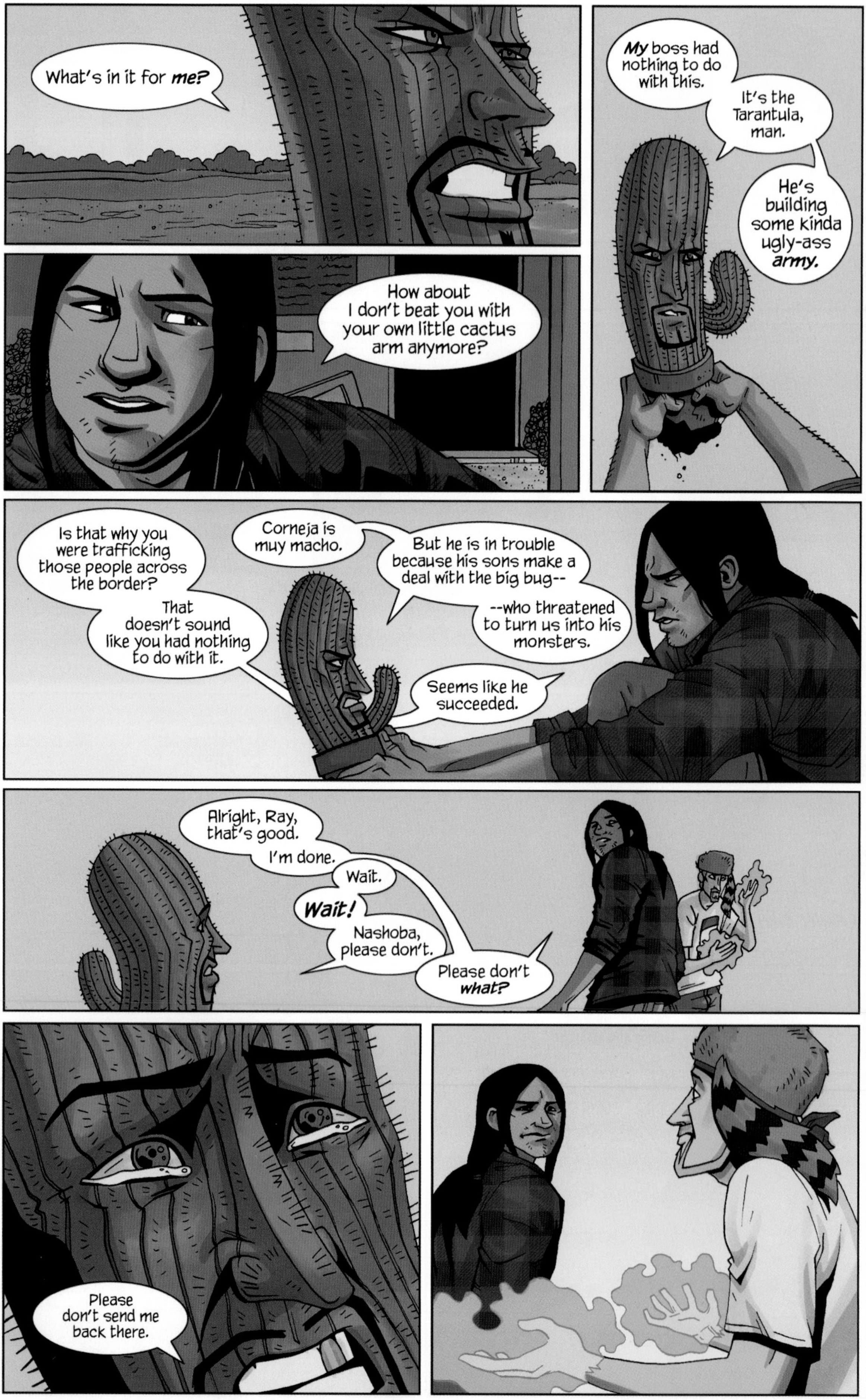
What's in it for *me?*
My boss had nothing to do with this.
It's the Tarantula, man.
He's building some kinda ugly-ass *army.*
How about I don't beat you with your own little cactus arm anymore?
Is that why you were trafficking those people across the border?
That doesn't sound like you had nothing to do with it.
Corneja is muy macho.
But he is in trouble because his sons make a deal with the big bug--
--who threatened to turn us into his monsters.
Seems like he succeeded.
Alright, Ray, that's good.
I'm done.
Wait.
Wait!
Nashoba, please don't.
Please don't *what?*
Please don't send me back there.

Alright, so Reuben's lair is in Bellmead.

How far is that from Sonora?

Whoa, hold on!

You're just gonna make me leave him there like that?

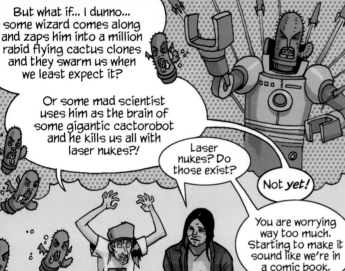

But what if... I dunno... some wizard comes along and zaps him into a million rabid flying cactus clones and they swarm us when we least expect it?

Or some mad scientist uses him as the brain of some gigantic cactorobot and he kills us all with laser nukes?!

Laser nukes? Do those exist?

Not *yet!*

You are worrying way too much. Starting to make it sound like we're in a comic book.

Billie, how far away do your parents live?

About six hours.

Why?

We're taking you home.

Hold up.

So you guys are dropping me off *then* hunting down the bad guys?

I just survived a diner full of bug zombies and saw *you* turn into some kind of... werewolf.

I just learned magic was *real,* y'all.

A woman who turns into a big white rabbit told me people are being kidnapped--

--by the same gang who just destroyed everything I had.

And you think I'm going back to Oklahoma?

Hell no!

I call shotgun.

You kids are out of control.

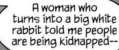

Are you kiddin' me?

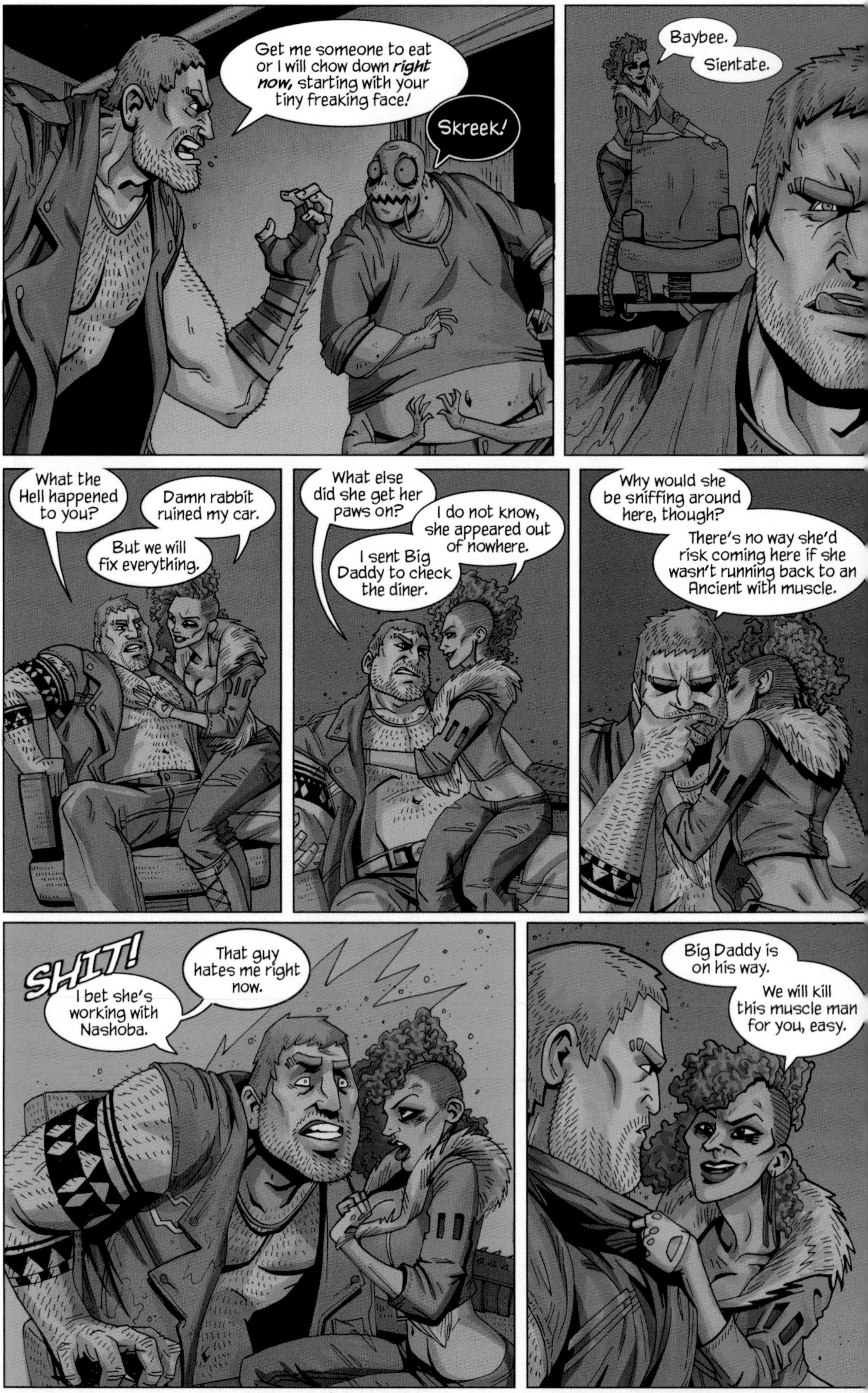
Get me someone to eat or I will chow down ***right now,*** starting with your tiny freaking face!
Skreek!
Baybee.
Sientate.
What the Hell happened to you?
Damn rabbit ruined my car.
But we will fix everything.
What else did she get her paws on?
I do not know, she appeared out of nowhere.
I sent Big Daddy to check the diner.
Why would she be sniffing around here, though?
There's no way she'd risk coming here if she wasn't running back to an Ancient with muscle.
SHIT!
I bet she's working with Nashoba.
That guy hates me right now.
Big Daddy is on his way.
We will kill this muscle man for you, easy.

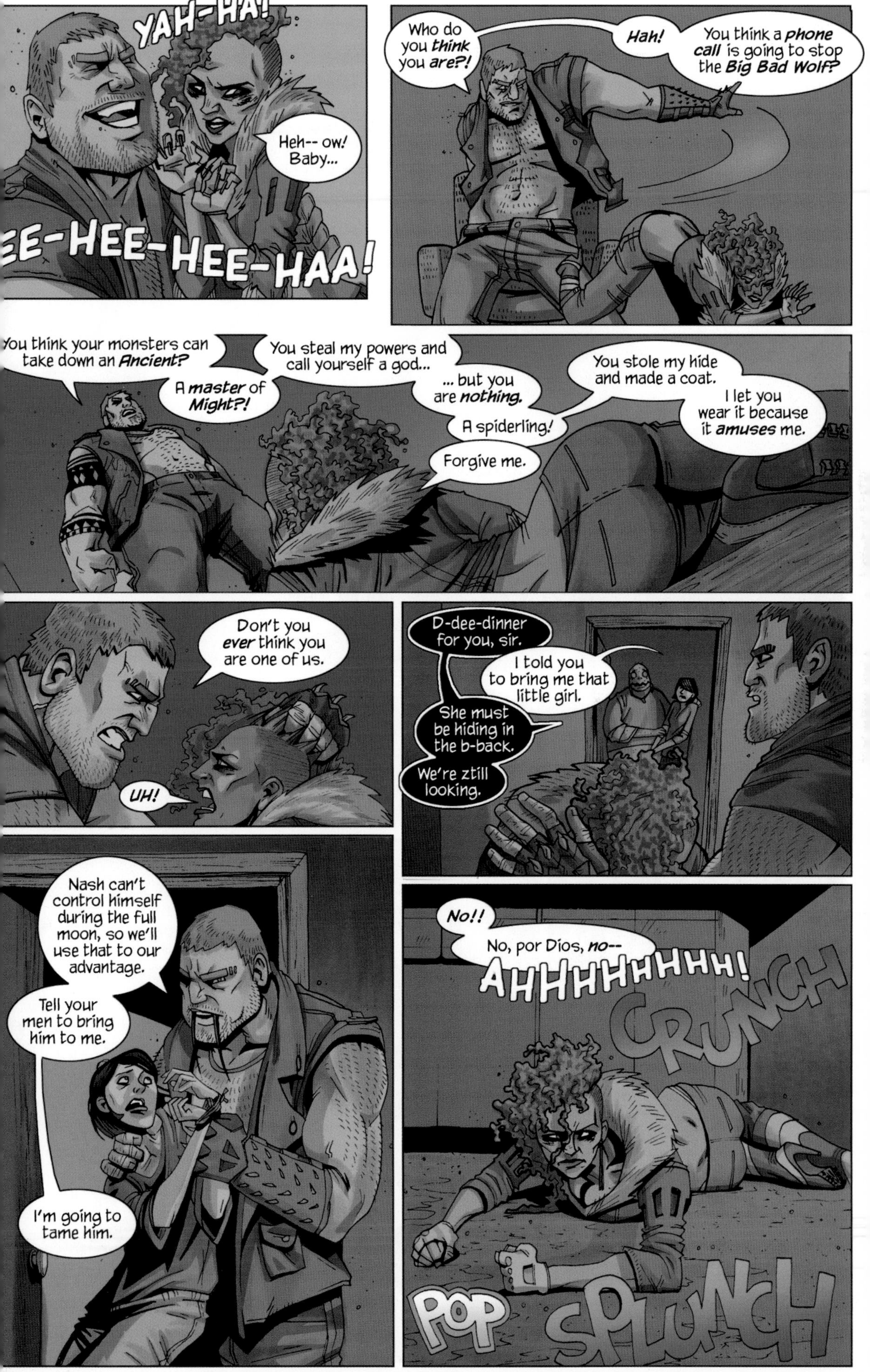
YAH-HA!
Heh-- ow! Baby...
EE-HEE-HEE-HAA!
Who do you think you are?!
Hah!
You think a phone call is going to stop the Big Bad Wolf?
You think your monsters can take down an Ancient?
A master of Might?!
You steal my powers and call yourself a god...
... but you are nothing.
A spiderling!
You stole my hide and made a coat.
I let you wear it because it amuses me.
Forgive me.
Don't you ever think you are one of us.
UH!
D-dee-dinner for you, sir.
I told you to bring me that little girl.
She must be hiding in the b-back.
We're ztill looking.
Nash can't control himself during the full moon, so we'll use that to our advantage.
Tell your men to bring him to me.
I'm going to tame him.
No!!
No, por Dios, no--
AHHHHHHHHH!
CRUNCH
POP
SPLUNCH

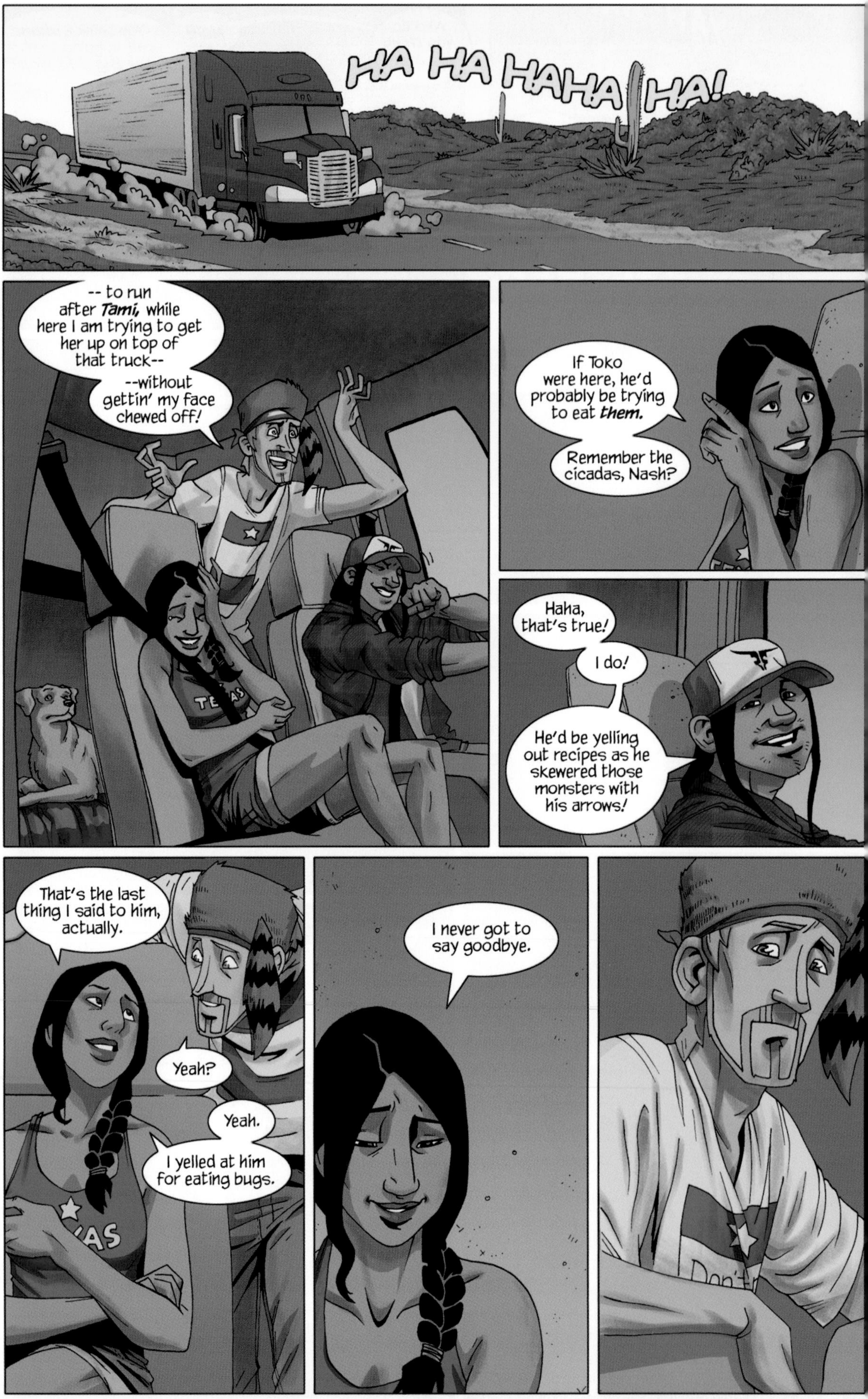
HA HA HAHA HA!
-- to run after *Tami,* while here I am trying to get her up on top of that truck--
--without gettin' my face chewed off!
If Toko were here, he'd probably be trying to eat *them.*
Remember the cicadas, Nash?
Haha, that's true!
I do!
He'd be yelling out recipes as he skewered those monsters with his arrows!
That's the last thing I said to him, actually.
Yeah?
Yeah.
I yelled at him for eating bugs.
I never got to say goodbye.

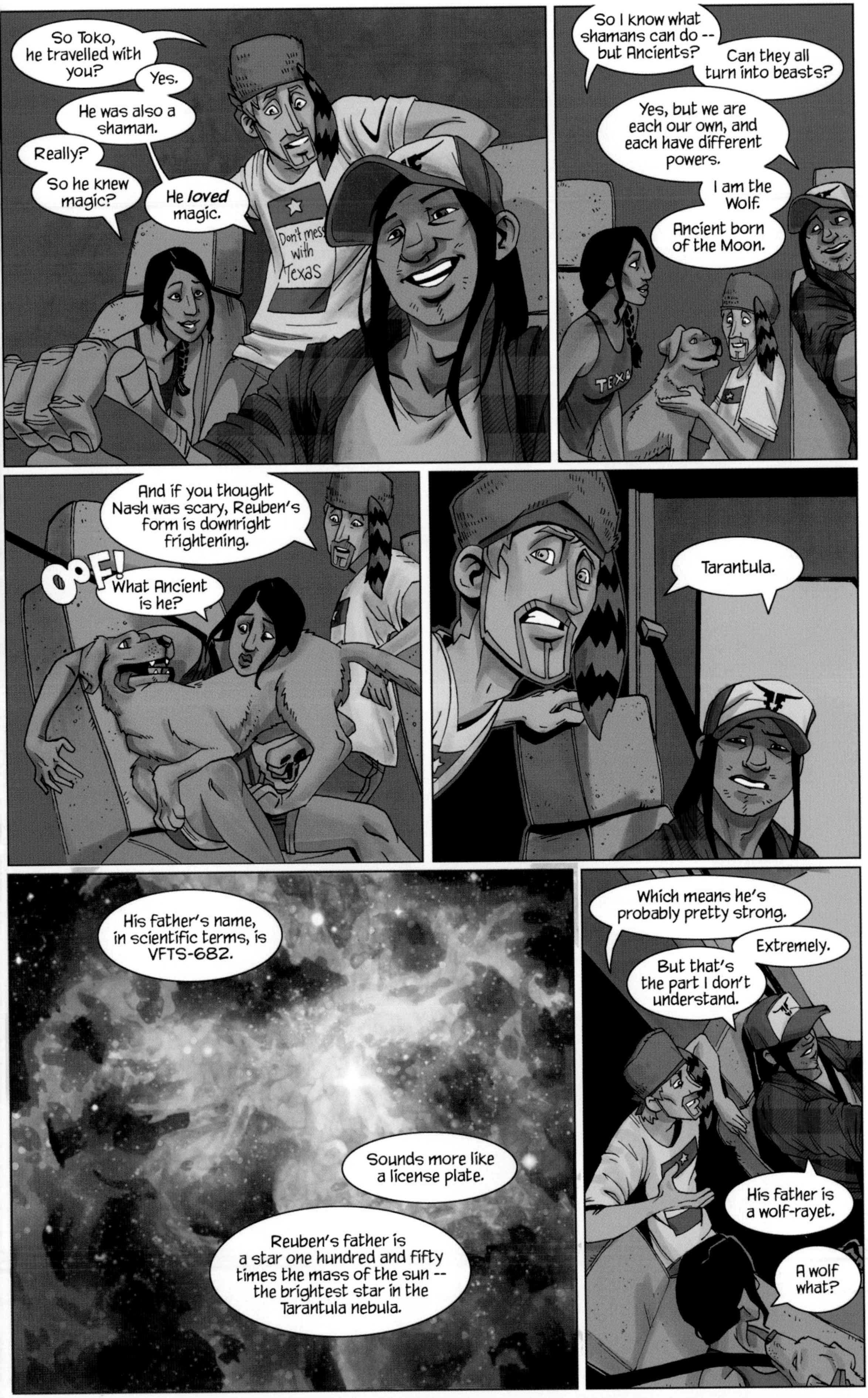
So Toko, he travelled with you?
Yes.
He was also a shaman.
Really?
So he knew magic?
He *loved* magic.
Don't mess with Texas
So I know what shamans can do -- but Ancients?
Can they all turn into beasts?
Yes, but we are each our own, and each have different powers.
I am the Wolf.
Ancient born of the Moon.
TEXA
And if you thought Nash was scary, Reuben's form is downright frightening.
OOF!
What Ancient is he?
Tarantula.
His father's name, in scientific terms, is VFTS-682.
Sounds more like a license plate.
Reuben's father is a star one hundred and fifty times the mass of the sun -- the brightest star in the Tarantula nebula.
Which means he's probably pretty strong.
Extremely.
But that's the part I don't understand.
His father is a wolf-rayet.
A wolf what?

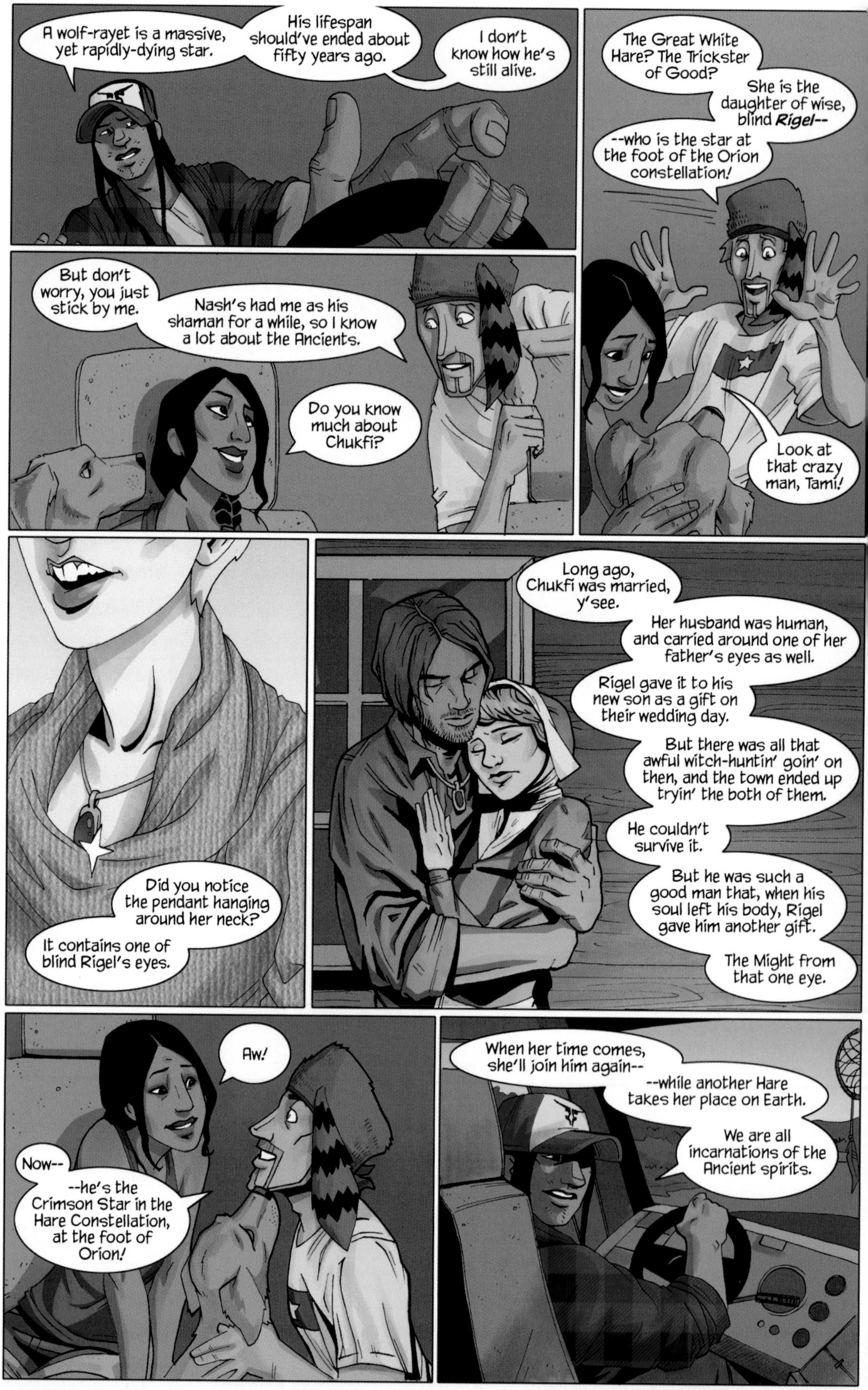
A wolf-rayet is a massive, yet rapidly-dying star.
His lifespan should've ended about fifty years ago.
I don't know how he's still alive.
But don't worry, you just stick by me.
Nash's had me as his shaman for a while, so I know a lot about the Ancients.
Do you know much about Chukfi?
The Great White Hare? The Trickster of Good?
She is the daughter of wise, blind *Rigel*--
--who is the star at the foot of the Orion constellation!
Look at that crazy man, Tami!
Did you notice the pendant hanging around her neck?
It contains one of blind Rigel's eyes.
Long ago, Chukfi was married, y'see.
Her husband was human, and carried around one of her father's eyes as well.
Rigel gave it to his new son as a gift on their wedding day.
But there was all that awful witch-huntin' goin' on then, and the town ended up tryin' the both of them.
He couldn't survive it.
But he was such a good man that, when his soul left his body, Rigel gave him another gift.
The Might from that one eye.
Aw!
Now--
--he's the Crimson Star in the Hare Constellation, at the foot of Orion!
When her time comes, she'll join him again--
--while another Hare takes her place on Earth.
We are all incarnations of the Ancient spirits.

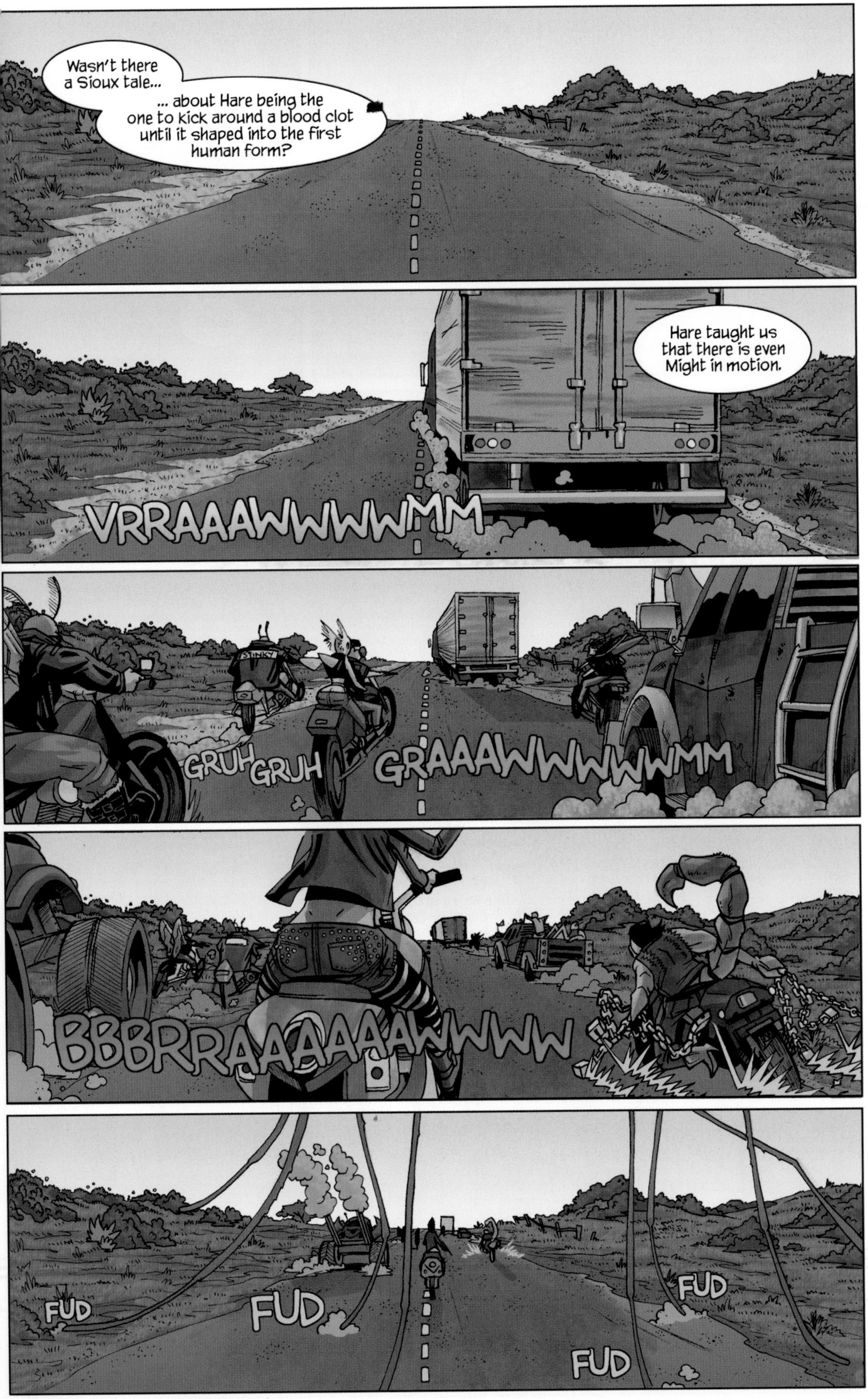
Wasn't there a Sioux tale...
... about Hare being the one to kick around a blood clot until it shaped into the first human form?
Hare taught us that there is even Might in motion.
VRRAAAWWWWMM
STINKY
GRUH GRUH
GRAAAWWWWWMM
BBBRRAAAAAAWWW
FUD
FUD
FUD
FUD

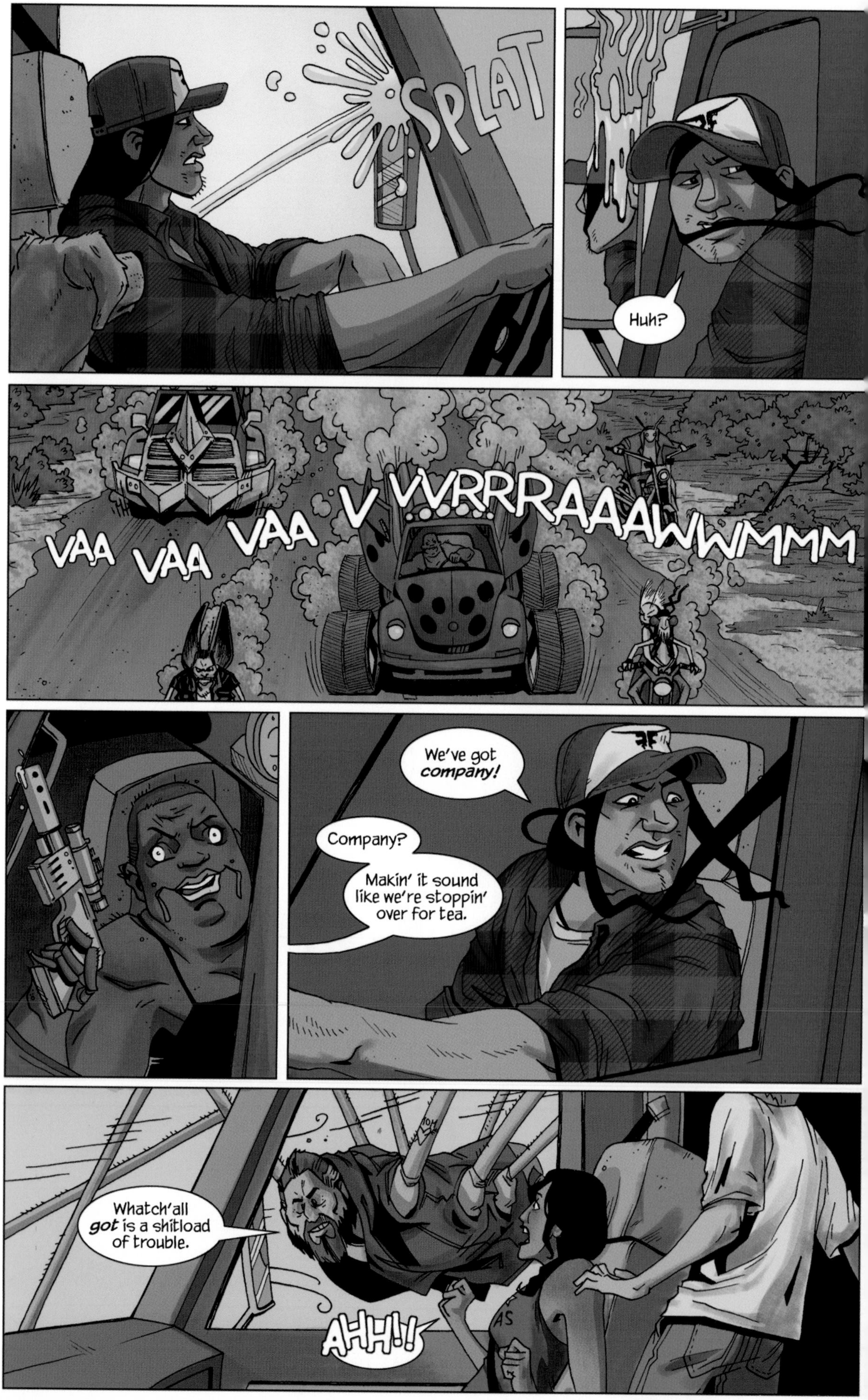
SPLAT
Huh?
VAA VAA VAA V VVRRRAAAAWWMMM
We've got *company!*
Company?
Makin' it sound like we're stoppin' over for tea.
Whatch'all *got* is a shitload of trouble.
AHH!!

Well, Shitload...

... say *hello* to *Uncle Charlie!*

BIG DADDY

BRRRRRRRRRAAAWWW

FUH-WHOOOM

VRRRRRR

VVVRR VRRRRRR

WHAM

I got this...

... just keep the pedal to the floor, brother!

It's been on the floor since I saw Miss Monster Bug's monster bug over here!

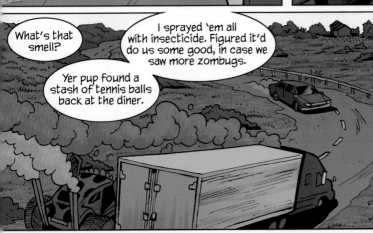

What's that smell?

I sprayed 'em all with insecticide. Figured it'd do us some good, in case we saw more zombugs.

Yer pup found a stash of tennis balls back at the diner.

Oh *no.*

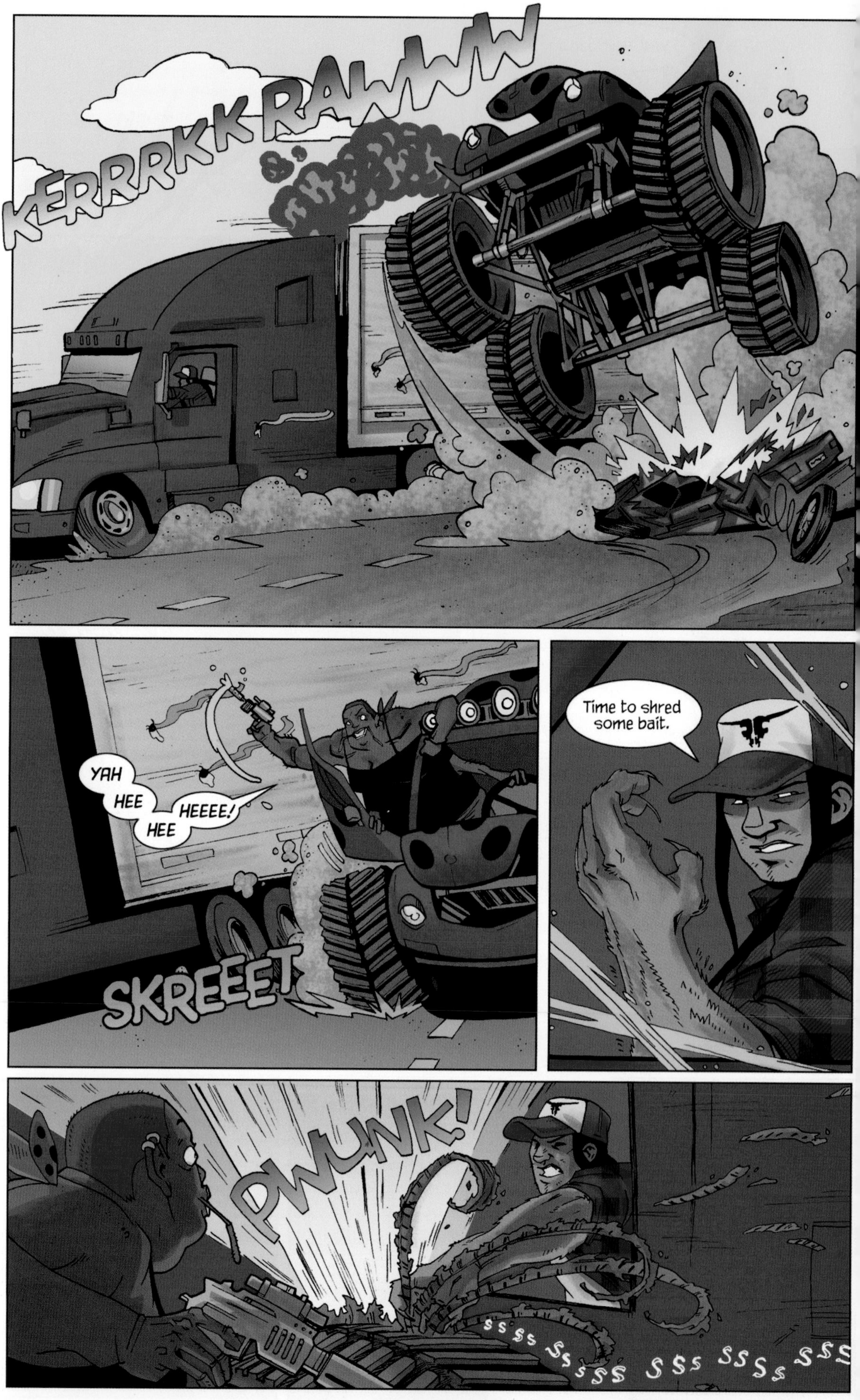
KERRRKK RAWWW
YAH
HEE
HEE
HEEEE!
SKREEEET
Time to shred some bait.
PWUNK!

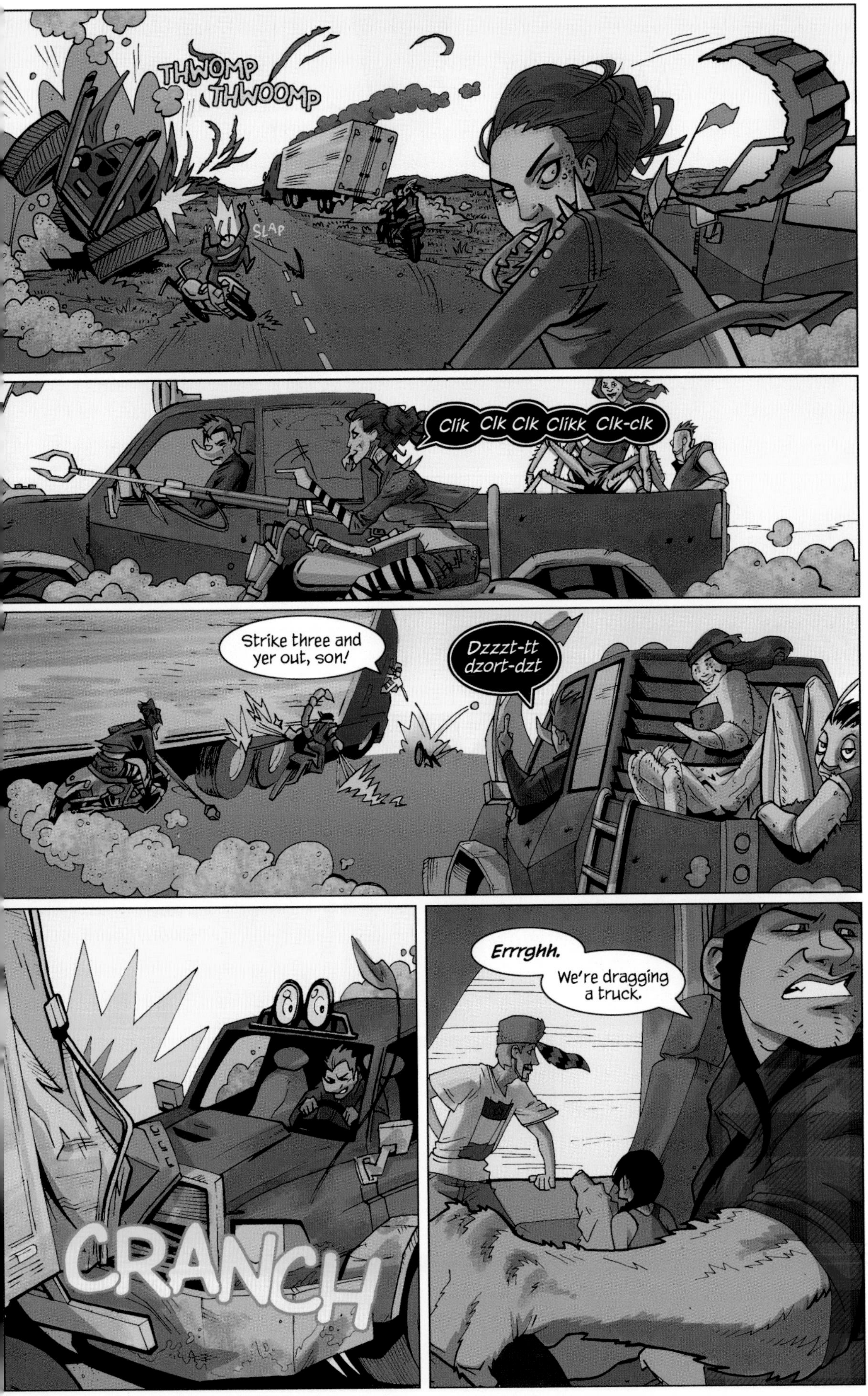
THWOMP
THWOOMP
SLAP
Clik Clk Clk Clikk Clk-clk
Strike three and yer out, son!
Dzzzt-tt dzort-dzt
CRANCH
Errrghh.
We're dragging a truck.

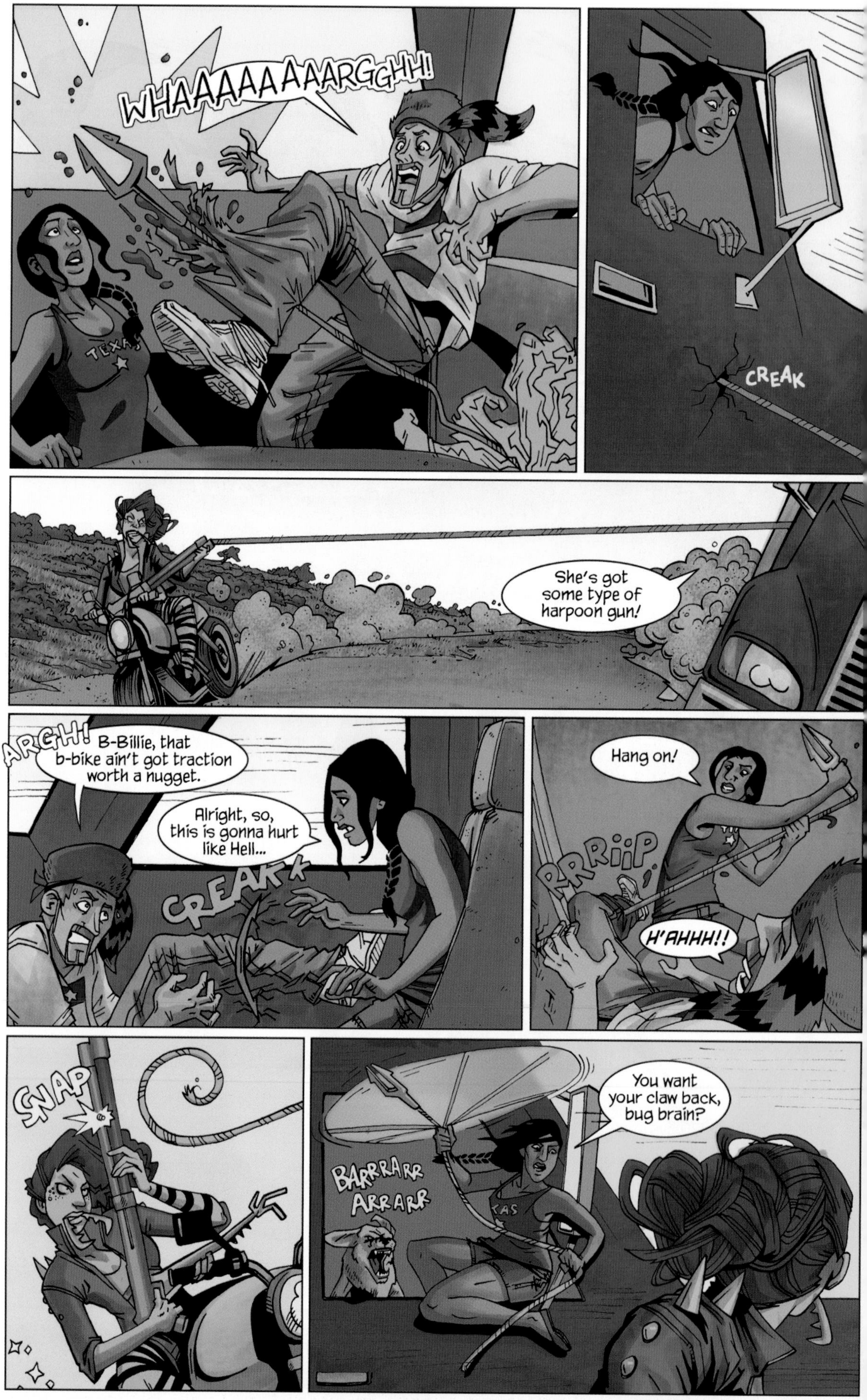
WHAAAAAAAARGGHH!
CREAK
She's got some type of harpoon gun!
ARGH! B-Billie, that b-bike ain't got traction worth a nugget.
Alright, so, this is gonna hurt like Hell...
CREAKK
Hang on!
RRRIIP
H'AHHH!!
SNAP
You want your claw back, bug brain?
BARRRARR ARRARR

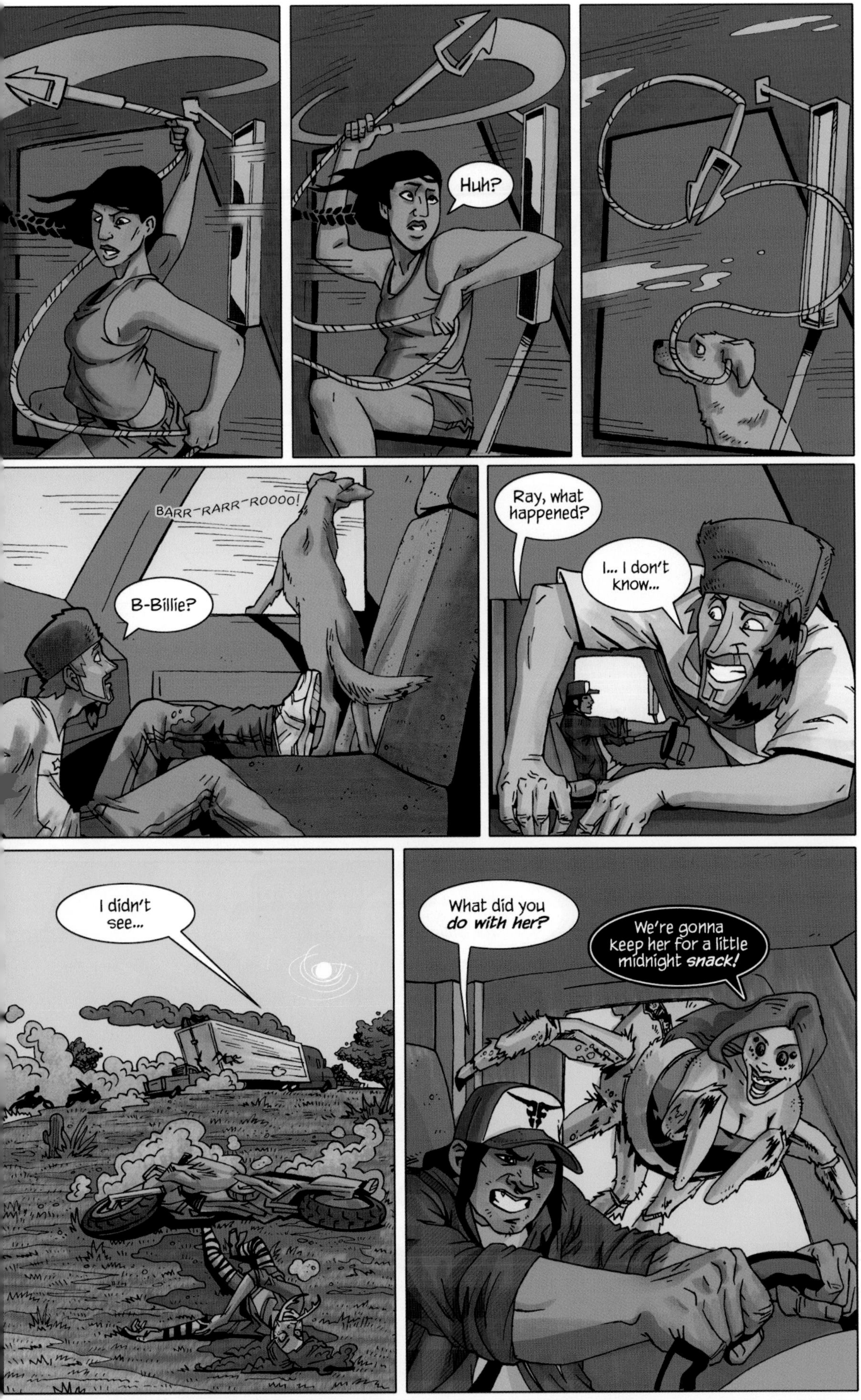
Huh?
BARR-RARR-ROOOO!
B-Billie?
Ray, what happened?
I... I don't know...
I didn't see...
What did you do with her?
We're gonna keep her for a little midnight snack!

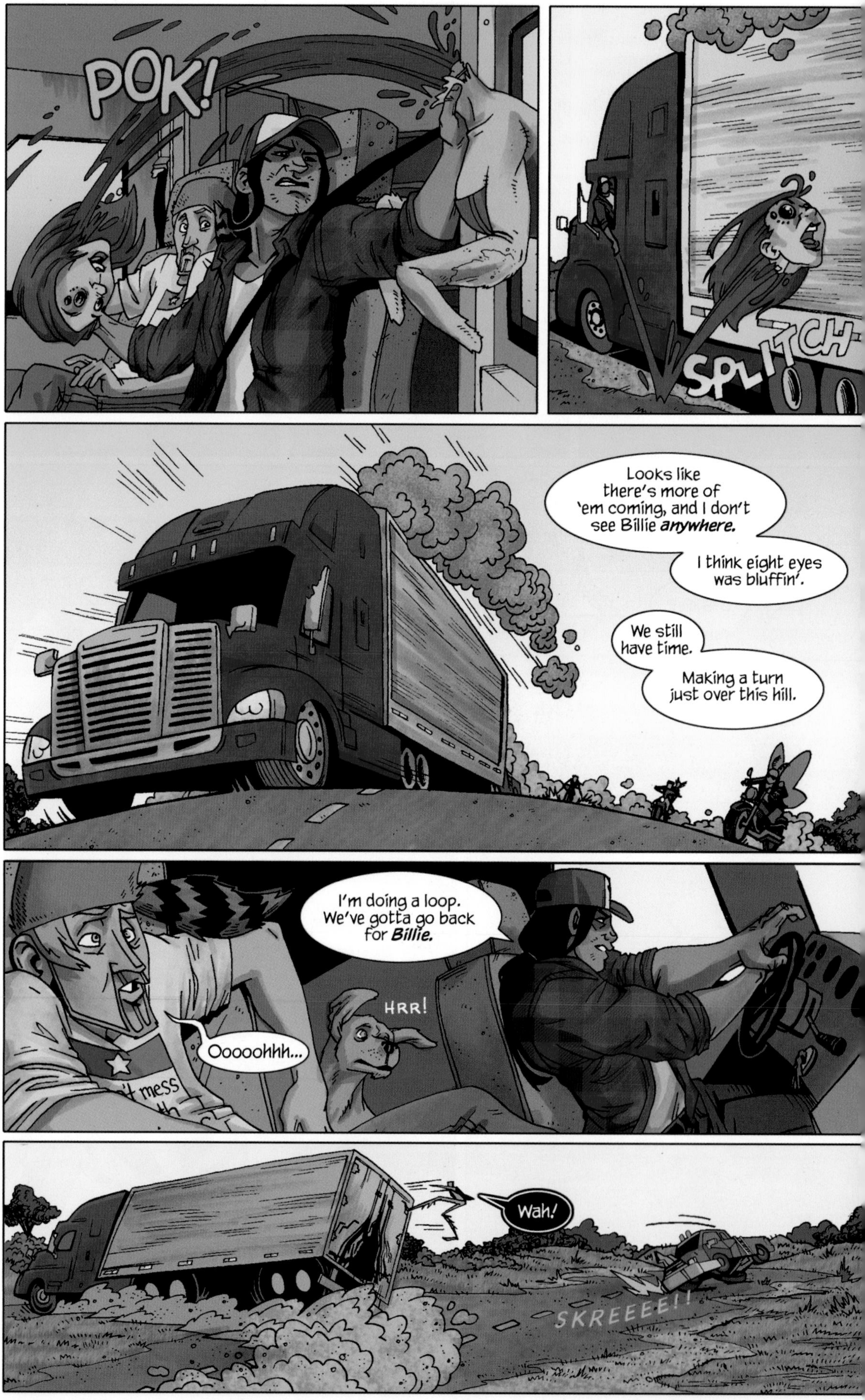
POK!
SPLITCH
Looks like there's more of 'em coming, and I don't see Billie *anywhere.*
I think eight eyes was bluffin'.
We still have time.
Making a turn just over this hill.
I'm doing a loop. We've gotta go back for *Billie.*
HRR!
Oooohhh...
Wah!
SKREEEE!!

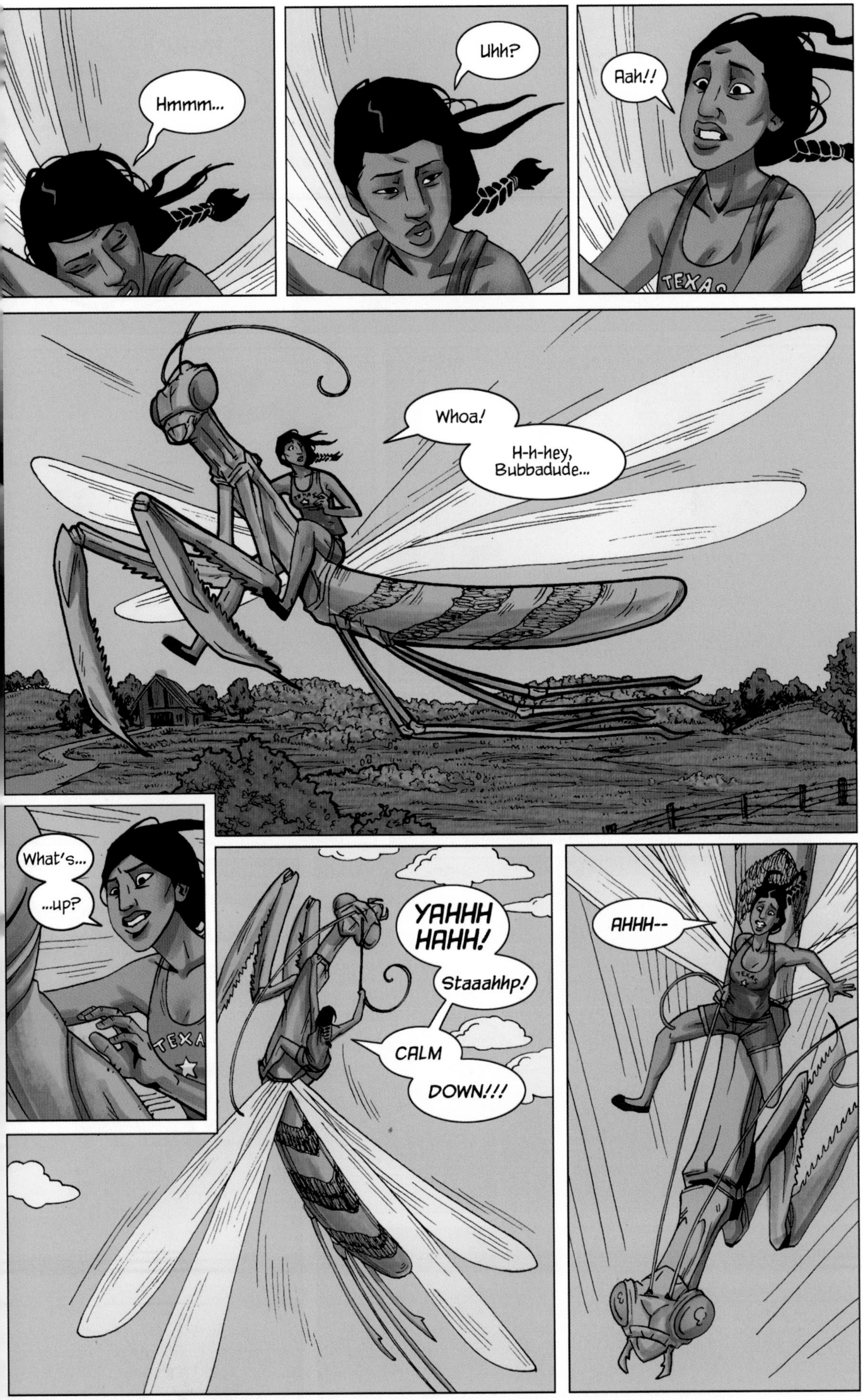
Hmmm...
Uhh?
Aah!!
Whoa!
H-h-hey, Bubbadude...
TEXAS
What's...
...up?
TEXAS
YAHHH HAHH!
Staaahhp!
CALM
DOWN!!!
AHHH--
TEXAS

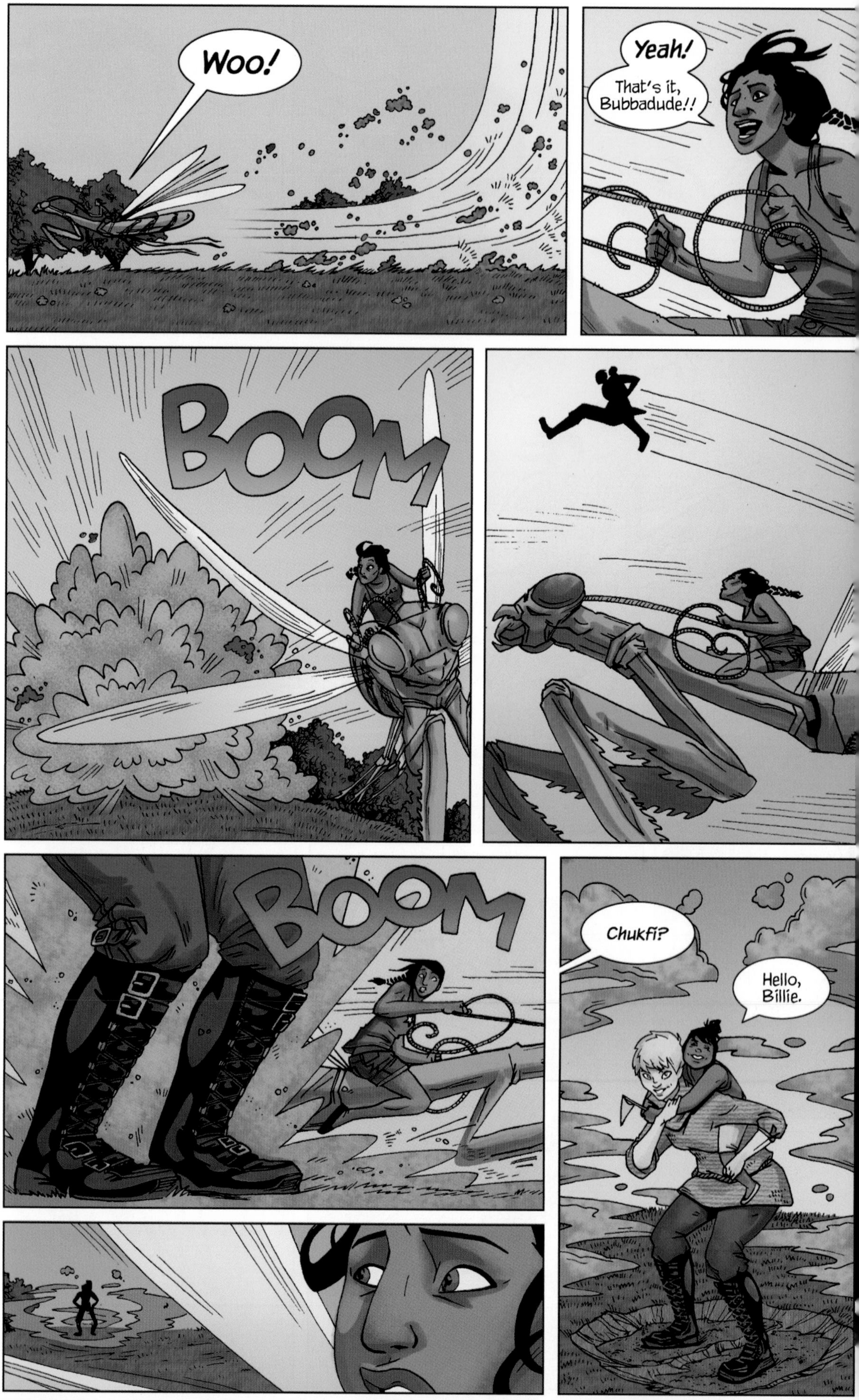
Woo!
Yeah!
That's it, Bubbadude!!
BOOM
BOOM
Chukfi?
Hello, Billie.

Good to see you again so soon.

Her name is Ezra! I freed her from Reuben's lair.

Now she's helping me find the next warehouse full of hostages!

It's good to see you too, even if you did scare the *Hell* outta me!

Who's the cute little tyke?

BOOM

Did you find out why he needs all these people?

Girl, you do *not* want to know.

That bad?

Oh yes. And from what I know, this is just one of many warehouses Señor Corneja is in charge of.

We've got to get there before he sends any more people to Reuben.

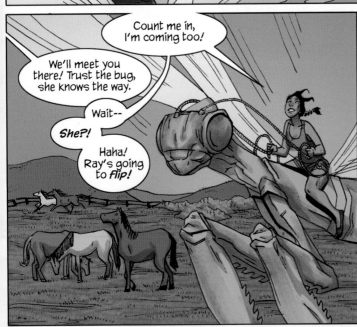

Count me in, I'm coming too!

We'll meet you there! Trust the bug, she knows the way.

Wait--

She?!

Haha! Ray's going to *flip!*

YA!

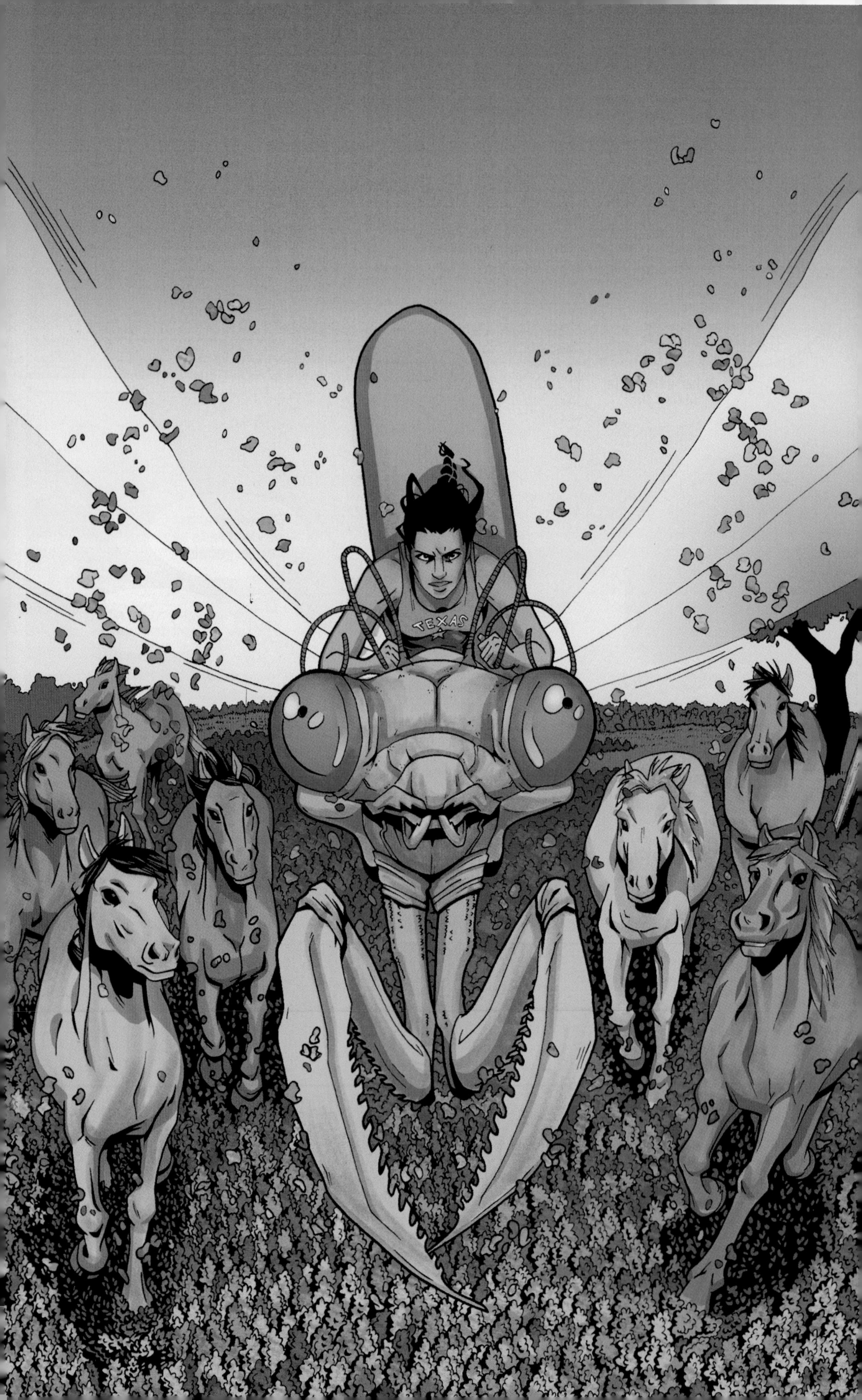
TEXAS

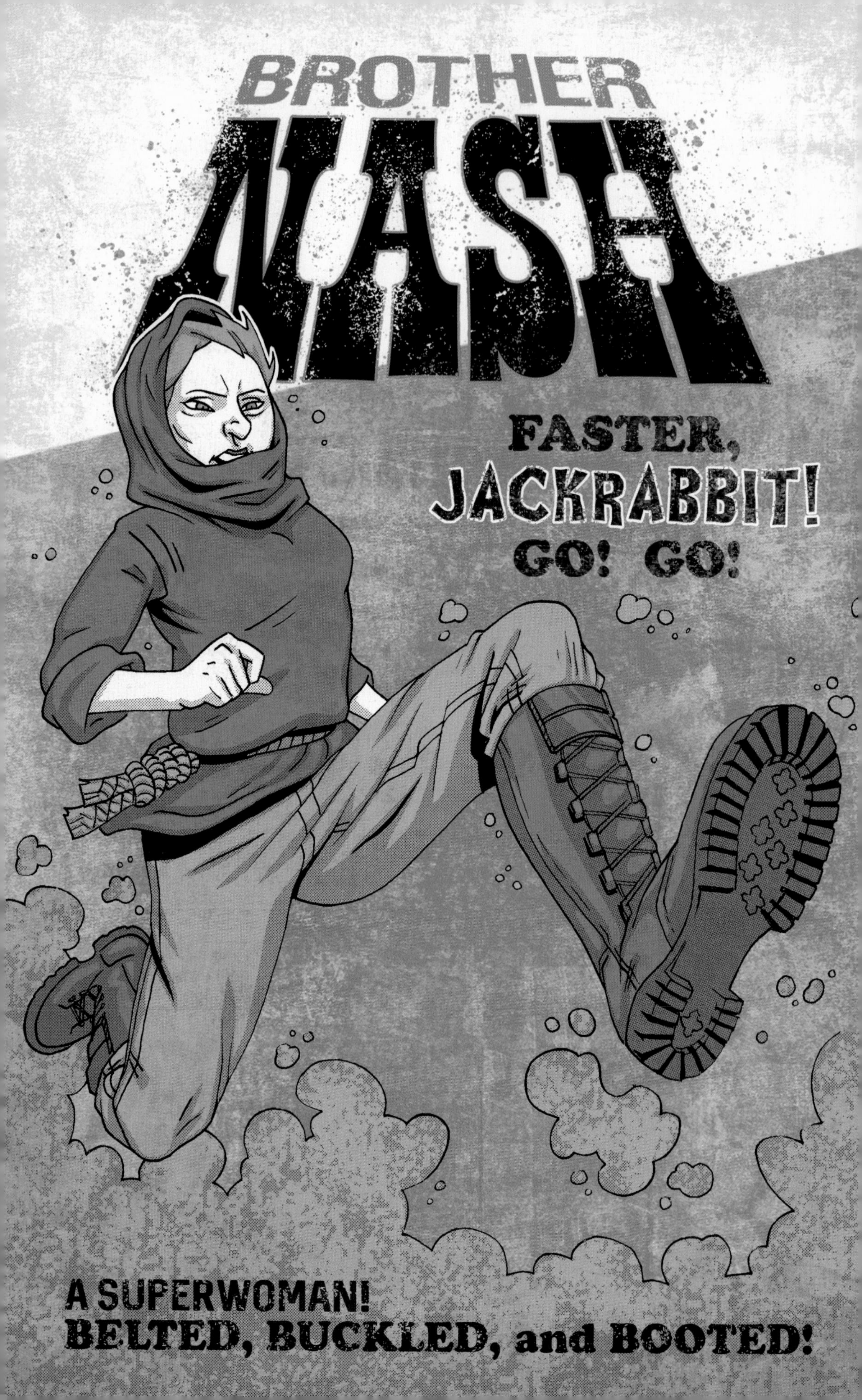
BROTHER NASH
FASTER, JACKRABBIT! GO! GO!
A SUPERWOMAN!
BELTED, BUCKLED, and BOOTED!

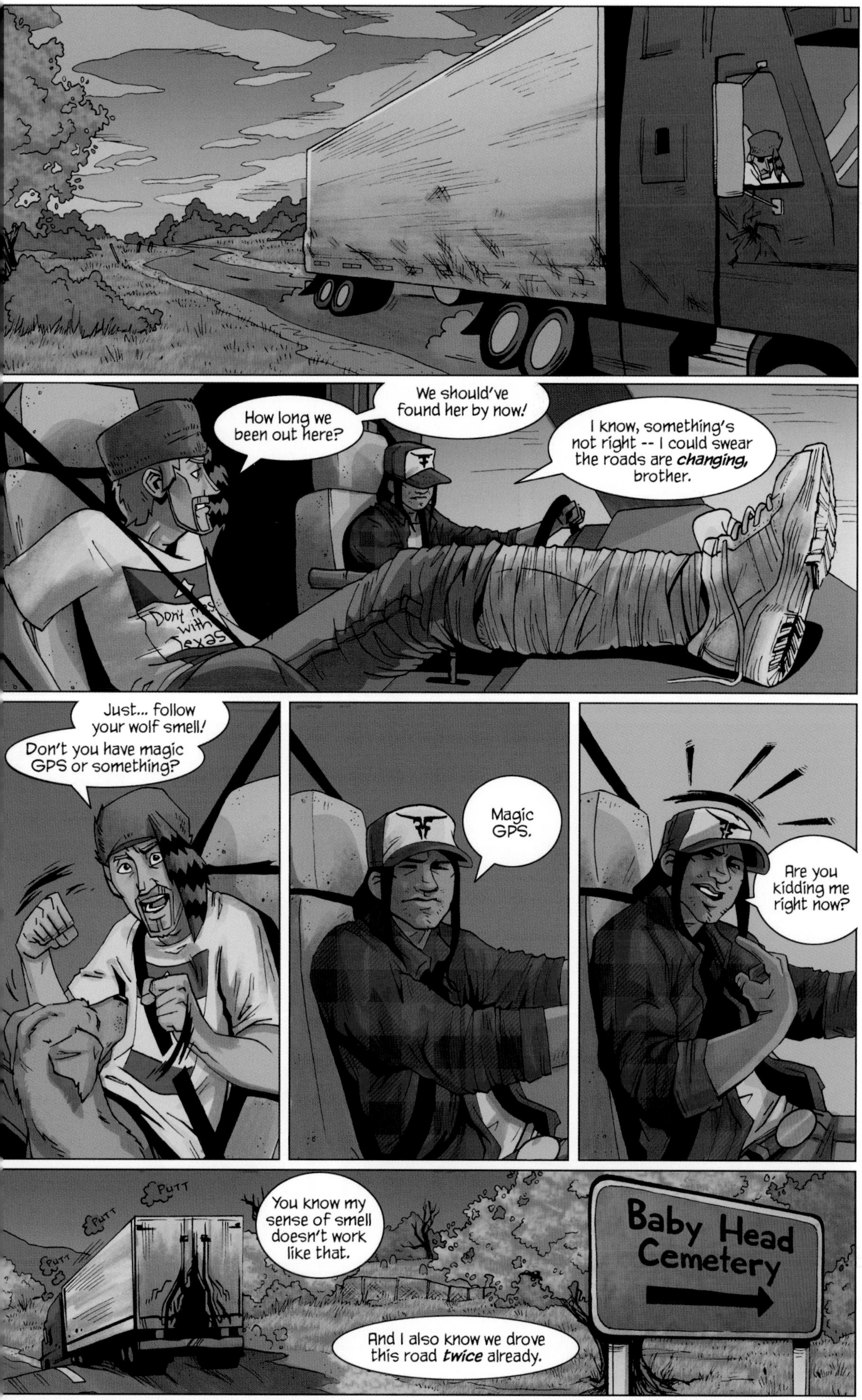
How long we been out here?
We should've found her by now!
I know, something's not right -- I could swear the roads are *changing,* brother.
Don't mess with Texas
Just... follow your wolf smell!
Don't you have magic GPS or something?
Magic GPS.
Are you kidding me right now?
PUTT
PUTT
PUTT
You know my sense of smell doesn't work like that.
Baby Head Cemetery
And I also know we drove this road *twice* already.

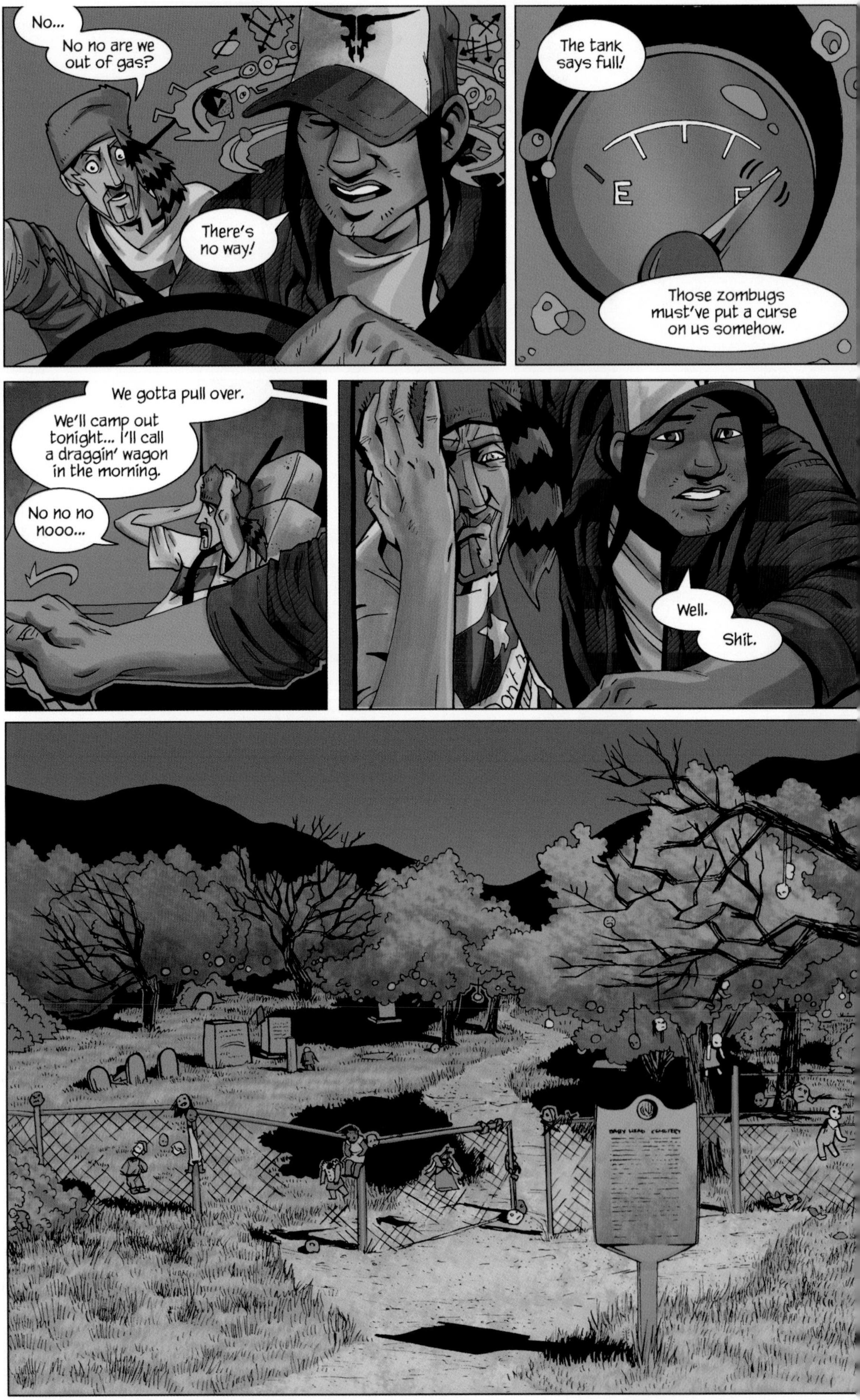
No...
No no are we out of gas?
There's no way!
The tank says full!
E
F
Those zombugs must've put a curse on us somehow.
We gotta pull over.
We'll camp out tonight... I'll call a draggin' wagon in the morning.
No no no nooo...
Well.
Shit.

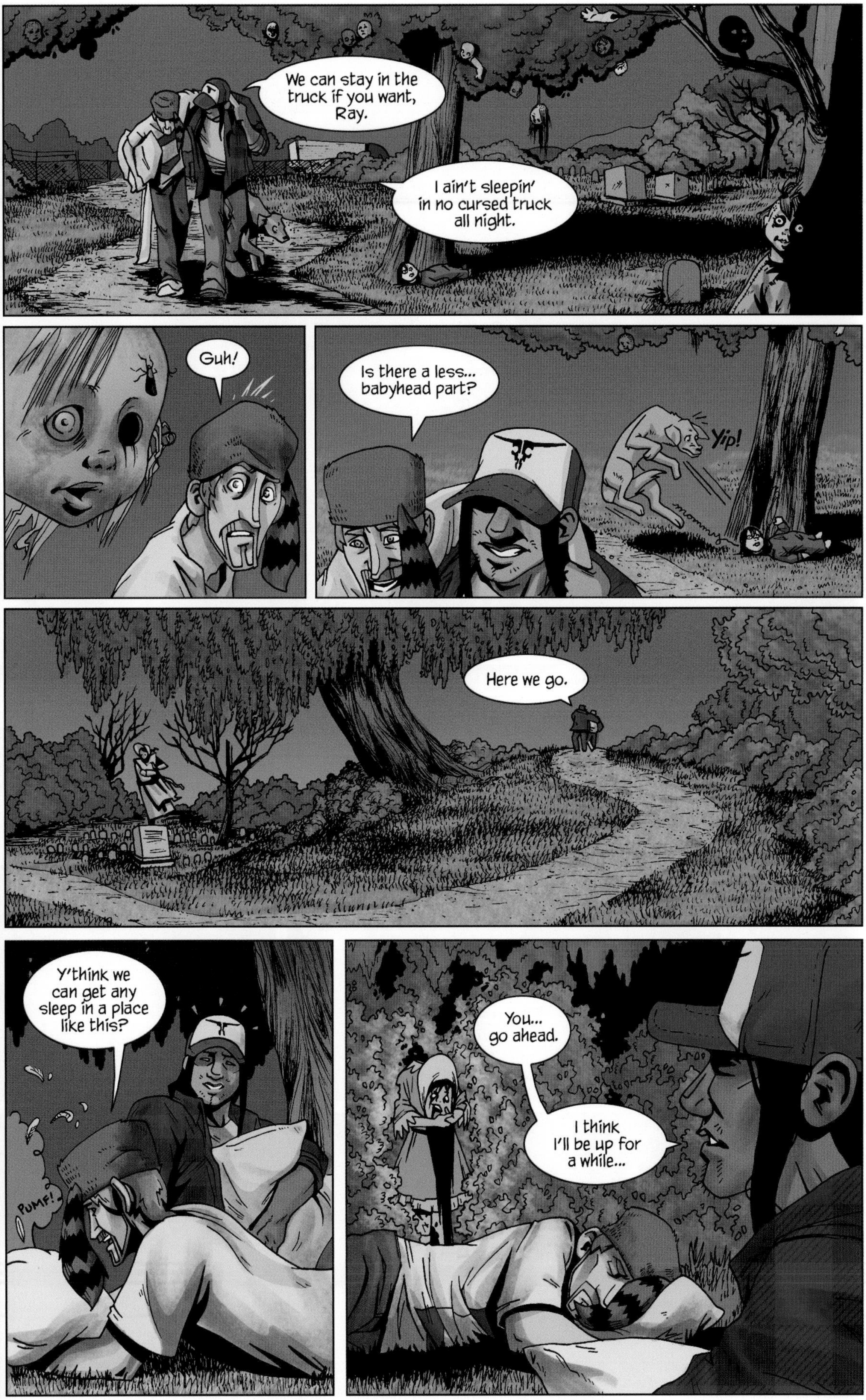
We can stay in the truck if you want, Ray.
I ain't sleepin' in no cursed truck all night.
Guh!
Is there a less... babyhead part?
Yip!
Here we go.
Y'think we can get any sleep in a place like this?
PUMF!
You... go ahead.
I think I'll be up for a while...

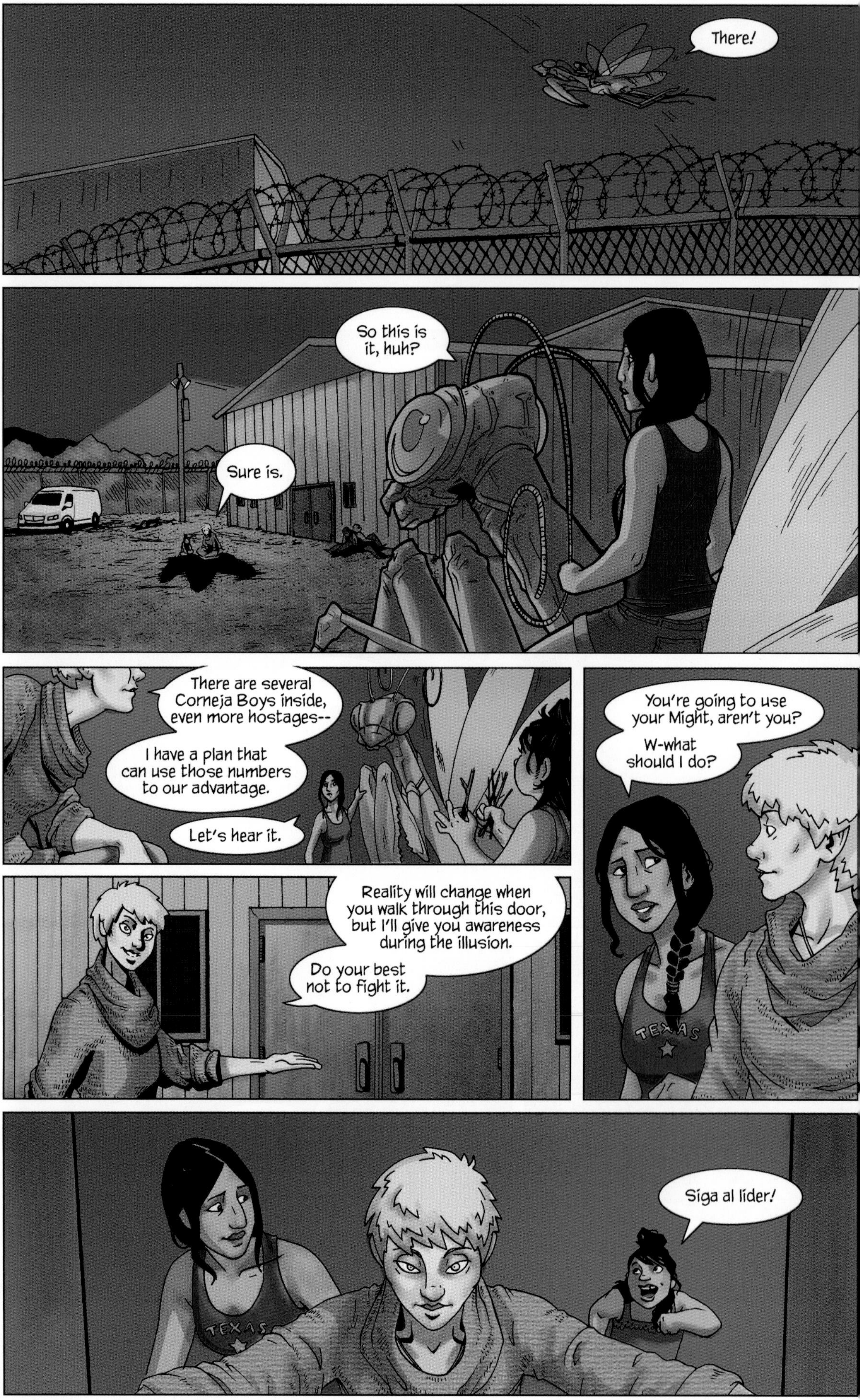
There!
So this is it, huh?
Sure is.
There are several Corneja Boys inside, even more hostages--
I have a plan that can use those numbers to our advantage.
Let's hear it.
You're going to use your Might, aren't you?
W-what should I do?
Reality will change when you walk through this door, but I'll give you awareness during the illusion.
Do your best not to fight it.
TEXAS
Siga al lider!
TEXAS

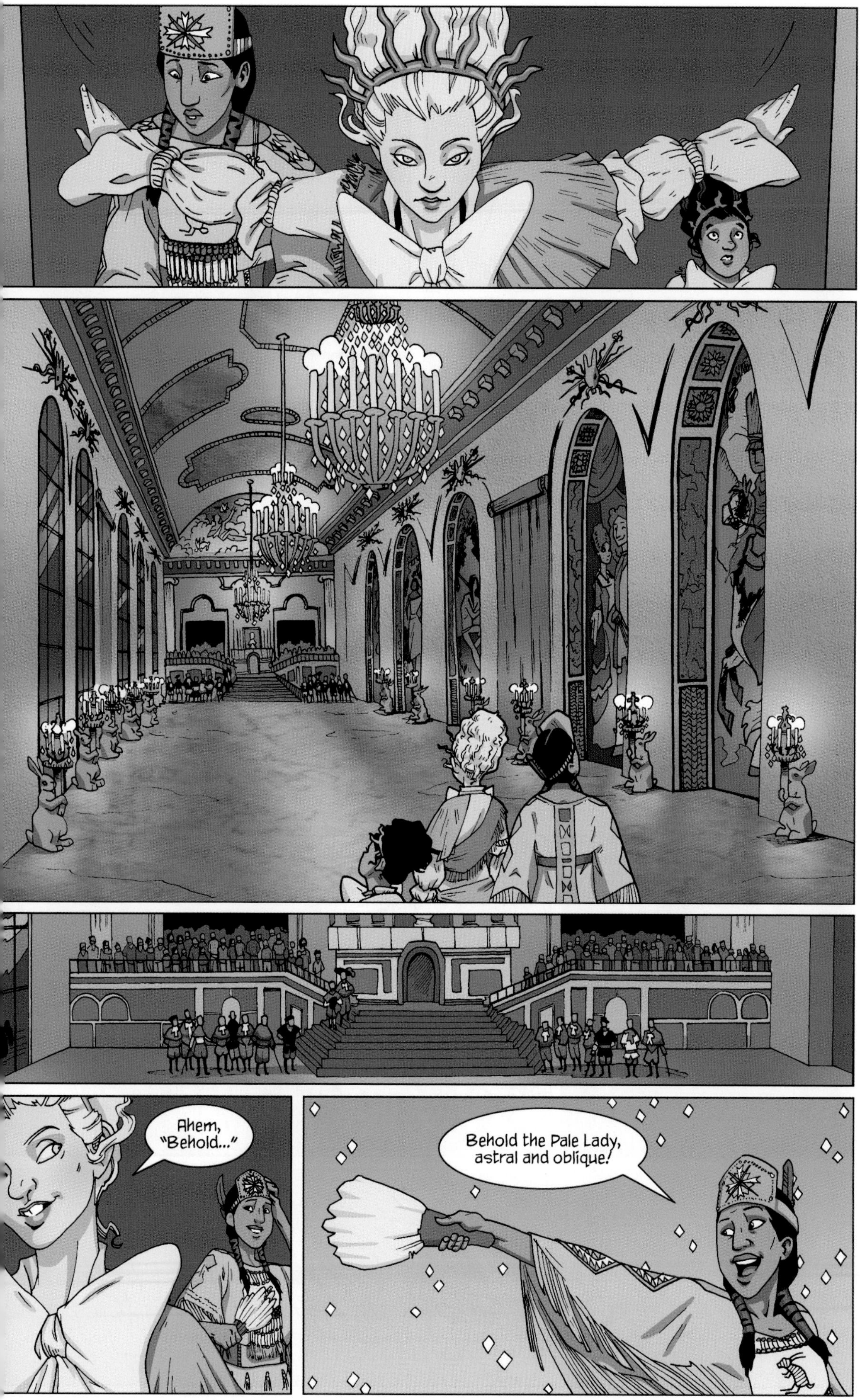
Ahem, "Behold..."
Behold the Pale Lady, astral and oblique!

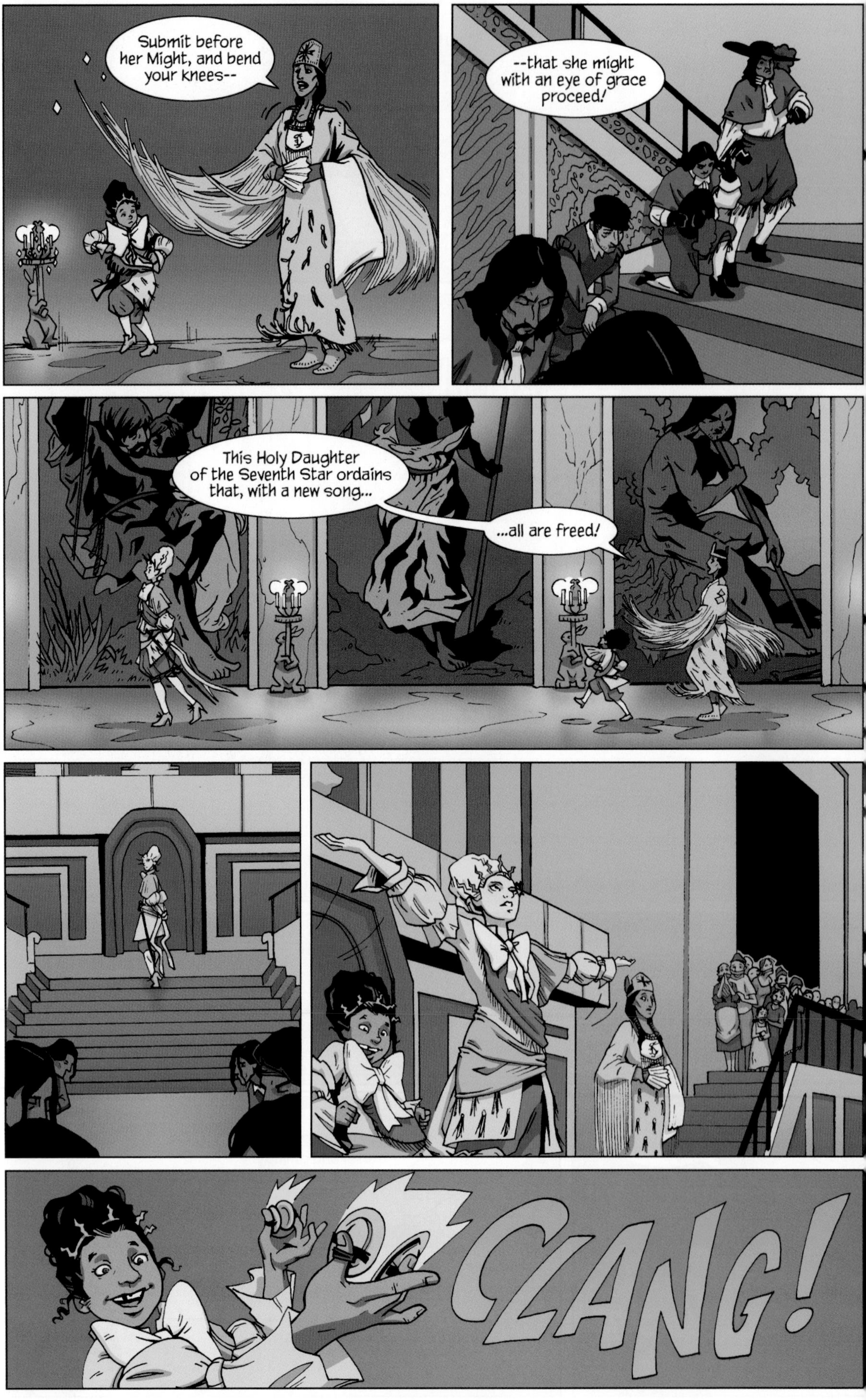
Submit before her Might, and bend your knees--
--that she might with an eye of grace proceed!
This Holy Daughter of the Seventh Star ordains that, with a new song...
...all are freed!
CLANG!

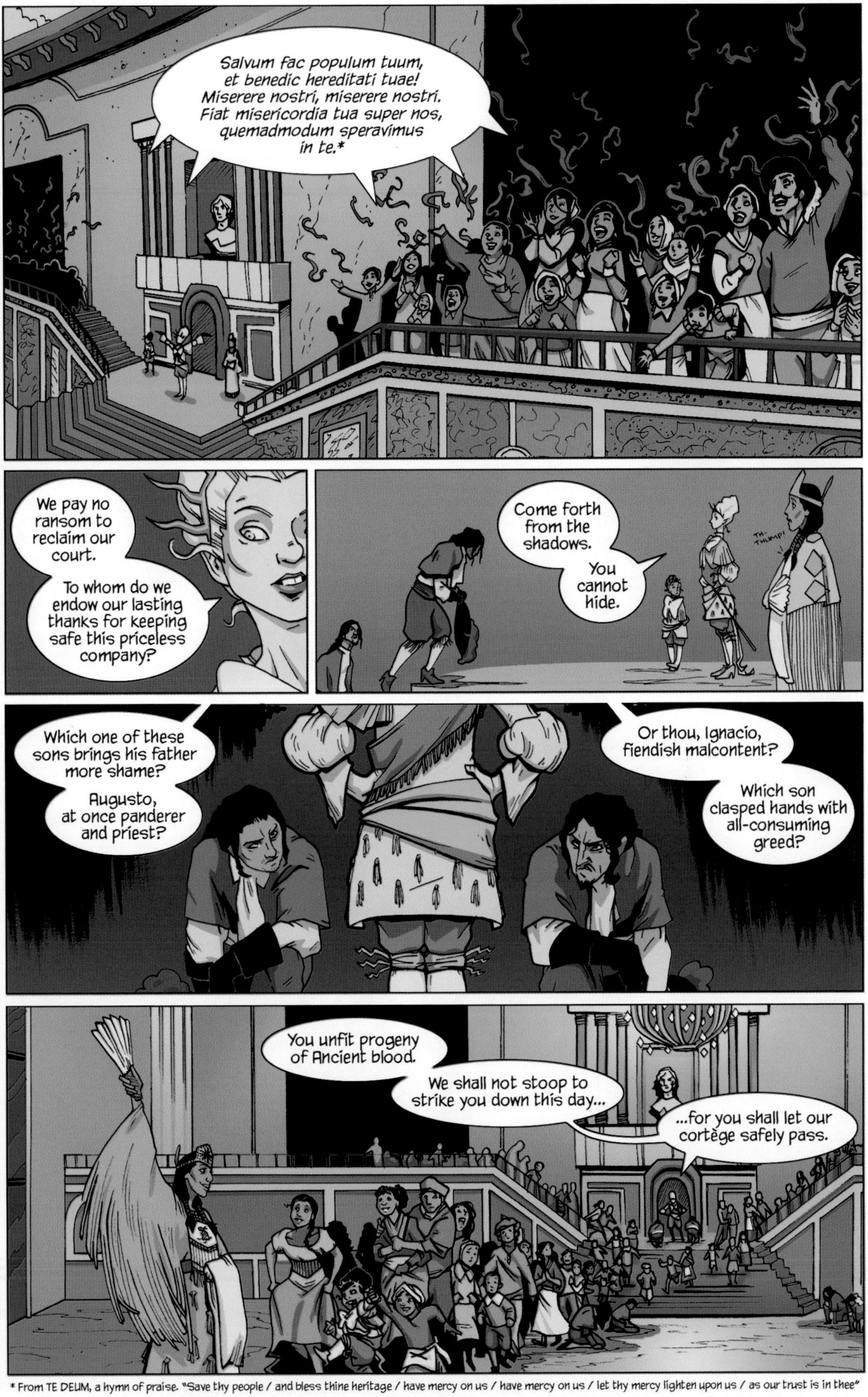
Salvum fac populum tuum, et benedic hereditati tuae! Miserere nostri, miserere nostri. Fiat misericordia tua super nos, quemadmodum speravimus in te.*
We pay no ransom to reclaim our court.
To whom do we endow our lasting thanks for keeping safe this priceless company?
Come forth from the shadows.
You cannot hide.
TH-THUMP!
Which one of these sons brings his father more shame?
Augusto, at once panderer and priest?
Or thou, Ignacio, fiendish malcontent?
Which son clasped hands with all-consuming greed?
You unfit progeny of Ancient blood.
We shall not stoop to strike you down this day...
...for you shall let our cortège safely pass.

* From TE DEUM, a hymn of praise. "Save thy people / and bless thine heritage / have mercy on us / have mercy on us / let thy mercy lighten upon us / as our trust is in thee"

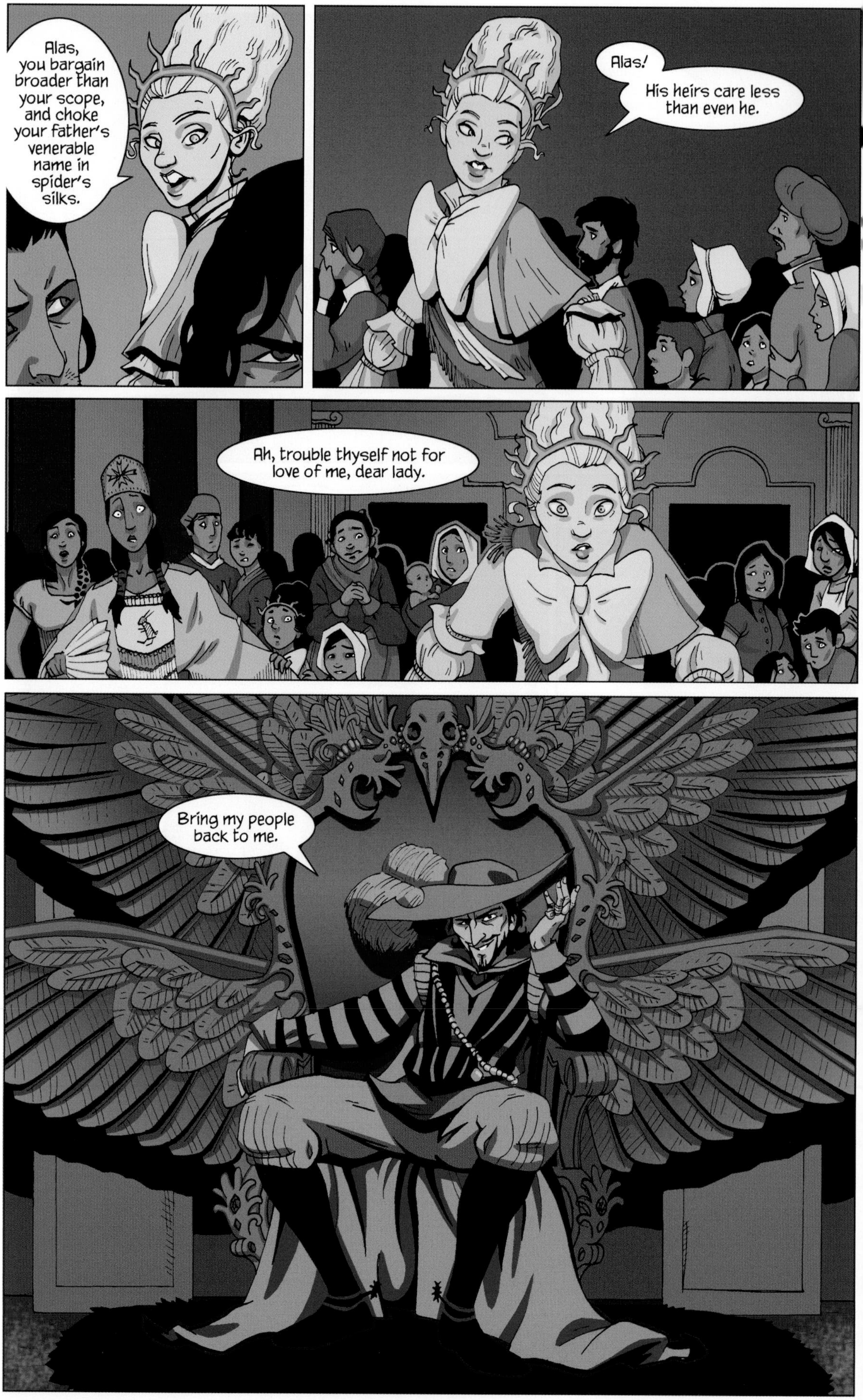
Alas, you bargain broader than your scope, and choke your father's venerable name in spider's silks.
Alas!
His heirs care less than even he.
Ah, trouble thyself not for love of me, dear lady.
Bring my people back to me.

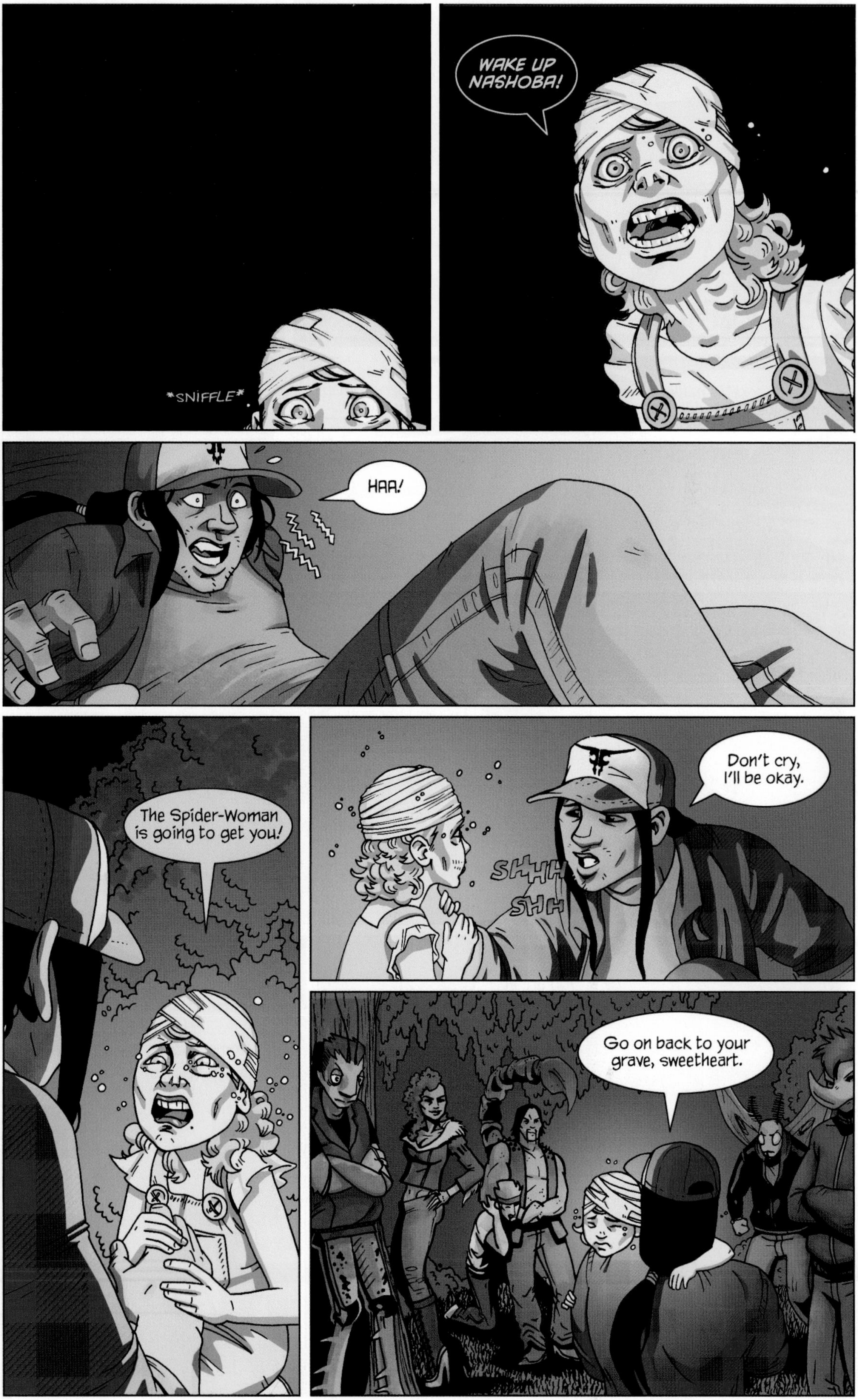
SNIFFLE
WAKE UP NASHOBA!
HAA!
The Spider-Woman is going to get you!
Don't cry, I'll be okay.
SHHH
SHH
Go on back to your grave, sweetheart.

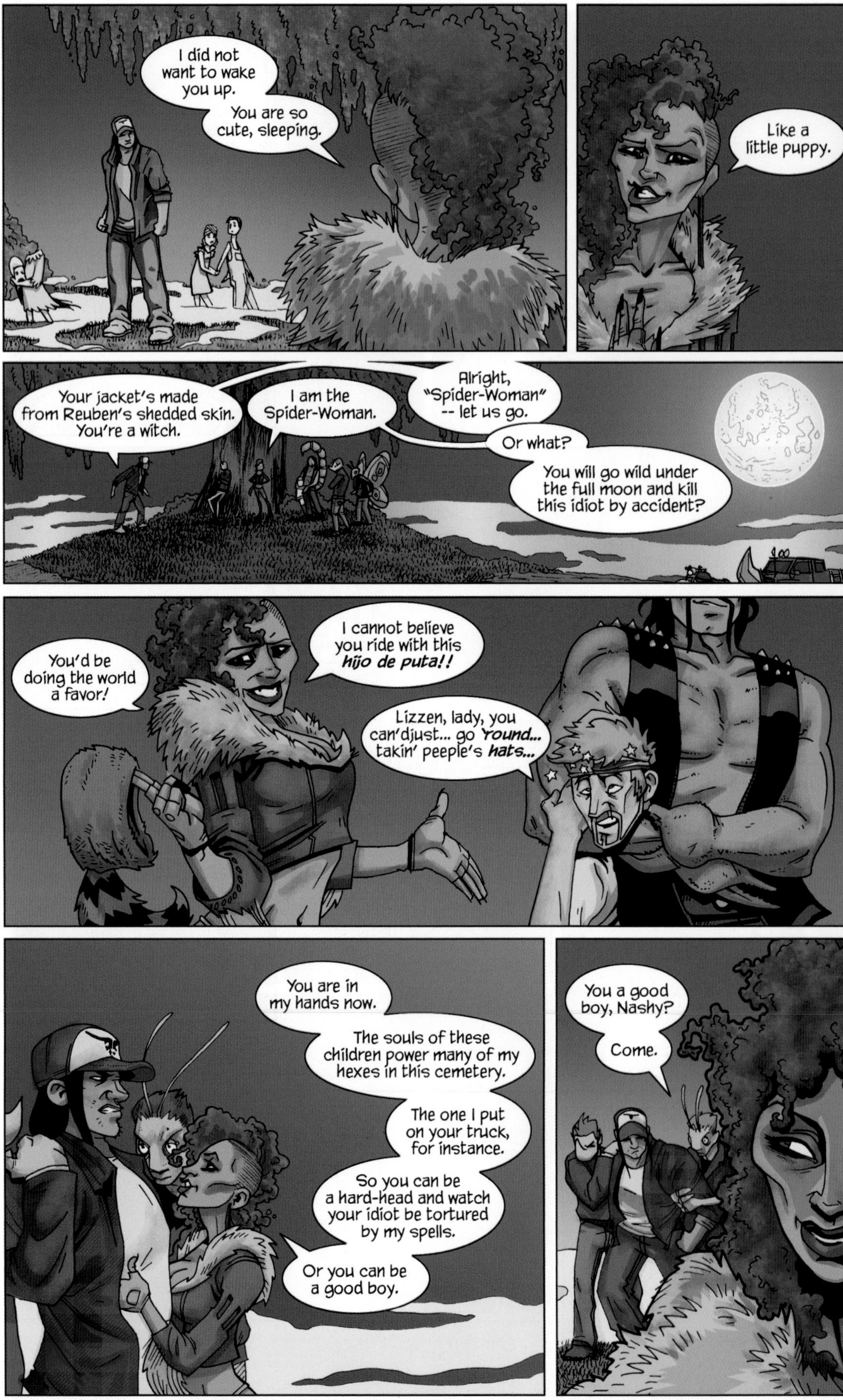
I did not want to wake you up.
You are so cute, sleeping.
Like a little puppy.
Your jacket's made from Reuben's shedded skin. You're a witch.
I am the Spider-Woman.
Alright, "Spider-Woman" -- let us go.
Or what?
You will go wild under the full moon and kill this idiot by accident?
You'd be doing the world a favor!
I cannot believe you ride with this *hijo de puta!!*
Lizzen, lady, you can'djust... go *'round...* takin' peeple's *hats...*
You are in my hands now.
The souls of these children power many of my hexes in this cemetery.
The one I put on your truck, for instance.
So you can be a hard-head and watch your idiot be tortured by my spells.
Or you can be a good boy.
You a good boy, Nashy?
Come.

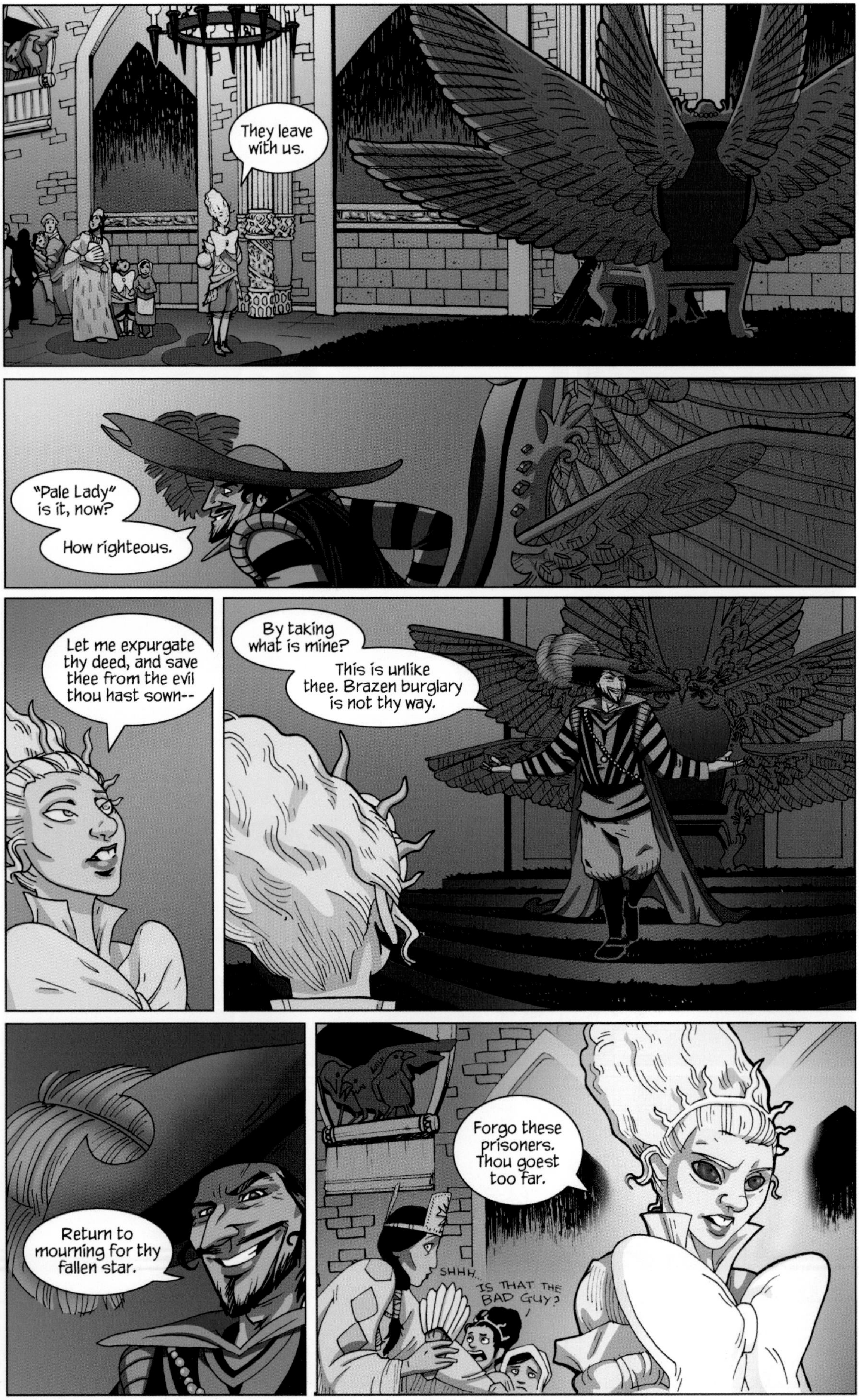
They leave with us.
"Pale Lady" is it, now?
How righteous.
Let me expurgate thy deed, and save thee from the evil thou hast sown--
By taking what is mine?
This is unlike thee. Brazen burglary is not thy way.
Return to mourning for thy fallen star.
Forgo these prisoners. Thou goest too far.
SHHH...
IS THAT THE BAD GUY?

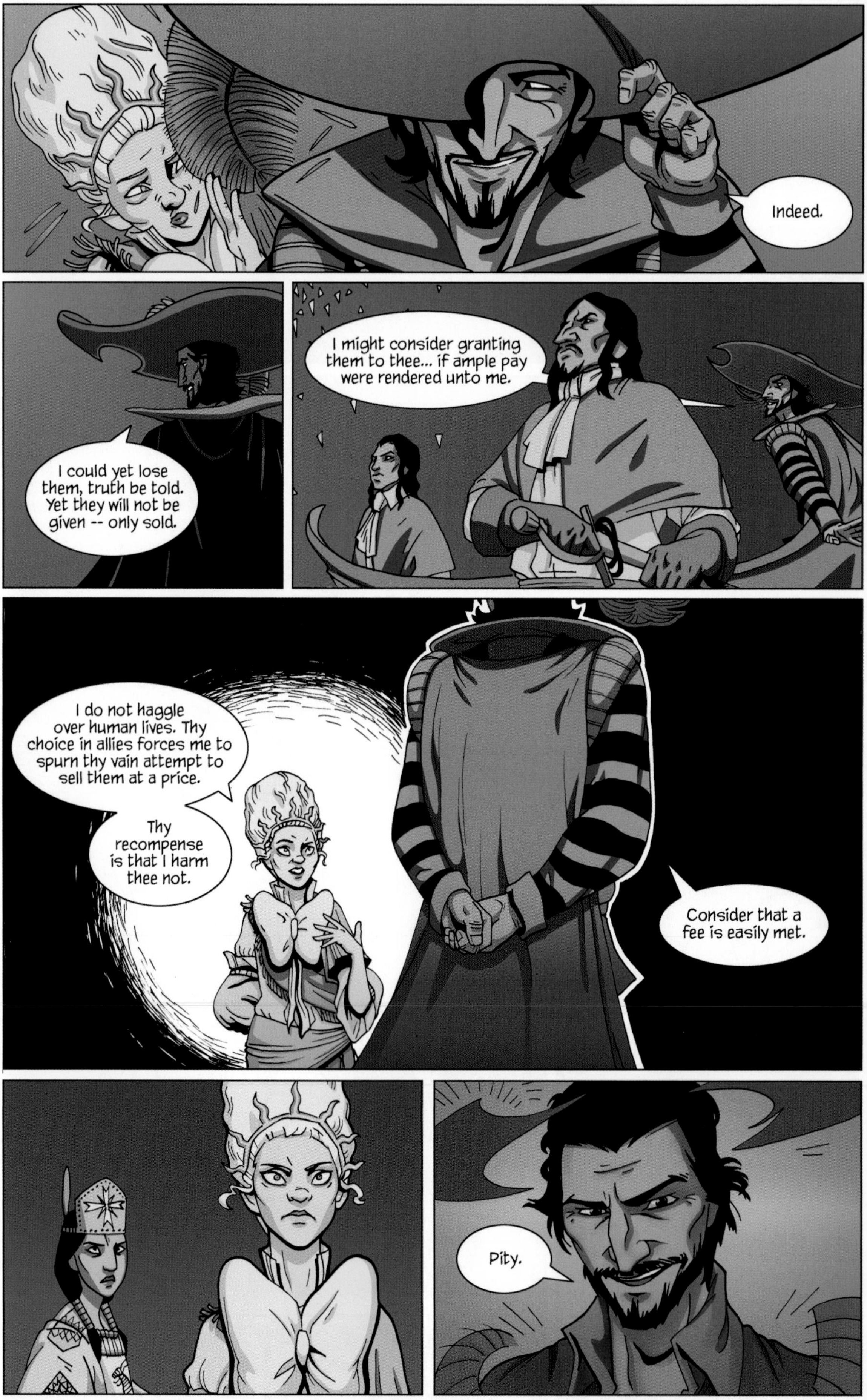
Indeed.
I could yet lose them, truth be told. Yet they will not be given -- only sold.
I might consider granting them to thee... if ample pay were rendered unto me.
I do not haggle over human lives. Thy choice in allies forces me to spurn thy vain attempt to sell them at a price.
Thy recompense is that I harm thee not.
Consider that a fee is easily met.
Pity.

It is good to see you again, Chukfi...

...even if you did just try to pick my pocket.

Augusto! Tell Reuben about our guest.

Tell him the deal's off.

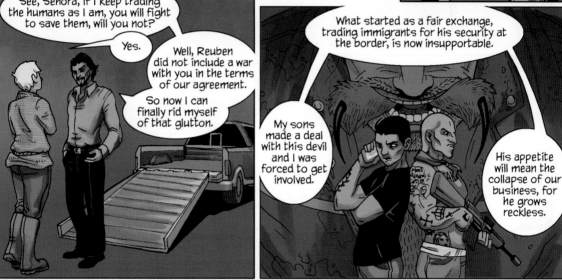

See, Señora, if I keep trading the humans as I am, you will fight to save them, will you not?

Yes.

Well, Reuben did not include a war with you in the terms of our agreement.

So now I can finally rid myself of that glutton.

What started as a fair exchange, trading immigrants for his security at the border, is now insupportable.

My sons made a deal with this devil and I was forced to get involved.

His appetite will mean the collapse of our business, for he grows reckless.

Gracias por todo.

Now kill the hostages. We have no further use of them.

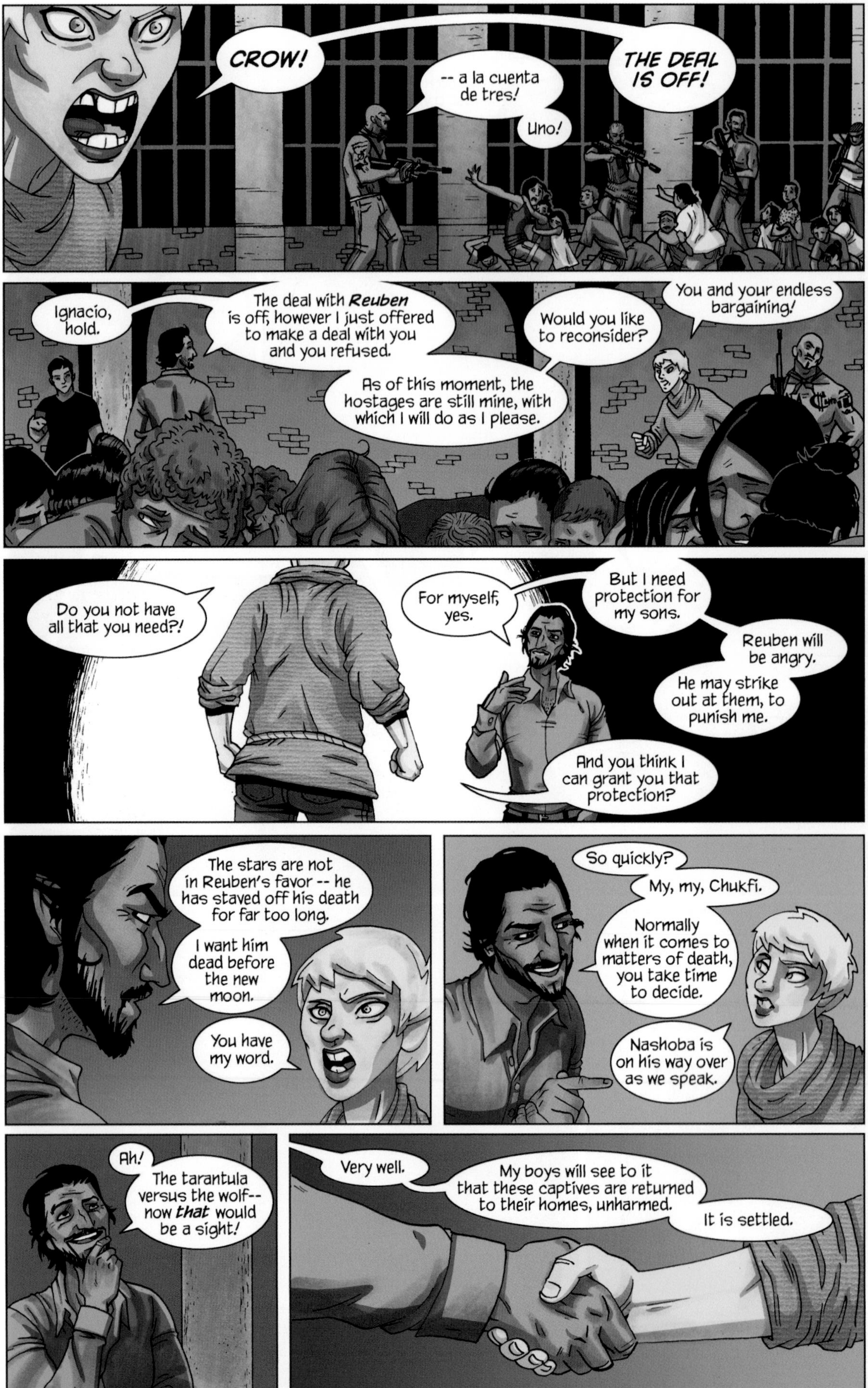
CROW!
THE DEAL IS OFF!
-- a la cuenta de tres!
Uno!
Ignacio, hold.
The deal with Reuben is off, however I just offered to make a deal with you and you refused.
As of this moment, the hostages are still mine, with which I will do as I please.
Would you like to reconsider?
You and your endless bargaining!
Do you not have all that you need?!
For myself, yes.
But I need protection for my sons.
Reuben will be angry.
He may strike out at them, to punish me.
And you think I can grant you that protection?
The stars are not in Reuben's favor -- he has staved off his death for far too long.
I want him dead before the new moon.
You have my word.
So quickly?
My, my, Chukfi.
Normally when it comes to matters of death, you take time to decide.
Nashoba is on his way over as we speak.
Ah!
The tarantula versus the wolf-- now that would be a sight!
Very well.
My boys will see to it that these captives are returned to their homes, unharmed.
It is settled.

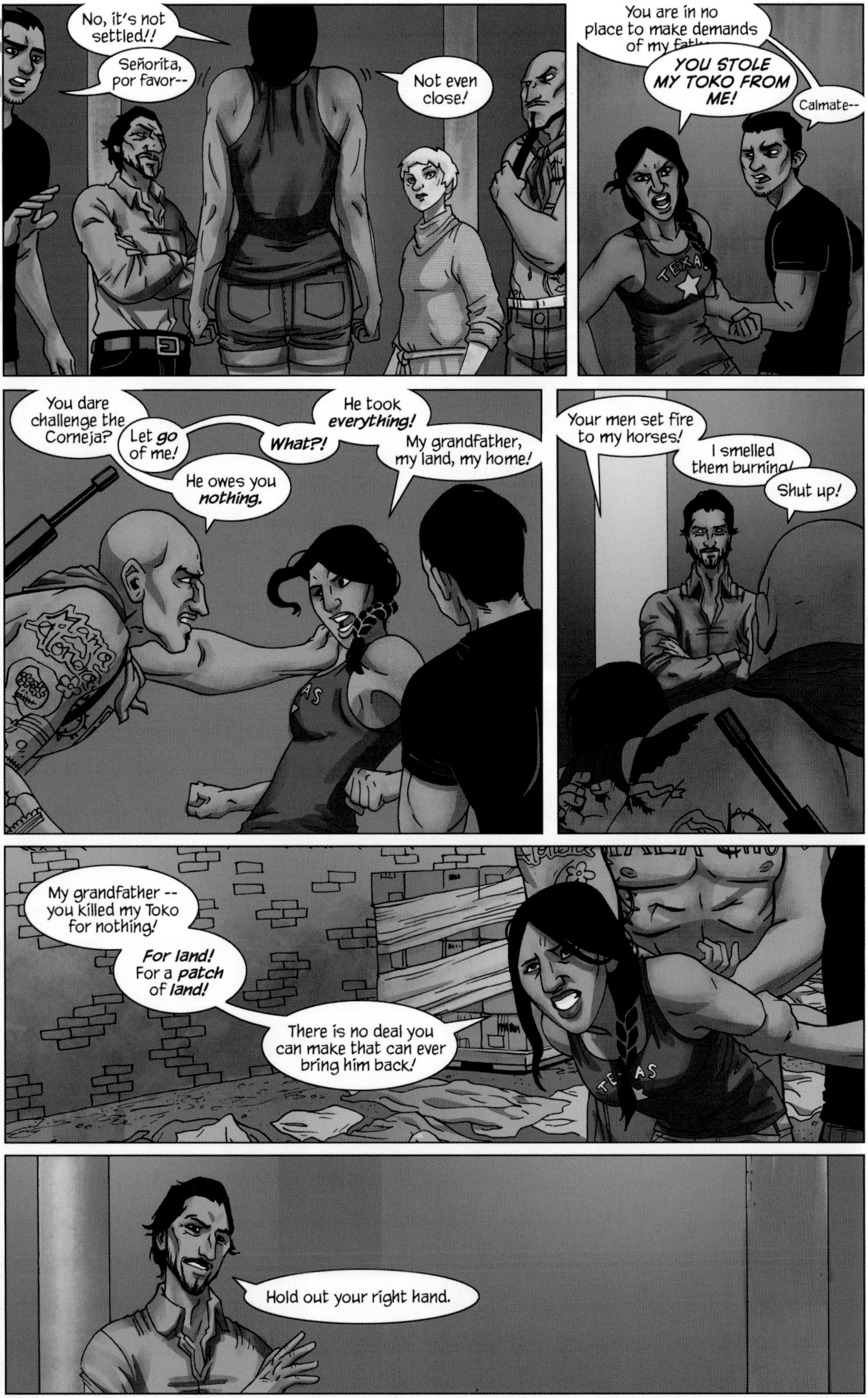
No, it's not settled!!
Señorita, por favor--
Not even close!
You are in no place to make demands of my fathe--
YOU STOLE MY TOKO FROM ME!
Calmate--
You dare challenge the Corneja?
Let go of me!
What?!
He took everything!
He owes you nothing.
My grandfather, my land, my home!
Your men set fire to my horses!
I smelled them burning!
Shut up!
My grandfather -- you killed my Toko for nothing!
For land! For a patch of land!
There is no deal you can make that can ever bring him back!
Hold out your right hand.

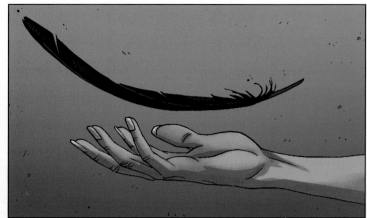

A feather that contains some of my Might.

You may use it once, and it will protect you.

Seriously?! There is nothing left of my ranch because of you!

Your gang stole away everything we worked for!

How *dare* you claim that your *feather* is worth the life of my grandfather?

THAT FEATHER IS WORTH ONE HUNDRED GRANDFATHERS!

FLAP!

TUG TUG

TEXAS

Go!

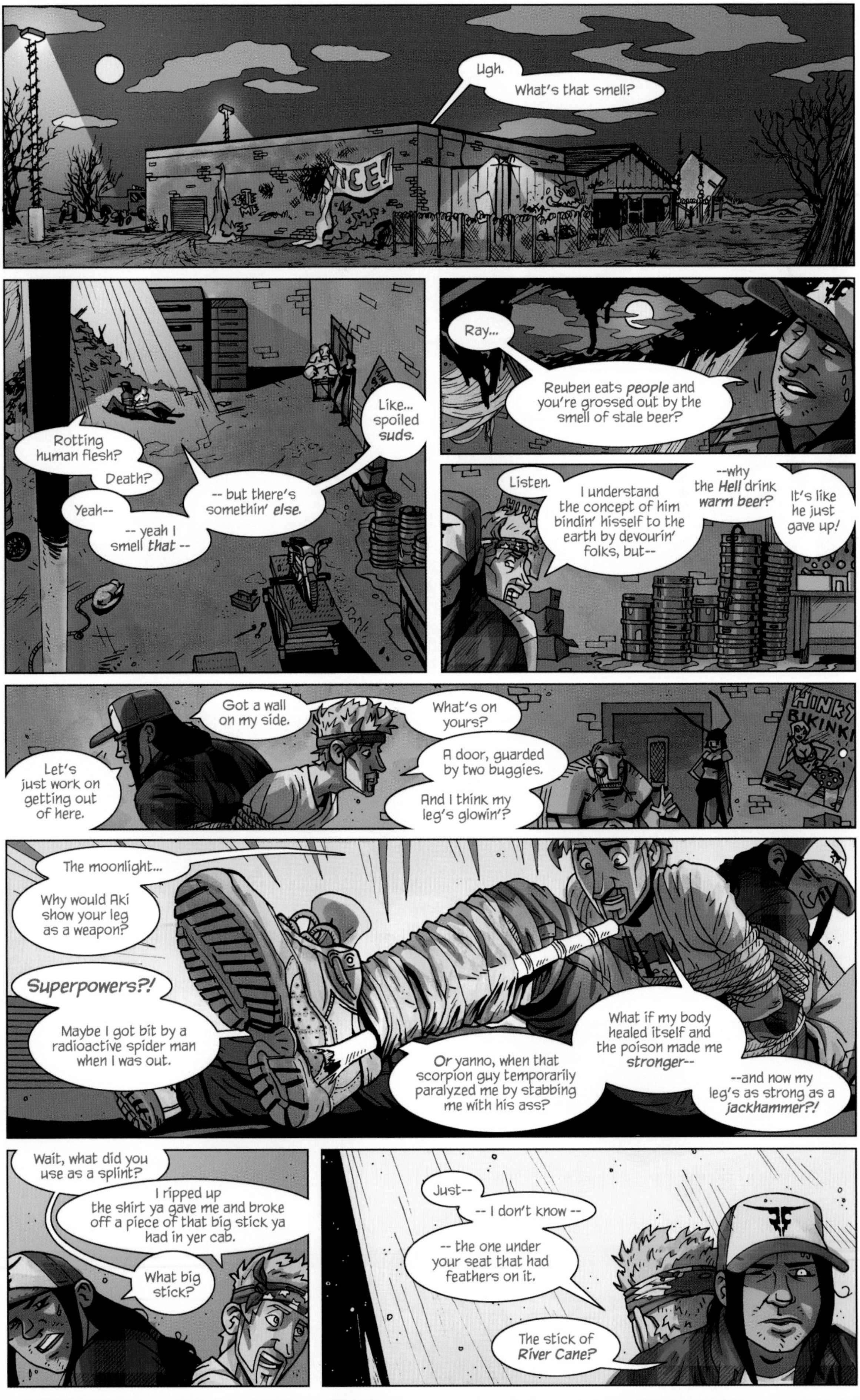
Ugh.
What's that smell?
VICE!
Rotting human flesh?
Death?
Yeah--
-- yeah I smell *that* --
-- but there's somethin' *else.*
Like... spoiled *suds.*
Ray...
Reuben eats *people* and you're grossed out by the smell of stale beer?
Listen.
I understand the concept of him bindin' hisself to the earth by devourin' folks, but--
--why the *Hell* drink *warm beer?*
It's like he just gave up!
Let's just work on getting out of here.
Got a wall on my side.
What's on yours?
A door, guarded by two buggies.
And I think my leg's glowin'?
HINKY BIKINKI
The moonlight...
Why would Aki show your leg as a weapon?
Superpowers?!
Maybe I got bit by a radioactive spider man when I was out.
Or yanno, when that scorpion guy temporarily paralyzed me by stabbing me with his ass?
What if my body healed itself and the poison made me *stronger--*
--and now my leg's as strong as a *jackhammer?!*
Wait, what did you use as a splint?
I ripped up the shirt ya gave me and broke off a piece of that big stick ya had in yer cab.
What big stick?
Just--
-- I don't know --
-- the one under your seat that had feathers on it.
The stick of *River Cane?*

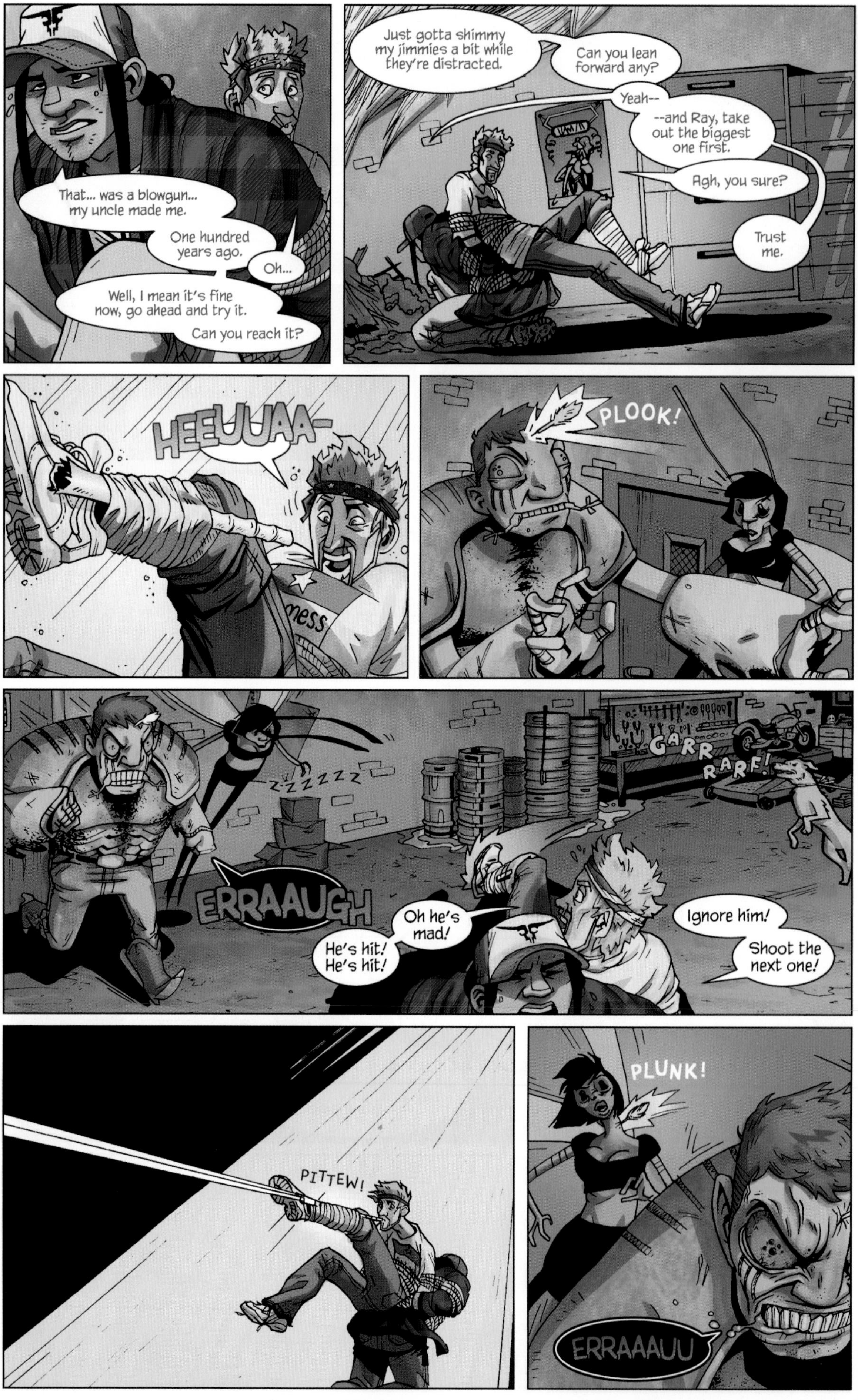
That... was a blowgun... my uncle made me.
One hundred years ago.
Oh...
Well, I mean it's fine now, go ahead and try it.
Can you reach it?
Just gotta shimmy my jimmies a bit while they're distracted.
Can you lean forward any?
Yeah--
--and Ray, take out the biggest one first.
Agh, you sure?
Trust me.
HEEUUAA-
PLOOK!
ZZZZZZ
GARR
RARF!
ERRAAUGH
He's hit! He's hit!
Oh he's mad!
Ignore him!
Shoot the next one!
PITTEW!
PLUNK!
ERRAAAUU

FWUMP!

DURR

SCRITCH
SCRITCH

Whew --
sleepy darts!

Thank goodness.

Was that someone
shouting just now?

The witch.
She's on her way.

Of course
she is.

Stay here
and be a good
boy, Tami.

We'll
be back.

WHIMPERRR

I'll take care of her,
you find Reuben.

But
your
leg--

Don't mess
with
Texas

Is busted.
I'm just thinking,
if he's got Billie...

You sure you'll
be okay?

You're right.

Be safer out
here fightin' a witch
than in there with
you fightin' him.

Now go
on n'get.

WATC PRO

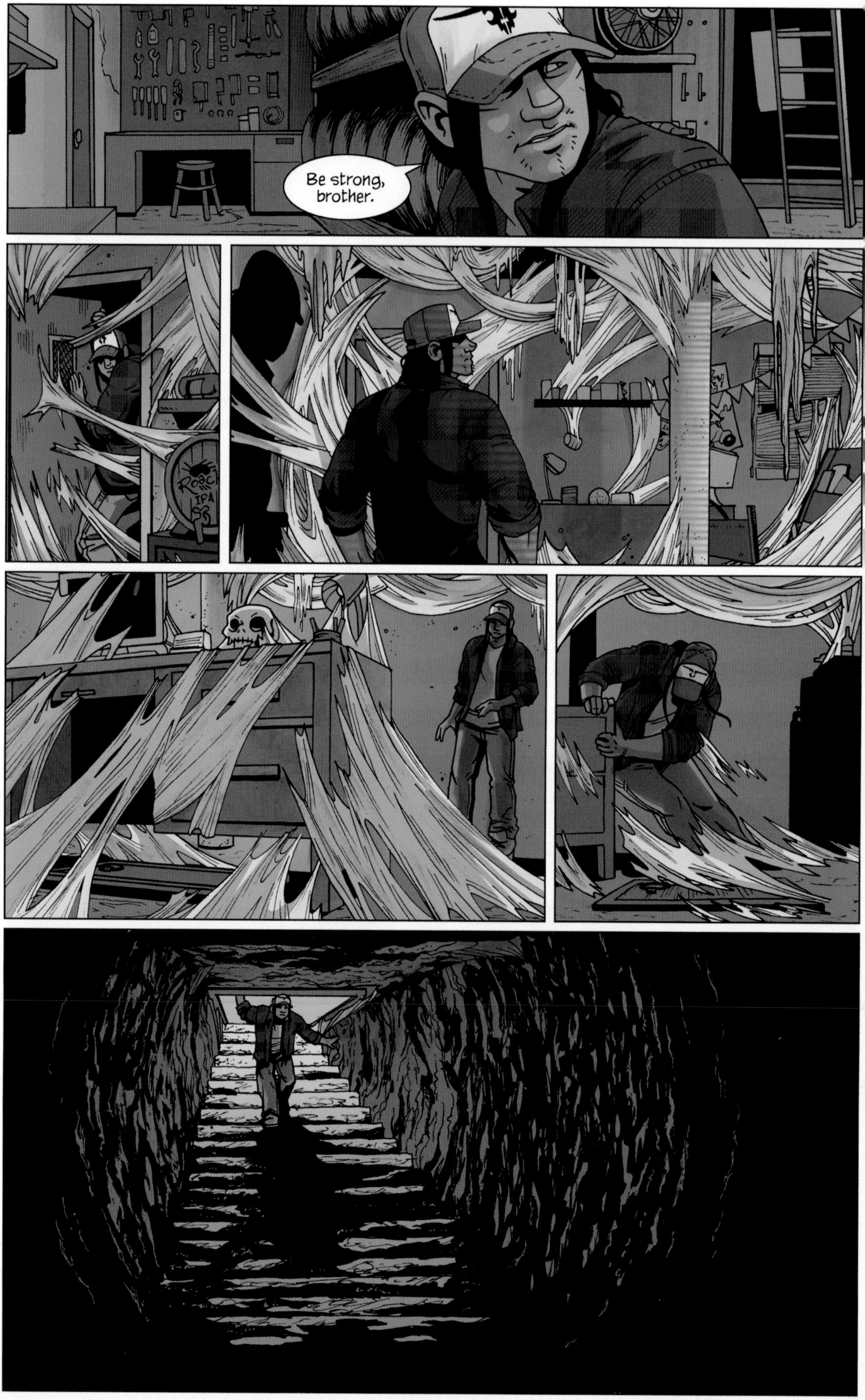
Be strong, brother.
Roach IPA

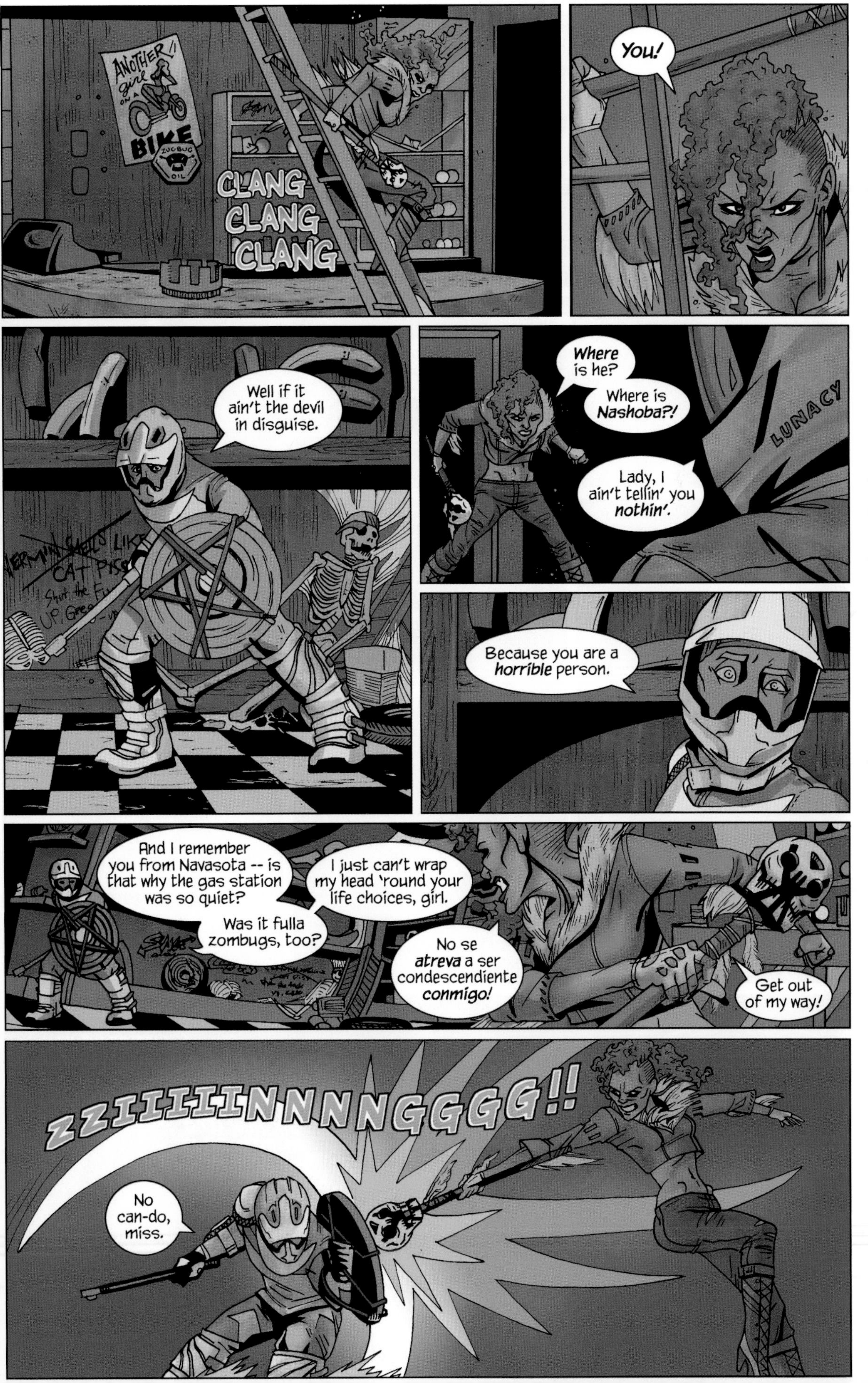
ANOTHER girl ON A BIKE
ZOMBUG OIL
CLANG
CLANG
CLANG
You!
Well if it ain't the devil in disguise.
Where is he?
Where is Nashoba?!
LUNACY
Lady, I ain't tellin' you nothin'.
Because you are a horrible person.
And I remember you from Navasota -- is that why the gas station was so quiet?
Was it fulla zombugs, too?
I just can't wrap my head 'round your life choices, girl.
No se atreva a ser condescendiente conmigo!
Get out of my way!
ZZIIIIIINNNNNGGGGG!!
No can-do, miss.

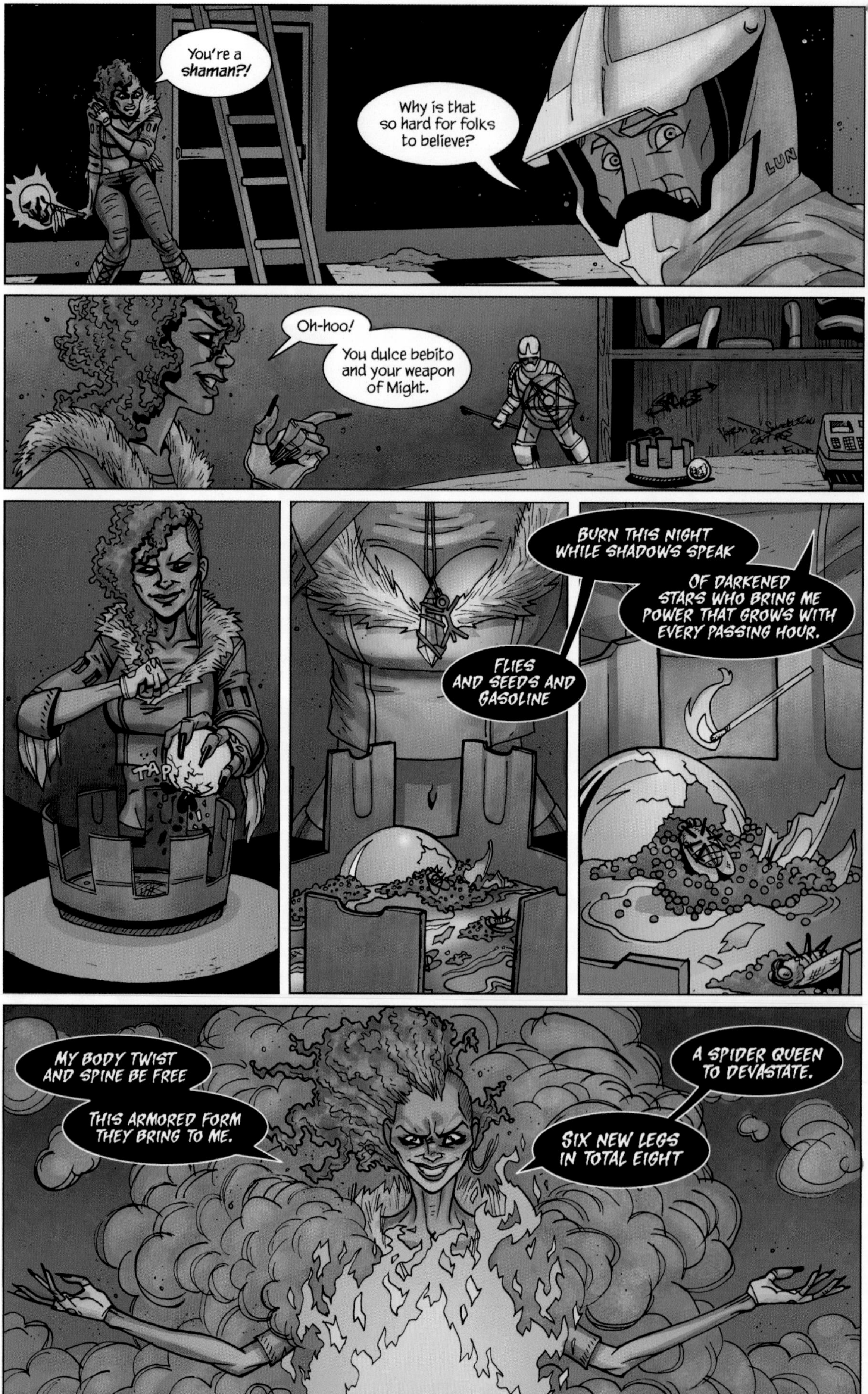
You're a shaman?!
Why is that so hard for folks to believe?
LUN
Oh-hoo!
You dulce bebito and your weapon of Might.
TAP
BURN THIS NIGHT WHILE SHADOWS SPEAK
FLIES AND SEEDS AND GASOLINE
OF DARKENED STARS WHO BRING ME POWER THAT GROWS WITH EVERY PASSING HOUR.
MY BODY TWIST AND SPINE BE FREE
THIS ARMORED FORM THEY BRING TO ME.
SIX NEW LEGS IN TOTAL EIGHT
A SPIDER QUEEN TO DEVASTATE.

HER
Oh Lord...
TAM
TING!
TAMM
You think you will break me with your *Moon charms?*
You're too--
MMPH!
--late!

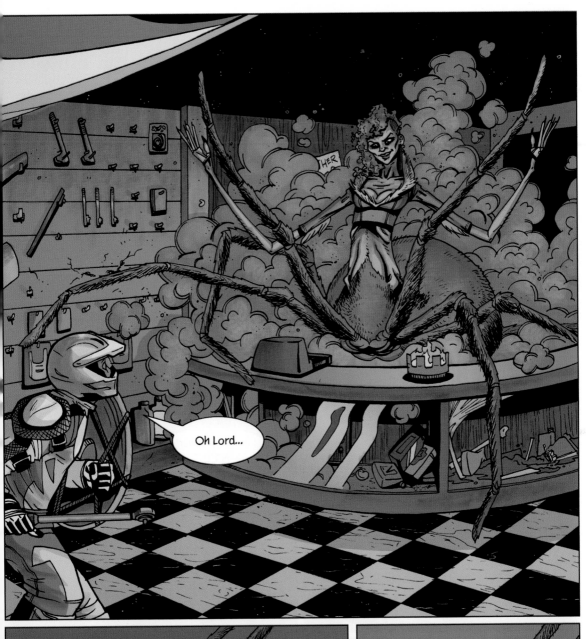

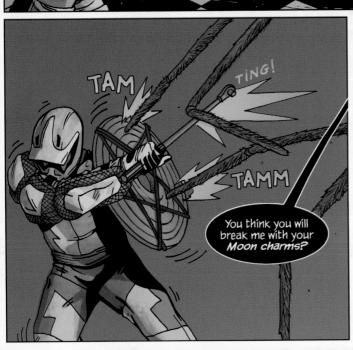

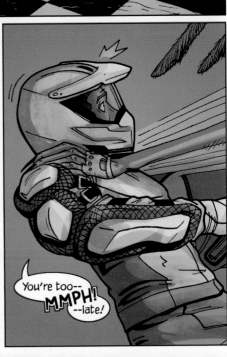

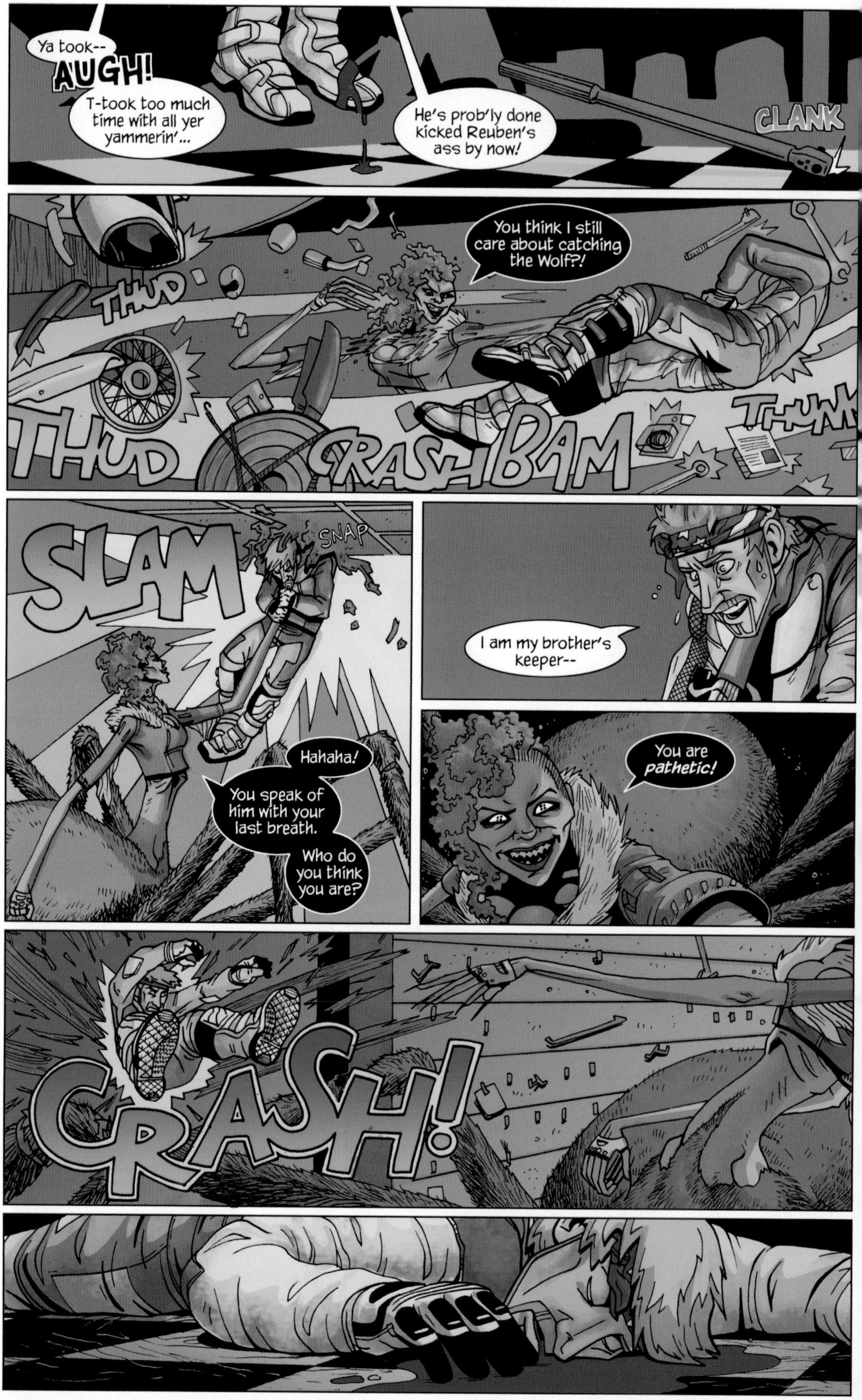
Ya took--
AUGH!
T-took too much time with all yer yammerin'...
He's prob'ly done kicked Reuben's ass by now!
CLANK
THUD
You think I still care about catching the Wolf?!
THUD
CRASH
BAM
THUNK
SLAM
SNAP
I am my brother's keeper--
Hahaha!
You speak of him with your last breath.
Who do you think you are?
You are *pathetic!*
CRASH!

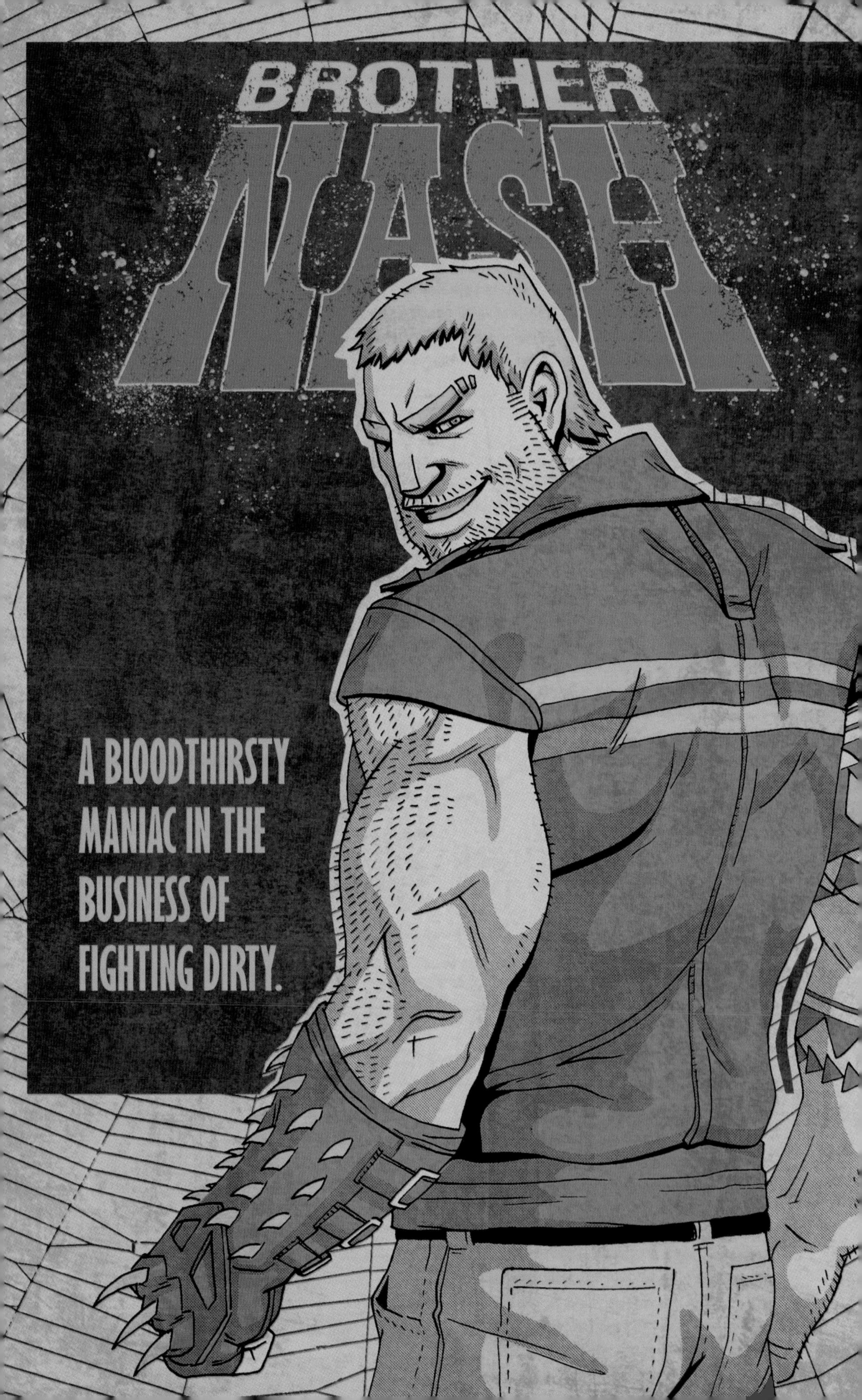
BROTHER
NASH
A BLOODTHIRSTY
MANIAC IN THE
BUSINESS OF
FIGHTING DIRTY.

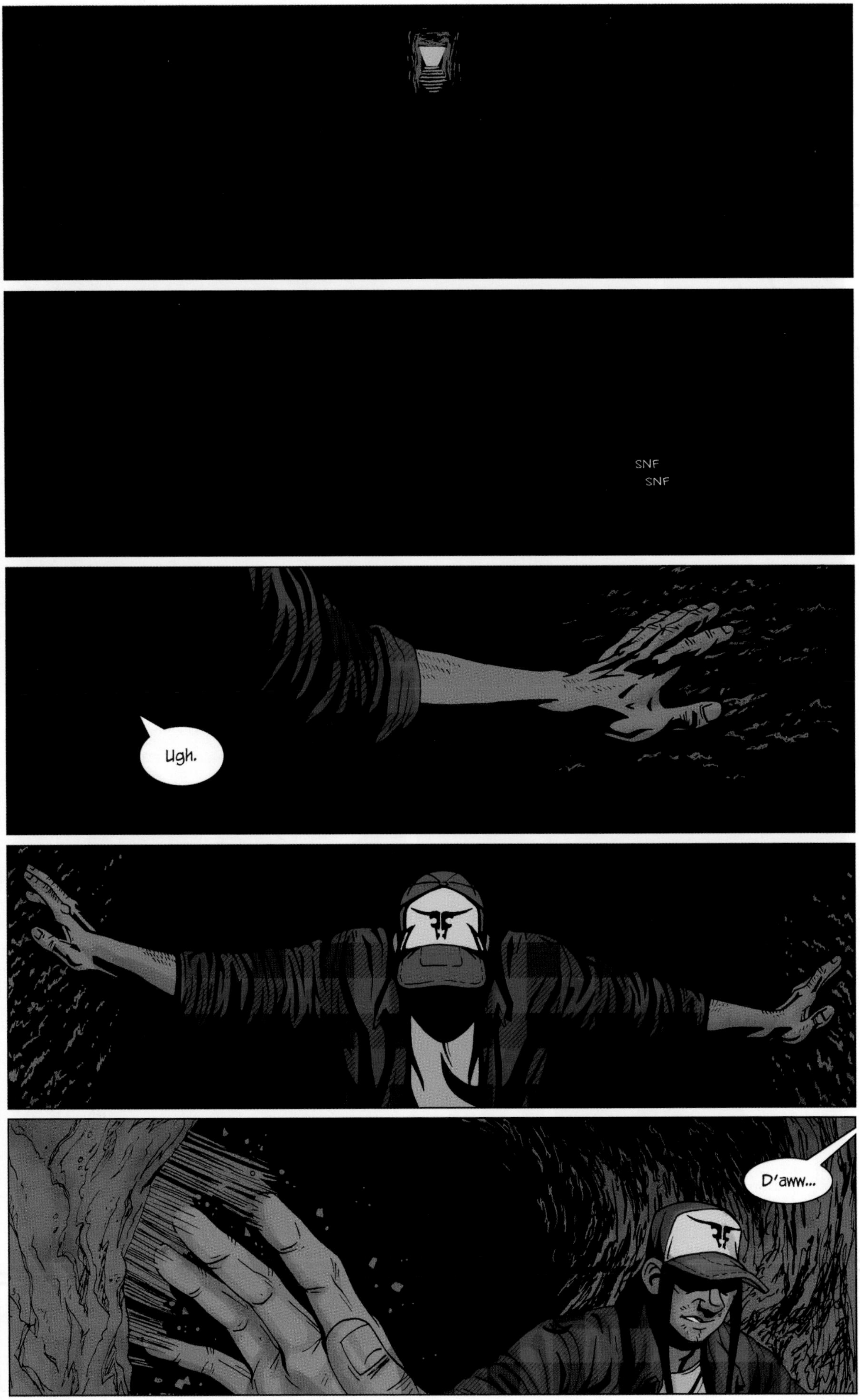
SNF
SNF
Ugh.
D'aww...

... Puppy wanna play?

Not here to play around, *Reuben*.

I'm here to end all of this.

The Hell do you mean "end all of this"? --

--the party just arrived!

Go get him, boys!

WOOSH

The witch in your lobby says you've been eating people.

POP!

And I feel more *alive* than *ever!*

They're actually pretty tasty.

WHAM!

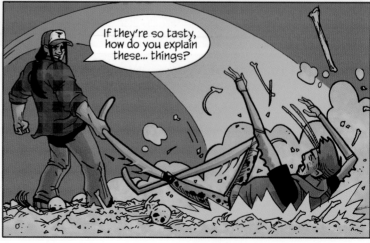

If they're so tasty, how do you explain these... things?

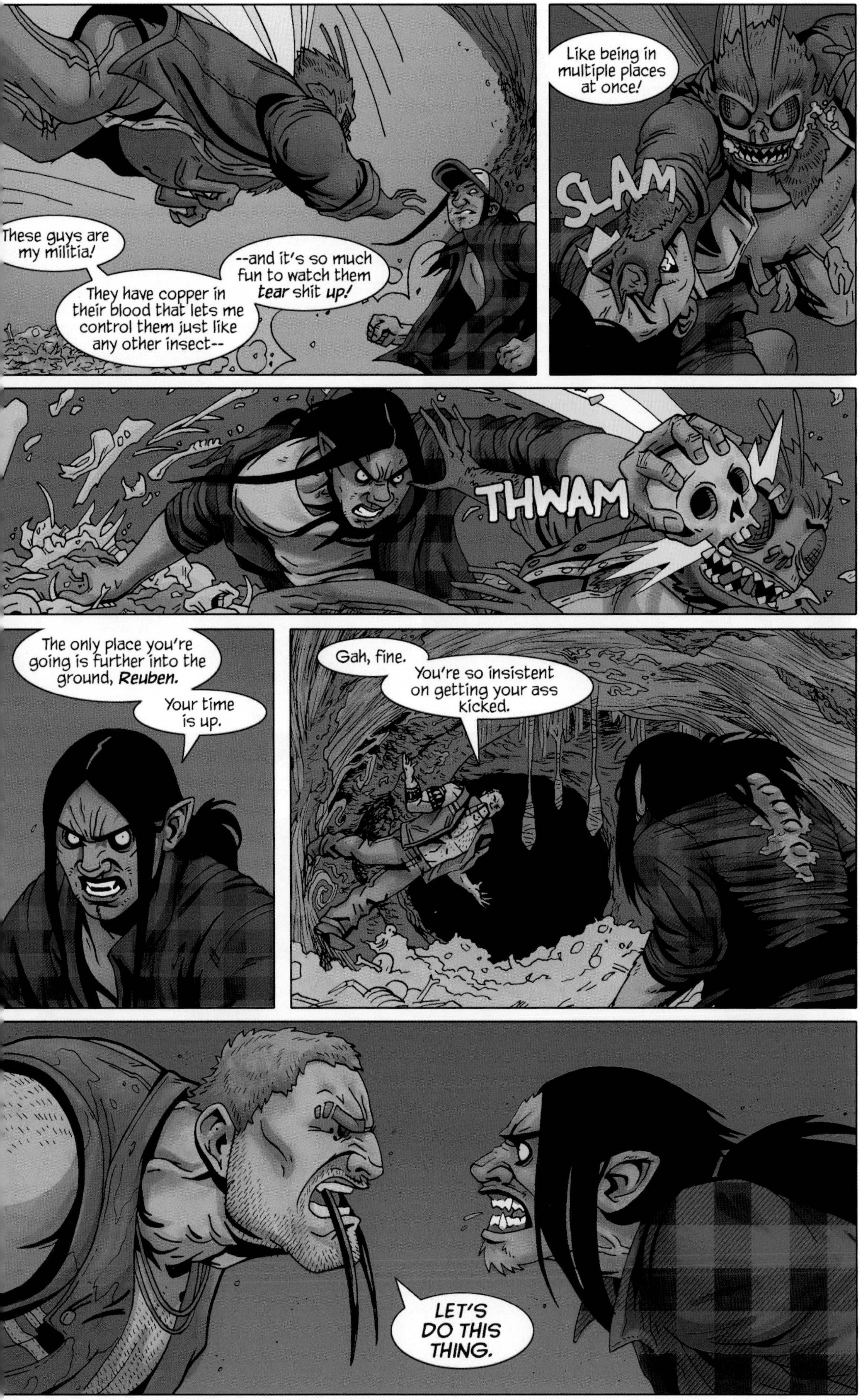
These guys are my militia!
They have copper in their blood that lets me control them just like any other insect--
--and it's so much fun to watch them *tear* shit *up!*
Like being in multiple places at once!
SLAM
THWAM
The only place you're going is further into the ground, *Reuben.*
Your time is up.
Gah, fine.
You're so insistent on getting your ass kicked.
LET'S DO THIS THING.

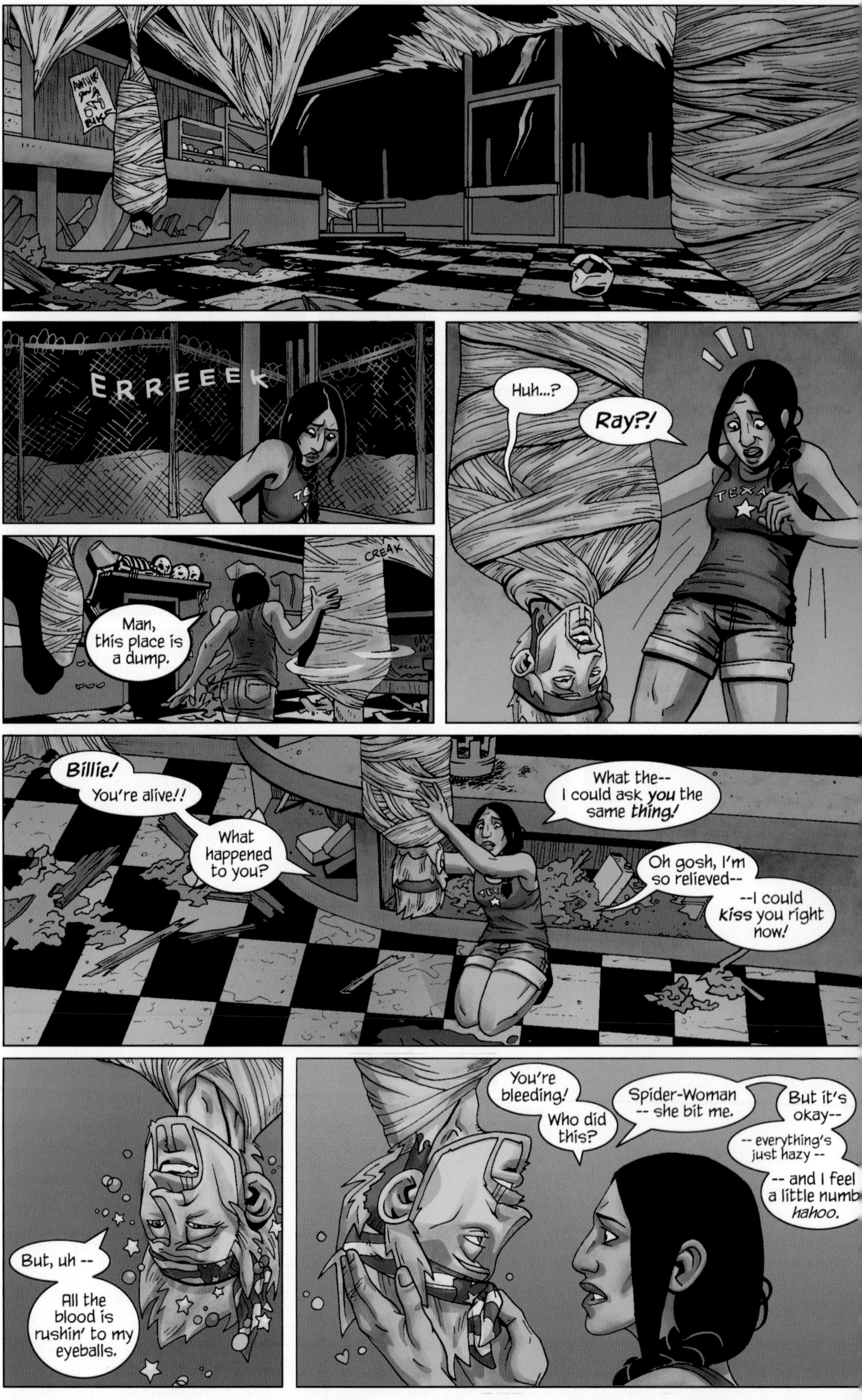
ERREEEK
Man, this place is a dump.
CREAK
Huh...?
Ray?!
Billie! You're alive!!
What happened to you?
What the-- I could ask you the same thing!
Oh gosh, I'm so relieved--
--I could kiss you right now!
But, uh --
All the blood is rushin' to my eyeballs.
You're bleeding!
Who did this?
Spider-Woman -- she bit me.
But it's okay--
-- everything's just hazy --
-- and I feel a little numb hahoo.

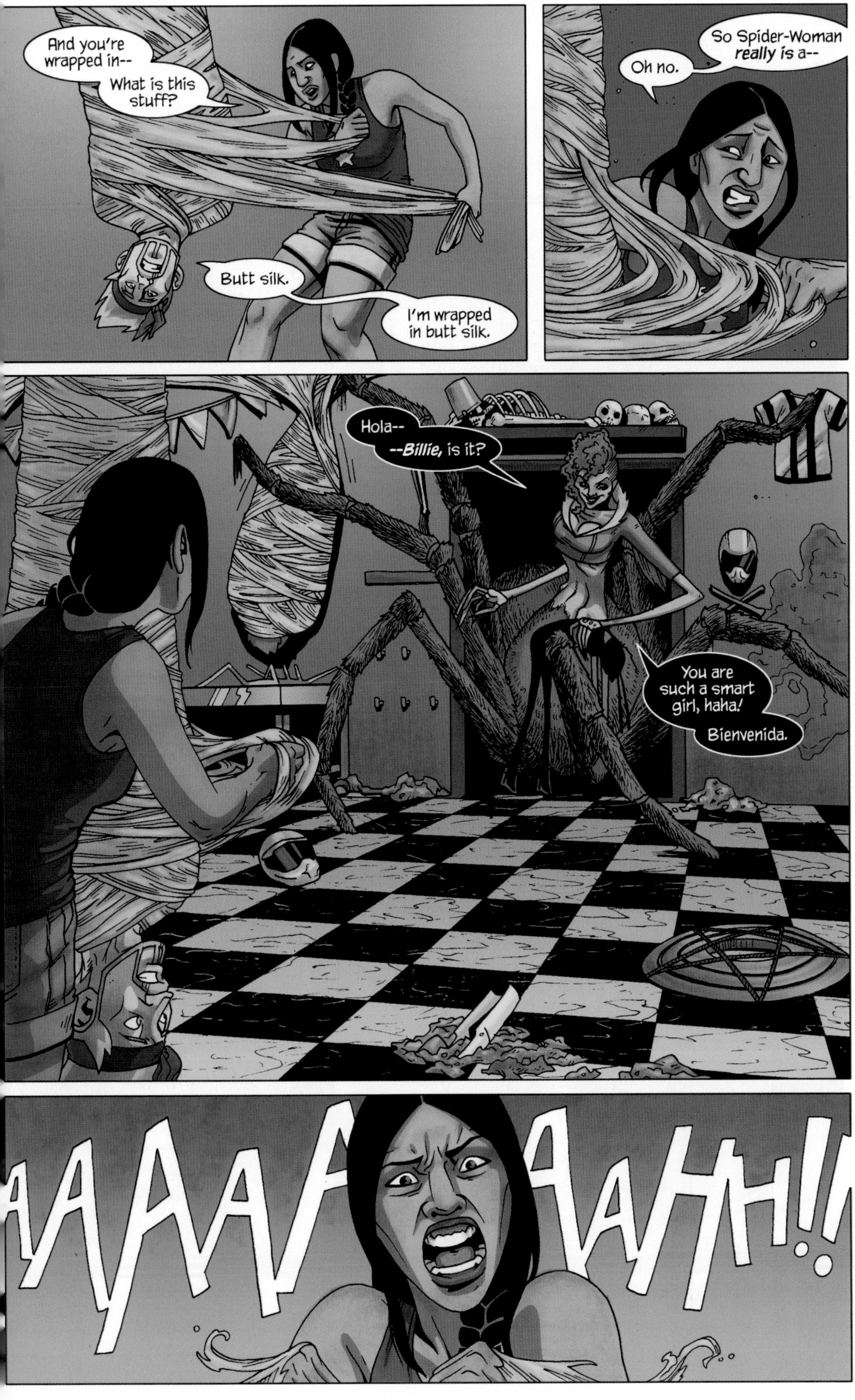
And you're wrapped in--
What is this stuff?
Butt silk.
I'm wrapped in butt silk.
Oh no.
So Spider-Woman *really* is a--
Hola--
--*Billie,* is it?
You are such a smart girl, haha!
Bienvenida.
AAAAAAAAAH!!!

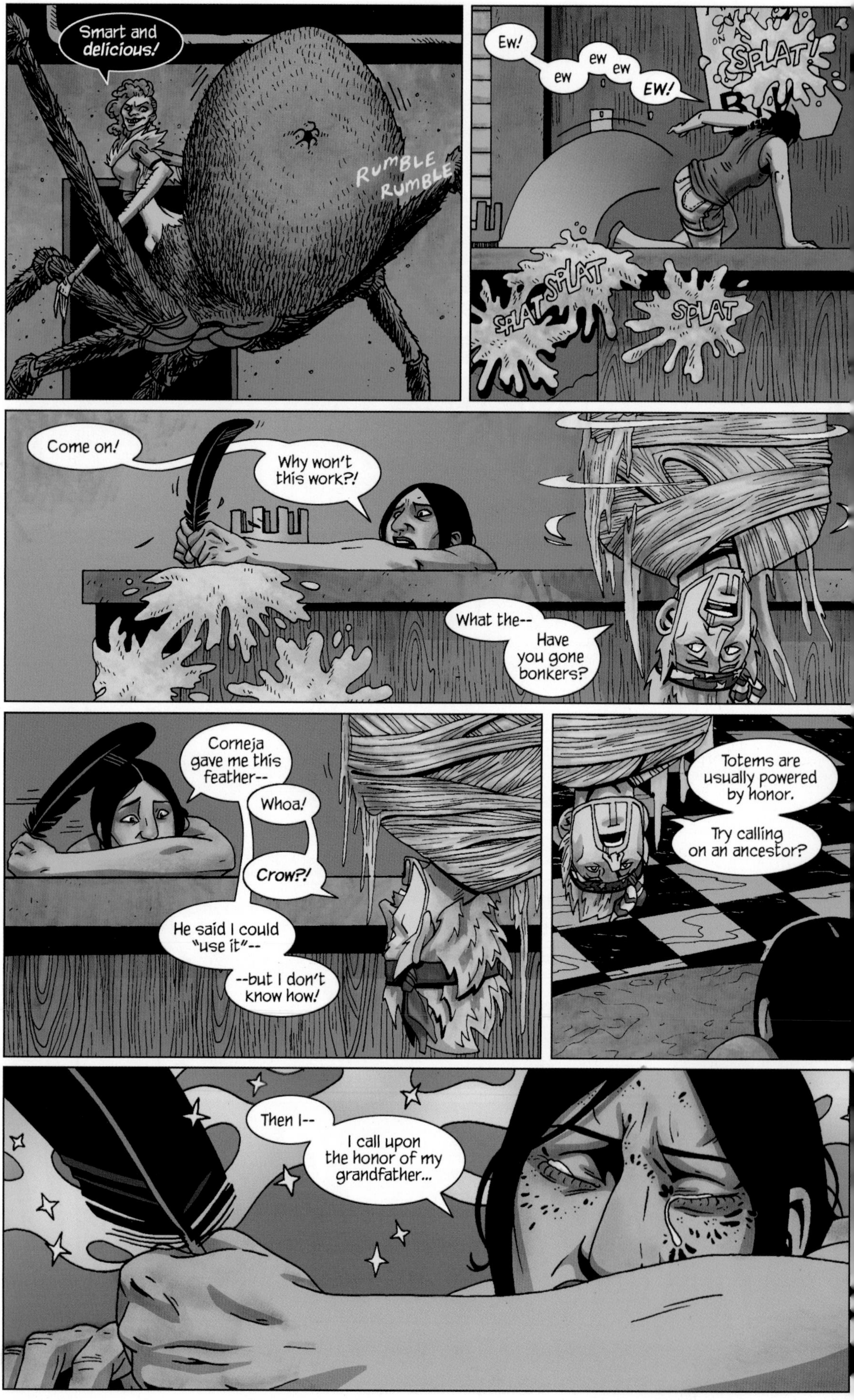
Smart and delicious!
RUMBLE RUMBLE
Ew! ew ew ew EW!
SPLAT!
SPLAT SPLAT
SPLAT
Come on!
Why won't this work?!
What the--
Have you gone bonkers?
Corneja gave me this feather--
Whoa!
Crow?!
He said I could "use it"--
--but I don't know how!
Totems are usually powered by honor.
Try calling on an ancestor?
Then I--
I call upon the honor of my grandfather...

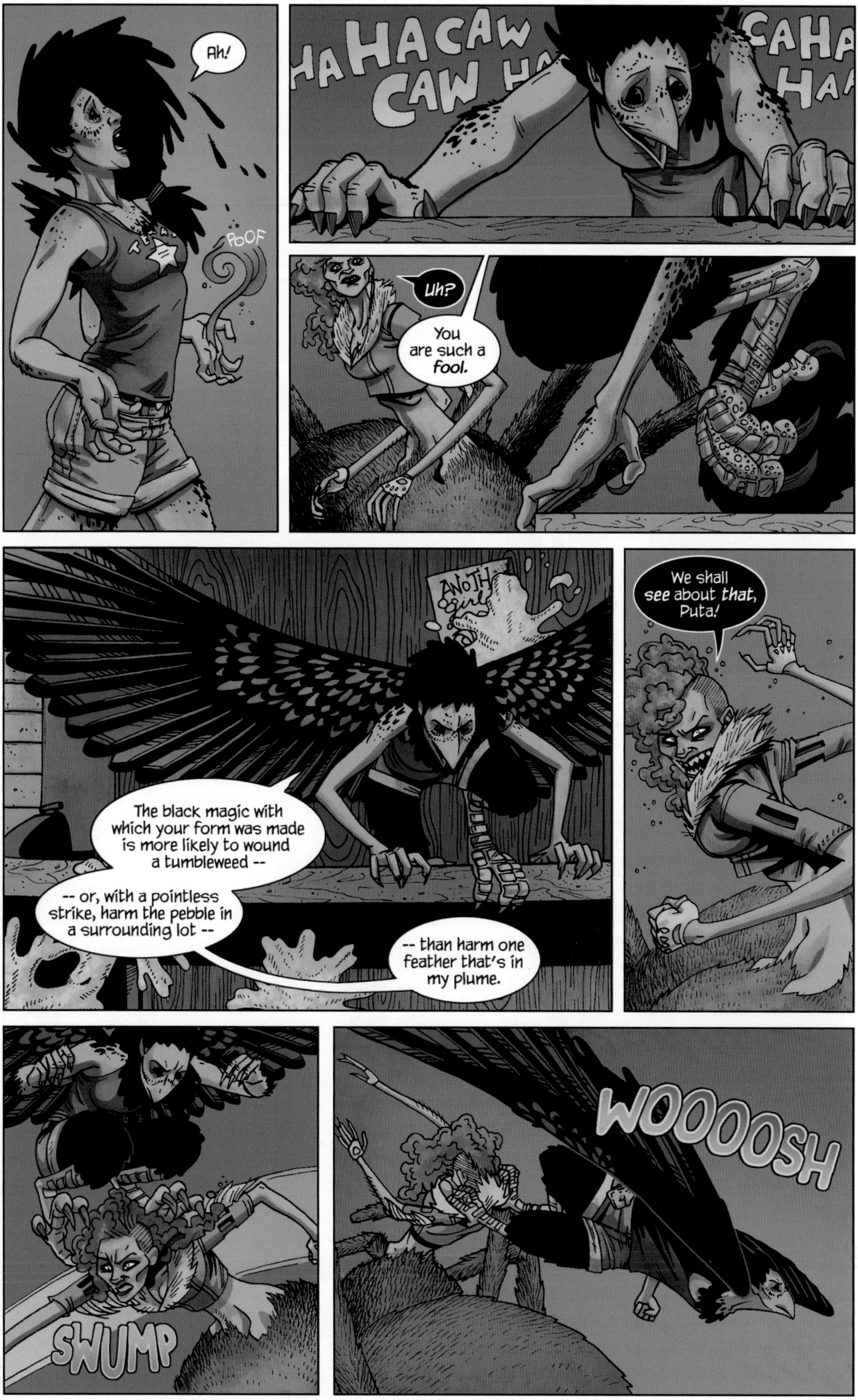
Ah!
POOF
HAHACAW
CAW HA
CAHA
HA
Uh?
You are such a *fool.*
ANOTH girl
The black magic with which your form was made is more likely to wound a tumbleweed --
-- or, with a pointless strike, harm the pebble in a surrounding lot --
-- than harm one feather that's in my plume.
We shall *see* about *that,* Puta!
SWUMP
WOOOOSH

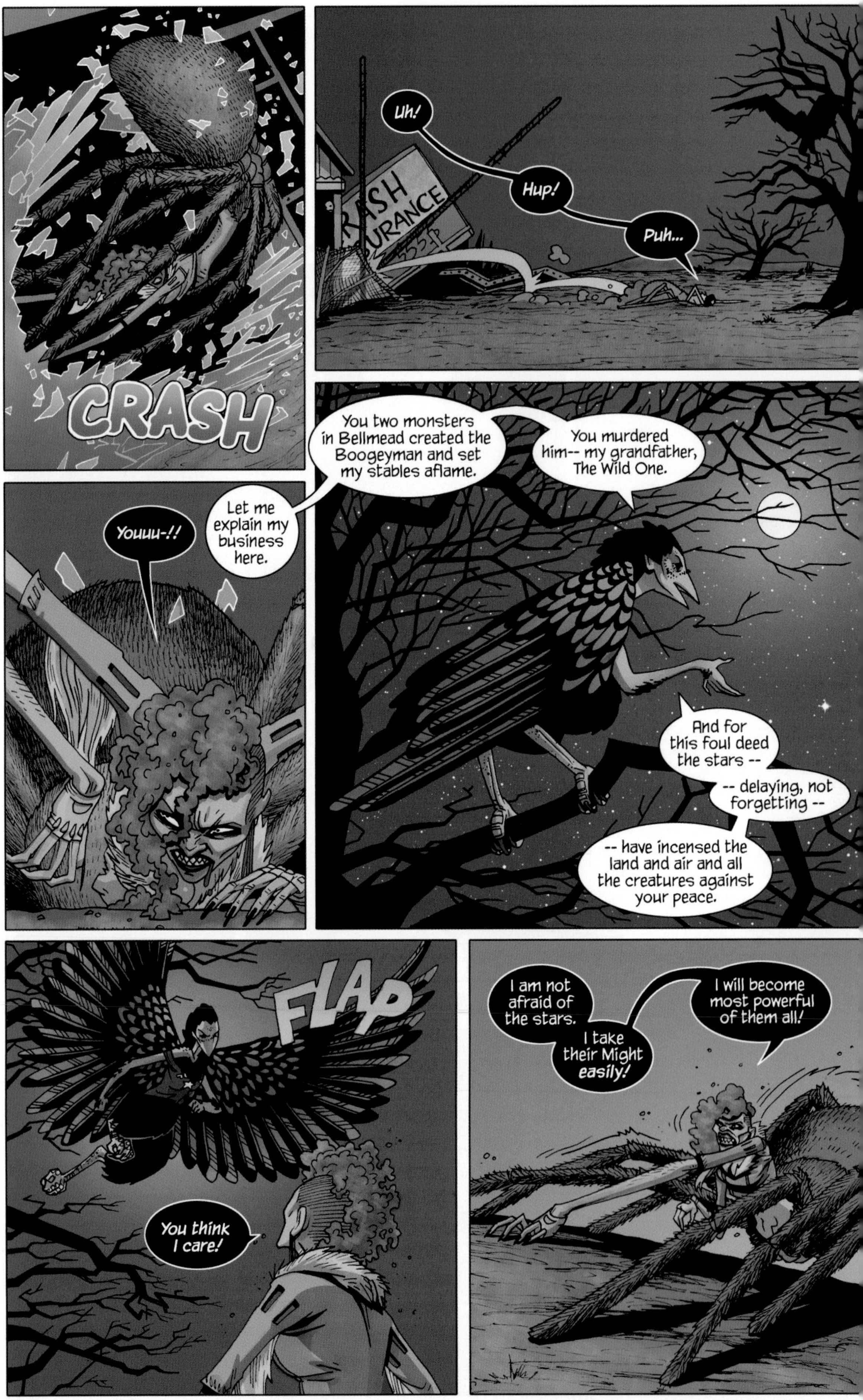
CRASH
Uh!
Hup!
Puh...
Youuu-!!
Let me explain my business here.
You two monsters in Bellmead created the Boogeyman and set my stables aflame.
You murdered him-- my grandfather, The Wild One.
And for this foul deed the stars --
-- delaying, not forgetting --
-- have incensed the land and air and all the creatures against your peace.
FLAP
You think I care!
I am not afraid of the stars.
I take their Might easily!
I will become most powerful of them all!

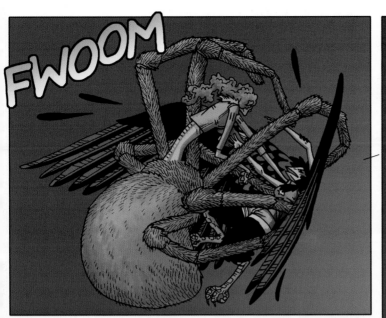

FWOOM

Aah?!

SNAP

Ee-yahh!

Crah!

CRACK

AAHHHHHHH!!!

Ray?

Ray, please...

Wake up...

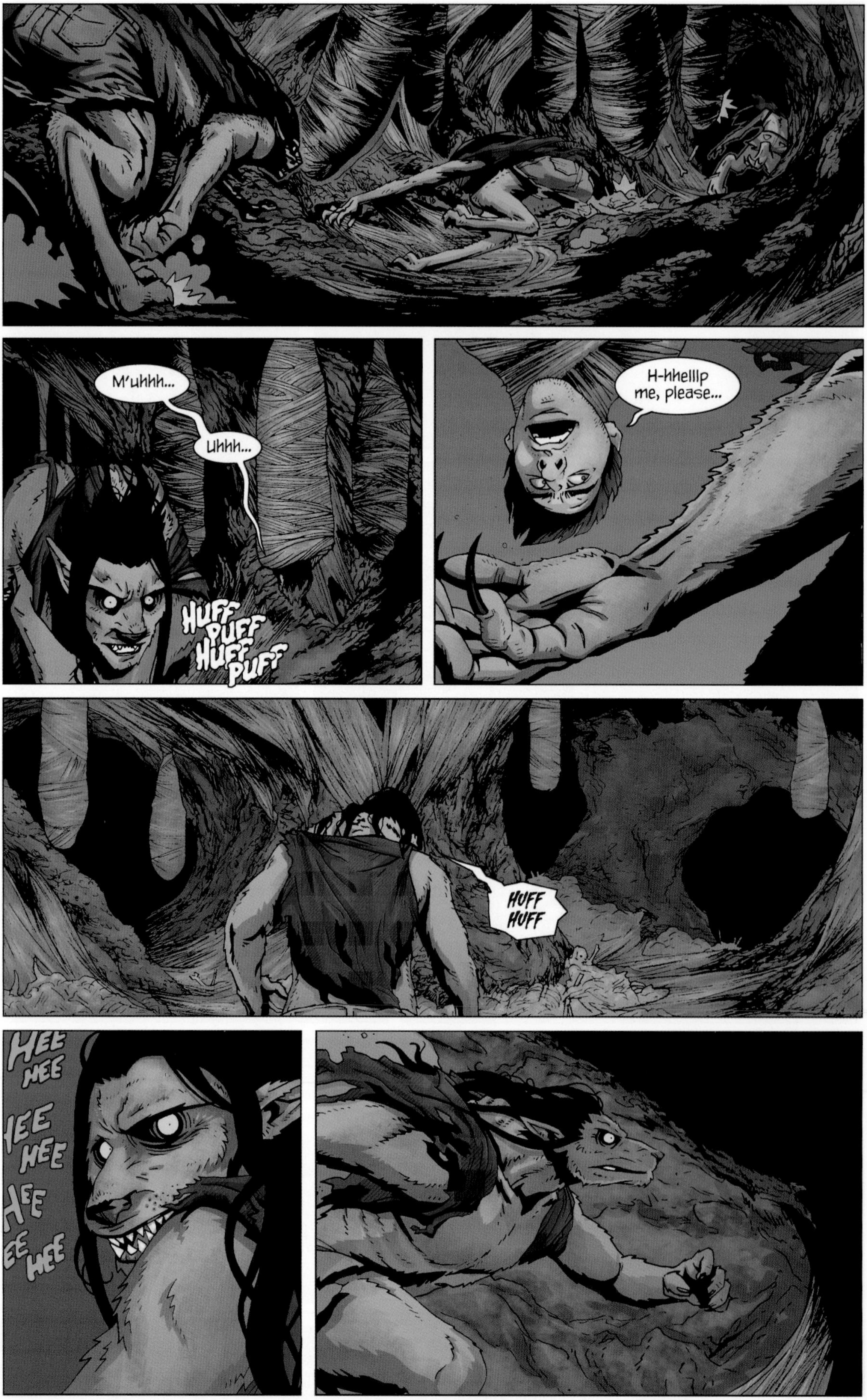

M'uhhh...
uhhh...
HUFF PUFF HUFF PUFF
H-hhelllp me, please...
HUFF HUFF
HEE HEE
HEE HEE
HEE
HEE HEE

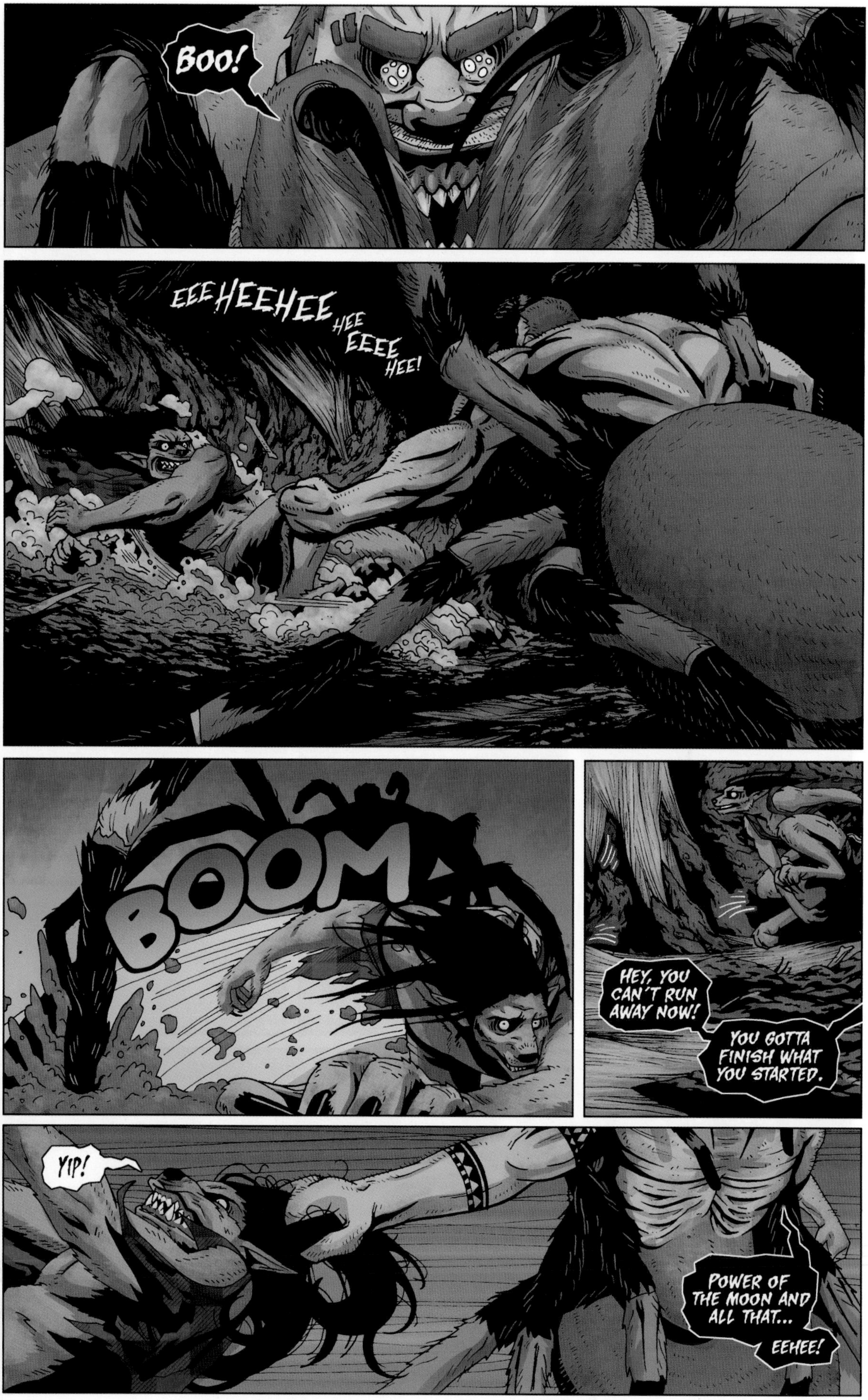
BOO!
EEE HEEHEE HEE EEEE HEE!
BOOM
HEY, YOU CAN'T RUN AWAY NOW!
YOU GOTTA FINISH WHAT YOU STARTED.
YIP!
POWER OF THE MOON AND ALL THAT...
EEHEE!

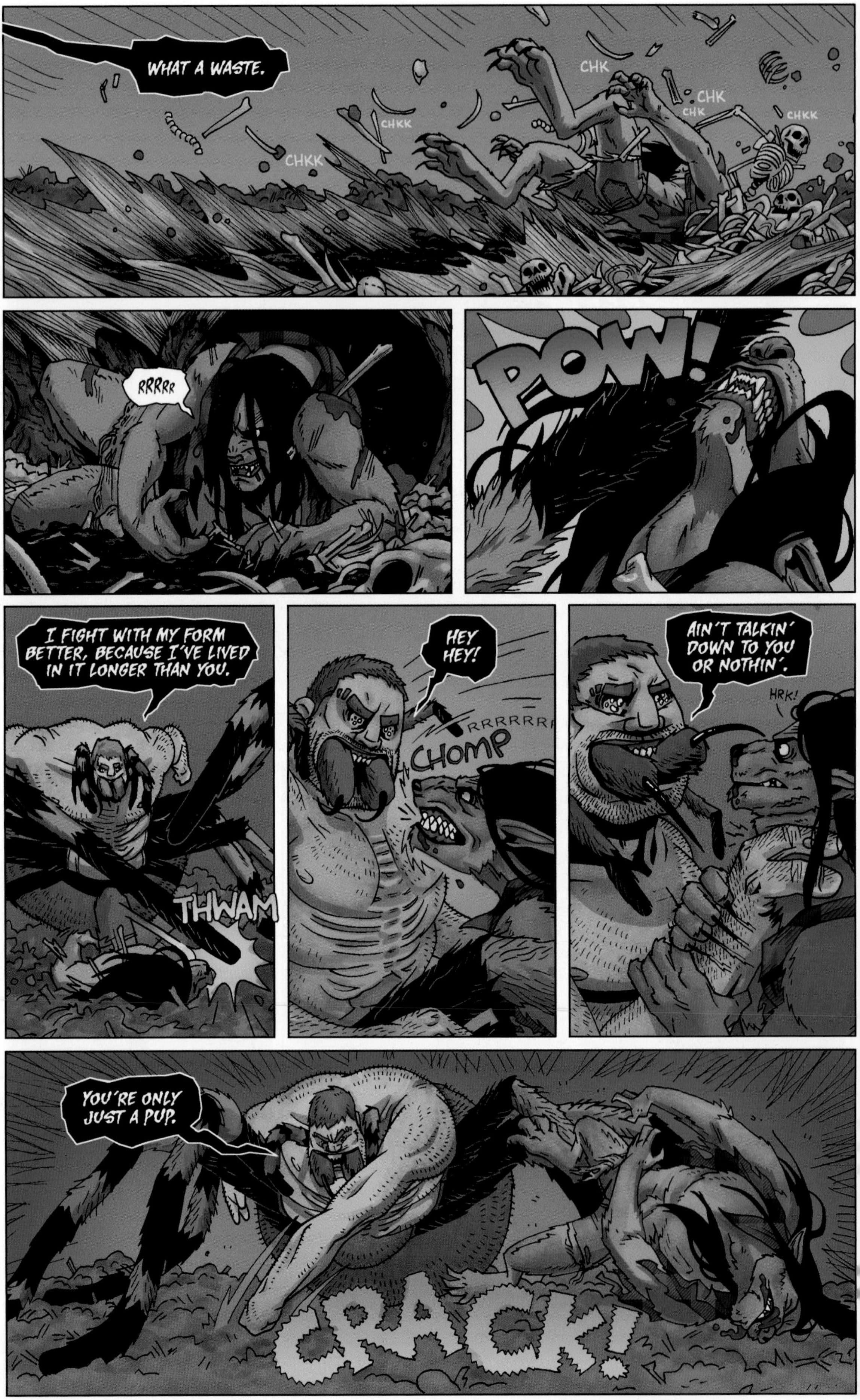
WHAT A WASTE.
CHK
CHK
CHK
CHKK
CHKK
CHKK
RRRRR
POW!
I FIGHT WITH MY FORM BETTER, BECAUSE I'VE LIVED IN IT LONGER THAN YOU.
THWAM
HEY HEY!
RRRRRRR
CHOMP
AIN'T TALKIN' DOWN TO YOU OR NOTHIN'.
HRK!
YOU'RE ONLY JUST A PUP.
CRACK!

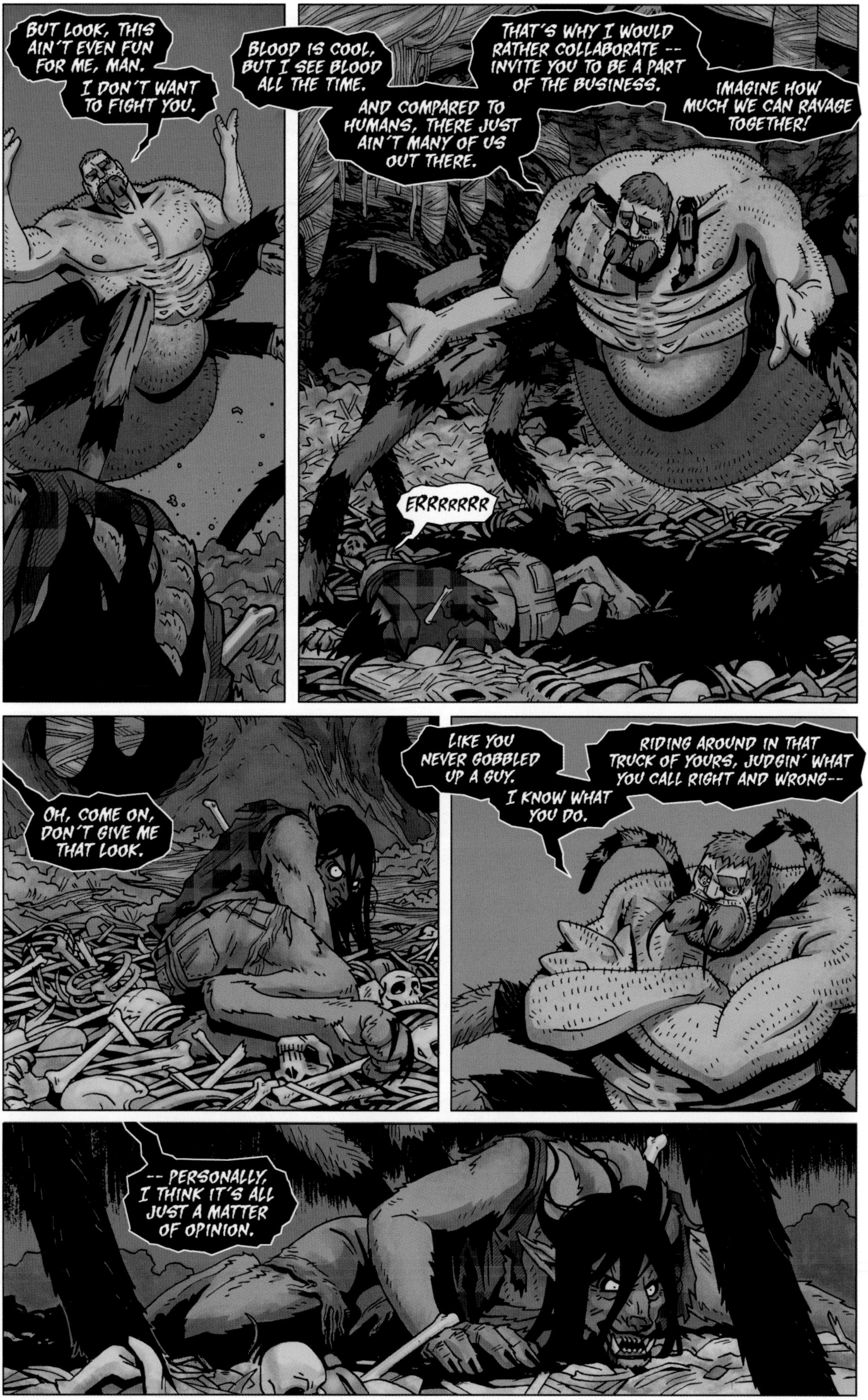
BUT LOOK, THIS AIN'T EVEN FUN FOR ME, MAN.
I DON'T WANT TO FIGHT YOU.
BLOOD IS COOL, BUT I SEE BLOOD ALL THE TIME.
AND COMPARED TO HUMANS, THERE JUST AIN'T MANY OF US OUT THERE.
THAT'S WHY I WOULD RATHER COLLABORATE -- INVITE YOU TO BE A PART OF THE BUSINESS.
IMAGINE HOW MUCH WE CAN RAVAGE TOGETHER!
ERRRRRRR
OH, COME ON, DON'T GIVE ME THAT LOOK.
LIKE YOU NEVER GOBBLED UP A GUY.
I KNOW WHAT YOU DO.
RIDING AROUND IN THAT TRUCK OF YOURS, JUDGIN' WHAT YOU CALL RIGHT AND WRONG--
-- PERSONALLY, I THINK IT'S ALL JUST A MATTER OF OPINION.

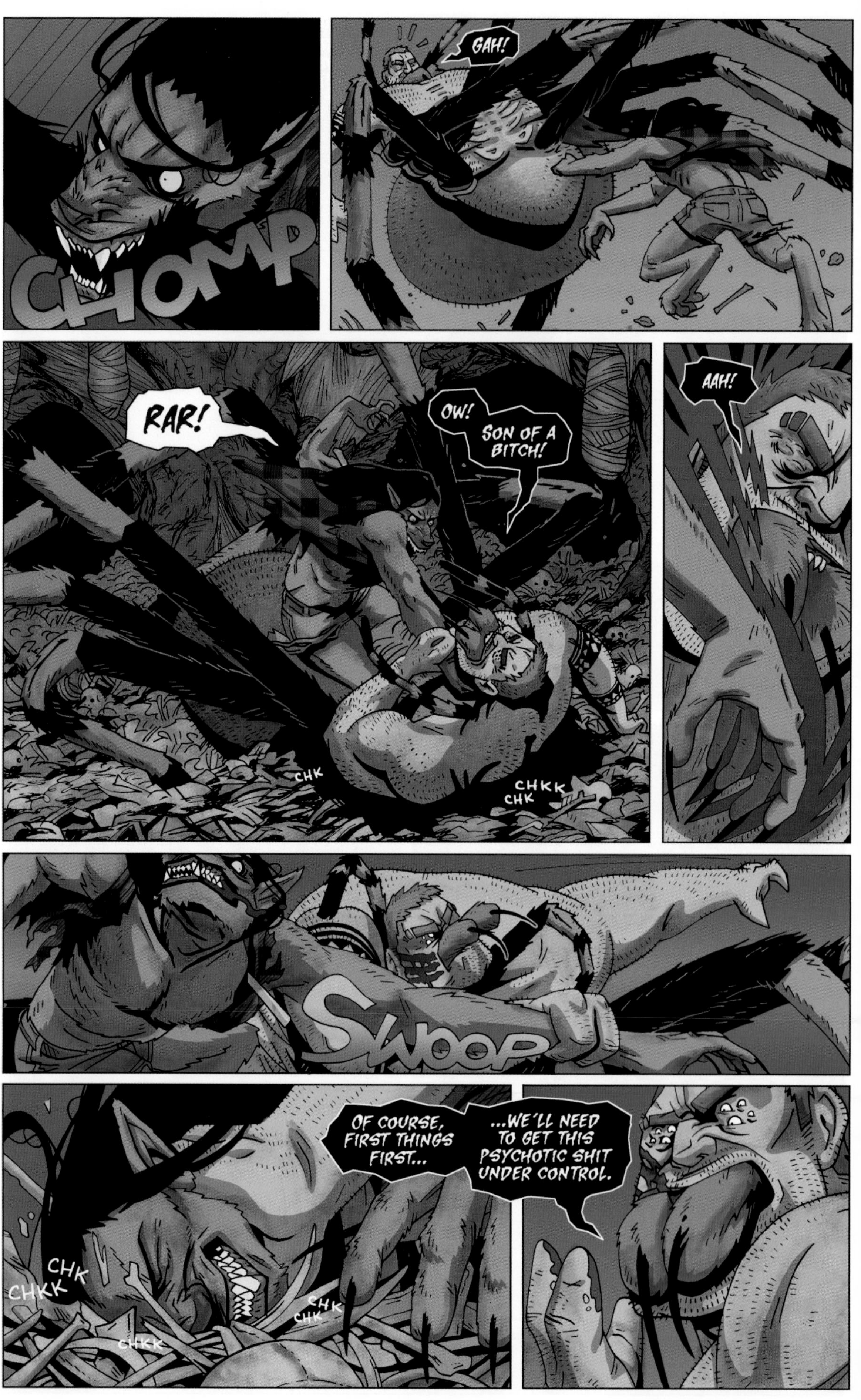
CHOMP
GAH!
RAR!
OW!
SON OF A BITCH!
CHK
CHKK
CHK
AAH!
SWOOP
CHK
CHKK
CHK
CHK
CHKK
OF COURSE, FIRST THINGS FIRST...
...WE'LL NEED TO GET THIS PSYCHOTIC SHIT UNDER CONTROL.

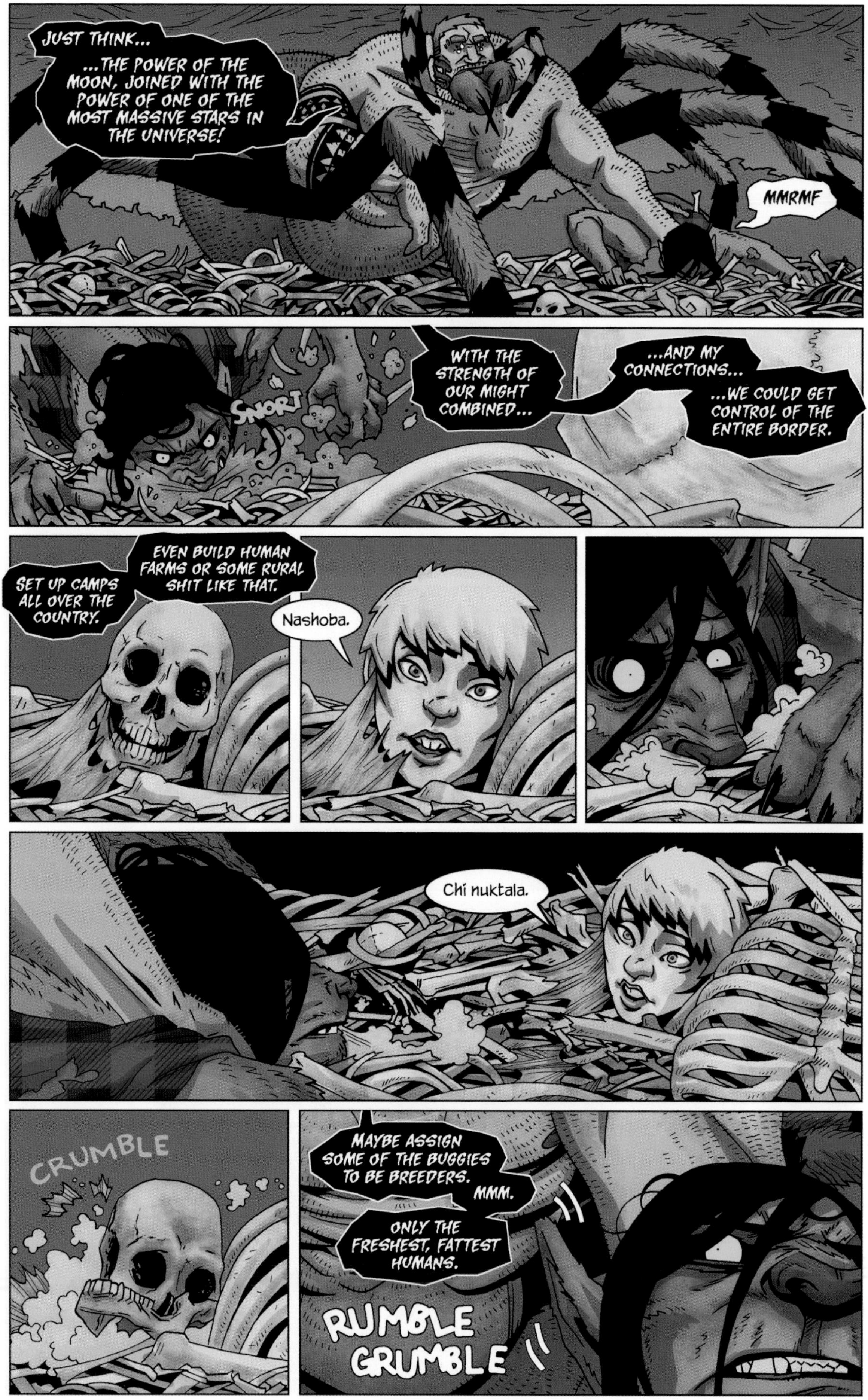

JUST THINK...
...THE POWER OF THE MOON, JOINED WITH THE POWER OF ONE OF THE MOST MASSIVE STARS IN THE UNIVERSE!
MMRMF
SNORT
WITH THE STRENGTH OF OUR MIGHT COMBINED...
...AND MY CONNECTIONS...
...WE COULD GET CONTROL OF THE ENTIRE BORDER.
SET UP CAMPS ALL OVER THE COUNTRY.
EVEN BUILD HUMAN FARMS OR SOME RURAL SHIT LIKE THAT.
Nashoba.
Chi nuktala.
CRUMBLE
MAYBE ASSIGN SOME OF THE BUGGIES TO BE BREEDERS.
MMM.
ONLY THE FRESHEST, FATTEST HUMANS.
RUMBLE GRUMBLE

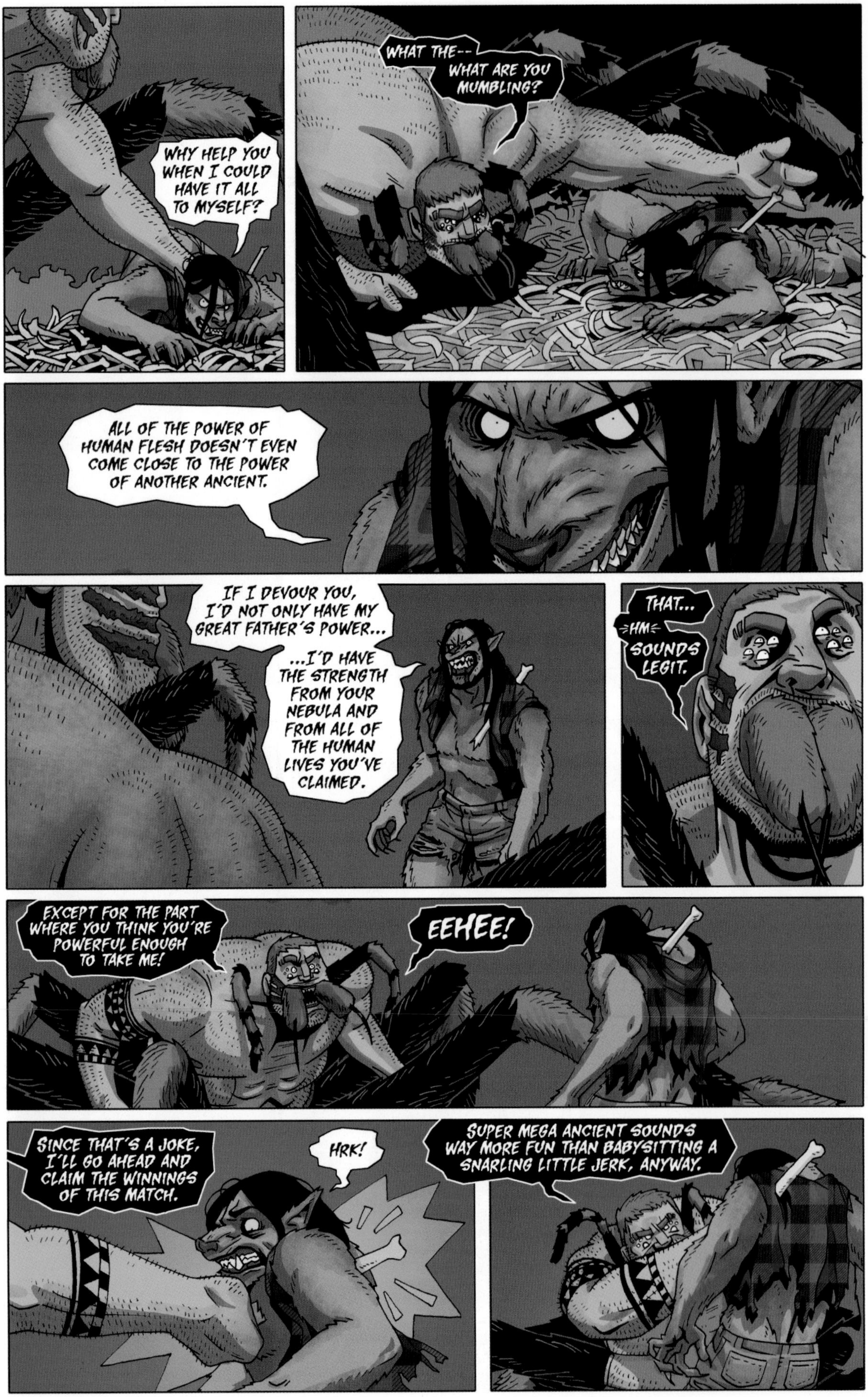
WHY HELP YOU WHEN I COULD HAVE IT ALL TO MYSELF?
WHAT THE--
WHAT ARE YOU MUMBLING?
ALL OF THE POWER OF HUMAN FLESH DOESN'T EVEN COME CLOSE TO THE POWER OF ANOTHER ANCIENT.
IF I DEVOUR YOU, I'D NOT ONLY HAVE MY GREAT FATHER'S POWER...
...I'D HAVE THE STRENGTH FROM YOUR NEBULA AND FROM ALL OF THE HUMAN LIVES YOU'VE CLAIMED.
THAT...
HM
SOUNDS LEGIT.
EXCEPT FOR THE PART WHERE YOU THINK YOU'RE POWERFUL ENOUGH TO TAKE ME!
EEHEE!
SINCE THAT'S A JOKE, I'LL GO AHEAD AND CLAIM THE WINNINGS OF THIS MATCH.
HRK!
SUPER MEGA ANCIENT SOUNDS WAY MORE FUN THAN BABYSITTING A SNARLING LITTLE JERK, ANYWAY.

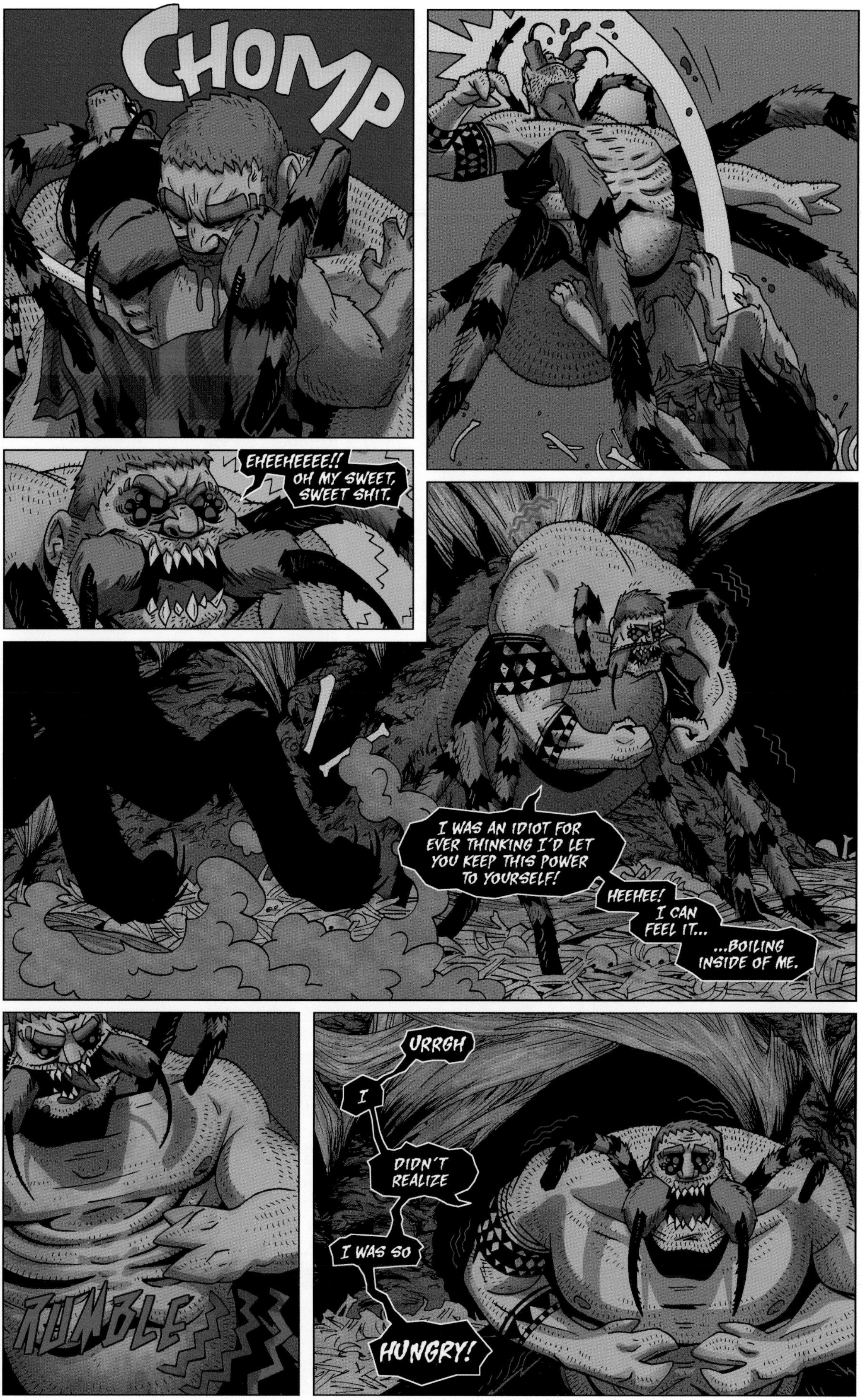
CHOMP
EHEEHEEEE!! OH MY SWEET, SWEET SHIT.
I WAS AN IDIOT FOR EVER THINKING I'D LET YOU KEEP THIS POWER TO YOURSELF!
HEEHEE! I CAN FEEL IT...
...BOILING INSIDE OF ME.
RUMBLE
URRGH
I
DIDN'T REALIZE
I WAS SO
HUNGRY!

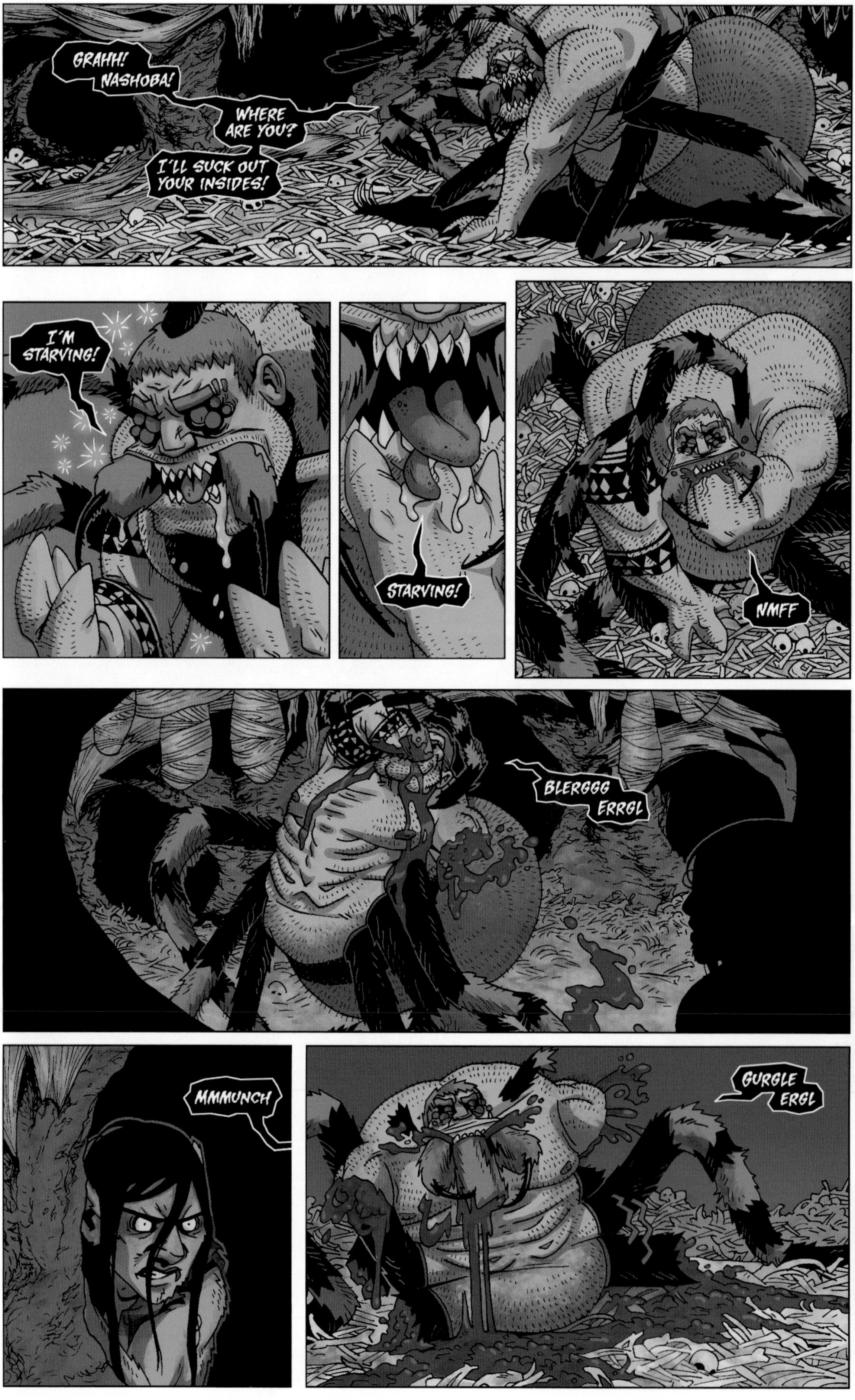
GRAHH! NASHOBA!
WHERE ARE YOU?
I'LL SUCK OUT YOUR INSIDES!
I'M STARVING!
STARVING!
NMFF
BLERGGG ERRGL
MMMUNCH
GURGLE ERGL

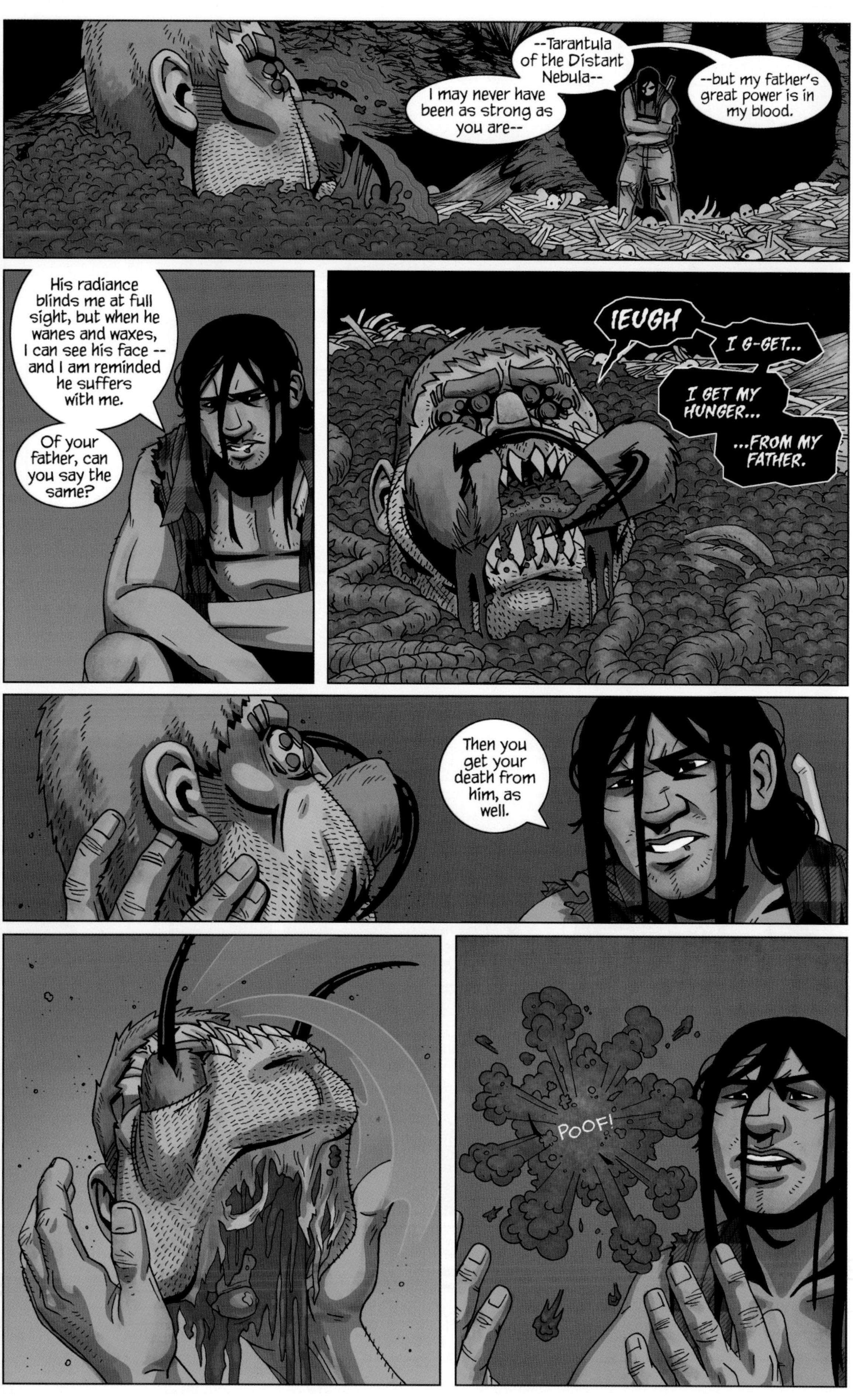
I may never have been as strong as you are--
--Tarantula of the Distant Nebula--
--but my father's great power is in my blood.
His radiance blinds me at full sight, but when he wanes and waxes, I can see his face -- and I am reminded he suffers with me.
Of your father, can you say the same?
IEUGH
I G-GET...
I GET MY HUNGER...
...FROM MY FATHER.
Then you get your death from him, as well.
POOF!

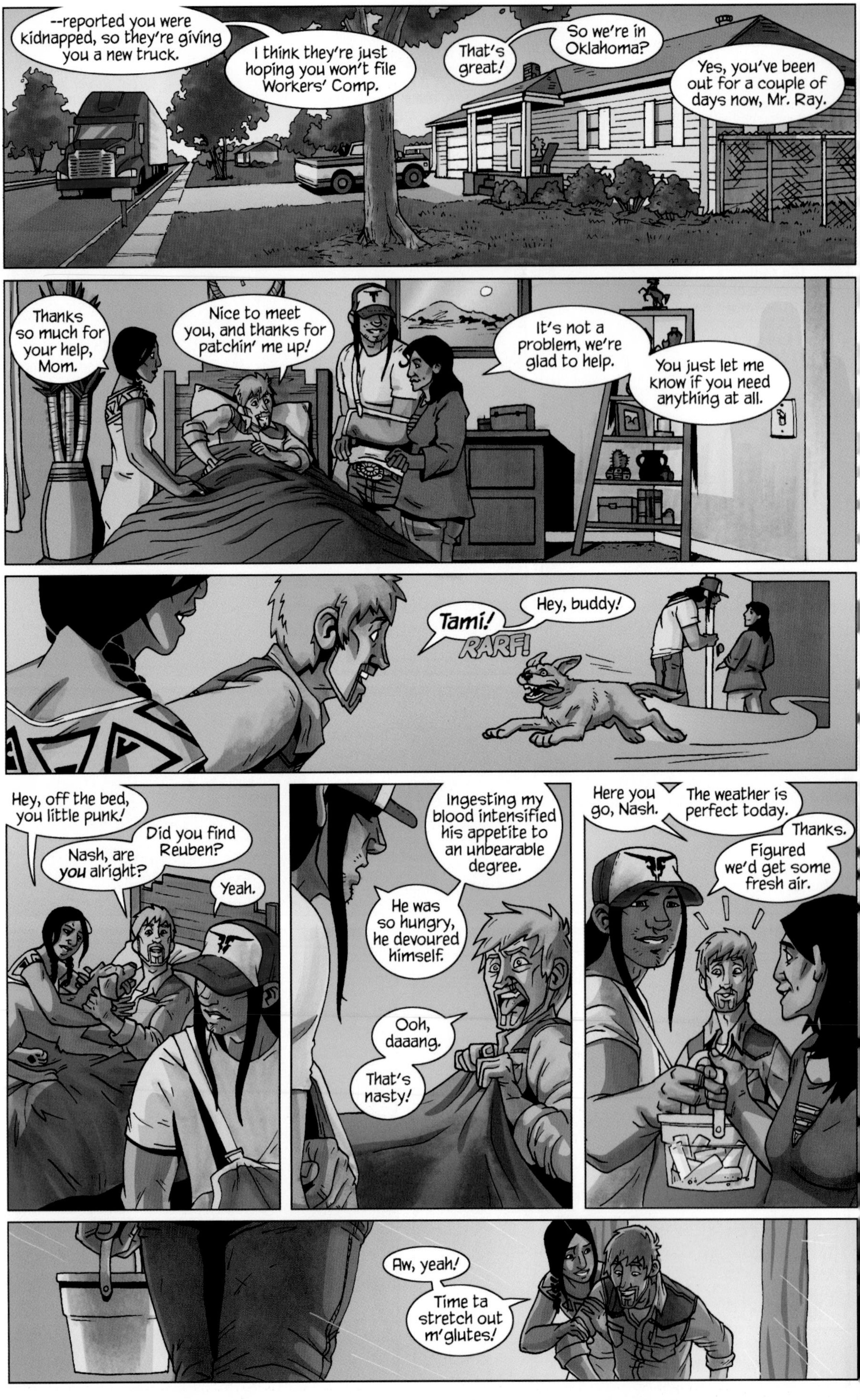
--reported you were kidnapped, so they're giving you a new truck.
I think they're just hoping you won't file Workers' Comp.
So we're in Oklahoma?
That's great!
Yes, you've been out for a couple of days now, Mr. Ray.
Thanks so much for your help, Mom.
Nice to meet you, and thanks for patchin' me up!
It's not a problem, we're glad to help.
You just let me know if you need anything at all.
Tami!
Hey, buddy!
RARF!
Hey, off the bed, you little punk!
Nash, are you alright?
Did you find Reuben?
Yeah.
Ingesting my blood intensified his appetite to an unbearable degree.
He was so hungry, he devoured himself.
Ooh, daaang.
That's nasty!
Here you go, Nash.
The weather is perfect today.
Thanks.
Figured we'd get some fresh air.
Aw, yeah!
Time ta stretch out m'glutes!

--and after we left, Chukfi searched through the rest of Reuben's lair.

She's working with Crow and his boys to return the rest of the hostages to their homes.

Wow, really?

Yup, Billie was with Chukfi the whole time.

Yeah, and it turns out--

Bubbadude?!

Aw *Hell* no!

Billie, get back.

That's one *evil sonnamabitch!*

No no, it's okay -- Bubbadude isn't evil!

Just big... and misunderstood.

When I was taken off the side of the truck, that was Bubbadude.

She flew me to meet Chukfi at one of Crow's warehouses.

TAP TAP TAP

Heh-hey!

She?!

Haha!

Aw, jeez, you're kidding me.

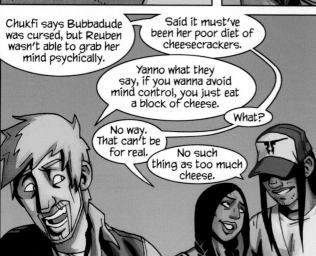

Chukfi says Bubbadude was cursed, but Reuben wasn't able to grab her mind psychically.

Said it must've been her poor diet of cheesecrackers.

Yanno what they say, if you wanna avoid mind control, you just eat a block of cheese.

What?

No way. That can't be for real.

No such thing as too much cheese.

Well, if Billie likes ya, Miss Dude, I guess you're okay in my book.

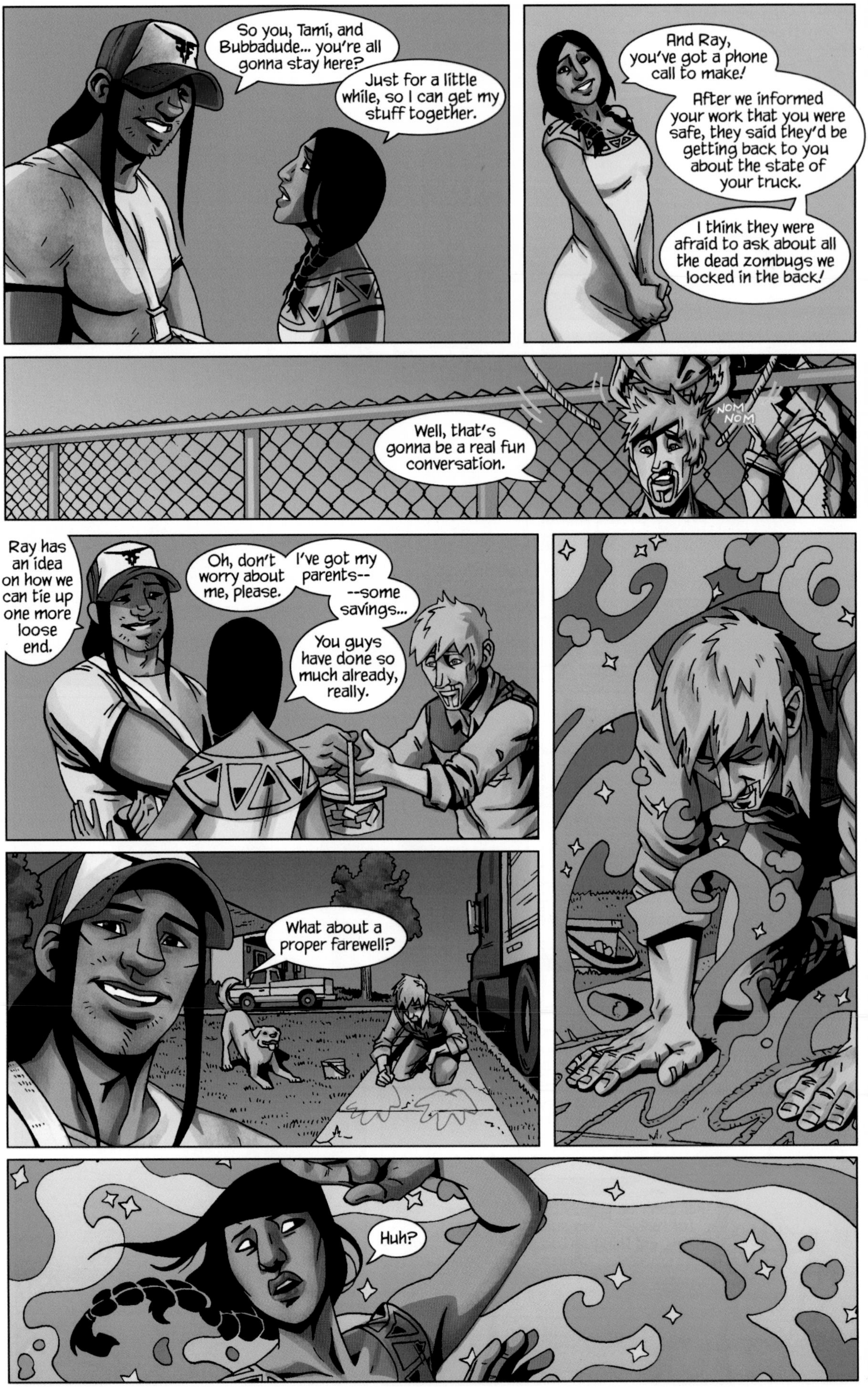
So you, Tami, and Bubbadude... you're all gonna stay here?
Just for a little while, so I can get my stuff together.
And Ray, you've got a phone call to make!
After we informed your work that you were safe, they said they'd be getting back to you about the state of your truck.
I think they were afraid to ask about all the dead zombugs we locked in the back!
Well, that's gonna be a real fun conversation.
NOM NOM
Ray has an idea on how we can tie up one more loose end.
Oh, don't worry about me, please.
I've got my parents--
--some savings...
You guys have done so much already, really.
What about a proper farewell?
Huh?

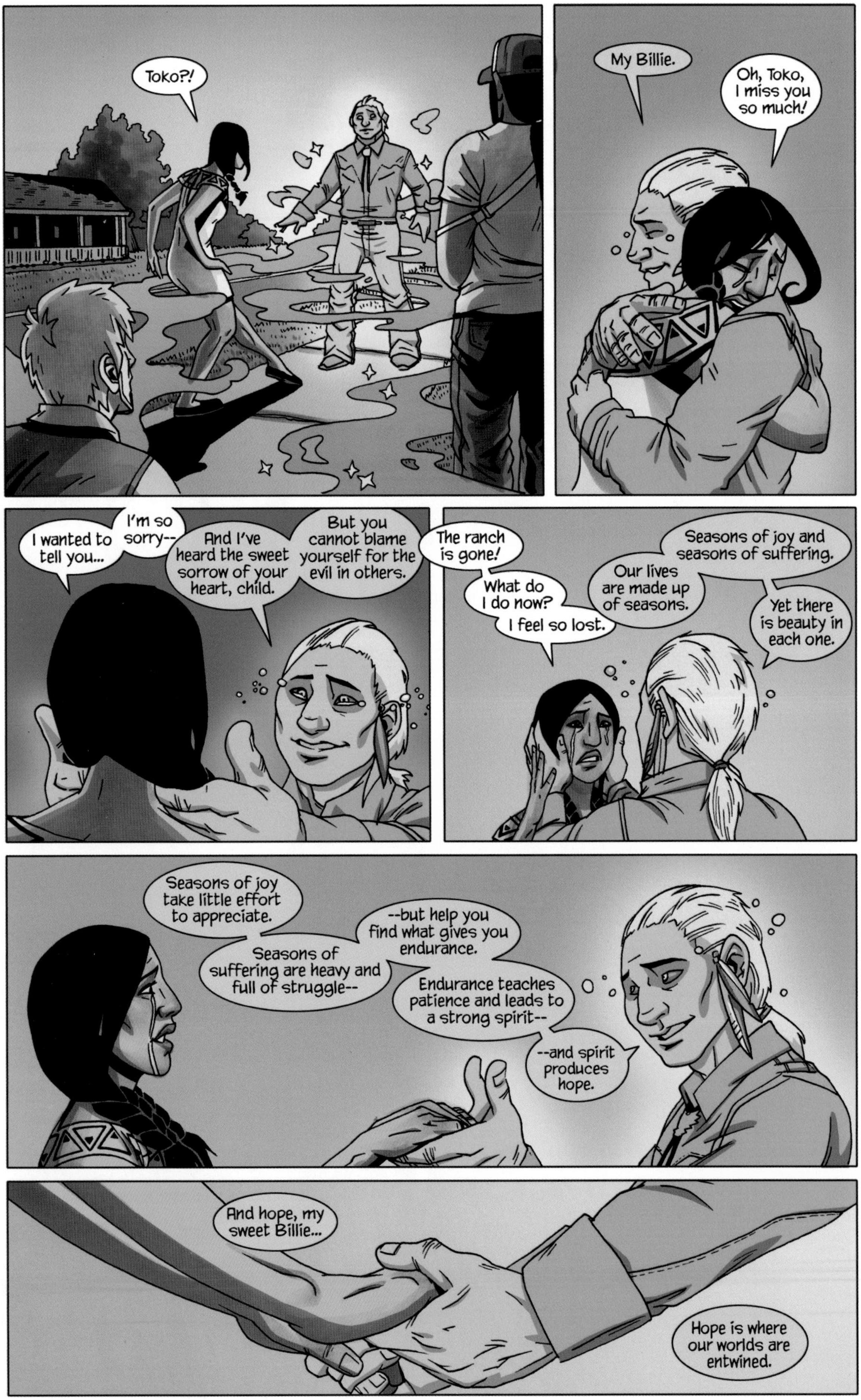
Toko?!
My Billie.
Oh, Toko, I miss you so much!
I wanted to tell you...
I'm so sorry--
And I've heard the sweet sorrow of your heart, child.
But you cannot blame yourself for the evil in others.
The ranch is gone!
What do I do now?
I feel so lost.
Our lives are made up of seasons.
Seasons of joy and seasons of suffering.
Yet there is beauty in each one.
Seasons of joy take little effort to appreciate.
Seasons of suffering are heavy and full of struggle--
--but help you find what gives you endurance.
Endurance teaches patience and leads to a strong spirit--
--and spirit produces hope.
And hope, my sweet Billie...
Hope is where our worlds are entwined.

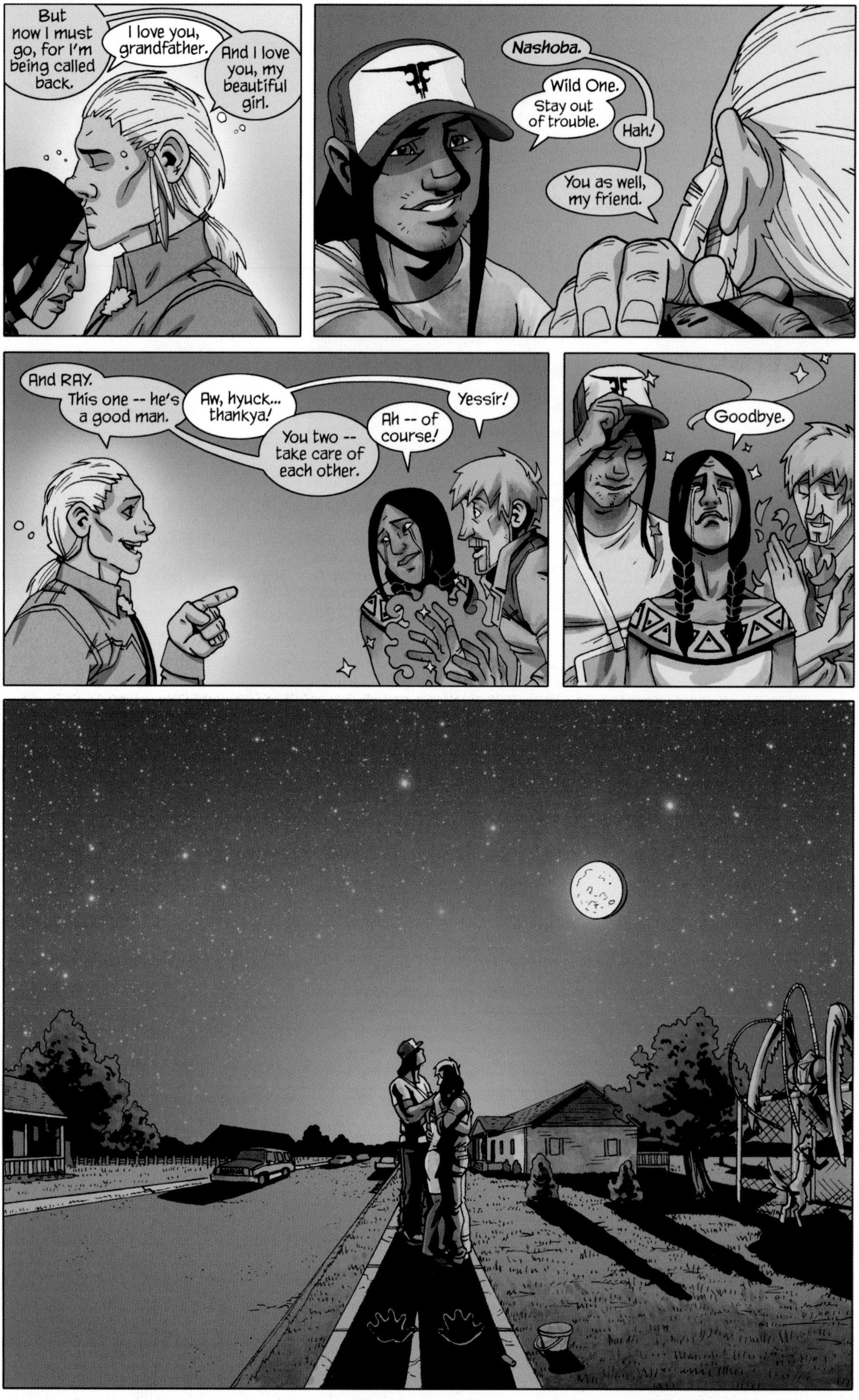
But now I must go, for I'm being called back.
I love you, grandfather.
And I love you, my beautiful girl.
Nashoba.
Wild One. Stay out of trouble.
Hah!
You as well, my friend.
And RAY. This one -- he's a good man.
Aw, hyuck... thankya!
You two -- take care of each other.
Ah -- of course!
Yessir!
Goodbye.

GUEST ART GALLERY

SAM SPINA
http://spinadoodles.com

JEREMY BROOKS
twitter @sketchbrooks

HENRY EUDY
http://oh-the-humanatee.deviantart.com/

ERAKLIS PETMEZAS
http://madtiki.deviantart.com

Collaboration with JUSTIN CROUSE, RICO RENZI
http://crousejustinb.deviantart.com
http://whoisrico.deviantart.com;
http://nolongermint.com

JAMES HARREN
http://jharren.deviantart.com;
http://the-bog.tumblr.com

ETHAN NICOLLE
http://ethannicolle.com
http://bearmageddon.com
http://axecop.com

AFUA RICHARDSON
http://www.afuarichardson.info

DOUG TENNAPEL
http://tennapel.com

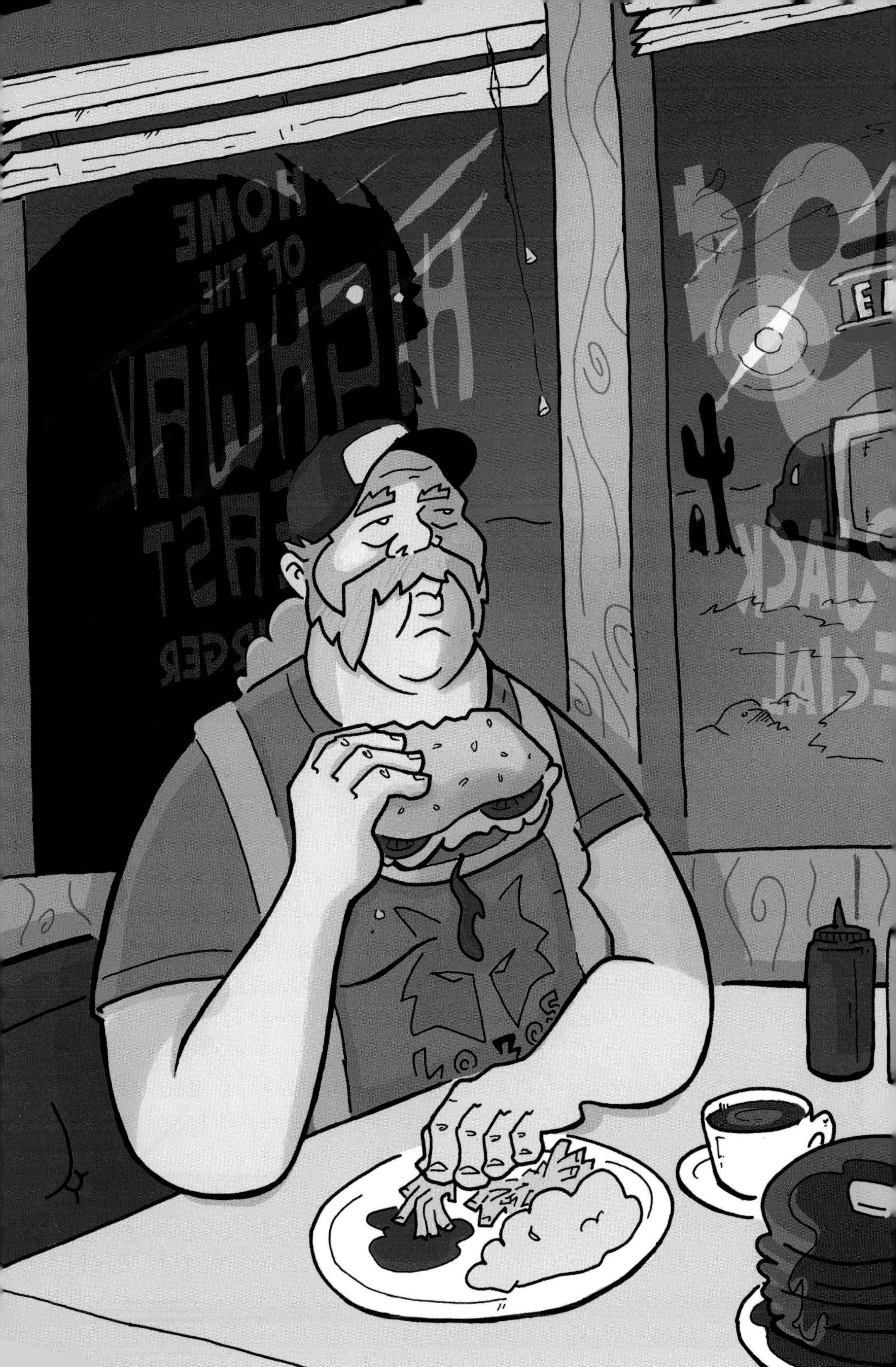

JEREMY BROOKS

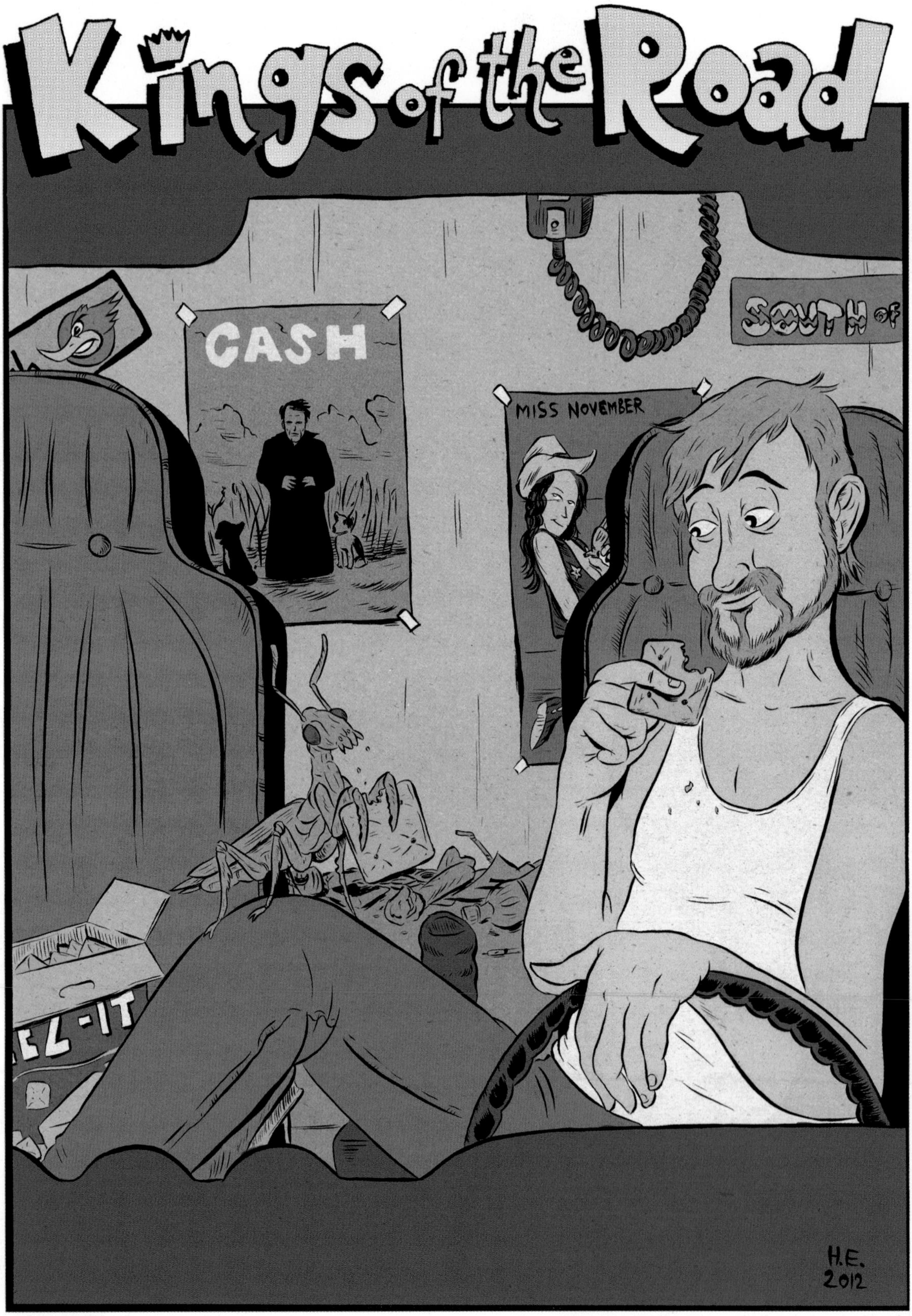
Kings of the Road
CASH
SOUTH of
MISS NOVEMBER
H.E.
2012

HENRY EUDY

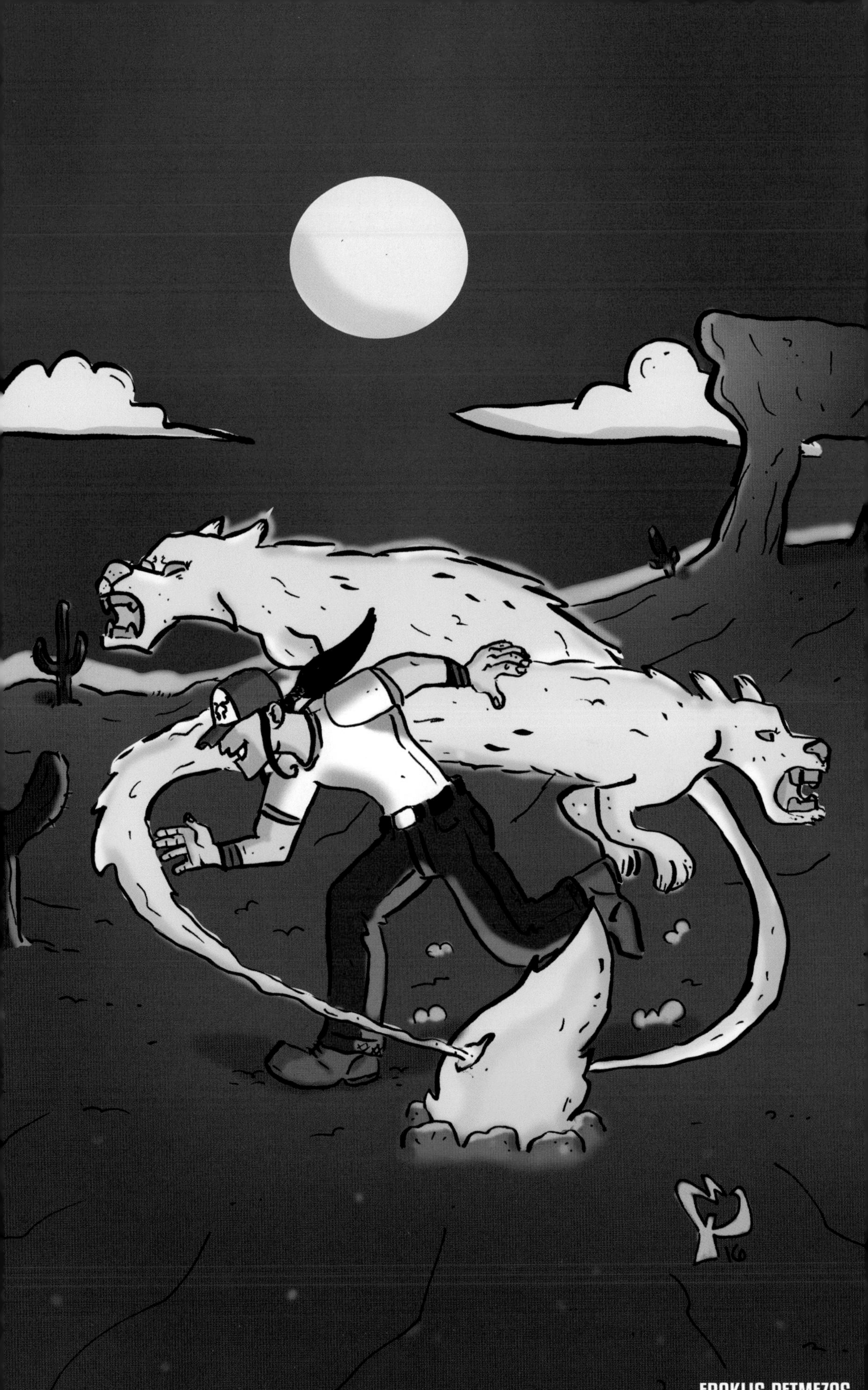

ERAKLIS PETMEZAS

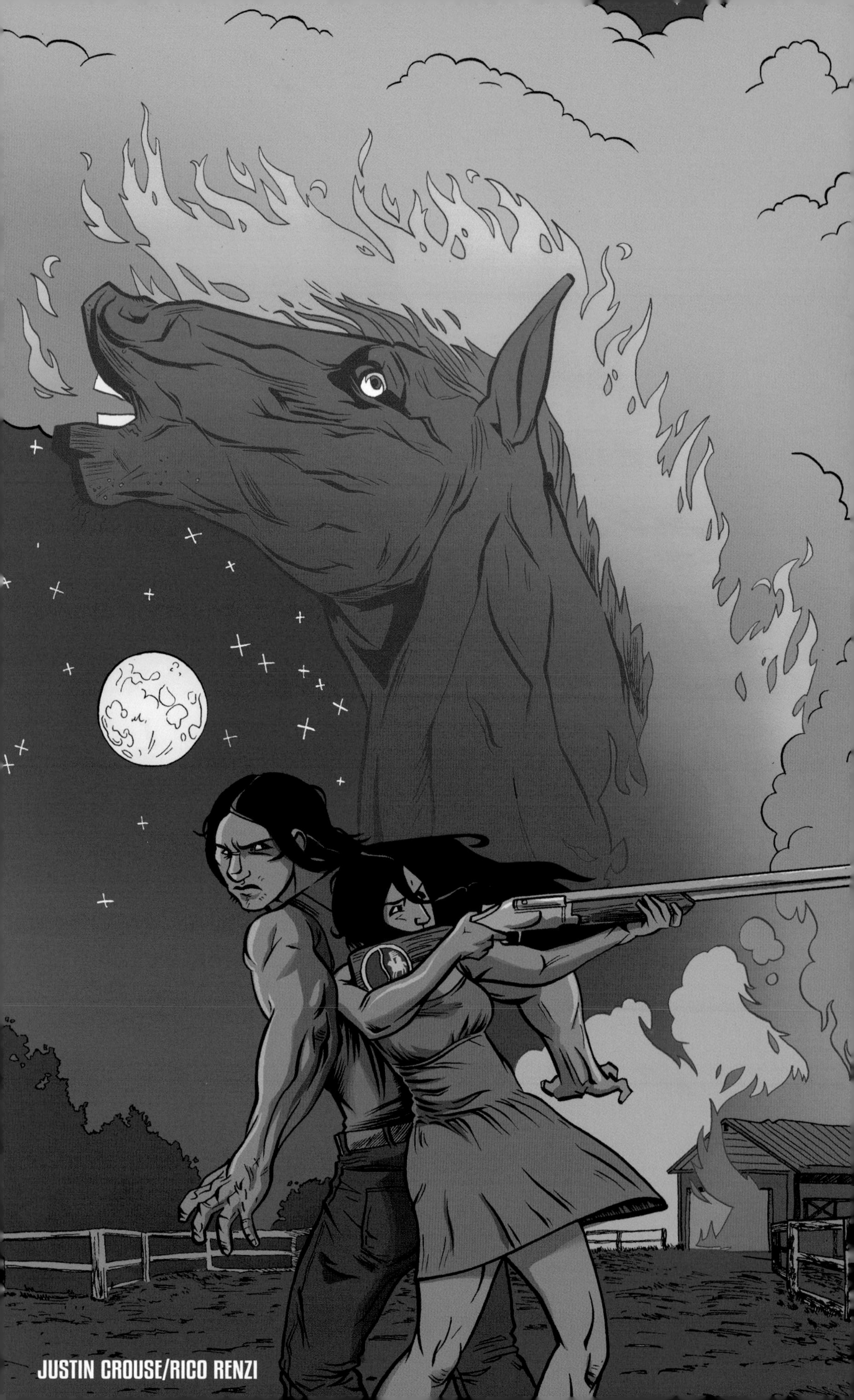
JUSTIN CROUSE/RICO RENZI

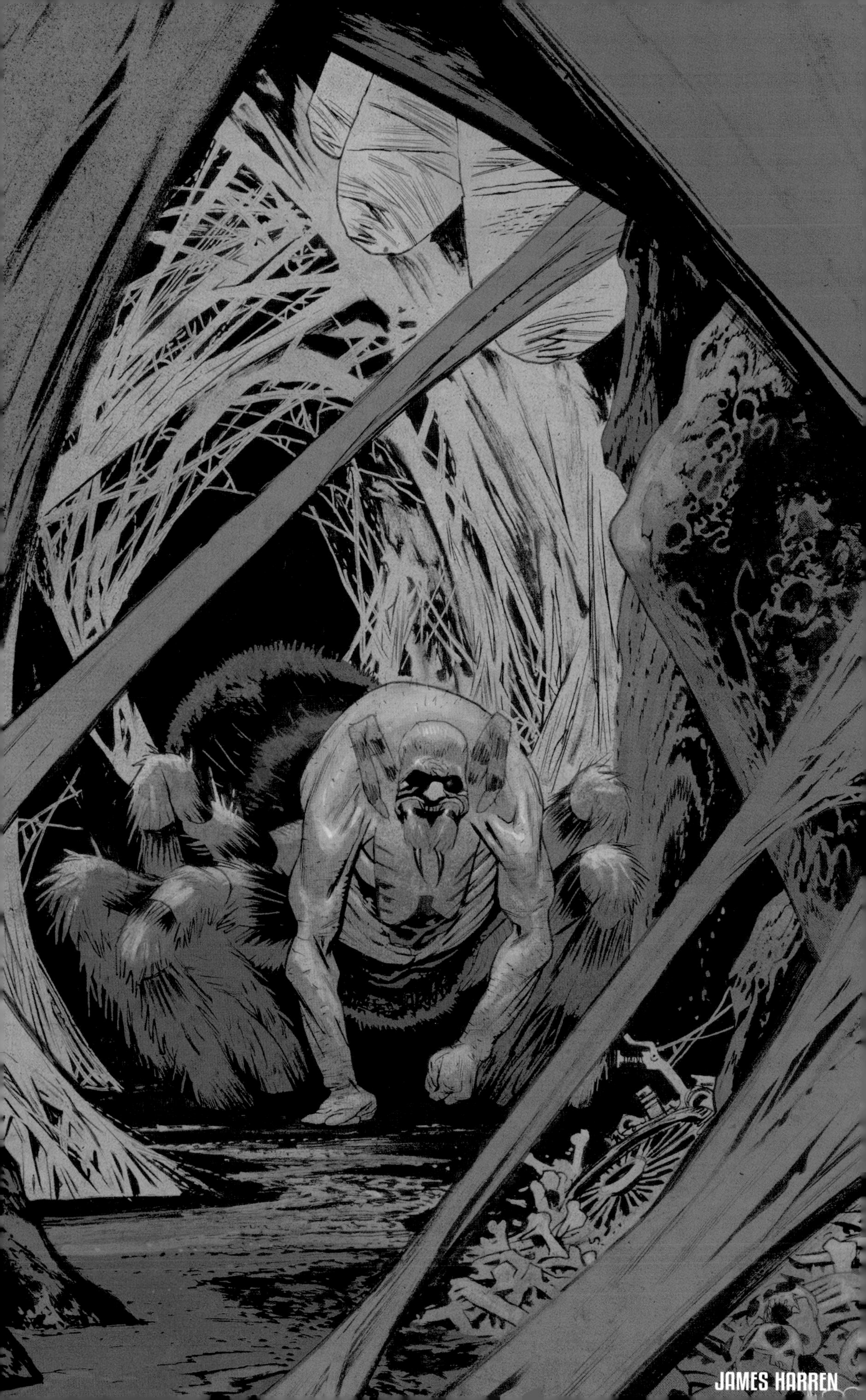
JAMES HARREN

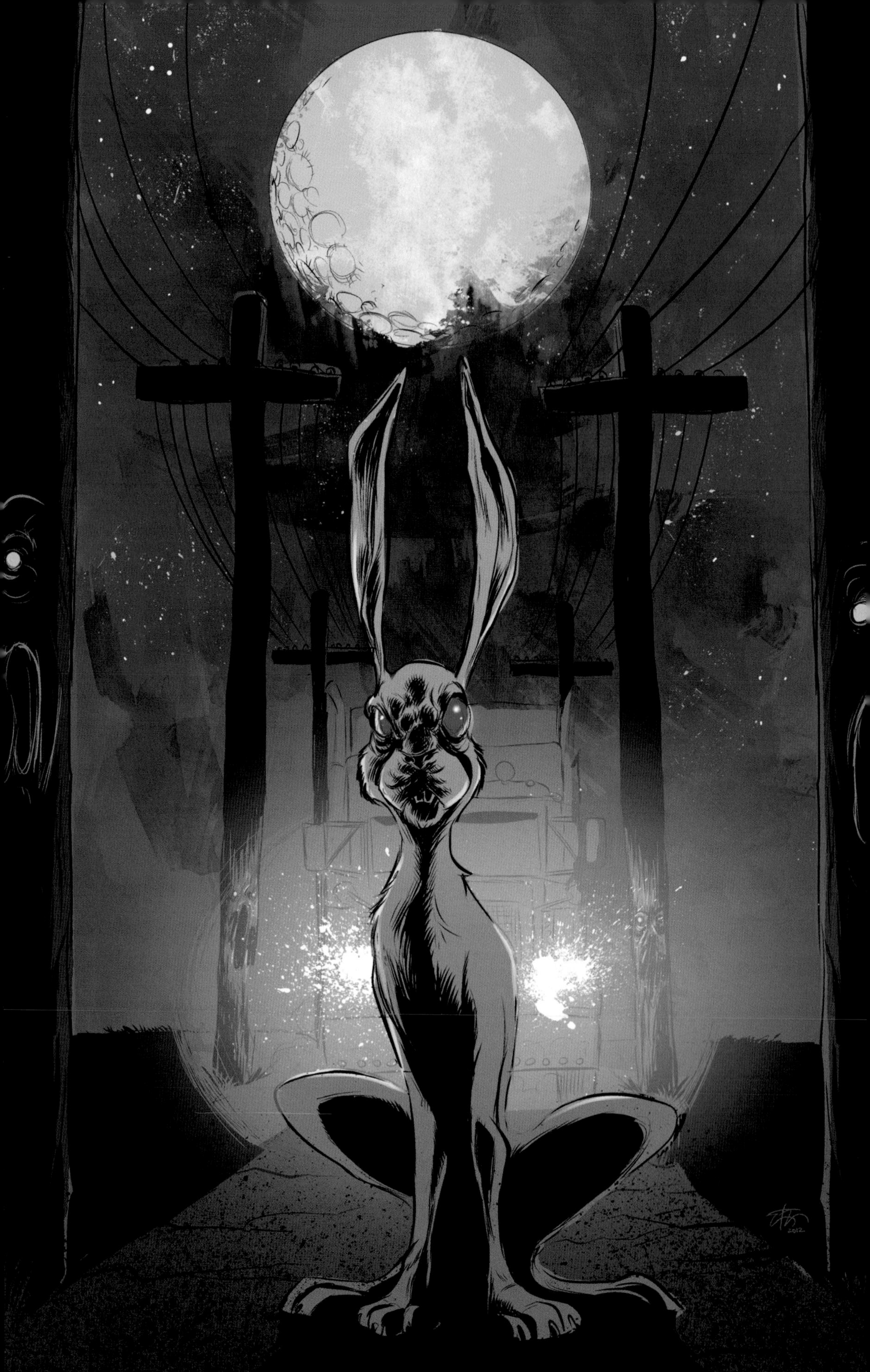

ETHAN NICOLLE

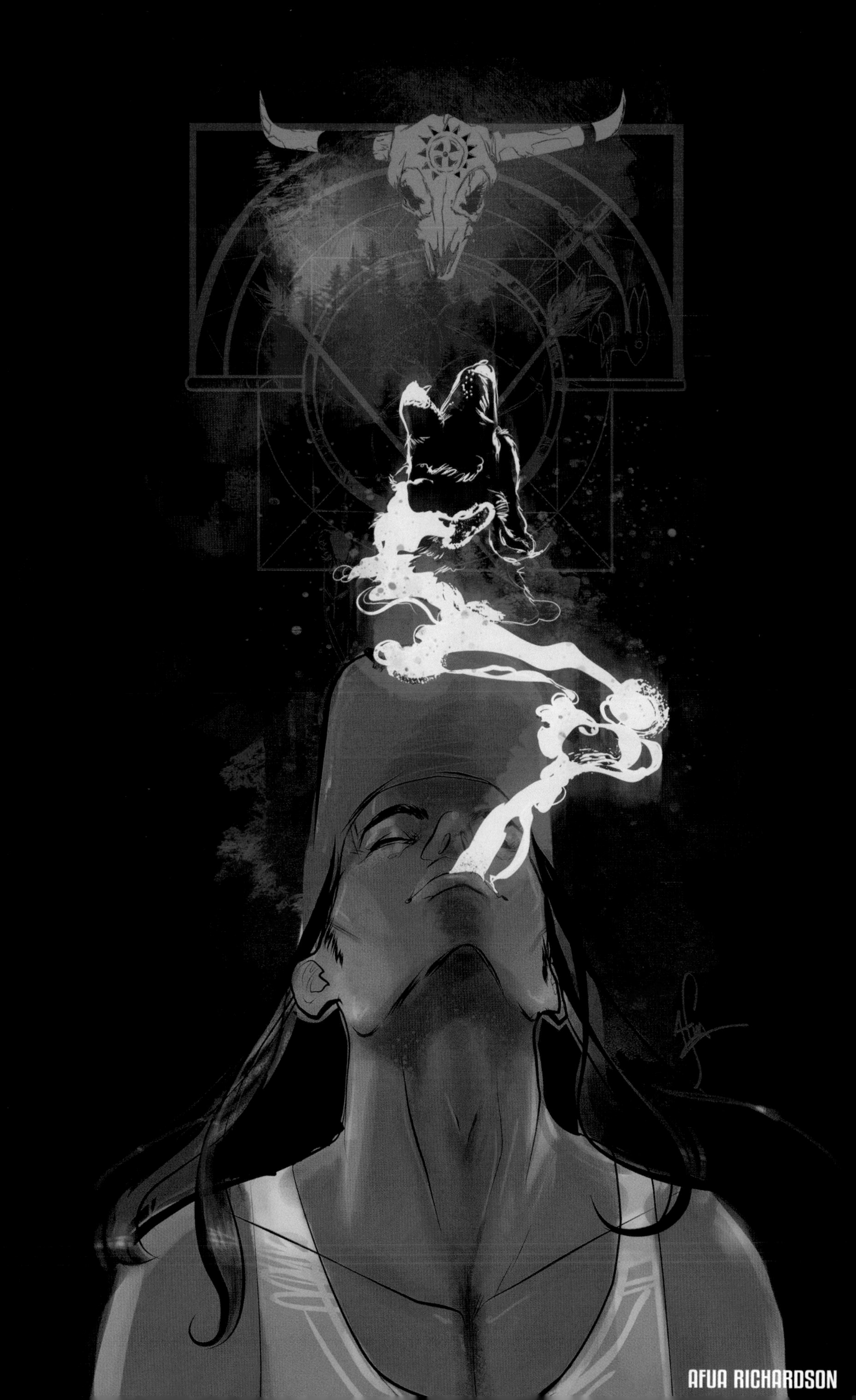

AFUA RICHARDSON

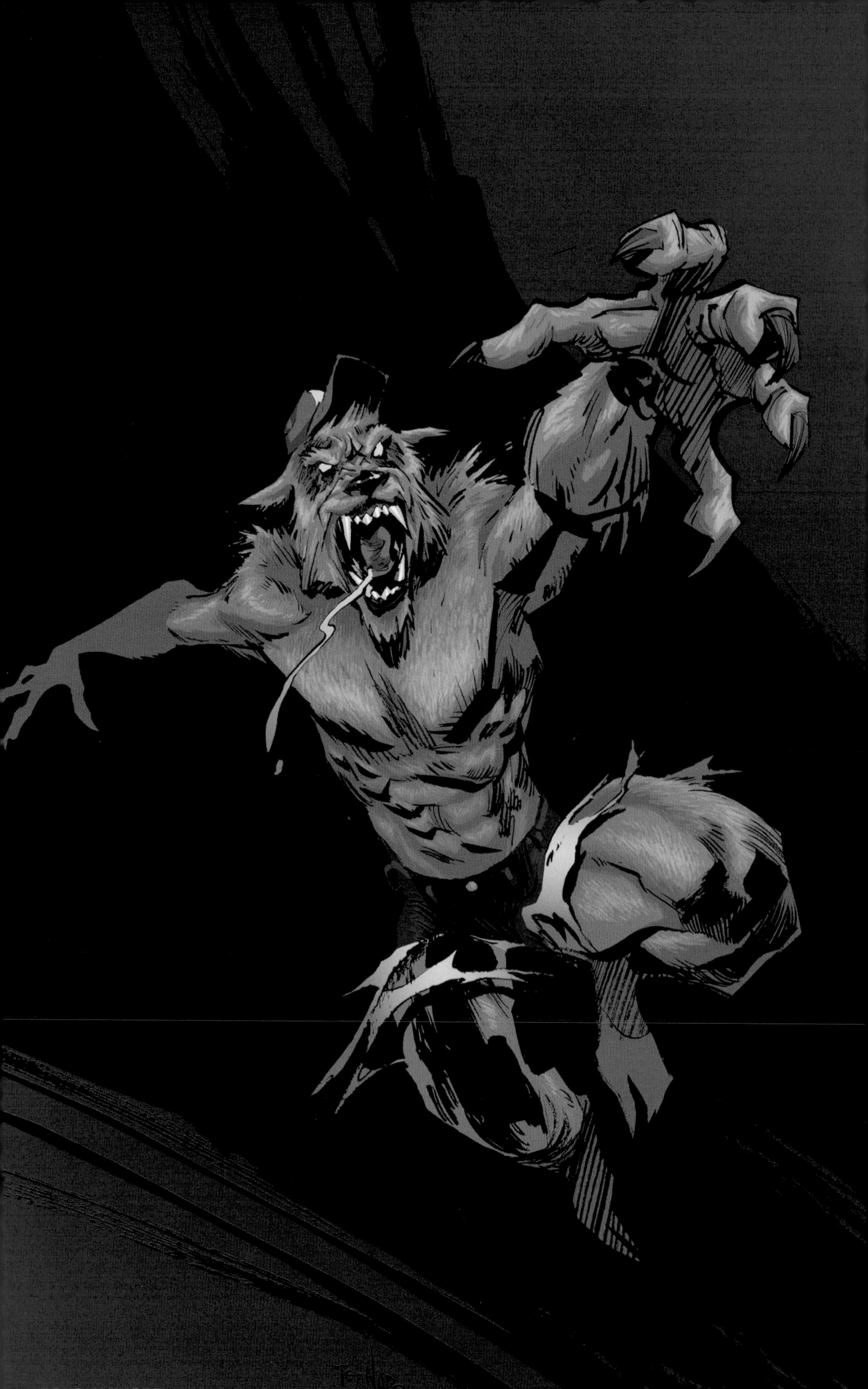

DOUG TENNAPEL

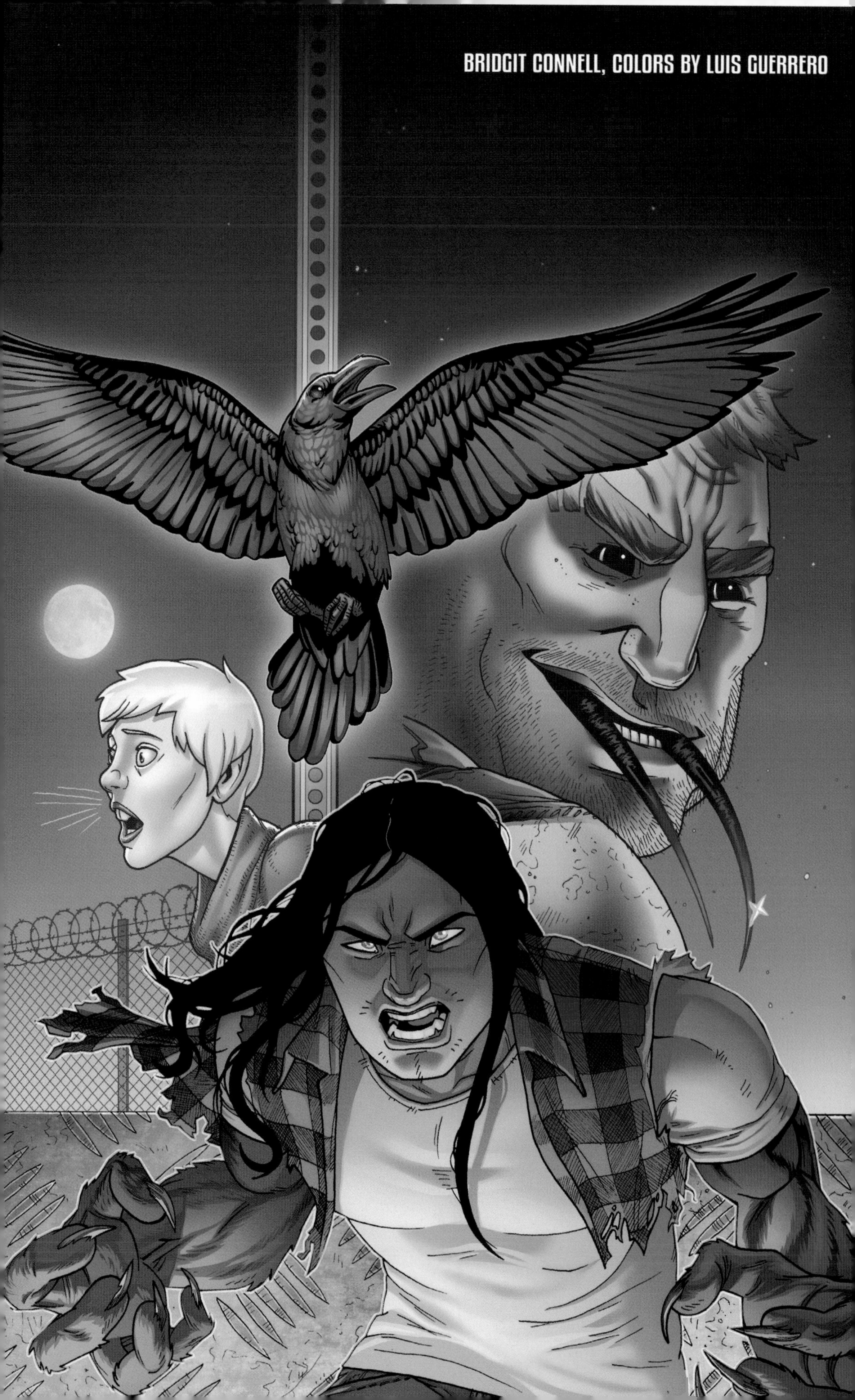
BRIDGIT CONNELL, COLORS BY LUIS GUERRERO

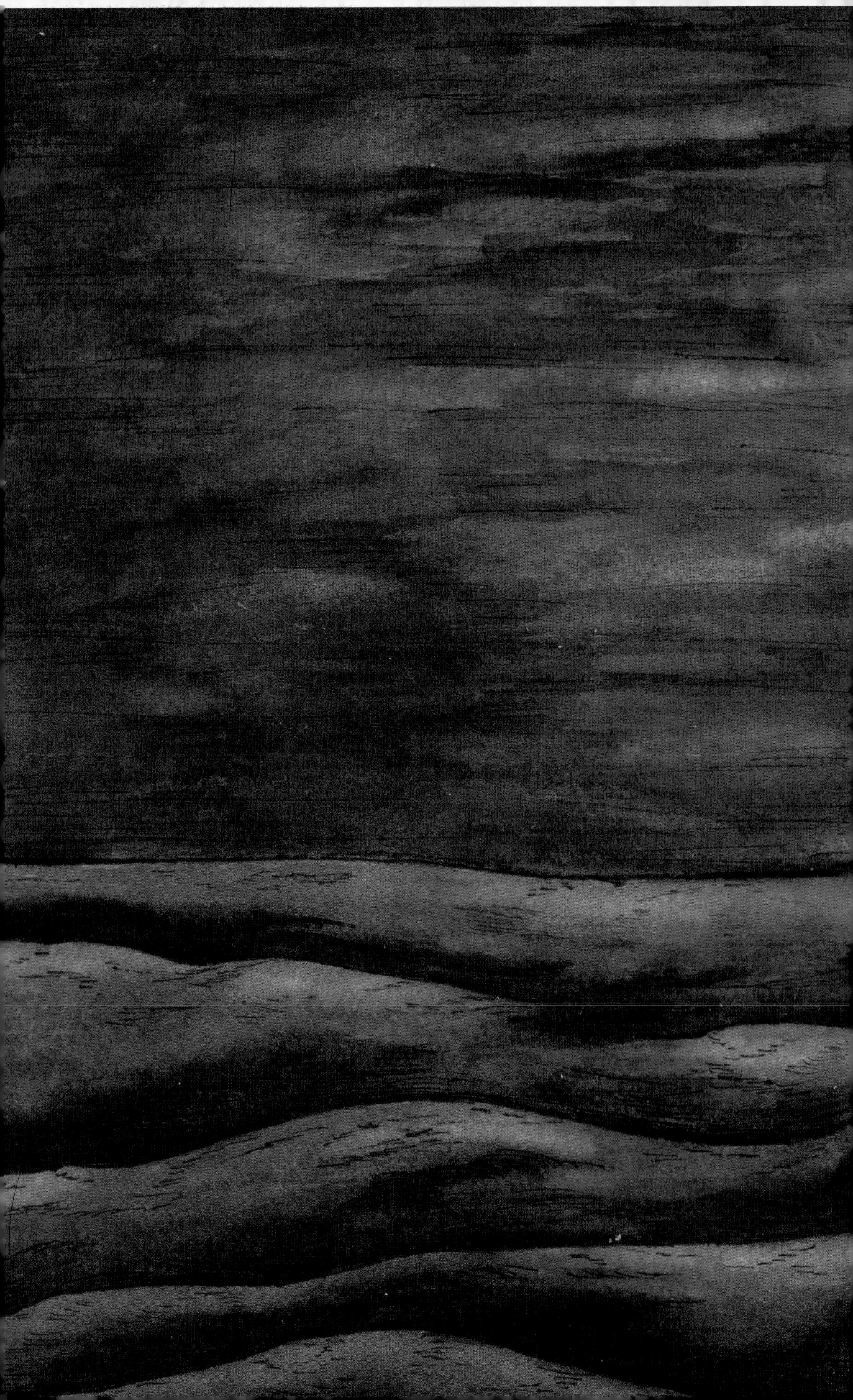

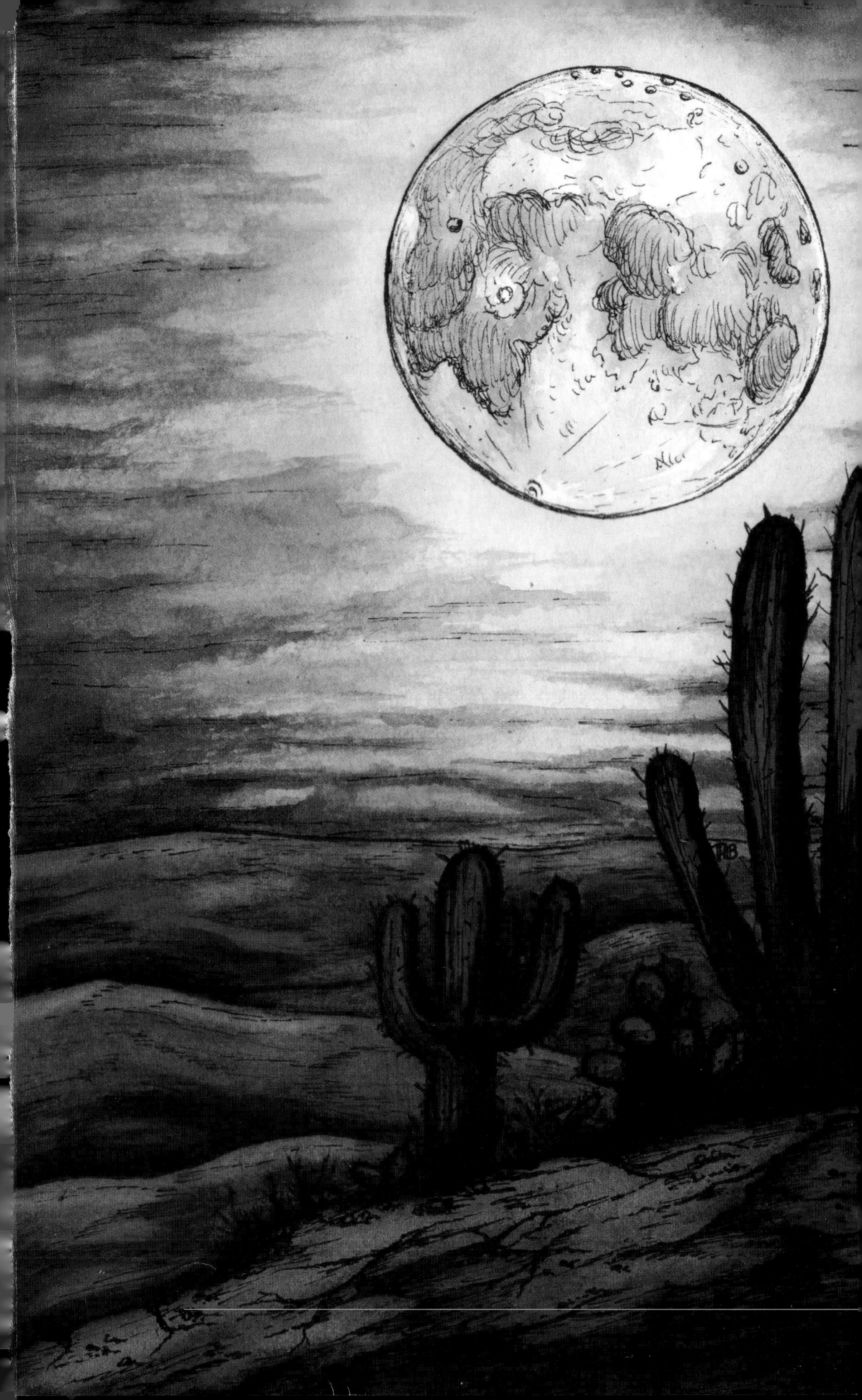

BRIDGIT CONNELL was born in 1986 in Wheaton, Illinois, and, in a few years and some hundreds of miles away, grew up in Matthews, North Carolina. She graduated at UNC Charlotte with a BFA in Illustration.

Currently working as a freelance comic book artist, Bridgit resides in Concord with her wonderful husband, Justin, and their puppy monster, Barnabas.

Website: http://www.bridgitconnell.com
Instagram: @bridgitconnell
Twitter: @bridgitconnell

For all inquiries related to original art or appearances, please contact Bridgit at
bridgitconnell@gmail.com